OXFORD EARLY CHRISTIAN STUDIES

General Editors

Gillian Clark   Andrew Lou

DATE DUE

THE OXFORD EARLY CHRISTIAN STUDIES series includes scholarly volumes on the thought and history of the early Christian centuries. Covering a wide range of Greek, Latin, and Oriental sources, the books are of interest to theologians, ancient historians, and specialists in the classical and Jewish worlds.

St John Damascene, the Skete of St Anne (early 14th cent.)

St John Damascene

Tradition and Originality in Byzantine Theology

ANDREW LOUTH

OXFORD
UNIVERSITY PRESS

OXFORD

UNIVERSITY PRESS

Great Clarendon Street, Oxford OX2 6DP

Oxford University Press is a department of the University of Oxford.
It furthers the University's objective of excellence in research, scholarship,
and education by publishing worldwide in

Oxford New York

Auckland Cape Town Dar es Salaam Hong Kong Karachi Kuala Lumpur
Madrid Melbourne Mexico City Nairobi New Delhi Shanghai Taipei Toronto

With offices in

Argentina Austria Brazil Chile Czech Republic France Greece
Guatemala Hungary Italy Japan South Korea Poland Portugal
Singapore Switzerland Thailand Turkey Ukraine Vietnam

Oxford is a registered trade mark of Oxford University Press
in the UK and in certain other countries

Published in the United States
by Oxford University Press Inc., New York

British Library Cataloguing in Publication Data
Data available

Library of Congress Cataloging in Publication Data

Louth, Andrew

St. John Damascene: tradition and originality in
Byzantine theology/ Andrew Louth.
p. cm.- (Oxford early Christian studies)
Includes bibliographical references (p.) and index.
I. John, of Damascus, Saint. I. Title: Saint John Damascene.
II. Title. III. Series.
BR65.J66 .L68 2002 230′.14′092-dc21 2002020025

ISBN 0-19-927527-0 (pbk)

Typeset in Garamond MT
by Regent Typesetting, London
Printed in Great Britain
on acid-free paper by
Biddles Ltd., King's Lynn, Norfolk

For Carol

Originality means to remain faithful to the originals
Zissimos Lorenzatos

PREFACE

St John Damascene has been oddly served by scholarship. On the one hand, we now have a fine critical edition, nearly complete for his prose works, the life-work of Dom Bonifatius Kotter, OSB. This is a signal mark of recognition, as yet extended to relatively few of the post-Nicene Greek Fathers (Gregory of Nyssa and Dionysios the Areopagite have been similarly honoured; a critical edition of Maximos the Confessor is well under way; and less complete editions, save in the case of Gregory Nazianzen and, more recently, Evagrios, are appearing in the series Sources Chrétiennes). But despite this, there has been little attempt to reflect on the theology of the Damascene. In the early years of the project fostered by the Byzantine Institute of the Abbey of Scheyern, under whose auspices Kotter's work proceeded, a number of works on aspects of John's theology appeared: notably, valuable studies of his theological method by Basil Studer, of his Christology by Keetje Rozemond, and of his logic by Gerhard Richter; but since then there has been little. Earlier still, attention to John's theology had been slight: there were monographs by Langen (1879), on his trinitarian theology by Bilz (1909), and on his theology of icons by Menges (1938), but in his *History of Dogma* Harnack (1884–9) devoted only a handful of pages to the Damascene. Still further back, the seventeenth-century scholar and advocate of union between the Orthodox Churches and Rome, Leo Allatius, wrote a good deal on John's works (or what he believed to be his works), but this scarcely amounted to a consideration of the Damascene's theology as a whole.

Kotter's edition has transformed our understanding of John, and demands renewed reflection on the theological *œuvre* of the Damascene, which this book attempts to provide. It improves on Le Quien's edition of 1712 (reprinted, with some additions, in Migne, PG 94–6) in several ways. First, as one might expect, it provides a more secure text, as well as revising the list of works by John thought to be authentic. But further, it makes clear both the nature of the tradition of John's works, several of which exist in different recensions which Le Quien's edition had tended to conflate, and also the nature of his sources; for John, like any theologian (or indeed any other kind of thinker) of Late Antiquity or the Byzantine period, was concerned simply to record the truth that had always been known and, he believed, generally better expressed by the 'Fathers', from whom he had received his faith. This he did in a particular historical situation, during the first century of the Arab Empire, ruled by the Caliph, whose servant he had been before embracing the monastic life: an empire founded on the ruins of the Persian Empire and the eastern and southern provinces of the Roman (or Byzantine) Empire. Much of the interest in studying John's theology lies in attempting to understand how John and the tradition to which he belonged coped with the transition from being the religious centre of the Christian Byzantine Empire to being the site of one of the holy places of the religion of Islam.

John has generally been dismissed, either explicitly or implicitly, as an unoriginal thinker, a mere compiler of patristic florilegia. Even if it is argued that there is nothing 'mere' about compiling florilegia, there soon comes the realization that John was often not even doing this much, but was using an already existing tradition of such compilation. This was not due to laziness, or carelessness. It was intentional: twice, towards the beginning of his great *Fountain Head of Knowledge*, John asserts that 'I shall say nothing of my own'. If we are to think through what is meant by 'tradition' and 'originality' in relation to John, we shall be forced to revise what we mean by these terms. The epigraph to this book, from the Greek writer and critic, Zissimos Lorenzatos, points towards a possible way of understanding John. The whole sentence, from an essay on the great writer Alexandros Papadiamandis, too little known outside his native Greece, runs as follows:

Originality means to remain faithful to the originals, to the eternal prototypes, to extinguish 'a wisdom of [your] own' before the 'common Word', as Heraclitus says (Fr. 2)—in other words, to lose your soul if you wish to find it, and not to parade your originality or to do what pleases you. (Lorenzatos 2000, 15)

John would have understood that; indeed, he would have been astonished that it needed saying. But it does need saying in our day, and if we are to make anything of John and the tradition to which he belonged (which continues to the present day), we need to try and understand it. The following pages are an attempt to do that.

The chapters are arranged in three parts. The first, 'Faith and Life', tells what we know of the life of John Damascene and sets it in its historical context; it also opens up discussion of the way in which John was not simply shaped by tradition but was also determinative for the form that the later theological tradition of Byzantium was to take. The second and largest part, 'Faith and Logic', is devoted to John's own presentation of

Orthodox Christian theology, especially in his three-part work *The Fountain Head of Knowledge*. The final part, 'Faith and Images', looks at the place of images in John's theology, both his defence of visual images in the context of the iconoclast controversy, and also his use of imagery, both in his homilies and in his liturgical poetry.

A few words are perhaps necessary about another aspect of presentation. John's Bible was the Greek translation, the Septuagint (abbreviated as LXX); my references are therefore to that text (with occasional indications of marked differences from the versions found in English Bibles, which, for the Old Testament, are based on the Hebrew). The numeration of the Psalms between 10 and 146 is therefore generally one less than that found in English Bibles. Note also that 1 and 2 Samuel and 1 and 2 Kings appear as 1–4 Kingdoms (Kgd.) in the LXX. For the same reason figures of the Old Testament are referred to by their Greek names, rather than the Anglicizations (which is what they mostly are, rather than transliterations) of the Hebrew forms, as in most English Bibles (e.g., Elias and Isaias, rather than Elijah and Isaiah). Greek names have been transliterated from the Greek, rather than *via* Latin, save when there is a familiar English form (so Athanasios and Maximos, but John and Cyril).

This book has been a long time in conception, if not in execution. My earlier books on Denys the Areopagite (1989) and Maximos the Confessor (1996) were undertaken, in part, because I wanted to clarify my mind about two of the Fathers whom John revered. They are very different thinkers from John, and precisely for that reason, perhaps, more accessible to present-day theology. Over the years I have incurred many debts, some of which I have probably now forgotten. First, I would mention my students, especially my graduate students over the last five years in Durham, who must think they have heard rather more about the Damascene than they might reasonably have expected. They have been too polite to criticize, but I am grateful to them, especially for their looks of incomprehension, which have forced me to think through my ideas more clearly. I am grateful, too, to the two universities that have employed me over the last ten years or so, Goldsmiths' College in the University of London and the University of Durham, and to the periods of research leave they have granted me, without which none of this would have been possible. I must also express my gratitude to the librarians of the libraries I have used, and those who service the Inter-Library Loan system, especially to Alisoun Roberts and the other librarians in the Palace Green Library of the University of Durham and Professors David Wright and Trevor Hart who made available to me a couple of rare books.

Several parts of this book have been offered as lectures or papers at conferences and seminars, where I have benefited from the wisdom of others. One chapter (Chapter 8) is a revised and expanded version of my contribution to a symposium, which later appeared as a chapter in the book *Preacher and Audience: Studies in Early Christian and Byzantine Homiletics* (1998); I am grateful to the publishers, Brill of Leiden, for permission to reuse the material here. Finally, I want to express my gratitude to all who have encouraged me: from the beginning, Professor A. M. Allchin and Bishop Kallistos of Diokleia, and along the way too many people to mention, but especially Averil Cameron, Charlotte Roueché, David Ricks (who introduced me to Lorenzatos), Brian Daley, Pauline Allen, Clare Stancliffe (who prevented me from making too many mistakes about Bede), Alexander Lingas and Archimandrite Ephrem Lash (who each knows more about Byzantine liturgical poetry and music than I ever shall), my former colleagues in the Department of Historical and Cultural Studies at Goldsmiths (who taught me to ask historical questions), and my present colleagues in the Department of Theology at the University of Durham (especially Sheridan Gilley on a few points of style). I would also like to thank Hilary O'Shea of Oxford University Press and my fellow editor of the Oxford Early Christian Studies series, Gillian Clark, for accepting this book for the series, and for the two anonymous readers who made a host of helpful suggestions. But I doubt if this book would have been ever finished without the constant encouragement of my wife and colleague, Carol, to whom it is dedicated.

ANDREW LOUTH

Darlington, Feast of St John Damascene, 2000

CONTENTS

PART III: *Faith and Images*

ILLUSTRATIONS

All illustrations are reproduced with the permission of the Holy Community of Mount Athos.

ABBREVIATIONS

Works of John Damascene (with English translation of the title,
as used in the text, and references to CPG and texts used)

Aceph.   *De natura composita contra acephalos* [On the Composite
           Nature, against the Acephali] (*CPG* 8051): Kotter iv.
           409–17
Anast.   *Laudatio s. Anastasiae* [Praise of St Anastasia] (*CPG* 8068):
           Kotter v. 289–303
Artem.   *Passio s. Artemii* [Passion of St Artemios] (*CPG* 8082):
           Kotter v. 202–45
Barb.   *Laudatio s. Barbarae* [Praise of St Barbara] (*CPG* 8065):
           Kotter v. 256–78
Barl.   *Vita Barlaam et Ioasaph* [Life of Barlaam and Ioasaph]
           (*CPG* 8120): G. R. Woodward-H. Mattingley, *St. John
           Damascene, Barlaam and Ioasaph*, introduction by D. M.
           Lang, LCL, 1967
Chrys.   *Laudatio s. Joh. Chrysostomi* [Praise of St John Chrysostom]
           (*CPG* 8064): Kotter v. 359–70
Dial.   *Dialectica* (*CPG* 8041): Kotter i. 47–146
Dorm. I–III *Homiliae* I–III *in dormitionem b. v. Mariae* [Homilies I–III on
           the Dormition of the Blessed Virgin Mary] (*CPG* 8061–3):
           Kotter v. 483–500, 516–40, 548–55
Elias   *Commentarius in proph. Eliam* [Commentary on the Prophet
           Elias] (*CPG* 8083): Kotter v. 406–18
Expos.   *Expositio fidei* [On the Orthodox Faith] (*CPG* 8043):
           Kotter ii. 7–239
Ficus   *Homilia in ficum arefactam* [Homily on the (Cursed) Fig-
           Tree] (*CPG* 8058): Kotter v. 102–10
Fides   *De fide contra Nestorianos* [On the Faith, against the
           Nestorians] (*CPG* 8054): Kotter iv. 238–53
Haeres. *Liber de haeresibus* [On Heresies] (*CPG* 8044): Kotter iv.
           19–67
Hypap.   *Sermo in Hypapanten Domini* [Homily on the Meeting of the

Lord (i.e. the Purification, in Western calendars)] (*CPG* 8066): Kotter iv. 381–95

Ieiun.   *De sacris ieiuniis* [On the Holy Fasts] (*CPG* 8050): PG 105, 64–77

Imag. I–III   *Contra imaginum calumniatores orationes tres* [Three Treatises against those who Attack the Icons, or: Against the Iconoclasts] (*CPG* 8045): Kotter iii. 65–200

Instit.   *Institutio elementaris ad dogmata* [Elementary Introduction] (*CPG* 8040): Kotter i. 19–26

Jacob.   *Contra Jacobitas* [Against the Jacobites] (*CPG* 8047): Kotter iv. 109–53

Manich.   *Dialogus contra Manichaeos* [Dialogue against the Manichees] (*CPG* 8048): Kotter iv. 351–98

Nativ. D.   *Sermo in nativitatem Domini* [Homily on the Nativity of the Lord] (*CPG* 8067): Kotter v. 324–47

Nativ. M.   *Homilia in nativitatem b. v. Mariae* [Homily on the Nativity of the Blessed Virgin Mary] (*CPG* 8060): Kotter v. 169–82

Nestor.   *Adversos Nestorianos* [Against the Nestorians] (*CPG* 8053): Kotter iv. 263–88

Palm.   *Homilia in dominicam palmarum* [Homily for Palm Sunday] (*CPG* 8086): Kotter v. 72–90

Rect.   *De recta sententia liber* [On Right Thinking] (*CPG* 8046): PG 94, 1421–32

Sabbat.   *Homilia in sabbatum sanctum* [Homily on Holy Saturday] (*CPG* 8059): Kotter v. 121–46

Sarac.   *Disputatio Saraceni et Christiani* [Dispute between a Saracen and a Christian] (*CPG* 8075): Kotter iv. 427–38

Transfig.   *Homilia in transfigurationem domini* [Homily on the Transfiguration of the Lord] (*CPG* 8057): Kotter v. 436–59

Trisag.   *Epistula de hymno Trisagio* [Letter on the Thrice-Holy Hymn] (*CPG* 8049): Kotter iv. 304–32

Volunt.   *De duabus in Christo voluntatibus* [On the Two Wills in Christ, or: Against the Monothelites] (*CPG* 8052): Kotter iv. 173–231

(In Geerard's view, largely supported by Kotter, *CPG* 8040–70 are authentic works by John Damascene, while *CPG* 8075–8100 are dubious, and *CPG* 8110–27 are spurious.)

Other abbreviations

ACO	*Acta Conciliorum Œcumenicorum*, ser. 1, ed. E. Schwartz (and later J. Straub and R. Schieffer), 19 vols. in 4, Berlin and Leipzig: Walter de Gruyter, 1927–74; ser. 2, ed. R. Riedinger, 4 vols. in 2, Berlin: Walter de Gruyter, 1984–95
BA	Bibliothèque Augustinenne, *Œuvres de St. Augustin*, Paris: Desclée de Brouwer, 1933– .
CCSG	Corpus Christianorum, Series Graeca, Turnhout: Brepols, 1977– .
CCSL	Corpus Christianorum, Series Latina, Turnhout: Brepols, 1954– .
CPG	*Clavis Patrum Graecorum*, 5 vols., ed. M. Geerard and F. Glorie, CCSG, Turnhout: Brepols, 1974–87 (cited by item number); supplement, ed. M. Geerard and J. Noret, 1998.
CSCO	Corpus Scriptorum Christianorum Orientalium, early vols. Paris, later vols. Louvain: E. Peeters
CSEL	Corpus Scriptorum Ecclesiasticorum Latinorum, Vienna: F. Tempsky, 1866 ff.
DCB	*A Dictionary of Christian Biography, Literature, Sects, and Doctrines*, ed. William Smith and Henry Wace, 4 vols., London: John Murray, 1877
DS	*Dictionnaire de Spiritualité*, ed. M. Viller *et al*, 16 vols. + index, Paris: Le Cerf, 1937–95
GCS	Die Griechischen Christlichen Schriftsteller der ersten [drei] Jahrhunderte, ed. by the Kirchenväter-Commission der Königlichen Preussichen Akademie der Wissenschaften [later, the Deutsche Akademie der Wissenschaften zu Berlin], Leipzig: J. C. Hinrich [later, Berlin: Akademie-Verlag], 1897 ff. [Neue Folge, 1995 ff.]
Kotter	Bonifatius Kotter, OSB (ed.), *Die Schriften des Johannes von Damaskos*, 5 vols., PTS 7, 12, 17, 22, 29, Berlin and New York: Walter de Gruyter, 1969–88
LCL	Loeb Classical Library, London: Heinemann/Cambridge, Mass.: Harvard University Press, 1912 ff.
Mansi	J. D. Mansi, *Sacrorum Conciliorum Nova et Amplissima Collectio*, 31 vols., Florence, 1759–98
OCT	Oxford Classical Texts

PG	J.-P. Migne (ed.), Patrologiæ Cursus Completus, Series Græca, 162 vols., Paris, 1857–66
PL	J.-P. Migne (ed.), Patrologiæ Cursus Completus, Series Latina, 221 vols., Paris, 1844–64
PTS	Patristische Texte und Studien, im Auftrag der Patristischen Kommission der Akademien der Wissenschaften zu Göttingen, Heidelberg, München und der Akademie der Wissenschaften und der Literatur zu Mains, ed. K. Aland and W. Schneemelcher, Berlin and New York: Walter de Gruyter, 1964– .
SC	Sources Chrétiennes, Paris: Le Cerf, 1942 ff.
SP	Studia Patristica
TU	Texte und Untersuchungen zur Geschichte der altchristlichen Literatur, founded by O. von Gebhardt and A. Harnack, Leipzig, 1882–1943; Berlin, 1951 ff.

In the footnotes, titles of works cited follow the abbreviations given in G. W. H. Lampe (ed.), *A Patristic Greek Lexicon*, Oxford: Clarendon Press, 1961 (for Greek Patristic writers); H. G. Liddell and R. Scott, *A Greek–English Lexicon*, 9th edn. with new supplement, Oxford: Clarendon Press, 1996 (for Classical Greek writers); and A. Blaise, *Dictionnaire Latin–Français des Auteurs Chrétiens*, rev. edn., Turnhout: Brepols, 1967 (for Latin Patristic writers). References to Plato and Aristotle give, as is normal, the page and line numbers of the Stephanos and Bekker editions, respectively, printed in the margins of most editions (and translations). Editions used (except for PG and PL) are listed in the bibliography.

PART I

Faith and Life

I

Life and Times

St John Damascene forms a strange, though by no means exceptional, case in the history of Christian theology. His influence is far-reaching, not only in later Byzantine theology, where eventually the pattern of John's theological synthesis became determinative, but also in later Western theology, beginning with the great *Summae* of the scholastic theologians, for whom his epitome of patristic doctrine (known in the West as *De Orthodoxa Fide*, 'On the Orthodox Faith') became their principal resource for the Trinitarian and Christological doctrines defined by the Oecumenical Synods of the early Church, and continuing through the Reformation era and the period of Protestant scholasticism, up to the systematic theology of the great Romantic theologian Schleiermacher. But if the ripples of his influence reach out throughout a millennium or more of Christian history, at the centre from which these ripples emanate there is found a mysterious figure. In fact, we know far more about the times of St John Damascene than about the events of his own life, and closer scrutiny of the sources in recent scholarship has only eroded the few fixed points that were thought to exist, without providing others. The hagiographical lives of John that survive are late and unreliable (though not without interest, as we shall see); his writings contain scarcely any personal clues; and references to him in other historical sources are sparse.

The general parameters of John's life, both temporal and geographical, however, seem clear: he lived the whole of his life in the Middle East in the period of the Umayyad caliphate (651–750), first in Damascus, where he was born, and latterly in Palestine, where he became a monk. The first of the Umayyad caliphs, Mu'awiya, made Damascus his capital in 651, and from there ruled the empire the Arabs had built up from their conquest of the eastern and southern provinces of the Roman (or Byzantine) Empire and their defeat of the Persian Empire in the three decades after the death of the Prophet Muhammad in 632.[1] This empire continued to expand. It crept along the North African coastline during the course of the seventh century until in 711 Spain was itself invaded by the Arabs. In the course of the same century, one by one, islands of the Mediterranean fell to Arab rule—Cyprus (649), Rhodes (654), though Crete and Sicily were successfully to resist the Arabs for some centuries. The Arabs also invaded Asia Minor with the ultimate intention of taking the Byzantine capital, Constantinople: Arab fleets blockaded the city from 674 to 678, and again in 717–18. The Umayyads also expanded towards the East, bringing under their control the more remote provinces of the defeated Sasanid Empire of Persia.

The Umayyad Empire was the beginning of a new configuration in the political geography of the Middle East. For the seventh century can be seen to constitute a watershed in the history of the Middle East—and in fact in the history of Europe and western Asia as far as northern India. In the course of this century two landmarks, clearly in place in the earliest history of the eastern Mediterranean world we possess—that of the Greek Herodotus—were swept away. The first landmark was the basic unit of society, the old city-state: a city with its public spaces and public life that, with its agricultural hinterland, formed a fairly self-sufficient economic unit. This was eroded over a period of time that critically includes the seventh century.[2] The other landmark was the—admittedly flexible—frontier that separated the Eastern Mediterranean world (eventually the Mediterranean empire known as the Roman Empire) from the Persian Empire, that ran—ideally, from the Greek or Roman point of view—along the upper Tigris valley and the lower valley of the Euphrates. This was ultimately swept away and replaced by a frontier that consisted of the Mediterranean itself, and the Taurus and Anti-Taurus mountains that separate Asia Minor—now western Turkey—from the rest of Asia. The ripples of that change of configuration spread throughout Europe and across Asia at least as far as India, but the epicentre, so to speak, was located in the Middle East—the area now covered by Syria, the Lebanon, Jordan, Israel, Iraq, and Saudi Arabia.[3] The Umayyad Empire was the first political entity based on this change.

[1] I shall, for convenience, use the dates of the Christian era (AD). John himself would have been unfamiliar with this system; he would have used dates of the Seleucid era, and was presumably aware of the Islamic system of dating from the Hijra, the migration of Muhammad from Mecca to Medina in AD 622.

[2] On this question see, from a rapidly growing bibliography, Rich 1992 and, more specifically on the eastern Empire, Cameron 1993, 152–75.

[3] For an important attempt to rethink the significance of this change, see Fowden 1993.

The background of the Umayyad caliphate is more relevant to John's life than one might expect, for his family had a long-standing role in the fiscal administration of Syria, which it retained under the new Arab rulers.[4] John's grandfather, Mansur ibn Sarjun, to give him the name by which he is known in the Arab sources, had been in charge of the fiscal administration at Damascus from early in the seventh century. He was evidently a survivor, for he maintained his position not only after the surrender of Damascus to the Arabs in 635, a surrender that Mansur himself is said to have negotiated,[5] but also during the earlier occupation by the Persians from 612 to 628: he retained his position when Herakleios retook Damascus in 628 only by paying an indemnity of 1,000 dinars.[6] He was succeeded by his son, Sarjun ibn Mansur, who is mentioned by the Byzantine chronicler Theophanes for the year 690/1 as a 'most Christian man' and the General Logothete (treasurer).[7] There is nothing surprising in John's family continuing to occupy such a position, at least for the first half-century or so of the Umayyad period, for part of the secret of the success of the Arab expansion was that the Arabs left the administration of the conquered provinces intact, and ruled as a military elite who kept themselves apart from their conquered subjects. From their names, it would seem that John's family was Semitic, probably Syrian rather than Arab;[8] but whatever their racial background, as members of the continuing administrative class in Damascus, they are likely to have been thoroughly Hellenized.[9]

That John was born in Damascus, son of a family prominent in the civil administration of Syria, is universally admitted. When he was born is less clear. The fact that he died around 750 (see below) suggests a date in the latter half of the seventh century, but attempts to define the date more precisely (Kotter suggested 650,[10] Nasrallah 655/60[11]) depend on giving greater credence to the assertions of later, hagiographical sources than they warrant (see the next chapter). The same is true for the hagiographical details about John's education (again, see the following chapter): all we can say is that John's later command, of both Greek verse

---

[4] For John's biography and the history of his family, see Jugie 1924; Richter 1982, 2–24; Le Coz 1992, 41–58; Auzépy 1994.

[5] Eutychios, *Annals*, 278–80 (Breydy, 114–17).

[6] Ibid. 271 (107).

[7] Theophanes, *chron.* A.M. 6183 (de Boor, 365; Mango and Scott, 510).

[8] According to D. J. Sahas, of 'semitic ancestry': 1992, 204. Le Coz seems to take a similar view: 1992, 43.   [9] *Pace* Sahas 1992.

[10] Kotter 1988, 127.

[11] Nasrallah 1950, 58.

and Greek prose, makes it clear that he had benefited from a classical education (the *enkyklios paideia*). His education finished, it seems that John, whose Arabic name was the same as his grandfather's, Mansur ibn Sarjun, also served in the fiscal administration of the Umayyads.[12]

At some stage, perhaps in the second decade of the eighth century, John resigned from his post in the administration at Damascus, and became a monk in Palestine, taking as his monastic name John, the name by which he has been known ever since. It seems not unlikely that this took place around 706, when, under Caliph al-Walid, the changeover from Greek to Arabic in the Umayyad civil service finally took place.[13] The tradition that his monastery was the famous Great Laura, the monastery of St Sabas (or Mar Saba), founded in 478 by St Sabas on the steep slopes of the Wadi Kidron in the Judaean desert, is a late tradition: there is no mention of this monastery in the account of John in the tenth-century *Synaxarion of Constantinople*; its earliest mention seems to be in the probably tenth-century Greek *vita*, composed by John, patriarch of Jerusalem. There is little doubt, however, that it was in the environs of Jerusalem that he became a monk, for one of the rare personal references in his works mentions his closeness to the patriarch (presumably John V, 706–35: *Trisag.* 26. 13–14).[14] There he lived to become an old man (he refers to himself 'in the winter of words': *Dorm.* II. 1. 30 f.). He seems to have been ordained a priest: Theophanes always refers to him as 'priest and monk',[15] which is how he is generally designated in the inscriptions to his works. Just once, in the title for the homily on the fig-tree, John is described as 'presbyter of the Holy Resurrection of Christ our God'. This suggests that John held some position in the Church of the Anastasis (as well, presumably, as belonging to his monastery, whichever it was); on this basis, Eustratiades asserts that he was the 'sacred preacher (*hierokēryx*) of the Church of the Anastasis',[16] and that as such he composed his liturgical poetry, and presumably also his homilies. Theophanes the Chronicler is also witness to a tradition that he had some fame as a preacher: he always calls him John *Chrysorrhoas* ('flowing with gold'), 'because of the golden gleam of spiritual grace that bloomed both in his discourse and in his life' (the same epiphet is used, as a variant for the

---

[12] That would seem to be a reasonable inference from the comparison between John and the evangelist Matthew in the *Acta* of the Seventh Oecumenical Synod (Mansi 13. 357B).

[13] See Hoyland 1997, 651.

[14] For the Judaean monasteries in the Byzantine period, see Hirschfeld 1992. For the monastery of Mar Saba, see Patrich 1994.

[15] Theophanes, *chron.* A.M. 6221 (de Boor, 408; Mango and Scott, 565).

[16] Eustratiades 1931, 497.

more usual *chrysostomos*, of St John Chrysostom himself).[17] Furthermore, Theophanes mentions that John delivered a sermon in praise of Peter of Maïuma, who was martyred for cursing Muhammad in 743.[18] A final reference to John occurs in his condemnation at the Synod of Hiereia in 754, preserved in the *Acta* of the Seventh Oecumenical Synod of 787:[19] there he was anathematized under his Arabic name, Mansur. He was condemned together with Germanos, the patriarch of Constantinople deposed by Leo III in 730, and an otherwise unknown George of Cyprus. The condemnation concludes by saying that 'the Trinity has deposed all three', which suggests that by then they were all thought to be dead.

John spent the last years of his life as a monk living in the shadow of Jerusalem, a city by then dominated by the Muslim mosques on the Temple Mount—the Mosque of the Dome of the Rock and the Al-Aqsa Mosque—though the Christian shrines, including the Church of the Anastasis (or the Holy Sepulchre), remained, and Christian pilgrimage to the Holy Places seems to have continued, though in a reduced form. It was during this period that John probably composed his large theological *œuvre*, though we cannot rule out the possibility that some of his works were composed during his time as an Umayyad civil servant in Damascus.

But if it is difficult to establish more than the barest outline of the events of John's life, it is scarcely less difficult to establish any chronology with respect to his works. In the rest of the book, whatever evidence there is will be discussed in its place. But, to anticipate these discussions, there is very little to go on. John was, as we have seen, well educated, and an interest in theological matters was something that a well-educated layman might pursue.[20] One might well surmise that, once John became a monk, he had more time to devote to theological matters, but in the absence of any way of establishing a chronology, we cannot trace the development of his theological learning. It is very likely that John's acquaintance with Islam (which, as we shall see, was not negligible) went back to his days at the Umayyad court;[21] but the monks of Palestine knew about Islam too.

[17] Theophanes, *chron.* A.M. 6234 (de Boor, 417; Mango and Scott, 578); see also, A.M. 6221 (de Boor, 408; Mango and Scott, 565); A.M. 6245 (de Boor, 428; Mango and Scott, 592). For the use of *chrysorrhoas* see Lampe 1961, 1535.

[18] Theophanes, *chron.* A.M. 6234 (de Boor, 417; Mango and Scott, 578).

[19] See the definition of the Council of Hiereia, preserved in the *Acta* of the Seventh Oecumenical Synod: Mansi 13. 356CD (Eng. trans.: Sahas 1986, 168–9). See also Theophanes, *chron.* A. M. 6234 (de Boor, 417; Mango and Scott, 578); A.M. 6245 (de Boor, 428; Mango and Scott, 592).

[20] *Pace* Eustratiades 1931, 393, who argues that John's learning in Damascus extended only to the *enkyklios paideia*, and that his theological learning came later, under the influence of John V, patriarch of Jerusalem.   [21] See below, Ch. 5(d).

There is one work which one might be tempted to date early: his treatise against the Manichees. There are two reasons for suggesting this: first, the very slight manuscript tradition this work has, which might be explained by the fact that it was not available at his monastery; secondly, its restrained use of patristic quotation, and greater reliance on arguments formulated by John himself. But, as the reader can see, the argument is in danger of becoming circular.[22] Two of John's works (*Against the Jacobites* and *On Right Thinking*) are associated with the name of Peter II, metropolitan of Damascus, whom an eighth-century Monophysite theologian, writing against John's Christology, refers to as '[John's] bishop' (the former treatise was written at Peter's request, the latter is dedicated to him).[23] But, since Peter lived until 743, when, according to Theophanes, he was martyred for his opposition to Islam,[24] long after John had become a monk, these treatises do not necessarily belong to his early period in Damascus. The only works we can date with some confidence are his treatises against the iconoclasts: if they are concerned with Byzantine iconoclasm (which seems to me certain), they must be later than 726, and their interrelationships and the precise historical references in the second treatise enable one to suggest some sort of chronology.[25] If that is a secure inference, then there is another date we can establish, for, as Eustratiades has pointed out, John writes in this treatise with the assured authority, not just of a monk, but of a priest.[26]

If the works themselves give little hint of their place in John's life and theological development, the same can be said for the light they shed on John's preoccupations and the preoccupations of those for whom he wrote, save in general terms. There is, clearly, a concern for doctrinal orthodoxy: practically everything John writes is concerned with this. What this concern amounts to is something we shall consider in some detail later on. But it is difficult to introduce much greater specificity. The doctrine of Christ is clearly of great importance, and he defends Orthodox teaching principally against the Monophysites; he is equally passionate in his attacks on Monothelitism, which can be found even in his homilies (Nestorianism seems much less pressing).[27] The Maronites, a group of Lebanese Christians who embraced Monothelitism, are

---

[22] See below, Ch. 5(b).
[23] See Kotter, iv, 100 f., and Roey 1944.
[24] Theophanes, *chron.* A.M. 6234 (de Boor, 416; Mango and Scott, 577).
[25] See below, Ch. 7(a).
[26] Eustratiades 1931, 398.
[27] See below, pp. 157–73.

specifically mentioned in *On Right Thinking.*[28] This brief treatise is perhaps, because of its very brevity, of interest here, for it contains a confession of faith, covering, first, the Trinity (betraying little anxiety about the procession of the Spirit, simply asserting that 'he has the Father as cause and fount, going forth from him, not by way of begetting but by way of proceeding'[29]); secondly, Christological doctrine, explaining Orthodox teaching very clearly, with Monophysites and Monothelites in view (*Rect.* 2–4); then, brief chapters on the Thrice-Holy Hymn (*Rect.* 5) and the Six Oecumenical Synods (*Rect.* 6), and a final chapter expressing his allegiance to Peter II, in which he mentions heretics he has proscribed, not only the Maronites, but also the Manichees. None of this is very surprising; it is in accordance with what is generally thought to have been the religious situation in Palestine and Syria in John's day. His homilies yield a few further details.[30] He mentions Origenism as a heresy (*Sabbat.* 6. 5–7). There are occasional places where he seems to have in mind Muslim objections to Christianity: the charge of idolatry (*Barb.* 4; *Dorm.* II. 15, where the charge is honouring Mary as a 'goddess'); the remark, or taunt, as John seems to take it, that Christ was a 'slave',[31] which might simply reflect the Muslim view of Christ as one of their prophets, and therefore a true 'Muslim' (which means 'slave of God'). These hints do not add up to much, but do suggest something of the concerns and preoccupations of John and his fellow Christians.

John's works fall into roughly three categories: exposition and defence of Orthodoxy, sermons, and liturgical poetry. In composing these works, he was entering into a tradition that extended back to the Apostles, but which in a particular way had evolved from the time of the establishment of monastic settlements in Palestine in the fifth century, and had assumed a special role in the century after the conquest of the Middle East by the Arabs in the seventh century. For from the fourth century onwards, Palestine had become a centre of pilgrimage for Christians. The monasteries that grew up in the region around Jerusalem gained much of their fame, and their wealth, from their connection with the Holy Sites. Their link with the pilgrims, and their patronage by the Emperor, also meant that they were aware of a wider Christian world beyond their immediate Palestinian context. A major consequence of this oecumenical awareness emerged in the years following the Synod of Chalcedon which met in 451. This synod issued a Christological Definition of Faith, according to which Christ was defined as a single person existing in two

---

[28] *Rect.* 8 (PG 94. 1432C). [29] *Rect.* 1 (1421A).
[30] See Ch. 8 below. [31] Which John finds offensive, despite Phil. 2: 7.

natures. Many of the Christians of the East, from Syria to Egypt, greeted with dismay this decision, as it seemed to them to introduce an ultimate duality into Christ, and thereby to betray the teaching of the great patriarch of Alexandria, St Cyril, whose clear emphasis on the unity of Christ had been vindicated at an earlier synod held at Ephesus in 431. The monks of Palestine, while yielding to none in their veneration of Cyril, supported the Synod of Chalcedon, and thereby found themselves at the heart of a controversy about the unity of Christ that was still alive in the days of St John of Damascus, nearly three centuries later.

A determining moment in this controversy occurred in 516, when imperial policy under the emperor Anastasios inclined towards those who abjured Chalcedon. The Orthodox patriarch of Jerusalem, Elias, had been deposed, and his successor John was being forced to anathematize Chalcedon. However, with the support of thousands of monks from the Judaean desert, led by St Sabas, the founder of the Great Laura, by tradition John's monastery, John the patriarch was able to withstand the coercion of the military ruler (the *dux*) of Palestine, also called Anastasios, so that, instead of anathematizing Chalcedon, John anathematized those who condemned the synod.[32] Such became the historic link between the monks of Palestine and Chalcedonian Orthodoxy, that, as Flusin has put it, 'the function of the monasteries of Palestine was to be one of the strongholds, perhaps, for the East, the very hearth of Chalcedonianism'.[33]

This link between Palestinian monasticism and synodical Orthodoxy took a new form in the seventh century. On the one hand, imperial policy, under the emperor Herakleios and his sons, once again sought, if not to disown Chalcedon, at least to make peace with those who had historically rejected it. By endorsing first Monenergism (the doctrine that Christ has a single 'theandric', divine–human activity) and then Monothelitism (the doctrine that Christ has but a single [divine] will), the Emperor was able to reconcile to the Imperial Church many of those who rejected Chalcedon. In reality, few had any illusions about the nature of this compromise, despite the careful way in which these doctrines were expressed: Theophanes records the Jacobites and Theodosians (the local names for those who rejected Chalcedon in Syria and Egypt respectively) boasting, 'It is not we who have communicated with Chalcedon, but rather Chalcedon with us by confessing one nature of Christ through the one energy.'[34] It was a Palestinian monk, a native of Damascus,

---

[32] See the account in Cyril of Scythopolis, *v. Sab.* 46.

[33] Flusin 1992, ii. 59.

[34] Theophanes, *chron.* A.M. 6121 (de Boor, 330; Mango and Scott, 461).

St Sophronios, elected patriarch of Jerusalem in 634, who led the opposition to Monenergism. In 638 Monothelitism was promulgated in the imperial *Ekthesis*, and it was Sophronios's disciple St Maximos the Confessor who was to take up the baton from his mentor (who died in 638), and lead the defiance to the imperial will, an act which was to lead to his death, condemned, mutilated, and in exile, in 662. After St Maximos's death, it was the monks of Palestine who almost alone in the East came to assume the role of guardians of Orthodoxy. For most of the eastern part of the Byzantine Empire abandoned Orthodoxy in obedience to the imperial will (the West was more steadfast, not least because most of the West was beyond the power of the Emperor, though, after initial defiance, culminating in the death in exile of Pope Martin, who had supported Maximos, in 655 Rome seems to have wavered, in the persons of Pope Martin's nearest successors), and even after the restoration of Orthodoxy at the Sixth Oecumenical Synod in 680–1 (the third to be held in Constantinople), the Christians in the capital seem to have yielded easily to the imperial will, acceding to a brief revival of Monothelitism in 712 under Philippikos, and then from 726 onwards the imperial imposition of iconoclasm.

The year 638, that of the Monothelite *Ekthesis*, was also the year in which Sophronios, as patriarch of Jerusalem, surrendered what was now the Christian holy city to Caliph Umar: which leads us to the other defining factor in the link between Orthodoxy and Palestinian monasticism in the seventh century. For the situation in Palestine itself changed—forever, as it turned out—as a result of the Arab conquest of the Middle East. Theological matters ceased to be a matter of the imperial will (or resistance to it): there was created, under the caliphate, a kind of level playing field so far as religious doctrine was concerned. To begin with the Arab rulers seem to have shown little inclination towards proselytism (save towards other Arabs), so that Christians of all varieties—those who accepted synodical Orthodoxy; those who rejected Chalcedon out of loyalty to St Cyril of Alexandria (often called 'Monophysites'); those who had been condemned at the Synod of Ephesus at which Cyril had been victorious, called by their enemies 'Nestorians' after the patriarch of Constantinople deposed at that council; Monenergists; and Monothelites—now existed alongside one another, and also alongside those belonging to other religions, not least Jews, who had been much encouraged by the fall of Christian Jerusalem, first to the Persians in 614 and then to the Arabs in 638, and probably also Samaritans and Manichees, both groups survivors of imperial persecution in the sixth century. It is probably this new situation that accounts for the sudden emergence of Christian–Jewish dialogue (or anti-Jewish vituperation) in the seventh century,[35] and also for the growth of controversial literature, often in the form of dialogues, in which the issues (mostly Christological) between the different varieties of Christianity were argued out. With the intra-Christian debate, in particular, the issues were often very technical, involving philosophical terms such as 'essence' and 'person', and concepts such as the will. Already in the writings of Maximos we find lists of definitions of such concepts, drawn both from the classical philosophers and their successors in Late Antiquity and from the writings of the Christian Fathers.[36] But it was not only a matter of definition of terms, the arguments themselves had to be sound, and so we find in the seventh century the development of simple books of logic designed for Christian controversialists, drawing on the logical treatises of Aristotle and later philosophers, such as Porphyry and the sixth-century Aristotelian commentators of Alexandria.[37] The monks of Palestine found themselves not only defending, almost alone in the East, the Orthodoxy of the Byzantine councils, but also refining that Orthodoxy and defining it more precisely in this new situation of open controversy.

This was the situation into which John entered: a process of refining and defining the tradition of Christian Orthodoxy. Both by his family background as a Syrian 'Melkite' (that is, a supporter of the imperial Orthodoxy of the Byzantine *basileus*, king, in Syriac, *malkâ*) and by becoming one of the Palestinian monks, with their historic attachment to synodical Orthodoxy, John was committed to that cause. We should see John not as a remarkable individual who was able to reduce the amorphous mass of traditional Orthodoxy to some kind of 'scholastic' form, but as the culmination of a tradition of definition that had entered on a new phase a decade or so before his birth, and consequently regard his works as the high point of this phase. But Palestinian monasticism was engaged in more than a prolonged bout of controversial theology: the Faith was not just defended and defined, it was also acclaimed in the weekly celebration of the paschal mystery, and in the celebration year by year of the great events of the history of salvation (or the 'economy', *oikonomia*, as Greek theology calls it), as well as the feast-days of the great

---

[35] See the recent survey by Averil Cameron (1996), and the literature cited there.

[36] See, e.g., Maximos the Confessor, *opusc.* 14, 17, 18, 23, 26 (the authenticity of some of these *opuscula* is not certain).

[37] For further detail see Ch. 3 below.

saints of the Christian Church. Homilies formed an important part of this celebration, but by the seventh century they were being overtaken by the liturgical poetry with which the worship of the Christian Church—and in particular the worship of the Christian monastery—was being increasingly embellished. John, as we have seen, was a preacher of renown in his day. He seems also to have been one of the greatest liturgical poets, who contributed particularly to a new development in the monastic office: the canon, a series of verses (or troparia), originally interwoven with the verses of the nine biblical odes, or canticles, that were the backbone of the monastic office of matins (or *orthros*, the 'dawn service').[38]

It is important not to isolate John the monk from the background of the Palestinian monasticism to which he belonged. It is necessary to emphasize this for several reasons. First, the later Byzantine tradition was happy to treat John in isolation, given that the Byzantine Church itself had responded so abysmally to iconoclasm. That one lone monk in Palestine spoke up against iconoclasm could be admitted, but not that he was but one member of a large Christian community that stood fast when Byzantium wavered. In the aftermath of iconoclasm, the Byzantines, especially the patriarchal court, rewrote the history of the period, bringing out the heroic role of the patriarchs Germanos, Tarasios, and Nikephoros in preventing a complete collapse before the imperial will. The resistance of the people and the monks of Palestine did not fit this picture, whereas an isolated voice like John's could be accommodated. Secondly, the community of Palestinian monks was important for John himself. He was no isolated genius, but a participant in an extended collaborative exercise. The history of the dissemination of his works, many of which exist in parallel forms, is, as we shall see in the course of this book, full of puzzles. It becomes less puzzling, if we see John writing for his contemporaries, even if it took a long time, perhaps not much less than a century, for his works to reach Byzantium. The different editions of his great work, *The Fountain Head of Knowledge*, the different forms of each of the three parts of this work, the different versions of his attack on iconoclasm (which is what the three different treatises really are), and the alternative versions of some of his other treatises (e.g., *On the Two Wills in Christ*) make sense if we see John writing for an immediate audience, amongst whom his works were quickly (and thereafter, irrevocably) distributed. Thirdly, John's eventual renown and his place in Byzantine theology are again probably to be seen as part of the general influence of Palestinian monasticism on Byzantium in the wake of iconoclasm. This is

---

[38] For a more detailed discussion, see Ch. 9 below.

usually regarded as part of the reform of Byzantine monasticism initiated in the lull between the two periods of iconoclasm by St Theodore of Stoudios, though it may well have been part of a more general influence of the traditions, not least the liturgical traditions, of the Holy Places on Constantinople.

It is John's theological work, the product of both the intellect and the heart, that is the subject of this book. The work of an individual, no doubt, but of an individual who cared nothing for his own individuality, and lost himself in the tradition that he was enriching and passing on. The immediate context of his theological task should not go unnoticed. When we think of Byzantine Orthodoxy, the theology of the Oecumenical Synods—that is, the synods that spoke for the *oikoumene*, the (whole) inhabited realm that the Byzantine Emperors claimed to rule under God—we are apt to think of a somewhat triumphalist progress of Orthodoxy, protected by the Emperor, and both able and willing to call on the power of the State to persecute those who opposed what they called Orthodoxy. There is some truth in this, and it is a truth that is often ugly. But it is a truth that does not apply at all to the theological task in which John was engaged. The process of refining, defining, and celebrating Orthodoxy that John took part in was the work of Palestinian monks, living and working almost literally in the shadow of the mosques of the Dome of the Rock and of Al-Aqsa, newly built on the Temple Mount in Jerusalem and overshadowing the Christian Holy Sites, Palestinian monks who belonged to a minority with diminishing power, attacked by other Christians (who called them 'Maximianists', followers of a monk who had been condemned for heresy by the Byzantine Emperor), and open to attack once again from Jews, Samaritans, Manichees, and eventually Muslims. This Christian Orthodoxy was not the expression of human triumphalism, but something fashioned in the crucible of defeat.

2

St John Damascene and Tradition

There are two ways of understanding St John Damascene's relationship to tradition. The first sees tradition as that which shaped his experience: both the historical and political context in which he was born, grew up, and served as a civil servant, and, within that, the life he lived as a monk and the theological tradition into which he thus entered. As we have seen, this tradition of theological thought and liturgical celebration already had a long history; in most respects John continued ways of theological thought and theological proclamation already established. John himself was well aware of this: he made no claim to any kind of theological originality, and indeed would have been horrified to have been thought original. As he put it in the dedicatory letter with which he prefaced what came to be called *The Fountain Head of Knowledge*, 'I shall say nothing of my own, but collect together into one the fruits of the labours of the most eminent of teachers and make a compendium' (*Dial.*, proem. 60–2). John is a representative of a determining period in the development of the Byzantine theological tradition, rather than an original thinker. This is more than a simple consequence of the horror with which the Byzantine world greeted any kind of innovation. Anything new was disguised as tradition, so that the genuinely original insights of a thinker such as St Maximos the Confessor were expressed as reflections—or commentary—on already existing tradition. But John was no Maximos. John developed a tradition of learning that knew where to look in the Fathers for answers to all theological questions, and he responded to these questions by reproducing the best that he could find. He had, one might say, a genius for selection; but even this was probably not simply a matter of his personal giftedness as a learned scholar: he belonged to a tradition that had been sifting the works of the Fathers for generations. Florilegia—that is, collections of extracts from the Fathers on all significant topics—abounded, and there is no doubt that John made use of such. It is this first sense of a shaping tradition—embracing both the historical and political context in which John lived and the developing religious tradition into which he entered—that will be explored in the course of this book.

But there is another sense of tradition, in which John's role is more active. For the theological tradition to which he belonged, in the narrower sense, may be said to have culminated in John, and it is John who represents this tradition in later theology. This later role, as pre-eminent bearer of accumulated tradition and the source of later influence, took some time to develop: there is little trace of it in the ninth-century cultural Renaissance in Byzantium, often referred to, in Lemerle's phrase, as 'le premier humanisme byzantin';[1] indeed, John may have appeared to the great scholars of the ninth century to be a mere epitomizer. But by the eleventh century John's role as the pre-eminent representative of the Byzantine theological tradition had become evident, and in the twelfth century and thereafter it made itself felt in the West. There are two works that constitute striking witnesses to this fact, in which we see John not so much as one shaped by tradition, but as one who has given shape to what others have received as tradition, especially in determining their perception of the theological achievement of what came to be regarded as the golden age of the Fathers. These two works are the Greek *vita* of St John Damascene[2] and a work once attributed to John Damascene himself, the popular theological romance, *Barlaam and Ioasaph*.

In my account of John's life in the first chapter, the Greek *vita* was ignored: there are good reasons for this, some of which will emerge in what follows.[3] But even if the Greek *vita* is worthless as a historical source for the life of John, it is not without interest. As is the case with much hagiography, if we cease to regard this *vita* as a kind of window, opening out on to the historical landscape of John's life, and instead see it as a mirror in which later attitudes to John, and indeed to Christian sanctity

[1] The title of Paul Lemerle's great work, *Le premier humanisme byzantin. Notes et remarques sur enseignement et culture à Byzance des origines au XE siècle*, Paris: Presses Universitaires de France, 1971.

[2] The Greek *vita* is reprinted in PG. 94. 429–89. It is said to have been written by John, patriarch of Jerusalem, and to have been based on an Arabic *vita*. Possible Johns of Jerusalem are John VII (964–6) and John VIII (1106–56). An Arabic *vita* of the eleventh century was discovered earlier this century. If this is the *vita* used by John, then it must be the later John (though two manuscripts of the Greek *vita* are dated to the tenth century, this dating is not beyond revision); but it is possible that an earlier Arabic *vita* (no longer extant) was the exemplar, which would make possible an earlier date for the Greek life. See Richter 1982, 2–12; Kazhdan and Gero 1989, 125–6; Le Coz 1992, 41–3.

[3] Other recent accounts of John have been much less dismissive of the Greek *vita* and indeed have supplemented the account it gives from Arabic sources: see Nasrallah 1950, Sahas 1972.

as such, are reflected, then it becomes not only interesting, but even informative.

After a few introductory paragraphs, the Greek *vita* tells us of John's ancestors, who, it says, were rulers of Damascus among the Saracens (as it regularly calls the Arabs, following normal Christian usage), and gives a glowing account of John's father, praising especially his devout Christian faith and his charitable munificence. We then learn of John's birth and baptism, and how he was brought up not to bear arms or go hunting, but to understand the things of God. There follows a story about a monk from Calabria, called Cosmas, who had been captured by the Arabs ('barbarians' as they are now called: another normal Greek usage), and was facing possible death. This fate he bewails, he says, not because he fears death, but because in the course of his life he has acquired much learning, and would like to pass it on to a disciple before he dies. As a result, John's father purchases Cosmas as a slave from the leader of the Saracens, so that he can teach his son, John, together with another youth, also called Cosmas, from Jerusalem, whom he had adopted as his spiritual son. We then learn of the education of John and Cosmas, and of John's pre-eminence in theology. At last, Cosmas the teacher tells John's father that he has taught them all he knows, and would now like to resume his monastic life. He is allowed to depart, and becomes a monk at the Great Laura of St Sabas. John's father soon dies, and the ruler of the Saracens (the Caliph) makes John his 'first counsellor' (*protosymboulos*), or vizier.

We now find ourselves in 726 or 730, for the Byzantine emperor Leo III has banned the holy icons. John writes treatises in defence of the veneration of icons, and these come to the ears of the Emperor and enrage him. Unable to touch John directly, he has a letter forged in John's handwriting in which John is made to say that Damascus is poorly defended and that he could deliver it into the hands of the Emperor. This letter the Emperor passes on to the Caliph, who is naturally incensed at the disloyalty of his trusted servant, and has John's right hand amputated as punishment. The hand is displayed publicly, but John begs it back from the Caliph, in order to bury it: a request which is granted. This hand John places before an icon of the Mother of God, while he prays to her—in anacreontic verses! The Mother of God takes pity on John, and when he falls asleep, she appears to him in a dream, and his hand is restored. John awakes, discovers his hand restored, and spends the rest of the night singing his thanks to the Mother of God—and waking up his neighbours. In the morning he is summoned before the Caliph, who sees John's restored hand (a suture round his wrist remains, showing where it was cut off), concludes that he must have been innocent, and so restores him to the post of first counsellor. John prostrates himself before the Caliph, and begs permission, as he puts it, 'to take another path, and follow him who said "I am the Way"'. It is only after John has successfully defended himself in a duel—the telling of which draws on traditional accounts of the experiences of the martyrs—that John is allowed to leave the service of the Caliph. John gives away his wealth, sets off to Jerusalem to venerate the Holy Places, and then goes out into the desert to the Laura of St Sabas, where, together with his fellow-pupil Cosmas, he becomes a monk.

John initially has great difficulty in finding a monk to act as his spiritual father, such is his worldly fame and education; but eventually a *geron* ('elder': the traditional term for a spiritual father) is found, who lays down strict conditions: no writing, no study of the 'outer wisdom' (that is, secular learning), he is to 'practise silence with understanding'. John's obedience is tested in various extreme ways, characteristic of the tradition of the Desert Fathers. At one point he is commanded to go back to Damascus with baskets made in the monastery that he is to sell for an absurdly high price: as he sits in the market-place, he is recognized by someone who knew him at court, and who buys the baskets for the price John is asking. The next event concerns the death of the brother of one of his fellow-monks. In his grief, the monk begs John to write a funeral verse to comfort him. Mindful of his *geron*'s command, John at first refuses, but then relents and composes a troparion (verse of liturgical poetry).[4] This act of disobedience outrages his *geron*, who expels him from the cell they shared. The other spiritual fathers of the monastery take pity on John and plead with his spiritual father, who relents only on the condition that John clean out the monastery's lavatories ('the little houses of filth and pollution', as the *vita* puts it). Such a penance is thought so humiliating that the fathers are reluctant to tell John; but he hears them talking about it, and willingly does it. John is restored to the cell of his *geron*. The *geron* then has a vision of the Mother of God, in which she tells him that John

---

[4] The *vita* gives the first words of the troparion: 'Futility is everything human'. In a footnote, the Migne edition gives a complete troparion beginning with these words from a homily by the thirteenth/fourteenth-century Constantine Acropolites. In his long poem 'Ioann Damaskin', based on the *vita*, the nineteenth-century Russian poet Alexei Tolstoy gave a central place to this episode, and composed a long *tropar'* for John (which is quite independent of whatever the *vita* referred to). The last stanza of Tolstoy's *tropar'* provided the text for a cantata by Sergei Taneyev (also called *Ioann Damaskin*), which was first performed in 1884 in the memory of the Russian pianist Nikolai Rubinstein.

should be allowed to write songs; so John is commanded by his *geron* to write liturgical poetry. There then follows an account of John's writings — not just his songs, but his theological treatises and sermons as well. We are told, too, that Cosmas, John's spiritual brother, shared John's gift, especially for the composition of songs. Cosmas, we learn, became bishop of Maïuma, and John himself was ordained priest; but even as a priest, John remained a humble monk of the monastery. We hear more about John's writing, and of his having been praised by St Stephen the Younger, the great iconoclast martyr, and the account comes to an end.

It is an elaborate piece of hagiography, and follows many of the conventions (or *topoi*) of the genre: the nobility of John's family, the severity of his ascetic training, his humility, the miracles. But, looked at more closely, we can begin to discern various questions with which those who composed the *vita* (both the original Arabic *vita* on which it depends, and the Greek *vita* itself) and those who read it approached the life of John of Damascus. Take, for instance, the account of John's education by the mysterious Calabrian monk with his profound classical learning, whom John's father purchases in the slave market. Writing at least three centuries later, Christians living under the Arabs were amazed at John's classical learning, for John, too, had lived under the caliphs. But his education is probably not all that surprising, for Hellenistic learning seems to have flourished in the Middle East in the seventh century, probably more so than in the beleaguered capital of the Byzantine Empire itself.[5] But to Christian Arabs living at the turn of the millennium it was amazing, and this story provides an explanation.[6]

The account of Emperor Leo's revenge for John's attack on his iconoclasm likewise reflects later reality: how could the Emperor not have known about John Damascene and his defence of the icons? later Arab Christians, well aware of John's renown, surmised. The comparatively friendly relations between Emperor and Caliph also reflect later reality. The miracle of John's restored hand was to give rise to a particular form of the icon of the Mother of God, the so-called icon of the *Theotokos Tricherousis*, the 'Mother of God with the three hands'. For John, in gratitude for the miracle, was said to have had a silver hand made which was placed on the icon that had worked the miracle, and in copies of that icon the 'third' hand was included. The original icon is said to

[5] See Mango, n.d.

[6] For a more detailed discussion of the evolution of the account of the teacher of the Damascene, see Kazhdan and Gero 1989, 128–9.

have been brought from the Great Laura to the Serbian Athonite monastery of Chilandar by the great Serbian saint, Sava, in the thirteenth century.

The story of the beginning of John's writing liturgical hymns may reflect the tradition, in fact false, that in early days monks had been opposed to singing and to liturgical song. There is a famous story about Abba Pambo rebuking one of his monks who had heard the wonderful singing in the churches of Alexandria and regretted that there was no such singing among the monks in the desert. Abba Pambo, in despair, prophesied that one day the monks would indeed sing troparia during their services, but 'what kind of contrition, what tears, come to birth from troparia? What kind of contrition does the monk feel, who stands in church or in his cell and raises his voice like the oxen?'[7] There are no such stories from authentic accounts of the early Desert Fathers, however, and it is now maintained that the story of Abba Pambo is no earlier than the sixth century.[8] It is interesting, nevertheless, that this story is first found in the *Synagoge* of Paul Evergetinos.[9] This collection of monastic wisdom belongs to the middle of the eleventh century; it is therefore very nearly contemporary with the Greek *vita* of the Damascene, and therefore very likely reflects the same attitudes to the monastic past as we are likely to find in the *vita*. And so it seems to be in this case: the author of the *vita* is clearly familiar with the idea that originally the singing of troparia was foreign to the monastic life, and in his story about John's initial reluctance, overcome by his love for one of his monastic brothers, and by the Mother of God's endorsement of his poetical gifts, he accounts for John's renown as a liturgical poet. But the story also serves to provide supernatural authentication of John's gift for liturgical poetry. Such authentication is not unusual: Romanos's gift for composing kontakia came about as the result of a dream of the Mother of God,[10] and similarly with Caedmon.[11] John's case, however, is more like that of Gerard Manley Hopkins, for both of them had a natural facility for writing poetry (the *vita* claims that John had composed anacreontics for the Mother of God while still a civil servant), which they renounced on embracing the religious life, and took up again only when expressly commanded to do

---

[7] From Wellesz's recounting of the famous story: 1961, 172 n. 2.

[8] McKinnon 1994, 508.

[9] *Evergetinos*, ii. 160–1. The monastery of the Theotokos Evergetis, for which Paul compiled his *Synagoge*, is currently the subject of a research project at the Institute of Byzantine Studies, Belfast: see Mullett and Kirby 1994, 1997.

[10] *Synaxarion* 96. 8–14 (1 Oct.).

[11] Bede, *Hist.* iv. 24 (Colgrave and Mynors, 414–16).

so.[12] For it is *primarily* as a poet that John is presented in the *vita*: in his dream, John's *geron* hears the Mother of God praising John's gifts as a poet. The *vita* treats his gift for writing liturgical poetry as overflowing into his composition of theological treatises and sermons.

The other work that reveals something of the esteem in which John was held in the eleventh century is the romance *Barlaam and Ioasaph*. Until very recently John's authorship of this work was still defended,[13] and John's modern editor, Dom Bonifatius Kotter, seems to have kept an open mind on the issue.[14] But it is very unlikely that the work was composed by John; rather, it seems that it is a Greek translation from a Georgian version, made in the tenth or eleventh century, by St Euthymios the Georgian, a monk of the Iveron (Georgian) Monastery on the Holy Mountain.[15] The story is an elaboration of the life of the Buddha (who becomes St Ioasaph), composed in Arabic under Manichaean inspiration, and given Christian adoption when it was translated into Georgian, whence, at the beginning of the eleventh century, came the Greek version. In its Greek dress, the story is expanded by the addition of a great deal of theological material: long speeches are inserted, one of which is the otherwise lost second-century *Apology of Aristides* (a Syriac translation survives, but the Greek original is lost). This theological material is often either derived from John Damascene or characteristic of him, and it is on this material that Dölger drew in his attempt to prove the Damascene authorship of the romance.[16] He drew attention to its theological and polemical standpoint, which he argued was identical with that of John (62–4); to the agreement of theological formulae in the romance with those of the Damascene (64); to the way in which both the romance and John have the habit of borrowing whole works, or substantial parts of such works, and inserting them in their own compositions (65); to the way in which the romance, like John in his authentic works, frequently cites word for word from known works by John (65–8); and the similar tendency in both the romance and John's authentic works to introduce brief definitions of terms (68–9). Dölger concluded his case with a long

[12] *The Correspondence of Gerard Manley Hopkins and Richard Watson Dixon*, ed. C.C. Abbott, London: Oxford University Press, 1935, 14.

[13] See Dölger 1953.

[14] Kotter 1988, 127.

[15] See Lang 1955 and, more briefly, his introduction to *Barl.*, pp. ix–xxxv. F. Halkin (1953) made many of Lang's points in his review of Dölger. More recent suggestions assign *Barlaam and Ioasaph* a tenth-century or Constantinopolitan provenance (Griffith 1986, 131–2) or locate it in Palestine around 800 (Kazhdan 1988).

[16] In what follows, references to Dölger are provided in parentheses in the text.

list of passages, giving parallels in the works of the Damascene and in the Damascene's favourite theological writers (notably St Basil the Great and St Gregory the Theologian) (69–104). But what Dölger shows is not, as he intended, that the romance is by John, but that, by the eleventh century, anyone wanting to show that he was theologically literate turned to the works of the Damascene both for a model and for theological material.

The significance of this is perhaps greater than might appear at first sight, for the romance *Barlaam and Ioasaph*, if the eleventh-century attribution is correct, is related to the broader project of producing an extensive collection of saints' lives, the *Menologion*, associated with Symeon Metaphrastes. What Symeon and his associates were doing was producing a uniform collection of saints' *vitae* in the literary Greek of the period, frequently working over older saints' lives that had been composed originally in the spoken Greek of ordinary people. It is possible that the working over of *Barlaam and Ioasaph* was done by Symeon Metaphrastes, or one of his colleagues, using a faithful translation from the Georgian by St Euthymios, though there is no reason to suppose that Euthymios could not have produced the farced translation himself: he may even have been an acquaintance of Symeon, and shared his hagiographical ideals. But this association suggests that John provided the theological bench-mark, as it were, for the whole Metaphrastic enterprise: further evidence of the pervasiveness of John's influence by the eleventh century.

It is interesting to note that it is somewhat less than a century after Euthymios, or one of his associates, made of the tale of Barlaam and Ioasaph the Greek version, redolent of the theology of St John Damascene, that we have the first evidence of a liturgical cult of St John at the monastery of Mar Saba. It occurs in the Russian abbot Daniel's account of his pilgrimage to the Holy Land in 1106–8. He visited Mar Saba, and there he tells us that 'in the beautifully executed chapel over the tomb' of St Saba there 'lie many holy fathers, their bodies as if still alive; the bishop St John the Silent, St John Damascene and St Theodore of Edessa and Michael his nephew lie here, and St Aphroditian and many other saints, their bodies as if still alive and exhaling an ineffable perfume'.[17]

Most of this book will be concerned with exploring the vortex in the

---

[17] Wilkinson *et al.* 1988, 140. St John the Silent was a bishop who resigned his see to become a monk under St Saba; St Theodore a ninth-century bishop; St Aphroditian (or Aphrodit) probably Aphrodisius, a disciple of St Saba, perhaps assimilated to a popular apocryphal tale about an Afroditian (see the notes to the translation).

development and formation of the Byzantine theological tradition represented by John. Although the *vita* presents John first as a poet, and then as a theologian (thereby faithfully represents the regard in which John is held in the tradition of Byzantine Orthodoxy up to the present day), we shall proceed in the reverse direction. The principal reason for this is the state of these texts. Dom Bonifatius Kotter devoted his life to producing a critical edition of the texts of John of Damascus. This project was undertaken by the Byzantine Institute of the Benedictine Abbey of Scheyern, to which Kotter belonged. The original project envisaged an edition of about eight volumes, covering all the Damascene's prose works.[18] Of these Kotter produced five volumes (1969–88). The first volume is devoted to John's logical treatises, principally his *Dialectica*, the second to *On the Orthodox Faith*, the first and last parts of his three-part work, *Pêgê Gnôseôs, The Fountain Head of Knowledge*. Volume 3 contains the treatises against the iconoclasts. Volume 4 gathers together his polemical writings: *On Heresies*, the central section of the *Pêgê Gnôseôs*, and his treatises against the Manichees and the Christological heresies of Monophysitism, Monothelitism, and Nestorianism. The fifth volume, published posthumously, contains John's homilies.[19] A final volume, devoted to John Damascene's exegetical works, has yet to appear. This magnificent edition is based on a thorough analysis of the tradition to which John belonged, in the two senses we have outlined: that is, the tradition John inherited and the one he shaped. For Kotter's edition makes clear the tradition on which John relied: his edition is furnished with an apparatus detailing the patristic works and other sources used by John in his own writings. But Kotter also explored the tradition of the manuscripts of John's works, revealing much of interest about the way John's works were valued by those who preserved them, as well as some differences between what seems to have been John's original intention and the way his works were read later. One striking finding of Kotter's research is how much John became assimilated to the tradition. He had, we have seen, renown as a preacher. But no one seems to have thought to make a collection of his sermons; the sermons that survive do so in liturgical manuscripts, *Menaia* and such like: John's extant sermons have become a continuing part of the liturgical celebration for which they were originally composed. The same is true of his poetry. Whereas with older

---

[18] See Hoeck's introduction to the first volume of the edition: Kotter i. pp. v–vii.

[19] For a list of John's works, with their traditional Latin titles and the English translations used in this book, together with their location in Kotter's edition (or Migne's *Patrologia Graeca*, for those works not edited by Kotter), see pp. xiv–xv, above.

writers such as St Gregory the Theologian, or even Synesios of Cyrene, there are collections of their poetry in manuscripts, with John there is nothing of the sort: his verse survives littered throughout liturgical manuscripts, sometimes ascribed to him, often not, simply part of the tradition of liturgical celebration to which, as we shall see, he made such a significant contribution.

Kotter's edition, however, was confined to the prose works of the Damascene: his theological treatises and sermons. Fundamental work remains to be done on his liturgical poetry, as on Byzantine liturgical poetry in general. Scholars have long lamented this: Dom Johannes Hoeck, in his survey of research on John of Damascus, preparatory to the edition to which his fellow-monk, Kotter, was to devote his life, remarked that 'anyone, possessed even of only a little familiarity with this material [that is, the poetry of the Eastern Church], knows how shifting much of the ground is here and how much pioneer work is still needed, before even the slightest semblance of order can be brought to this chaos'.[20] The situation has not changed dramatically in the last half-century. Nevertheless, there was already a series of articles, based on liturgical manuscripts mainly in Jerusalem and Paris, published in 1931–3 by the former bishop of Leontopolis, Sophronios Eustratiades,[21] that Hoeck seems to have overlooked, as well as the now rather elderly *Heortodromion* ('Guide to the Feasts') by St Nikodimos the Agiorite (*c.*1749–1809; better known perhaps for his contribution to the compilation of the *Philokalia*) which provides a commentary on the canons for ten of the Twelve Great Feasts, together with those for Holy Week and Easter, several of which are by John Damascene, in which Nikodimos explores the theology of the canons and analyses their patristic sources.[22]

Besides the works edited by Kotter and the liturgical poetry, there are other genuine works by the Damascene. These mainly comprise the exegetical works, destined for the final volume of the Scheyern edition. Most imposing is the *Hiera*, or *Sacra Parallela* (*CPG* 8056), which is something like the scriptural *catenae* (that is, collections of extracts from the Fathers, arranged in 'chains' as commentary on verses of Scripture), save that it is arranged thematically, rather than following the order of the scriptural text.[23] This genre is by no means peculiar to the Damascene; similarly arranged are the *Pandects* of Antiochos, a monk of the monastery

---

[20] Hoeck 1951, 53.   [21] Eustratiades 1931–3.
[22] Nikodimos 1987.   [23] On the *Hiera*, see also Odorico 1990, 14–21.

of Mar Saba at the beginning of the seventh century,[24] and the *Kephalaia theologica* or *Loci communes*, falsely ascribed to Maximos the Confessor. Karl Holl, long ago, demonstrated the close links that exist between these two works and John's *Hiera*.[25] Tradition has not been kind to the *Hiera*. Originally it seems to have consisted of a massive florilegium of biblical verses, accompanied by passages of patristic exegesis, arranged in three books: the first on God, the second on human nature, and the third on the virtues and vices. (The title, 'Sacred Parallels', seems to derive from the parallel arrangement of this last book.) In this form little has survived (and even less edited). Other versions, in which the three books were conflated and the material arranged alphabetically (as in the first two books), have survived, but in this form the editorial intentions of the Damascene are to some extent obscured.[26] It is an enormously important work, in which, as Karl Holl put it, John 'created for the ethics of the Greek Church something similar to what he did for its dogmatics with his *Pêgê Gnôseôs*'.[27] Nevertheless, I shall have little to say about the *Hiera* and John's contribution to scriptural exegesis in this book. This may seem a serious omission, but so little scholarship has been devoted either to establishing a critical text of the *Hiera* (if that is any longer possible) or to exploring John's method in compiling it, that the balance of this book, intended as a general survey of John's theological endeavour, would be skewed if I were to attempt such an assessment here. Besides the *Hiera*, there is a commentary on the Pauline Epistles, ascribed to the Damascene, which presents itself as extracted from the homilies of John Chrysostom. This seems to be not entirely the case, though it is not clear what other Fathers have been drawn on. The authenticity of this as a work of the Damascene is dubious, however, so I shall ignore it.[28] What I have to say about John's interpretation of Scripture will be mostly found in the chapters on his sermons and his liturgical poetry.

There are two short treatises, not edited by Kotter, generally recognized as being authentic, *On Right Thinking*, a brief exposition of the Christian faith, addressed to Peter II, metropolitan of Damascus, and *On Fasting*, as well as a table for calculating Easter (*Canon Paschalis*: *CPG* 8055),

---

[24] Antiochos's *Pandects* can be found in PG 89. 1428–1849 (*CPG* 7843), and the *Loci communes* in PG 91. 721–1017 (*CPG* 7718).

[25] Holl 1897, 277–390.

[26] This summary is based on Holl 1897; Richard 1964, 476–86; and *CPG* 8056, which gives details of what is published of the *Hiera*.

[27] Holl 1897, 392.

[28] The commentary can be found in PG 95. 441–1033 (*CPG* 8079). See also Hoeck's comment on it: 1951, 30 n. 2.

and three prayers (*CPG* 8081), the first two of which still form part of the
Orthodox Office of Preparation for Holy Communion; though generally
categorized as dubious, they may well be genuine.

It is a serious question, however, as to what is meant by 'authorship'
and 'authenticity' in a case like John Damascene's. By modern standards,
with our high evaluation of originality and the 'right of the author', John
was scarcely an author at all: he was simply a skilful plagiarist. We have
already noted that John makes no claim to originality, thereby simply
reflecting the abhorrence of originality characteristic of Byzantine society
as a whole.[29] Further, it is even difficult to know how far John's skill in
selecting and organizing is really his own. The post-modernist notion of
the 'death of the author' may seem to have been anticipated by John: for
he never even lived as an author in that sense. But the corollary of the
'death of the author' is the 'birth of the reader'.[30] This may be an illuminating notion for understanding John—except that the notion of the
reader here is not that of the *individual reader*, as nowadays, but rather that
of a tradition of *reading*, a tradition that sets out for the reader certain
Fathers for certain subjects: Gregory of Nyssa for Trinitarian theology,
perhaps, or Cyril of Alexandria for Christology. The florilegia are already
a beginning of this process, and various other works that John knew and
used can also be seen as developing such a guide for discriminating reading. It is within such a tradition of reading that John the 'author' is to be
understood. What John contributes of his own is perhaps seen most
clearly in his sermons and in his poetry. Studer has remarked that 'not
only the songs, but also his sermons, especially those for the feasts of the
Transfiguration of the Lord and the Dormition of the Mother of God,
give eloquent witness of his poetical talent, even if there were models for
these sermons'.[31] That last caveat is important, for even in his sermons,
and, one might say especially in his songs, John does not seek to surprise
his listener or reader by what he says: what engages them is the way he says
it. Eustratiades spoke of 'the sweetness of his rhythm and line and the
simplicity of his expression'.[32]

The plan of the rest of this book finds its structure in the most
important of John Damascene's works. The next part, 'Faith and Logic',

[29] For the question of originality in Byzantine culture in general, see Littlewood 1995. Only
one of the contributions to this symposium, that by Mary Cunningham, concerns matters
theological, and her contribution deals with an earlier period than that of John.

[30] Cf. Roland Barthes: 'the birth of the reader must be at the cost of the death of the
Author', in his 'The Death of the Author': 1977, 148.

[31] Studer 1956, 15.

[32] Eustratiades 1931, 500.

takes as its guide the shape of the Damascene's main set of theological treatises, his *The Fountain Head of Knowledge* (*Pégé Gnôseôs*—logic : heresies : orthodoxy—as envisaged by John in the dedicatory letter to the then bishop of Maïuma, Cosmas (*Dial.*, proem. 43–60). Taking that as a framework, we shall discuss, first, John's textbooks of logic that provided a basis for the concepts and arguments in his theological works (Chapter 4); secondly, his engagement with heresies both in his *On Heresies*, and in some of his shorter treatises, paying greater attention to those heresies about which John seems to have something of his own to say, notably Manichaeism, Messalianism, and Islam (and largely passing over here the doctrinal heresies, which will be treated in the context of John's exposition of the Christian faith) (Chapter 5); and thirdly, John's own exposition of the Orthodox doctrine, principally in his *On the Orthodox Faith*, but also in those opuscula in which he attacks Christian doctrinal heresies (Chapter 6). This second part will thus trace John's building up of his edifice of Orthodoxy, both as a positive recapitulation of the tradition and as something to be defended against error.

The final part of the book, 'Faith and Images', begins with the great new challenge which John encountered to his vision of Orthodoxy: the proclamation of iconoclasm in Byzantium, that empire in which he never set foot, though he seems to have felt he belonged there. In his treatises against the iconoclasts we can see in operation John's defence of, and definition of, Orthodoxy: his use of argument and rhetoric, his appeal to the Christian tradition, and his amassing of texts from the Fathers in support of his position. But John's defence of Orthodoxy, I shall argue, was more than an *ad hoc* defence. John saw Orthodoxy as a seamless whole, the rejection of any part of which entailed destruction of the whole. So his defence does more than counter iconoclast arguments; it demonstrates the central place of images in the faith professed by men and women created in the image of God as beings with body and soul. I shall argue that the implications of this position can be seen in John's proclamation and celebration of the Christian faith in his sermons and his poems: in both, at best, John reveals himself to be a poet capable of drawing on the vast resources of the imagery of the Scriptures and the liturgy, a theologian who, in passing beyond the conceptual, uses imagery to express the inexpressible. Like Dionysios the Areopagite, one of his favourite theologians, John had a profound sense of the ineffability of God, and regarded the apophatic tradition, the way of negation, as fundamental if we are not to reduce God to an idol. But, precisely for that reason, John draws on images, in all their bewildering and seemingly contradictory variety, to find ways of capturing for the human imagination a sense of the richness of God's manifestation and helping the heart to turn to God in praise, a praise ultimately expressed in the silence of prayer.

PART II

Faith and Logic

3

The Fountain Head of Knowledge:
Nature and Development

In this second part, we shall adopt as a framework the threefold programme John set himself in the introductory letter that precedes the
Dialectica. In that letter John says,

First, I shall set forth what is most excellent among the wise men of the Greeks,
knowing that anything that is true has been given to human beings from God, since
'every good endowment and every perfect gift is from above, coming down from
the Father of lights'. If anything is opposed to the truth, then it is a 'dark invention'
of Satanic error 'and an invention of the mind of a wicked demon', as Gregory
said, who is rich in theology. Imitating therefore the ways of a bee, I shall gather
together what belongs to the truth and pick the fruits of salvation from the enemies,
and reject everything that is evil and falsely called knowledge. Then I shall set forth
in order the chattering nonsense of the heresies hateful to God, so that by recog-
nizing what is false we may cleave the more to the truth. Then, with the help of God
and by his grace, I shall set out the truth, truth that destroys error and drives away
falsehood, and is adorned and made beautiful, as with golden tassels, by the
words of divinely inspired prophets and divinely taught fishermen, of God-bearing
shepherds and teachers, that truth, the glory of which shines from within and illu-
minates by its rays those who encounter it with due purification and having set aside
troubling trains of thought. (*Dial.*, proem. 43–60)

It is a threefold programme of, first, what can be derived from the
Greek philosophers, secondly, an account of the errors of heresy, and
thirdly, an exposition of the truth. This threefold programme is what we
are familiar with in modern editions and translations of the *Pêgê Gnôseôs*,
or *The Fountain Head of Knowledge*, consisting of the *Dialectica*, or 'philosophical chapters', the treatise on heresies, and the *Exact Exposition of the
Orthodox Faith*. The manuscript tradition, however, tells a different tale:
this threefold programme is found in only one of the manuscripts,[1]

---

[1] The eleventh-century Venice manuscript, Venet. Marc. gr. II, 196: see Kotter 1959, 86.

and the extension of the title *Pêgê Gnôseôs* to the whole trilogy (rather than to the *Dialectica* alone, as John's own use is commonly held to imply: *Dial.* 2. 8–9) seems to be no older than the seventeenth-century Greek Catholic scholar, Leo Allatius.[2] In the manuscripts, the *Dialectica* is usually followed immediately by *On the Orthodox Faith*; if the treatise on heresies appears at all, it is appended to these two, so upsetting the order which John seems to envisage in his prefatory letter.[3] One of the earliest references to this work, by a certain Elias who sharply criticized John's exposition of Christology, refers to it as '150 chapters',[4] which would seem to be the shorter version of the philosophical chapters, followed by the 100 chapters of *On the Orthodox Faith*, which is indeed one of the commonest arrangements found in the manuscripts.

It further seems that the idea of a dogmatic treatise prefaced by philosophical chapters was not without precedent in John's time.[5] As an appendix to his edition of the *Dialectica*, Kotter published the collection of philosophical chapters contained in a manuscript in the Bodleian Library in Oxford (Cod. Oxon. Bodl. Auct. T. 1. 6).[6] The rest of this manuscript contains a text of the first forty-one chapters of a work known as the *Doctrina Patrum* (in full, *Doctrina Patrum de Incarnatione Verbi*: 'The Teaching of the Fathers on the Incarnation of the Word'), a lengthy patristic florilegium arranged in chapters dealing with different aspects of Christology (after the first, which deals with the doctrine of the Trinity).[7] The *Doctrina Patrum* dates from the turn of the seventh to the eighth century, and is therefore most likely earlier than John's own work. What we have in the manuscript in the Bodleian Library, then, seems to be a precursor of the combination of the *Dialectica* with *On the Orthodox Faith*, called by Elias the '150 chapters', and well represented in the manuscript tradition.[8] This makes it likely that John at some stage envisaged such a combination of philosophical and theological chapters, a likelihood reinforced by the fact that both the 'Oxford chapters' and the *Doctrina Patrum* seem to be witnesses to the same tradition that emerges in John's

[2] Studer 1956, 18. For Allatius, see his *Prolegomena* to St John Damascene, PG 94. 117/118–191/192: he discusses *The Fountain Head of Knowledge* on 133/4.

[3] There is a further complication, in that both *Dial.* and *Expos.* exist in two different forms in the manuscripts, a matter we shall deal with in the later chapters focused on these works.

[4] See Van Roey 1944, 8.

[5] This paragraph draws on Richter 1964, 23–30; and more briefly, Richter 1982, 64.

[6] Kotter i. 147–73.

[7] Edited by Franz Diekamp: see *Doctrina Patrum* in Bibliography.

[8] But see Roueché 1974, 67: Cod. Oxon. Bodl. Auct. T. 1. 6 'manifestly based on the *Dialectica*'. In support of statement in the text see Richter 1982, 64.

work: Kotter's apparatus to his edition makes evident how much material is common to the 'Oxford chapters' and the *Dialectica*, and the passages from the Fathers cited in the *Doctrina Patrum* are of, let us say, the same complexion as the sources for the Damascene's *On the Orthodox Faith*.

So far I have said nothing about the likely date of *The Fountain Head of Knowledge* (to use this way of referring to the whole work for convenience). Readers already familiar with John's work may find this surprising, for the prefatory letter has commonly been interpreted as providing a rare clue to the date of the work that it prefaces, since it is addressed to Cosmas, bishop of Maïuma. However, the date given, AD 743, the year, it is said, of the accession of Cosmas to his see, is based on a long-standing error.[9] For this date is based on a misreading of the passage in Theophanes' *Chronographia*, which tells of the martyrdom of Peter, metropolitan of Damascus, in 743/4, and at the same time of the martyrdom of another Peter, from Maïuma, whose panegyric was delivered by St John Damascene himself.[10] But Peter is not described as a bishop; on the contrary, Theophanes says that he was a tax official, and it has further been suggested that this 'Peter of Maïuma' is the Peter of Capitolias (in Transjordan) who is commemorated as a martyr.[11] Whoever this Peter was, there seems no reason to suppose that he was bishop of Maïuma, and therefore no reason to suppose that Cosmas succeeded him. This work of John's, then, joins the ranks of most of his other works: one for which we have no real clue as to its date.[12]

Nevertheless, the idea that *The Fountain Head of Knowledge*, in its three-fold form, was both John's intention and belonged to the later years of his life can be defended by other arguments.[13] To anticipate what will be demonstrated in later chapters, it seems to me that the following is the likely situation. As remarked above, the earliest form of this work seems to have consisted of 150 chapters, combining the short version of the *Dialectica* and *On the Orthodox Faith*. It is not possible to be definite about the date of this work, but it could well be in the 720s or 730s.[14] Later on,

[9] See Kotter ii. p. xxv, who cites Van Roey 1944, 9 n. 28; Richter 1982, 161.

[10] Theophanes, *chron.* A.M. 6234 (de Boor, 416–17; Mango and Scott, 577–8).

[11] See Mango's n. 5, ibid. 579.

[12] Kazhdan and Gero have advanced reasons for doubting whether the dedicatory letter was originally addressed to Cosmas at all: 1989, 123.

[13] What is set out here differs sharply from the view of the development of *The Fountain Head of Knowledge* advanced by Thümmel (1981). I have set out my arguments against Thümmel's views in Louth (2003a).

[14] One reason for thinking that this early version belongs to the early 720s (or perhaps even earlier) is *Expos.* 89, the chapter on iconoclasm. As will be argued below, there is nothing in this chapter that compels one to date it after the beginning of Byzantine iconoclasm (726, or

John undertook a revision, the pattern of which is set out in the prefatory letter to Cosmas. Immediately following the passage quoted at the beginning of this chapter, John remarks, 'I shall say nothing of my own, *as I have said*' (*Dial.* proem. 60; my emphasis). This seems to be a pre-echo of what he says in the second chapter of the later, longer version of the *Dialectica* ('I shall therefore say nothing of my own': *Dial.* 2. 9). Kotter noted this, and drew the conclusion (rightly, in my view) that the letter to Cosmas was written to preface the longer version of the *Dialectica*.[15] If this inference is valid, then it suggests that the threefold version of *The Fountain Head of Knowledge* was envisaged when John revised the *Dialectica*. In the next chapter I shall argue that John never completed his revision of the *Dialectica*, and the likely reason for that is that it was cut short by his death, which, as we have seen above, can probably be dated to *c*.750. Thus the threefold version of *The Fountain Head of Knowledge* was envisaged by John towards the end of his life, but was never finished, and therefore never published by him, which would explain why it had such a limited circulation that it has made virtually no impact on the manuscript tradition. After his death the prefatory letter was added to some manuscripts of the '150 chapters', and later copyists, noticing what it said, often supplied the lacking section on heresies, though most commonly as an appendix. The incompletely revised version of the *Dialectica* also circulated, and sometimes displaced the shorter version. Only one copyist, so far as we know, attempted to reconstruct *The Fountain Head of Knowledge* as John finally envisaged it. Such a development explains most features of the manuscript tradition of *The Fountain Head of Knowledge*.[16] Quite what John had in mind in revising his 150 chapters, we shall probably never know; but it is likely that John undertook the revision for a different audience than the original one, an audience for whom the account of heresy was important, rather than because of a subjective change of mind. Nevertheless, we may regard the threefold structure—philosophical foundation : exploration of heresy : exposition of Orthodoxy—as reflecting the mature intentions of the Damascene; it will therefore be

perhaps 730); rather, it seems to envisage the objections to icon veneration that we know had already been made by Jews in the seventh century. On the other hand, the different genre represented by *Expos.* means (I would argue against Thümmel 1981, 26–7) that one cannot be sure that it was written before the outbreak of Byzantine iconoclasm.

[15] See Kotter ii. p. xxvi.

[16] If this is true, then it is possible that Allatius was right, and that the title *Pēgē Gnōseōs*, which occurs in *Dial.* 2, is meant to refer to the whole three-part work, since John says that the aim of the book is 'to begin with philosophy . . . and to set down all kinds of knowledge (*pantodapēn gnōsin*)' (*Dial.* 2. 6–7).

used as a structure for the central section of this book. But before we look
at what John has to say about these subjects, we need to pay some attention to the literary genre he adopted.

All three works are collections of 'chapters' (*kephalaia*), a long-
established philosophical genre, in which, as Studer put it, 'a question
could be handled in a relatively limited manner, without taking into
account the whole context'.[17] Further, these chapters rarely contain
John's own discussion of the question in hand; rather, they contain a
discussion that John has borrowed from elsewhere, and made his own.
They are, in fact, disguised florilegia ('disguised', because in a genuine
florilegium such as the *Doctrina Patrum*, the authors of the passages
selected are generally given). To understand what John is doing in
these works, we need to know a little more about the (in this case, not
altogether separable) literary genres of the 'chapter' and the florilegium.[18]

John is a notable contributor to the genre of the florilegium in his
Hiera, not to mention the florilegia he appended to his treatises against
iconoclasm, which we shall discuss later. But collections of memorable
sayings or passages (the Greek word 'anthology' is an exact equivalent
[a 'calque'] of florilegium) are of some antiquity. Florilegia of passages
from poets and philosophers were common from the Hellenistic period
onwards, and Christian thinkers, from the apologists on, made use of
them. The first properly Christian florilegia are the so-called *testimonia*,
collections of passages from what Christians came to call the Old Testament, that were used by them to support their claim (primarily against
Jews, but also against non-Christian gentiles) that Jesus is the fulfilment
of the promises and prophecies of the Old Testament. It is evident from
these *testimonia* that their compilation and use constitute an appeal to
authority: these passages justify the Christian use of the Hebrew
Scriptures as the Old Testament (i.e., that which found its fulfilment in
the New Testament). Patristic florilegia, which emerge in the fifth
century, and flourish thereafter, augment scriptural authority with the
notion of patristic authority, the authority of the 'Fathers'. They first
emerge in the fifth century in the context of the Christological controversy: both sides, Cyril and his supporters (the so-called Alexandrians)
and the eastern bishops, whose most important representative was
Theodoret (the 'Antiochenes'), drew up lists of passages from the Fathers
that supported their interpretation of the doctrine of Christ.[19] The post-

[17] Studer 1956, 21. See also Ivánka 1954.
[18] For florilegia, see Chadwick 1969, Richard 1964, and Odorico 1990.
[19] Richard 1951.

Chalcedonian period saw a striking development of such florilegia.[20] Patristic florilegia facilitated appeal to the Fathers, who became the most immediate authorities in Christian theology: Scripture was, henceforth, to be interpreted through the witness of the Fathers.[21] To facilitate this, there emerges another kind of florilegium called *catenae* ('chains'), consisting of strings of patristic passages excerpted from commentaries and elsewhere that hang, as it were, from the verses of Scripture.[22] All of this makes possible a way of thinking theologically in which authority is found in 'following the Holy Fathers', to quote the phrase used by the Fathers of the Council of Chalcedon to introduce their famous definition of the Faith.[23] It was this tradition of theological thinking that John Damascene inherited. As Lionel Wickham has put it, in his characteristically lapidary way, 'Patristic theology may be said to aspire to the condition of the florilegium and in its last representative John of Damascus, whose *De Fide Orthodoxa* is a mosaic of quotations, attains its goal.'[24]

The use of a genre approximating to the florilegium tells us something, then, about the kind of authority to which John Damascene sought to lay claim in his *The Fountain Head of Knowledge*. But the component parts of the work also conform to another genre, though this becomes apparent only as a result of Kotter's editorial work. Hitherto the treatise on heresies has appeared to have 103 chapters, and *On the Orthodox Faith* to be divided into four books. But Kotter's edition reveals that the treatise on heresies originally consisted of 100 chapters, and that *On the Orthodox Faith*, similarly, is a work of 100 chapters, the division into books, which disguises this, being unknown in the Greek tradition and introduced into the Latin tradition only in the thirteenth century.[25] The shorter form of the *Dialectica* contains 50 chapters. It becomes clear that in these works John is adopting the way of presenting chapters as a group of 100: that is, as a century (in Greek: *hekatontas*). This was an already established genre, introduced into Christian circles probably by Evagrios (d. 399), the great theorist of the monastic life of ascetic struggle and contemplation. Thereafter it became a popular genre for monastic writing: Diadochos of Photike and Mark the Hermit composed centuries, both probably in the fifth century, as did Maximos the Confessor in the seventh.[26] The

[20] See Grillmeier's detailed study of such florilegia: 1987, 51–78.
[21] For the way in which florilegia facilitated appeal to patristic authority, especially in the synods of the Church, see Alexakis 1996, 1–42.   [22] See Grillmeier 1987, 87–8.
[23] For this notion of patristic authority, see Florovsky 1972, esp. 105–20.
[24] Lionel Wickham in Ebied and Wickham 1985, 117.
[25] Kotter 1959, 4–5; Kotter ii. pp. xxiii–xxiv.
[26] On the century as a literary form see Balthasar 1961, 482–4.

primary purpose of most of these monastic chapters was to present the monk with material for reflection in prayer: the subjects are mostly matters of ascetic theology. But Evagrios's *Gnostic Chapters* go beyond ascetic matters, and introduce questions of theological doctrine, and in this Maximos follows him. So again John Damascene is doing nothing original in casting his epitome of Christian doctrine in the form of a monastic century (though, as we shall see, *On the Orthodox Faith* covers issues such as human psychology that bear very directly on asceticism): but what he is doing is casting all three parts of his trilogy in a monastic mould. This, I think, is worth noting: John's *The Fountain Head of Knowledge* is not really a proto-scholastic summary, as it is often taken to be; rather, it is concerned with shaping and moulding the monastic vocation of its readers, or, more widely, with defining what it is to be a Christian, understood less as a set of beliefs (despite the high doctrinal content) than as a way of life. To realize this is to recall the context in which John composed his works: as a member of a monastic community in Palestine, writing primarily for his fellow-monks, and in his *Pēgē Gnōseōs*, in particular, providing a recapitulation of Christian doctrine in its Chalcedonian form, of which the Palestinian monks had proved themselves to be such doughty defenders.

4

Settling the Terms

The *Dialectica* itself exists in two different forms, a shorter version of fifty chapters and a longer version of sixty-eight chapters; in addition, there is a much briefer work of similar content called *Elementary Introduction*,[1] which is described as being 'from the voice' (*apo phônês*) of John of Damascus, a phrase which at this date usually means that it is an account of someone's oral teaching.[2] This is much shorter than either form of the *Dialectica*, and probably represents an early stage in John's attempt to provide the basic logical and conceptual tools for the understanding of theology.

(a) *Elementary Introduction*

The chapters of the *Elementary Introduction* give a very clear idea of the kind of material John wanted to introduce to his students (presumably more intellectually inclined novices). There are ten chapters, as follows:

1. On essence (*ousia*), nature (*physis*), and form (*morphê*): they are said to be the same.
2. On *hypostasis*, person (*prosôpon*), and individual (*atomon*): again they are the same.
3. On difference (*diaphora*), quality (*poiotês*), and property (*idiotês*): again they are the same.
4. On essential and non-essential difference, and on natural difference and accident.
5. On separable and inseparable accident.
6. On things of the same essence (*homoousion*), and of different essences (*heteroousion*).
7. On genus (*genos*) and species (*eidos*).

---

[1] Kotter i. 19–26.   [2] See Richard 1950. But see Richter 1982, 20.

8. On activity (*energeia*).
9. On affection (*pathos*).
10. On will (*thelêma*).

It is not difficult to work out the background to this list of concepts needed for the study of theology. One simply has to cast one's mind back over the theological controversies behind the Oecumenical Synods up to the time of John. The Synod of Nicaea introduced the term *homoousios*, and once that term became accepted in theological discourse, both it and its root, *ousia*, essence or being, needed some definition. The so-called Cappadocian settlement, that marked victory for the Nicene position, made a provisional distinction in Trinitarian theology between *ousia*, used to refer to the oneness of the Godhead, and *hypostasis*, used to designate Father, Son, and Holy Spirit, *hypostasis* being distinguished from *ousia* by characteristic properties (*idiômata*).[3] The Synod of Chalcedon in 451 made a distinction between *hypostasis* and *physis* (nature) to affirm that in Christ both divine and human natures are united in a single *hypostasis* and *prosôpon* (person). Later defenders of Chalcedon sought to bring these two distinctions together, so that there would be a uniform terminology in both Trinitarian theology and Christology: the two distinctions—between *hypostasis* and *ousia*, and between *hypostasis* and *physis*—were to be regarded as identical.

This clarification did not go uncontested: the opponents of Chalcedon resisted it with an array of arguments which we shall explore later, in Chapter 6, in our discussions of Trinitarian theology and Christology. But this clarification of terminology focused attention on the term *hypostasis*, and led to an attempt to work out a notion of person, or *hypostasis*, as something more than simply an instance of some universal kind (such as human kind), a discussion that involved an exploration of what constituted difference, the nature of qualities, and so on. The first three chapters of the *Elementary Introduction* with their categorical identification of essence with nature and form, of *hypostasis* with person and individual, and of difference with quality and property represent an attempt to lay down the basic ground rules for an understanding of the notion of person, or *hypostasis*, and the next four chapters introduce some of the terms involved in this endeavour. The seventh century saw an attempt at final reconciliation with the Monophysites, in the doctrines of Monenergism and Monothelitism—the theories that Christ's unity was constituted by a single divine–human activity (*energeia*) or by a single

---

[3] See, e.g., Basil, *ep.* 236 (Deferrari, iii. 400–4).

divine will (*thelêma*) respectively. Much of this discussion revolved around what could be meant by the divine Logos subjecting himself to being affected from outside ('suffering', in the widest sense). The terms used to elucidate these issues are defined in the last three chapters of the *Elementary Introduction*. This set of ten chapters is, then, very focused: a very basic introduction to the terms needed for the theological arguments still raging at the time of John of Damascus.

(b) *Dialectica*

The *Dialectica* proper, in both its forms, is more elaborate. There is no doubt that both forms go back to the Damascene, and, as mentioned in the last chapter, it would seem that the short version (*Dialectica brevior: Dial. brev.*) was put together first, and that the longer version (*Dialectica fusior: Dial. fus.*) is a reworking of this earlier version.[4] The underlying structure of the *Dialectica* can be set out as follows (the numbers refer to the chapters of *Dial. fus.*):[5]

1–8	Introduction
9–14	Porphyry's logical concepts
19–29	What Porphyry's concepts have in common and how they differ
32–9, 47–63	Aristotle's categories

(The 'missing chapters' are either 'errant'—e.g., 'Aristotelian' chapters inserted into a Porphyrian block—or concerned with concepts of interest to Christian theologians, but ignored by Porphyry or Aristotle, notably those connected with the term *hypostasis*.)

The basis of the *Dialectica* is thus lifted from Porphyry's *Isagoge* ('Introduction' [to Aristotle's *Categories*]) and from Aristotle's *Categories*: it represents the basic logic that was taught in Late Antiquity. Gerhard Richter

---

[4] In what follows I shall refer to the chapter divisions as found in Kotter's critical edition. Le Quien's edition, which is reprinted in PG 94. 521–676, is aware of the fact that there are short and long versions of *Dial.*, but inserts the variant chapters as supplements in what is effectively *Dial. fus.* This procedure is followed in the only English translation of *Dial.*, that by F. H. Chase. The order and division of the chapters is not precisely that of Kotter's *Dial. fus.* The numbering of the chapters is the same in both editions for 1–15; 16 (PG) combines 16 and 17 (Kotter); 18–45 (PG) = 19–46 (Kotter); 46 and the beginning of 47 (PG) = 47 (Kotter); the rest of 47 (PG) = 48 (Kotter); 48–63 (PG) = 49–64 (Kotter); 64–5 (PG) = 65 (Kotter); 66 (PG) = 67 (Kotter); 67–8 (PG) = 66 (Kotter); and a final unnumbered chapter (PG 94. 673–6) = 68 (Kotter).

[5] See Richter 1982, 76.

has argued that the stages in the development of the *Dialectica* can be reconstructed.[6] The basic layer consisted of chapters 1–6, 10, 11, 23–9, 32, and 50 (using the numbering of *Dial. brev.*). Here we have a collection of concepts, drawn from Porphyry's *Isagoge*, introduced without very much philosophical discussion. Richter argues that this raft of material already existed, having been put together at the end of the seventh or the beginning of the eighth century. John has supplemented this basic level from a source consisting of chapters 7–9, 12–14, 20–2, 30, 31, 33–49, and 15–19 (again in the enumeration of *Dial. brev.*). This source draws on Aristotle's *Categories*, and brings to the *Dialectica* a somewhat higher level of philosophical discussion. The work, thus constituted, circulated as the shorter version of the *Dialectica*, as an introduction to the dogmatic *On the Orthodox Faith*.

Later on—maybe much later on—John returned to his *Dialectica* and further augmented it. Chapters 1, 2, 9, and 12 were reworked and came to constitute chapters 4, 10, 18, and 6 in the enumeration of *Dialectica fusior*; chapters 12–14 in the short version became chapters 6–8 in the long; new chapters 5, 9, and 19–29 were added (which add much greater detail to the Porphyrian material present in *Dial. brev.*); chapters 4 and 5 were enlarged to form chapters 12 and 13 in the new version, and chapter 8 was divided into new chapters 16 and 17; chapter 49 (a discussion of the nature of philosophy) was reworked and appeared as new chapter 3; and entirely fresh chapters were composed to begin the work as chapters 1 and 2 (the prefatory letter probably also belongs to this revision).[7] The revision, it will be noticed, concerns the first half of the treatise (up to *Dial. fus.* 29); the latter half of the treatise is largely left alone, not to say neglected. Chapter 47 (= 30 in *Dial. fus.*) was slightly altered, and chapter 49, which had already been transferred to chapter 3, still appeared towards the end of the longer version as chapter 66. It is not unlikely that the final version of the *Dialectica* represents an incomplete revision of the *Dialectica brevior*.

From this reconstruction we can see that John was very little more than a compiler: *Dialectica brevior* is made up of two sources, one basically Porphyrian, the other based on the concepts discussed by Aristotle in his *Categories*; the revision represented by *Dialectica fusior* is mainly a reworking of already existent material, the 'new' chapters 5, 9, 19–29 providing, as mentioned above, a further injection of Porphyrian material. The only chapters that can be assigned to John are the introductory chapters 1 and 2, together with the prefatory letter. But this is what John intended: twice

---

[6] See Richter 1964, 222–35, and Richter 1982, 74–8.
[7] See Ch. 3 above.

in his 'own' material John says that 'I shall say nothing of my own' (*Dial.*, proem. 60; 2. 9). John belongs, even in his philosophical chapters, to a tradition, and a Christian tradition at that. We have already encountered two examples of this tradition, in the *Elementary Introduction* and in the first part of the manuscript in the Bodleian Library, discussed in the last chapter. But these are part of a wider tradition of which we can still catch glimpses.

(c) 'Christian' Logical Handbooks

This tradition was an eclectic tradition, in that it selected material from textbooks on logic. But one must not think of a series of learned scribes making their own selections, rather of a tradition of selected excerpts. What they selected from was, as we have seen, Porphyry's *Isagoge* and Aristotle's *Categories*, but they did not go back to the original sources; rather, they drew on the body of commentary on Aristotle's works (including Porphyry's introduction) that had been produced in Alexandria in the fifth and sixth centuries, by philosophers such as Ammonios, Elias, David, and others. Unlike the commentaries, however, which discuss the text of Aristotle and its interpretation, taking further a tradition of philosophical reflection, these textbooks of logic had a largely practical aim. As Mossman Roueché, to whose research we owe our knowledge of these textbooks, remarks, 'from the content of these texts we can be certain that the student who used them was one who was not making a careful study of logic, but one who wanted, or was required to know a few of its most fundamental elements'.[8] What Roueché's research has laid bare is a tradition of logical texts, consisting of excerpts from the Alexandrian commentaries on Aristotle's logical treatises, in which Roueché detects three stages: 'the simple excerpt, the topical collection of a number of excerpts, perhaps slightly rewritten with examples, and the collection of several shorter collections, comprising a logical handbook',[9] of which John's *Dialectica* constitutes a (late) example. These collections were Christian, a fact revealed in two ways: first, that in the examples names such as Socrates and Plato are replaced by names such as Peter and Paul, and secondly, and more significantly, that the terminology converges on terms like *ousia* and *hypostasis*, and concepts such as activity and will, that were important in Christian controversy in

---

[8] Roueché 1974, 63–4. In addition, see Roueché 1980, 1990.
[9] Roueché 1974, 63.

the sixth and early seventh centuries. What this tradition of Christian logical handbooks reveals is the need to be able to formulate clear concepts and conduct convincing arguments in this period, a need that bears witness to the historical situation of Christians in a period in which, if they were to survive, they had to be able to define and defend their faith with some conviction. Roueché's research has shown, by careful comparison of these texts, that what we have in John's *Dialectica* is a collection of excerpts, but not excerpts that John himself made from the Aristotelian commentators, rather a compilation made by John from this earlier tradition of Christian logical handbooks.

It is most likely that such logical handbooks were compiled not just by Christians belonging to John's tradition of the Byzantine Orthodoxy of Palestinian monasticism, but by other Christian traditions, too: those the Orthodox called Monophysites, Monothelites, and Nestorians, and also by other groups with whom Christians engaged in argument, such as Jews and Samaritans. What survives, however, seems mostly to belong to the Orthodox tradition (which is hardly surprising as they are preserved in medieval manuscripts written by later scribes who embraced Byzantine Orthodoxy). Some of the surviving collections of definitions are attributed to Maximos the Confessor, which is significant, since Maximos was the pre-eminent theologian of this tradition: such are his 'Theological and Polemical Opuscula' 14 (PG 91. 149–53), 18 (ibid. 213–16), and 23 (ibid. 260–8). It is not likely that these opuscula were published by Maximos himself, though they may be collections of definitions he made for private use, included among his works after his death. Other published examples of such logical material include the collections of definitions in the *Doctrina Patrum*[10] and in chapter 2 of the *Hodegos* ('Guide' or *Viae Dux*) of St Anastasios of Sinai,[11] both from the late seventh century, the late sixth-century *Proparaskeuē* of Theodore of Raïthu,[12] and the even earlier collections of definitions of terms put together by Athanasios of Antioch (559–98) and Ephrem of Antioch (527–45).[13] In the articles already referred to, Mossman Roueché has discovered several other examples of such logical handbooks, mostly anonymous, though some attributed again to Maximos, some of which he has published. It also seems to be the case that, whatever the immediate purpose of these logical handbooks, it was by such means that the tradition of Greek

---

[10] *Doctr. Patr.* 33 (Diekamp, 249–66).

[11] Anastasios, *hod.* 2 (Uthemann, 23–75).

[12] Diekamp 1938, 173–222.

[13] On such collections, see Grillmeier 1987, 82–7.

philosophy was continued during the eclipse of learning in Byzantium from the sixth to the ninth centuries, and was also transmitted to the Muslim world in the ninth and tenth centuries.[14]

(d) John's Purpose

Though John seems to have been neither the author nor even, save in a very minor way, the compiler of the *Dialectica*—he simply represents a tradition of the use of logical terms and conceptual definitions in which no one thinker had any decisive role—it does seem, if Richter's analysis is correct, that chapter 1 of the final version was composed by John himself. This chapter is about knowledge (*gnôsis*), and he begins by praising it: 'Nothing is more honourable than knowledge, for if knowledge is the light of the rational soul, then contrariwise ignorance is darkness.' Knowledge is the proper state of rational beings, so for rational beings, lack of knowledge renders them worse than irrational beings. John then comments that 'knowledge is the true knowledge of beings'. Consequently, knowledge of what is not is not knowledge at all, but is simply ignorance. However, in this life the soul is clothed with the veil of the flesh, and though it possesses an intellect (*nous*), which is 'a kind of eye, that sees and knows and is receptive of the knowledge and understanding (*epistêmê*) of beings', the intellect does not possess knowledge of understanding from itself; rather, it stands in need of a teacher. Therefore, John says, 'let us approach the teacher who is free of all deceit, truth itself—that is Christ—and let us hear his voice in the divine Scriptures and let us learn the true knowledge of everything that is'. To do this, it is necessary to purify the 'intellectual eye of the soul' from the passions, for even the purest and clearest eye is scarcely able to attain the truth. It is not enough to reach the gate, we have to knock hard on it, so that

when the door of the bridal chamber is opened to us, we may see the beauties within. For the gate is the letter, and the bridal chamber within the gate is what is hidden by the letter, the beauty of thoughts, the spirit of truth. Let us knock hard, let us read once, twice, many times, so that by digging we may find the treasure of knowledge and delight in its riches. Let us seek, let us search, let us examine, let us enquire; 'for everyone that asks receives, and everyone who seeks finds and to everyone who knocks it shall be opened'. (*Dial.* 1. 37–46)

John then goes on to say that in every task, one needs helpers. So, too, in

[14] See Roueché 1980, 73–6.

this task of seeking knowledge: let us not be afraid to make use of anything that is good, for such things are, as it were, the 'favourite slaves' who serve the queen. So rhetoric and argument can be used, in subordination to the truth. With Christ as our guide, we are embarking on a journey, the purpose of which is 'to be led upwards by the senses to that which is beyond everything belonging to the senses and beyond any apprehension, to the one who is the source and maker and creator of everything'. John quotes Wisdom 13: 5 and Romans 1: 20, which speak of the way we may pass from the creation that we can perceive to the Creator who is beyond perception, and then finally reminds his reader of the need for a way of thinking (*phronêma*) that is humble and free from being puffed up by self-regard, if we are to learn from one who himself taught the way of humility (John quotes John 5: 44 and Luke 14: 11).

This is the voice, not so much of the scholar, as of the monk: knowledge, the pursuit of truth, is to follow Christ, the Truth. The way demands humility and purification: it demands one's whole life, not just one's committed intellect. The focus of this search is not the subject of the *Dialectica* itself; rather, it is a careful and repeated reading of the Scriptures, a reading that enables one to hear the voice of Christ, the Truth, speaking in the Scriptures. It is the kind of meditative reading of Scripture that was called *lectio divina* in the Western monastic tradition. The content of the *Dialectica* itself is nothing more than 'favourite slaves' or 'maids' (*habrais*) of the 'queen'.[15] This reading and pondering the Scriptures is a work of love: the one who pursues it enters into a bridal relationship with Christ, and delights in the truth discovered in the bridal chamber. John is drawing on a long tradition, going back at least to Origen, in seeing meditation on Scripture as leading to a loving relationship with Christ, such as is celebrated in the Song of Songs.[16] We shall encounter the language and ideas of this chapter later on in chapter 90 of the *Expositio*, on the Scriptures. Such an emphasis on learning through the Scriptures has another important consequence. The ideas of this chapter are very Platonic—the necessity for purification, the intellect as the soul's organ of knowing, etc.—but Richter points out that this Platonism is subtly modified. When John uses the word 'immaterially' (*aülôs: Dial.* 1. 35), he does not mean, following Plato, that pure knowledge is free from the always deceitful perceptions, but rather that the intellect has freed itself from the storm of distracting thoughts. Similarly,

---

[15] In Kotter's text (*Dial.* 1. 58) *abrais* needs amending to *habrais*: see Liddell and Scott 1996, 3, and supplement, 1, *s.v.* 'habra'.

[16] See Louth 1981, 64.

at the end of the chapter, John envisages the soul attaining transcendent reality through the senses, rather than by abandoning the senses.[17]

John's procedure does not reflect his monastic setting simply in general terms; there are clear allusions to monastic wisdom in the details of his presentation. The first words about knowledge echo almost word for word a chapter from one of the centuries composed by St Thalassios the Libyan, friend of Maximos the Confessor: 'Holy knowledge is the light of the soul; bereft of it, "the fool walks in darkness".'[18] The idea of the soul's nakedness being veiled by the body is an image found in Diadochos of Photike's *Century on Spiritual Knowledge*.[19] So both John's general presentation and some of his detailed allusions together make it clear that, from the very beginning, John is writing as a monk, and inviting others to a search for knowledge that is fundamentally monastic, in that it involves a life of ascetic struggle and purification, so that the mind and heart may be attentive to God.

Commentators on the *Dialectica* often remark that the matters discussed do not seem to have any real bearing on the rest of *The Fountain Head of Knowledge*, or even constitute any kind of preparation for the rest of John's theological *œuvre*. Richter, for instance, says that 'the *Expositio* makes no use of the *Philosophical Chapters*'.[20] It is true that there are many chapters of the *Dialectica* that are rarely referred to in John's other writings, if at all. But this does not mean that the *Dialectica* has nothing really to do with *On the Orthodox Faith*. Presumably the purpose of the *Dialectica*, in John's eyes, was to help novice theologians to think clearly and argue convincingly, abilities that are necessary to read *On the Orthodox Faith* profitably, and build on the positions set out in that treatise. To say that *On the Orthodox Faith* makes no use of the *Dialectica* is a bit like saying that Beethoven's piano sonatas make no use of the piano exercises of Hanon's *The Virtuoso Pianist*: it is certainly true that few of Hanon's exercises appear in Beethoven's sonatas, not even all the scales in their various forms, and yet someone who has not mastered Hanon would certainly be ill-prepared to play Beethoven's sonatas.

[17] See Richter 1982, 165 n. 30, 166 n. 38.

[18] Thalassios, *cent.* I. 51 (*Philokalia* 1782, 459; *Philokalia* 1979 ff., ii. 310), noted by Richter 1982, 164 n. 19.

[19] Diadochos, *perf.* 71 (des Places, 131; *Philokalia* 1979 ff., i. 277), noted by Richter 1982, 164 n. 24.

[20] Richter 1982, 82.

(e) The Central Role of *hypostasis*

The *Dialectica* and the Christian logical handbooks on which it relies are not, however, simply collections of logical terms and methods: as we have noticed several times, they focused on the terms important in Christian controversy in the sixth and seventh centuries. One might go a stage further and say that these logical handbooks lead one to the notion of *hypostasis* and its place in a kind of topology of being. At the beginning of the chapter, we noticed how the *Elementary Introduction* concentrates on the terms necessary for the definition of *hypostasis*, and other terms like activity, passions, and will that assumed significance in the attempts by Maximos and his followers to defend their understanding of the Chalcedonian doctrine of the hypostatic union against Monenergists and Monothelites. The shorter form of the *Dialectica* closes with a chapter on the hypostatic union, and the longer version would probably have ended in a similar way, if its revision had been completed. All this points to the notion of *hypostasis*, and the terms necessary to define its meaning, as being the narrower focus of the *Dialectica*, and if this is something that John's handbook shares with other Christian logical handbooks, we should hardly be surprised.

Let us pursue a little further what this might entail.[21] Among the terms defined in the Christian logical handbooks, *hypostasis* is unusual in that the compilers found no help in their normal ultimate sources: Porphyry's *Isagoge*, Aristotle's *Categories*, and commentaries on these works. In his account of the use of *ousia* and *hypostasis* at the Synod of Alexandria in 361, the fifth-century historian Socrates remarked, 'Those who expound the hellenic wisdom of the Greeks [= pagans] defined *ousia* in many ways, but they made no mention at all of *hypostasis*.'[22] He goes on to remark that 'though the ancient philosophers neglect this word, the more modern philosophers frequently used the word *hypostasis* instead of *ousia*'.[23] The Cappadocian Fathers, in order to avoid the confusion that had arisen from different traditions in Greek Christian theology in which *hypostasis* was sometimes used to designate the members of the Trinity, sometimes, as an equivalent of *ousia* to designate the unity that the members of the Trinity shared, introduced a distinction between *ousia* and *hypostasis*: *ousia* was to refer to what the members of the Trinity had in common (*koinon*),

---

[21] For this see Ică 1995.

[22] Socrates, *h.e.* III. 7. 17 (Hansen and Sirinjan, 199, 4–6).

[23] Ibid. III. 7. 20 (Hansen and Sirinjan, 199, 12–14).

whereas *hypostasis* was to refer to what was particular (or proper: *idion* is the word most commonly used) to each member of the Trinity.[24] Other suggestions were made as to what it was that constituted a *hypostasis*: Basil, for instance, introduced the idea of a *hypostasis* being constituted by its 'mode of existence' (*tropos tês hyparxeôs*), a term used more confidently by his brother, Gregory of Nyssa.[25] But the Cappadocians only sketched out a notion of what *hypostasis* meant.

The next century saw the term *hypostasis* assume a still more central theological role when the Synod of Chalcedon, in its Christological Definition, used it, together with *prosopon* (or 'person'), to designate the unity of the Incarnate Christ. Further development took place in the following century, when the Trinitarian and Christological uses of *hypostasis* were explicitly identified by making it clear that the one *hypostasis* of the Incarnate Christ is identical with the second *hypostasis* of the Trinity (one of the key principles of so-called Neo-Chalcedonianism or, better, Cyrilline Chalcedonianism). All this led to further reflection on what constituted the notion *hypostasis*, a process that affected the Greek East much more than the Latin West, as the Latins had, since Tertullian, adopted a settled vocabulary that spoke of the Trinity as *unam substantiam in tribus [personis] cohaerentibus*, and of Christ as *una persona* from *duae substantiae*.[26]

It is this tradition of metaphysical reflection focusing on the notion of 'person' or *hypostasis* that John inherited. But it was a tradition that found little direct help in the logical treatises to which it customarily looked for guidance. Various definitions could be culled from such sources for all the other terms: genus, species, difference, property, accident— Porphyry's 'five terms', or *quinque voces*—and *ousia*, individual, quality, and so on. But for *hypostasis*, John and the tradition he inherited were obliged to look to the Fathers, to the great debates of the fourth century between the councils of Nicaea and Constantinople, and also to the efforts of such sixth-century theologians as Leontios of Byzantium.[27] Because of the key position that *hypostasis* occupied in theological discourse, it came to be conceded a key role in matters ontological. The young Romanian

[24] For the development of the distinction between *ousia* and *hypostasis*, see Régnon 1892–8, i. 167–215, and Halleux 1984.

[25] For more detail on the development of the idea of *tropos tês hyparxeôs* up to Maximos, see Sherwood 1955, 155–66.

[26] See Tertullian, *Prax.* 12, 27 (Evans, 102. 18; 124. 37–125. 3).

[27] The ecclesiastical provenance of the terms *hypostasis* and *prosopon* is confirmed by John Philoponos's remark in one of the extracts from his *Diaitetes*, preserved by John Damascene in an appendix to Haeres. 83 (and also in *Doctr. Patr.* 36): 'these [i.e., individuals] are what the teachers of the Church call *hypostaseis*, or sometimes *prosopa*' (Haeres. 83, addit. 38–9).

theologian Ioan Ică has interpreted this process thus: 'in Greek patristics there emerged a process of transformation of some notions of classical ontology towards an adequate expression of the personal aspect of the realities revealed to us in the mystery [of the Incarnation].'[28]

One can see something of what this means if one looks at the two places in the *Dialectica* devoted to *hypostasis*. The first consists of two chapters, *Dialectica fusior* 30–1 (= *Dial. brev.* 10–11), belonging to the earliest stratum of the *Dialectica*. The first of these chapters asserts that *hypostasis* is used in two senses: the first simply meaning being, equivalent to *ousia*, the other, *hypostasis* in itself, meaning the 'individual and the distinct *prosopon*'. The next chapter first of all explains the different ways in which 'the philosophers outside' (*hoi exô philosophoi*)—that is, the non-Christian (or pagan) philosophers—used *ousia* and *physis*, and distinguished between them. The next paragraph then abruptly asserts that the holy Fathers paid no attention to these 'many quarrels',[29] and made a simple distinction between the common (*to koinon*) and the particular (*to merikon*): the former they called indifferently *ousia*, nature, form (*morphê*), and species (*eidos*), while the latter they called individual, *prosopon*, or *hypostasis*, such as Peter and Paul. The chapter continues: '*hypostasis* needs to have *ousia* with accidents, and to subsist by itself, to be beheld by being perceived, that is, actually' (*Dial. fus.* 31. 29–31).

The other place belongs to the final version of *Dialectica brevior*. This chapter (*Dial. fus.* 43, *Dial. brev.* 26) starts in a similar way, by saying that *hypostasis* is used in two ways: first, as simple existence, and in that sense is identical to *ousia*, adding that this use is found in some of the Fathers who use *physis* and *hypostasis* in the same way (an important concession, as we shall see when we come to discuss the Damascene's Christology), and secondly, as existence on its own and by itself, which designates the individual, which is numerically distinct from other individuals. Then follows an important statement: 'It is necessary to know that *ousia* cannot subsist without any specific form, nor can there be any real difference, or species, or accident, but there are only *hypostaseis* or individuals and it is in them that *ousiai* and real differences and species and accidents are beheld' (*Dial.* 43. 8–11).

It is *hypostasis* that is the fundamental ontological reality. It is this emphasis that leads to two new logical terms *enypostatos* and *anypostatos* that

---

[28] Ică 1995, 116.

[29] This sharp contrast between the 'philosophers' and the 'Fathers' over definition of philosophical terms is also found in Maximos, *opusc.* 26 (PG 91. 276AB), though John does not seem to be following Maximos here; cf. also *opusc.* 21 (248B).

are defined along with *hypostasis*, with the meaning of 'having true [or concrete] reality' in relation to a *hypostasis*, or failing to have that reality: these terms evolved in theological (and especially Christological) contexts and will be discussed more fully later. Here it is important to see the way they help to define a notion of ontological reality focused on, and stemming from, the primary ontological reality, *hypostasis*.

We can perhaps take a little further the way in which logical, or ontological, topology is altered by giving the term *hypostasis* a central role, by drawing on some observations in Th. de Régnon's classic study. One way in which Régnon portrays the contrast between scholastic ontology and the ontology found among Greeks such as John of Damascus is by discussing the different ways in which they make use of the so-called Tree of Porphyry: the tree of classification in which the trunk of most general substance is divided into different boughs representing the genera, and the bough of each genus into different species, and the species into sub-species, and ultimately to individuals.[30] The scholastics, he suggests, start from the top and work their way down, from the most general to the most particular (the tree, it is to be noted, is upside-down with its roots in the heavens); whereas the Greek tradition we find in John works the reverse way, starting from the bottom, the individual, and working its way up, towards nature and being in its most general form. The individual is indefinable for the scholastics; it is the cusp, as it were, between existence and non-existence. But the Greeks start with the concrete individual reality, and discern (*theôrein*) in it the nature that it instantiates. Régnon comments:

This opposition of view-point between the two schools is manifest in a curious opposition of language. Unceasingly, we hear the scholastics using the following formulae: 'The substance requires the accidents; the individual nature needs this subsistence as its natural complement.' It really seems as if substance were already existing, like a liquid, needing however to be distributed in vases in order to remain in equilibrium. It is quite on the contrary with the Damascene Saint: for him, it is the

---

[30] Note that Régnon's studies—'plus souvent louées que lues', as Halleux puts it (1984, 313 n. 1)—are easily misrepresented in summary. The two traditions he contrasts in the studies in vol. i, that of Latin scholasticism and the Greek tradition represented primarily by John Damascene, are regarded as complementary, and are betrayed if characterized as 'Latin West' and 'Greek East'. Having introduced this contrast, Régnon remarks, 'Mais je laisse au lecteur le soin de vérifier cette assertion. Car, dans une question de nuance délicate comme celle-ci, quelques textes sont insuffisants; et pour se former une conviction, il faut lire les ouvrages dans leur entier, si l'on veut en bien saisir l'esprit': 1892–8, i. 263. On Régnon, see Barnes 1995, a rare study of the French Jesuit, although it has little relevance to our concerns.

hypostasis that requires, that needs. 'The *hypostasis*, he says, needs, *thelei*, to have a nature with accidents; it needs, too, to subsist in itself.'[31]

This insistence that reality is fundamentally hypostatic—that everything exists as, or in relation to, *hypostasis*—may be regarded as the starting-point of Greek patristic ontology. But how far does John himself develop this insight? It is important to be clear about this, as some recent theologians have made very high claims for the notion of person or *hypostasis* developed by the Fathers. Ică, as we have seen, speaks of the prospect of an ontology that 'gives adequate expression to the personal'; others, perhaps most influentially John Zizioulas (Metropolitan John of Pergamon), claim to find a personalist and existentialist ontology explicit in patristic theology, in which person is opposed to nature, existence to essence, in existentialist fashion.[32] We shall find this notion of *hypostasis* and the nature of hypostatic reality running like a silver thread through our exposition of John Damascene's theology: we shall return to it again in our discussion of the Damascene's doctrine of the Trinity,[33] and also of his Christology.[34] But here we are concerned with the *Dialectica*: how far does John develop a distinctively personal ontology here? The focus on *hypostasis* is complemented by the stand we noticed John taking earlier in the introductory chapter to the final form of the *Dialectica*, where he modifies his Platonic language to insist that it is through perception of reality, not by transcending reality, that we attain to the transcendent. It is an important point, sometimes obscured in Fathers less careful in their use of Platonic language and categories, and provides, as we shall see, a metaphysical foothold for John's defence of icons. Ică claims that in John we find a middle way between the essentialism of Platonism and the existentialist personalism advocated by such theologians as Zizioulas:

> From its fundamental axiom: *ouk esti ousia (physis) anhypostatos* ['there is no being separate from *hypostasis*'], patristic philosophy reveals itself to be of a type profoundly *existential*, not however existentialist; it is an ontological, existential realism in which essence is indissociable from existence, is always the essence of something existing. Platonic transcendental realism is an essentialism that separates existence from essence, and considers existence as an accident added to essence. But, if essentialism is insupportable, likewise unacceptable is existentialism, concentrated in the axiom: existence precedes essence.[35]

---

[31] Régnon 1892–8, i. 279. The passage quoted from the Damascene has been cited above.

[32] See Zizioulas 1985, esp. 27–65. But see Halleux's criticisms of Metropolitan John's historical arguments: 1986, esp. 133–55.   [33] See below, pp. 96–100, 111–14.

[34] See below, pp. 158–61.

[35] Ică 1995, 121.

But can this really be called a 'personalist ontology', even in the nuanced form suggested by Ică? The Latin philosopher-theologian and senator Boethius, who probably had a Greek philosophical education,[36] tells us that the 'Greeks' do not use *hypostasis* of irrational animals, but only of 'things of higher value, in order that in some way what is more excellent might be distinguished'.[37] If this were the case, then perhaps we could speak of the beginnings of a personalist ontology. But although Boethius presumably knew what he was talking about (and is likely to have known more than we ever shall about Greek logic at the beginning of the sixth century), there is no extant evidence to support Boethius's claim: *hypostasis* seems to be used to refer, quite generally, to a particular instantiation of an essence or *ousia*, if it is distinguished from *ousia* at all. This is certainly the case with John: for example, at *Dialectica* 44. 13, where he gives the example of a particular horse as an example of a *hypostasis*. So far as the *Dialectica* goes (and I am not clear that the situation is fundamentally different elsewhere in the Damascene's *œuvre*, though we must leave any such conclusion to its proper place), the focal role of *hypostasis* does not entail anything that we might call a 'personalist ontology'. For, as we have seen, John simply identifies *hypostasis*, individual (*atomon*), and *prosopon*, and contrasts this particular use of ontological terms with the use of *ousia*, nature, and form as applying to what things have in common. He does not restrict the designation *hypostasis* or even *prosopon* to beings that we might call 'personal' (which is one reason why I have avoided translating *prosopon* as 'person'): the distinction between common and particular ontological terms has quite general relevance, applying not just to what we might regard as persons, but also to animals, and even to inanimate objects, like houses or stones. There is no attempt here to work out an ontology of self-conscious, rational beings in terms of *hypostasis*.

There are, perhaps, some signs in some of John's precursors of attempts to work out a notion of personal reality, but these seem to focus on the term *prosopon* rather than *hypostasis*. Already, sixth-century theologians such as Theodore of Raïthu had distinguished between *hypostasis* as indicating the subsistent character of the reality expressed and *prosopon* as indicating possession of its own characteristics.[38] Theodore's distinction, however, certainly applies more generally than to 'personal reality'. But John does not follow up on any of this; he ignores any idea of a

[36] Chadwick 1981, 20.

[37] Boethius, *Eut.* 3. 71–8 (Rand *et al.*, 90).

[38] See Fraigneau-Julien 1961, 394, referring to Theodore of Raïthu, *praep.* (Diekamp, 205–6), and Ps-Cyril, *Trin.* 13 (PG 77. 1140B).

distinction between *hypostasis* and *prosopon*. A more striking anticipation of 'personalist' ontology can be found in Boethius, in a passage a little earlier than the one cited above. For Boethius famously defined *persona* as *naturae rationabilis individua substantia*, the 'individual substance of a rational nature'.[39] Whatever the limitations of this definition,[40] it clearly restricts 'person' to what we would call personal (indeed, Boethius makes this explicit in the previous chapter). It is also possible to find hints of a 'personalist metaphysics' in the reflections of Neoplatonic philosophy (which, however, John probably encountered only indirectly through theologians such as Dionysios the Areopagite and Maximos the Confessor), for the notion of the 'self-constituted' (*authypostatos*) explores the ontological reality of beings that are at least 'personal' (e.g., capable of self-reflective consciousness).[41] But there is nothing of this in John. At least so far as the *Dialectica* is concerned, it would seem rash to speak too confidently of any accomplished (as opposed to inchoate) 'transformation of some notions of classical ontology towards an adequate expression of the personal aspect' of reality.

[39] Boethius, *Eut.* 3. 4–5 (Rand *et al.*, 84). See Chadwick 1981, 190–5.
[40] See Chadwick 1981, 195.
[41] Proklos, *Inst.* 40–51 (Dodds, 42–50), and Dodds's commentary in Dodds 1963, 223–7.

5

Defining Error

The second part of the threefold programme that John set out in his dedicatory letter to Cosmas concerned 'the chattering nonsense of the heresies hateful to God'. In this chapter we shall first look at John's treatise on heresies, and then look in more detail at the three 'heresies' that John treated at length: Manichaeism, Messalianism, and Islam (the heresy of the 'Ishmaelites', also called Hagarenes or Saracens). All three heresies are included in the treatise on heresies (*Haeres.* 66, 80, 100), though the section on Manichaeism is no more than a brief paragraph, while the sections on Messalianism and Islam are both substantial—indeed, they are the only substantial chapters in the treatise. There are, however, separate treatises, in dialogue form, on both Manichaeism and Islam (the dialogue on Islam is of questionable authenticity, but it is certainly possible that it is by John). Manichaeism is also the object of four chapters in *On the Orthodox Faith* (92–5).

(a) Heresiology and *On Heresies*

We have seen that the treatise on heresies only once appears in the manuscript tradition in the place apparently intended by John: between the *Dialectica* and *On the Orthodox Faith*. It seems almost to have had a life of its own, and is found, as Kotter demonstrated, in three contexts in the manuscript tradition. First, it occurs in a lacunose form in a manuscript of the *Doctrina Patrum*, as chapter 34. Secondly, it appears together with the *Dialectica* and the *Expositio*, but tagged on at the end. Thirdly, it is found in heresiological or canonical collections, or on its own.[1] This fits well with the theory of the development of *The Fountain Head of Knowledge* suggested above, according to which the first version consisted of the short form of the *Dialectica*, followed by *On the Orthodox Faith*, as a work of 150 chapters,

[1] Kotter 1959, 214.

matching the number of the Psalms, whereas the 'final' version appeared only much later, prefaced by the dedicatory letter to Cosmas, and never really established itself. The addition of the letter, however, as a preface to the earlier version, revealed that John had intended to include a work on heresies, so completeness was restored by appending the text of the treatise on heresies, which John may well have composed quite independently, to the already existing coupling of the *Dialectica* and *On the Orthodox Faith*.

The presence of the treatise on heresies in the *Doctrina Patrum* raises other problems, for that work seems to be earlier than the Damascene. Could it be that John simply lifted *On Heresies* from the *Doctrina Patrum* and placed it in his threefold *The Fountain Head of Knowledge*? If so, interesting possibilities suggest themselves, for neither the long chapter on Messalianism nor most of the chapter on Islam is included in the text of chapter 34 of *Doctrina Patrum*. Is that chapter the original form of *On Heresies*, which was then augmented by John himself? Diekamp put forward such a suggestion in his edition of the *Doctrina Patrum*.[2] But Kotter has argued convincingly against this, pointing out that the sole manuscript of the *Doctrina Patrum* that contains chapter 34, though early, belongs to the late eighth century at the earliest, so that it is at least possible that chapter 34 was taken from the Damascene by the scribe, who abridged it and inserted it into the *Doctrina Patrum*.[3] Whichever way round it was, the close similarity of *Doctrina Patrum* and John's *On Heresies* points to the common tradition to which both John and the *Doctrina Patrum* belong. This is borne out by another striking parallel: namely, that three extracts from John Philoponos's *Diaitetes*, forming chapter 36 of the *Doctrina Patrum*, also appear together in some manuscripts as an appendix to *On Heresies*, 83, the chapter on the Monophysites. What is even more interesting is that this extract is the only part of Philoponos's *Diaitetes* to survive in the original Greek.

The history of the manuscript tradition of *On Heresies* is still more complicated, for in some manuscripts the *Dialectica* and *On the Orthodox Faith* are supplemented not by John's *On Heresies*, but by another, somewhat longer text, usually referred to as *Haereses Auctae* ('Heresies augmented'). It is now clear, however, that this alternative version of *On Heresies* is a later work, not by John himself.[4] We shall therefore not mention it further.

[2] Diekamp, *Doctr. Patr.*, pp. lxix–lxxiv.
[3] Kotter 1959, 211–14.
[4] See Kotter iv. 7–10.

But to ask who wrote *On Heresies* is, as the reader will now anticipate, a question to which the answer is likely to be somewhat oblique. For the first 79 chapters of the treatise, together with the first few lines of chapter 80, can be identified as the epitome (or *anakephalaiosis* as it is called) of an unmentioned, but easily recognizable, work (and not only recognizable to modern scholars, but, I suspect, well known to many of John's contemporaries), that work being the greatest treatise on heresiology from the early Christian period, the 'Medicine Chest', or *Panarion*, of St Epiphanios, bishop of Salamis or Constantia in Cyprus at the end of the fourth century. The *Anakephalaiosis*, a kind of table of contents with each chapter given a brief summary (a practice still quite common in the last century) prefacing each of the seven books of the treatise, was probably composed not by Epiphanios himself, but by a disciple, perhaps at the beginning of the fifth century.[5] Even the conclusions of each section, marking the division of the *Anakephalaiosis* into seven sections corresponding to the seven parts of Epiphanios's *Panarion*, are preserved in the text of 'John's' *On Heresies*.

Epiphanios[6] himself was a learned, if not altogether likable, person, who in his youth became an ascetic, and after a tour of the Egyptian desert founded a monastery near Gaza, which he ruled for thirty years, before becoming bishop of Constantia in 365. He had an ill-tempered intolerance of error, and stirred up the controversy about Origen at the end of the fourth century, as well as intemperately tearing down an embroidered icon (though it may have been a cloth embroidered with a pagan god) in a church,[7] and writing against the growing devotion in Christian circles to religious pictures (the iconoclasts took great delight in citing passages critical of icons from such a redoubtable saint, though John Damascene may have been right in doubting their authenticity).[8]

---

[5] For the *Anakephalaiosis*, see Holl, i. 162–8 (heresies 1–20), 234–7 (heresies 21–33); Holl and Dummer, ii. 1–4 (heresies 34–46), 211–14 (heresies 47–64), iii. 1–2 (heresies 65–9), 230–2 (heresies 70–6), 415 (heresies 75–80). Recently it has been argued (Knorr 1998) that the Damascene's use of the *Anakephalaiosis* is more complex, and betrays knowledge of the full text of the *Panarion*. He argues that the different recensions of the *Anakephalaiosis* (see *CPG* 3765) indicate different versions, one authentic by Epiphanios (as Holl argued), the other a later summary. It is a fundamental fault of Kotter's edition, Knorr argues, that these two recensions are confused, and that Kotter excludes the possibility of John's having had access to the full text of the *Panarios*. John's knowledge of the *Panarios* cannot have been very extensive: see below, p. 60.

[6] For Epiphanios and his *Panarion*, see Pourkier 1992.

[7] Epiphanios's letter to John, bishop of Jerusalem, containing the story was translated into Latin by Jerome, and is included in his correspondence (*ep.* 51. 9 (Labourt, i. 171–2)). The letter mainly concerns the errors of Origen.   [8] See below, Ch. 7.

This obsession with deviation from Christian truth bore fruits in his *Panarion*, a lengthy work that presents a kind of analysis, or better diagnosis, of heresy. There are eighty such heresies in all, an allusion to the number of concubines of the bridegroom in the Song of Songs (Cant. 6: 8).[9] The Greek word *hairesis* was originally quite neutral in its connotation: it indicated a choice, a way of life or way of thought.[10] It was used of the schools of philosophy and, by extension (by Josephus, for instance), of the different groups within Judaism. In Christian usage it came quickly to mean a *wilful* choice, a chosen departure from the one orthodox tradition. It is perhaps first used in this sense by Hegesippos, who, according to Eusebios, named seven 'heresies' among the Jews, 'all hostile to the tribe of Judah and the Christ', which, introduced into the 'virgin Church', spawned the heresies of various groups that scholars generally nowadays call 'gnostic'.[11] Many of the names of these heresies, as recorded by Eusebios, are preserved in the early parts of Epiphanioss' *Panarion*. It is a picture of an original unitary purity—that of Orthodoxy—splitting up into a multiplicity of heresies. Drawing on earlier attempts—as well as on Hegesippos, Justin Martyr's lost work on heresies, the now-lost Greek original of Irenaeus's *Adversus Haereses*, and Hippolytus's *Syntagma*—Epiphanios seeks to provide a genealogy of this process.

Epiphanios, however, provides an elaborate prehistory of heresy. He is not content to trace the manifold declension of heresies from the historic Gospel proclaimed by Jesus in the first century; rather, he sees heresy as the declension from an aboriginal faith, as old as creation. In this, Epiphanios is simply following one of the lines of the Christian apologists of the second century: that Christianity is no new-fangled superstition, but an ancient faith that had been overlaid with corruption in the course of time and was now newly revealed in its pristine clarity in the Gospel of Christ. This idea had provided the structure for the first book of Eusebios's *History of the Church*.

Epiphanios begins with the 'four mothers' of pre-Christian heresy (derived, it seems, from Col. 3: 11), and the sixteen heresies that have flowed from them. The first is 'barbarism', the antediluvian heresy that

---

[9] Epiphanios, *haer.* proem. 1. 3 (Holl, i. 155). Quite what the eighty concubines of Cant. 6: 8 have to do with the number of heresies is unclear: also contrasted with the 'one dove' of Cant. 6: 9 are 'sixty queens' and 'countless young girls'. It would seem unlikely to have anything to do with Solomon's 'foreign women . . . who turned away his heart after their gods' (3 Kgd. 11: 4), for in that account there were '700 princesses and 300 concubines' (3 Kgd. 11: 1).

[10] John Damascene still knows this neutral sense: see *Dial.* 65. 60–1.

[11] See Eusebius, *h.e.* iv. 22 (Schwartz, i. 368. 18–372. 21).

prevailed from the Fall, proceeding from Adam's disobedience. The second is 'Scythism', which prevailed from the Flood until the Tower of Babel (or Terah, the first potter, who made possible idolatry— Epiphanios's account is not at all clear), marked by 'error proceeding from the nature of the individual will, not from what was taught or written'.[12] The third mother of heresy is Hellenism, which is identified with idolatry, and the fourth Judaism, marked by circumcision. None of these was properly a heresy, but rather opposition, in various forms, to 'the faith, so to speak, which now holds sway in the holy Catholic church of God, so recently founded, a faith which was in the beginning and which later was revealed again'.[13] From these flow the sixteen pre-Christian heresies: four philosophical schools (Stoics, Platonists, Pythagoreans, and Epicureans) and twelve Jewish sects (Hegesippos's seven, augmented). There follows an interlude, telling of the Incarnation of the Word, after which Epiphanios embarks on his account of the sixty Christian heresies: from assorted gnostics to the various Trinitarian heresies of the fourth century, closing with the Mariolatrous Collyridians and the Messalians. Epiphanios's structure is an elaboration of the apologists' claim to the pristine nature of the Catholic faith: it is a kind of sociology of knowledge establishing the authenticity of Orthodoxy (it is surely no coincidence that this elaborate structure was conceived in the buildup to the victory of Nicene orthodoxy, and its endorsement as the ideology of the Christian Roman Empire by the emperor Theodosius, at the Second Oecumenical Synod, held in 381).

Much of this elaboration is lost in John Damascene's *On Heresies*, in which Epiphanios's vast work is reduced to little more than a list. But, as a list, its purpose perhaps becomes even clearer. In recent decades sociologists, not least Mary Douglas, have taught us the importance of lists as a way of organizing potentially bewildering arrays of perceptions. A list helps us to classify things and get them in proportion: potential bewilderment is reduced to comforting order, an order imposed by the one who makes the list.[14] The formation of societies depends on such classification, which is one of the ways of creating and articulating a sense of identity. This is the purpose of John's list, and the order still preserved from Epiphanios's more elaborate account provides reassurance of the historical pristineness of the Christian faith.

[12] Epiphanios, haer. 2. 3 (Holl, i. 174. 14–16).
[13] Ibid. (Holl, i. 174. 17–19).
[14] See Douglas 1970, esp. 54–72. Cameron (1994) also notes the significance of lists in the ecclesiastical literature of the period. For the role of lists in articulating Byzantine identity, this time against the Latins, some centuries later, see Kolbaba 2000.

In extending the *Anakephalaiosis* of Epiphanios's *Panarion*, John brought it into line with his other works. Until Kotter's edition appeared, this had been obscured by a history of later additions to the text, notably a chapter on iconoclasm.[15] But Kotter makes it clear that the original version of *On Heresies* was, like *On the Orthodox Faith*, a century of 100 chapters. Like the rest of *The Fountain Head of Knowledge*, it conformed to this monastic literary genre. But the genre of a century also makes a claim to a kind of completeness, and so here: it is not just a list that puts all Christian deviation in its place, but a list that aspires to some kind of completeness, symbolized by the number 100. The last heresy, Islam, completes the tale of heresy. But with this completion, John may well have been looking, not to the many future generations whom his work of summary was to serve so well, but to some kind of final consummation: the last heresy is introduced as the 'forerunner of the Antichrist' (*Haeres.* 100. 2). In harbouring such apocalyptic forebodings, John would not have been at all unusual amongst his fellow Palestinian monks, for the end of the seventh century saw a rebirth of apocalyptic.[16]

But the tally of 100 had to be attained, so John supplemented the list he took from Epiphanios. In the two cases of Messalianism and Islam, as we have seen, he had a great deal to say, but for the other chapters he conformed more closely to his model and produced brief paragraphs. Some of these chapters simply extend the history of heresy on from Epiphanios's time: such are the chapters on the Nestorians, followers of the patriarch of Constantinople condemned at the Third Oecumenical Synod held at Ephesus in 431 for separating the two natures of Christ (81); the Eutychians, followers of Eutyches, condemned at the Fourth Oecumenical Synod of Chalcedon in 451 for denying that Christ's human nature was 'consubstantial with us' (82); the Monophysites, those who refused to accept the Synod of Chalcedon in the conviction that it separated the two natures of Christ (83); the Aphthartodocetists, Monophysites who held that Christ's human nature was incorruptible even before the Resurrection (84); the Agnoêtai, who held that Christ was truly ignorant of the day of judgement (85); the somewhat more mysterious Barsanouphitai (86);[17] and the Monothelites, who held that, although

---

[15] Such additions began very early: Nikephoros, the patriarch of Constantinople at the beginning of the ninth century, cites the chapter against the iconoclasts as chapter 102: *antirr.* 3. 84 (PG 100. 528C–533A).

[16] See Alexander 1985, Reinink 1992, and pt. III by Sebastian Brock in Palmer 1993, 222–53.

[17] An eponymous monophysite sect (see *DCB* i. 267), condemned by Sophronios in his synodical letter (*ACO*, ser. 2, 2. 2, 484. 11). Its leader, a fifth-century bishop, is not to be con-

Christ had two natures—one human, one divine—he possessed only a single (divine) will (99). Another chapter (95) includes a sect that Epiphanios had missed (or rather included under the 'Cathars' in *Panarion* 59, but they are not mentioned in the *Anakephalaiosis*, which suggests that John did not know the *Panarion* itself, or at least not very well): the Donatists, the North African sect which held that the Catholic Church had forfeited its sacred authority by compromising in the Diocletian persecution at the beginning of the fourth century. Other chapters list sects that followed odd practices: the Heïkitai (87), who indulged with women in sacred dance; the Heliotropites (89), who venerated the sunflower or heliotrope, believing it to have occult properties; the Agonyklitai (91), who abjured any kind of kneeling in prayer; the Ethnophrones (94), who followed some pagan practices, while remaining Christian (there must have been many of these, judging by the decrees of the Quinisext Synod of 691–2); the Ethikoproskoptai (96), with their unspecified moral failings; and the Lampetians (98), who seem to have upheld the freedom of Christians to adopt any form of life, whether coenobitic or eremitical. Other chapters list sects with odd beliefs: the Thnêtopsychitai (90), who held that the human soul is mortal; the Theokatagnostai (92), who found fault with Christ; the Christolytai (93), who maintained that, after the Resurrection, Jesus left his body and soul here below and ascended into heaven in his Godhead alone; and the Parermeneutai (97), who misinterpreted certain passages of Scripture. It seems unlikely that any of these last two classes of 'heresies' concern sects that had any real organization, though there may have been individuals or small groups who embraced such practices or beliefs. A final category (88) identifies a group that is certainly popular nowadays, whatever its popularity in John's own time: the Gnôsimachoi, those who opposed all sacred knowledge, maintaining that nothing more is required of a Christian than good deeds! It looks as if a certain amount of ingenuity, as well as genuine historical information, went into the compilation of John's century of heresies.

But for three heresies, as we have already mentioned, John has a great deal more to say. Let us look at them one by one.

---

fused with the great recluse of the sixth century, though such confusion did occur: see Theodore of Stoudios, *ep.* 34. 126–143 (Fatouros, 98–9).

(b) Manichaeism

John included Manichaeism in his *On Heresies*, as it was present in the epitome of Epiphanios's *Panarion*. There is also a longer work that has come down to us, a dialogue between a Manichee and an Orthodox Christian (called 'Orthodoxos'), but more accurately described in the title as 'Against the Manichees', as well as, as already mentioned, four chapters in *On the Orthodox Faith*. The chapter in *On Heresies* reads thus:

> Manichees, also Aconites. These are the disciples of Mani the Persian, who say that Christ only appeared in a form; they worship the sun and moon, and pray to stars and powers and daimons; they introduce two eternally existent principles, one good the other wicked; they hold that Christ was only born and suffered in appearance, and blaspheme against the Old Testament and the God who speaks in it, maintaining that it is not the whole cosmos that has been created by God, but only a part of it. (*Haeres.* 66)

This is a fifth-century summary of how Manichaeism appeared to Christians. At that time, it was an active missionary movement that constituted a serious threat to Christianity: indeed, at the time when Epiphanios was compiling the chapter of his *Panarion* on Manichaeism, in the mid-370s, Augustine, the future bishop of Hippo, was a Manichee of a few years' standing. To Christians, Manichaeism meant first of all a docetic understanding of Christ. The Manichees also held astrological beliefs, including the idea, common in Late Antiquity, that the heavenly bodies were intelligent beings,[18] and offered some form of worship to the sun and the moon. Another important aspect of the Christian view of the Manichees was their dualism; like the dualistic gnosticism of the second century, which lingered long in the minds of Christians, the Manichees also rejected the Old Testament and its God.

The same kind of picture of Manichaeism emerges from other contemporary Christian accounts, such as what we read in Athanasios, his friend Serapion, Cyril of Jerusalem, Basil the Great, Nemesios of Emesa, and even Augustine himself. To Christians, Manichaeism represented dualism, a dualism in which matter was evil, whence the rejection of the Old Testament, and a docetic view of Christ: for most fourth-century Christians it is mentioned in the same breath as gnostic heresies of the second century such as Valentinianism and Marcionism. Alongside dualism, another Manichaean doctrine prominent in Christian accounts from the fourth century appears to be a kind of panpsychism: the idea

---

[18] For the classical and Hellenistic background to this idea, see Scott 1991, 3–110.

that everything has a soul, including the earth, the stars, and the planets. This is all that Manichaeism seems to mean to Nemesios,[19] and it features alongside dualism in Basil's attacks on Manichaeism in his commentary on the six days of creation, his *Hexaemeron*.[20]

This picture of Manichaeism is not erroneous, though the reality was a lot more complicated. It now appears that the Fathers were right in associating Manichaeism with second-century gnosticism, for Mani seems to have been brought up in the early third century among a Jewish–Christian sect called Elchasaïtes, and when he came to formulate his own teaching, he did so under the influence of Marcionism and the doctrine of the Syrian teacher Bardaisan. Mani himself, a Persian, as *On Heresies* asserts, seems to have preached his new teaching as far afield as India, but soon returned to Persia and secured the support of the Sasanian shah, Shapur I (240–*c.*272), during whose reign Manichaeism became a vigorous missionary movement, supervised by Mani from within Persia and reaching beyond its borders. But Shapur's successor-but-one, Vahram I (273–6), was an enthusiastic supporter of the national religion of the Sasanians, Zoroastrianism, and in the last year of his reign, Mani was martyred.

Mani's teaching is elaborate, and no more than a brief sketch can be given here.[21] As the basis of his doctrine, Mani taught two principles and three 'moments'. The two principles are light and darkness, which exist in eternal and irreducible opposition. The three moments are the former time, the present time, and the future time. In the former time, light and darkness existed side by side without encroaching on each other. The present time was inaugurated when some denizens of the realm of dark caught sight of the realm of light, were entranced by what they saw, and invaded it. The realm of light, characterized by love, faith, fidelity, benevolence, and wisdom, was not suited to the violence of warfare, so 'evocations' from the Father of the realm of light invaded the realm of darkness to overthrow the 'Great Calamity'. They were conquered by the powers of darkness, but this defeat was part of a long-term strategy on the part of the forces of light, to make the powers of evil dependent on the light, and prepare the way for the enslavement of the powers of darkness and the redemption of the elements of light that have been trapped in the realm of darkness.

The rest of the history of the present time is a complicated account of

---

[19] See Nemesios, *nat. hom.* 2. 69, 110–11 (Morani, 17. 10–14, 32. 20–33. 19).

[20] See Basil, *hex.* 2. 2, 4 (dualism), 8. 1 (panpsychism) (Giet, 142–8, 152–8, 428–30).

[21] For more detail, see Lieu 1988, Burkitt 1925, Widengren 1961.

this process. The sun and the moon, for instance, were formed from elements of light that had escaped defilement, the stars from elements that had been only slightly defiled: hence the importance of the heavenly bodies in Manichaeism. So far as the realm of earth is concerned, the struggle between light and darkness imposed a life of ascetic struggle on those committed to the realm of light, for it is the material world that enslaves the light here below, and the mechanism of desire through which the soul becomes entangled in the body and bodily processes. This struggle is maintained only by the revelation of the meaning of the cosmic struggle through the teaching of various prophetic figures, who include the Buddha, Jesus, and Mani himself, and the spread of this teaching through the missionaries of the Manichaean movement.

The ascetic struggle took different forms for the two main classes of the sect, the elect and the hearers. The elect lived out the principles of Manichaeism to the full. They were committed to personal poverty, lived lives of sexual continence, and were the teachers and missionaries of the teaching of Mani. They were not permitted to prepare their own food, lest they caused suffering to the light particles contained in the plants and vegetables that formed their diet. Their food was prepared by the hearers, the lower class of Manichee, who were allowed to own property, and marry or have mistresses (though they were to avoid having children), though, like the elect, they were committed to vegetarianism. The meals which the hearers prepared for the elect were regarded as a kind of sacrament, and in the West were generally referred to as the Eucharist. On death, the soul of the elect passed directly to the realm of light, whereas the soul of the hearer remained on earth to pass through a series of reincarnations—in the luminous bodies of fruits and eventually in the body of one of the elect—before finally returning to the realm of light. The present moment will come to an end as the liberation of light reaches completion, leaving an earth consisting almost entirely of matter, and therefore dominated by sin and strife. The result of this final great war will be the final separation of light from darkness again, which ushers in the future moment, marked by the restoration of the original division between light and darkness.

Manichaeism constituted a powerful challenge to Christianity just as the Church was coming to provide the Roman Empire with its religious ideology. Within the Empire, Manichaeism seems to have emphasized its undeniable affinities with Christianity. Pope Leo also knew a good deal about Manichaeism, and regarded it as a peculiarly insidious threat to Orthodoxy. He treated it as a Christian heresy, and it has recently been argued that his association of the 'Monophysitism' of Eutyches, condemned at the Synod of Chalcedon in 451, with Mani (and Valentinus) is more than an attempt to malign a misguided Christian by associating his Christology with docetism, but rather a serious effort to analyse the nature of docetism in terms of what he knew from his own experience.[22] Eventually Christianity won the allegiance of the Empire, and Manichaeism came to be persecuted as its most dangerous rival. In 527, an edict of Justinian's made Manichaeism a capital offence.[23] It seems that Manichaeism did not survive in the Byzantine Empire beyond the end of the sixth century.[24] Elsewhere, however, towards the East, it flourished as far as China, and continued to do so for many centuries.

What of John's attack on Manichaeism in his *Dialogue against the Manichees*? Kotter reports that this dialogue is contained in few manuscripts, and those relatively late, and remarks that this may be because of the lack of relevance ('geringe Aktualität') of the subject.[25] This does not seem very likely, for though Manichaeism itself may have been of little concern to the Byzantines after the religion was exterminated within the bounds of the Empire after the sixth century, John's main concern (as Kotter states) is dualism, which was far from being of little relevance to the Byzantine mind. Indeed, one might argue that the Byzantines were obsessed by the threat of dualism, in the forms of Paulicianism (which had already made its appearance in John's lifetime) and Bogomilism, both of which were regarded by Byzantine heresiologists as themselves forms of Manichaeism.[26]

If it is a puzzle why John's treatise against the Manichees attracted so little later attention, it is also worth asking why he composed it. Manichaeism, as we have seen, had been exterminated in the Byzantine Empire. John, however, was not writing in the Byzantine Empire, but in the Umayyad Empire, and there is some evidence that the tolerance of the Umayyads for other faiths, especially 'people of the book' (which Manichees could claim to be with some justification), led to a revival of Manichaeism within the former eastern provinces of the Byzantine Empire, and perhaps the return of some exiled Manichees to Mesopotamia.[27] It is thus possible John's engagement with Manichaeism was a matter of immediate concern rather than being simply theoretical.

---

[22] See Grillmeier 1987, 172–94.

[23] *cod.* I. 5. 12; Eng. trans.: Coleman-Norton 1966, 567 (see also *cod.* I. 5. 15, 16, 18: ibid. 572, 573, 575). See Lieu 1988, 170.   [24] Lieu 1988, 175.

[25] Kotter iv. 334.

[26] See, most recently, Hamilton and Hamilton 1998. An older general study is Runciman 1947.   [27] Kotter iv. 334; Lieu 1988, 82–3.

The evidence from the treatise itself is at first glance ambivalent. The dialogue begins on an authentic note. The Orthodox Christian (let us call him John, for there is no doubt with whom John identifies) begins by asking what they are seeking in their rational enquiry together. The Manichee replies, 'To lay bare the rational structure of the faith, that we may find the truth' (*Manich.* 1. 2–3). One recalls Augustine's words to Honoratus:

For what other reason could have persuaded me for nearly nine years to abandon the religion that had been instilled into me by my parents when I was a child, and to follow those men and diligently listen to them, save that they said that our superstition made us afraid and ordered us to put faith before reason, whereas they required faith of no one without the truth first being discussed and explained?[28]

There follows a quick-fire argument about the nature of truth and error, in which they readily come to an agreement, and then John asks the question: 'Do you say that there is one principle or two?' The Manichee replies that he believes in two principles that were originally separate, and then explains how it came about that they are now mixed. This is one of only two places where the Manichee is allowed to hold forth for more than a few lines without interruption (though perhaps it would be more accurate to say: until he is interrrupted):

Once the Good was in its own place, in all goodness and blessedness, and matter or wickedness was lifeless, unmoved, shameful, malformed darkness, insensible, and so throughout many ages. Latterly, matter rose up against itself, and its fruits fought one against another, some in pursuit, others in flight, and they came to the regions of the light and seeing the light desired its beauty and ceased from their mutual warfare, and making an agreement together they attacked the light. The Good sent a power from itself, and in the thick of the struggle the rulers of darkness ate part of the light. For the Good in its fear allowed the power from itself to be seized lest they gain dominion over its own place. This he did, so that through the portion that he had delivered to them he might gain dominion over wickedness. And thus there came about the mixture of good and evil; for from the portion of the good souls came to be, and from the substance of wickedness bodies. (*Manich.* 2. 11–24)

John now interrupts, saying, 'Let us discuss these things to begin with'. He continues: 'In how many ways is principle (*archê*) understood?' To which the Manichee obligingly replies, 'You tell me.' So he does. The section that follows is characteristically Johannine. We have already seen his interest in compiling definitions of particular terms. Here he is concerned with the different ways in which the single term *archê* can be taken

---

[28] Augustine, *Util. cred.* 1. 2 (Pegon, 210).

(which connotes a greater range of meaning than the normal English equivalent 'principle', as *archê* has other connotations, such as 'beginning'):

That which does not have an *archê* is said to be *anarchon* (without beginning), and the word *archê* is equivocal, for it means many things. For we can speak of *archê* in respect of time, as we say the rising of the sun is the beginning of the day, or speak of the beginning of the year. We can speak of *archê* in terms of space, as we speak of the beginning of a road, or say that the river Phison has its origin (*archê*) in Paradise. We can speak of *archê* in respect of worth or authority, as when we say that the king is the head (*archê*) of his subjects. We can speak of *archê* as that which is by nature first, as in the case of number. For if two exist, then one must necessarily be, whereas if one exists, two does not necessarily follow; for two is one plus one, but one is not two. One is therefore the principle (or beginning) of two. We can speak of principle in respect of order, as the rank of reader is first, then subdeacon, then deacon, and so priest, and bishop. We can speak of principle in respect of origin (*aition*) and that in three ways: naturally as father is the principle of son, creatively as creator is the principle of creation, and mimetically as what is depicted is the principle of the image. In such ways, therefore, what is said to be a principle is that which is said to be really without beginning, and it is said to be without beginning in all these ways. How therefore do you say that there are two principles without beginning? (*Manich.* 3. 2–18)

The Manichee replies, 'in all these ways', and John seeks to reduce this position to absurdity, by showing that two entails a prior monad (or unit), which thus becomes a principle behind the two so-called principles: how can this be? The Manichee astutely side-steps the question by raising the issue of the Trinity: 'You say that there are three *hypostaseis*, and how can you say that they must begin from a monad? (4. 1–2). John attempts a reply by utilizing the distinctions he has already made: the Word and the Spirit are from the Father, but not after him, because they are from the Father by origin (*kat' aitian*), not in time. The argument continues for several pages, and the Manichee is allowed to press John quite hard, particularly over the problem of the way in which to speak of Son and Spirit deriving from the Father seems to entail change in God. John has a great deal to say, the Manichee's part being confined to brief questions, but the questions are relevant and probing. One wonders if the real intellectual context with which John is engaging here is not so much Manichee objections to Christianity, as Muslim objections. The paradoxes of Trinitarian belief would be an obvious opening to Muslim controversialists,[29] perhaps more so than to a Manichee, whose own

---

[29] See below on *Sarac.*, and also the earliest extant Muslim attack on the Christian doctrine of the Trinity, Abū 'Īsā al-Warrāq's *Against the Trinity*: Thomas 1992.

beliefs included 'consubstantial' evocations from the Father, brought
into being to further the war against the powers of darkness after the
'Great Calamity'. The argument passes beyond the issue of the Trinity, as
John returns to the question of two original and opposed principles and
tries to get the Manichee admit the absurdity of the notion.

The principles behind John's arguments are those worked out in the
second and third centuries against gnostic dualism, not just by Christian
thinkers, but by Neoplatonists such as Plotinus. Behind much of this
thinking lay a conviction, enhanced at the time by the revival of interest in
the ideas of the ancient philosopher Pythagoras (often called 'Neo-
pythagoreanism'), that the origin of everything lay in unity, multiplicity
being a declension from primal unity. And that original unity was good,
either, for Christians, because it was God's creation, its goodness
reflecting the Creator's goodness, or, for Neoplatonists, because the hierarchies of being and goodness were parallel and convergent. A corollary
of this was the doctrine of evil as privation of the good. On these
principles, John argues that if there is any good at all, then there must be
an original single principle, the source of this goodness, evil being a
declension from original goodness.

The first section of the dialogue comes to an end as John allows the
Manichee once again (but for the last time!) to have his say, and explain
the reason for the mixture of good and evil that is found in the world. The
Manichee continues from where he left off:

There was,[30] as I said, God and matter, each within its own borders, the good God
together with life, light, movement, knowledge, understanding and everything
good, and matter together with wickedness, corruption, darkness, death, completely still and silent and motionless. Then, after many aeons, matter rose up
against itself, and its fruits one against another, and thus some were pursued and
some pursuing, and there was, as I have said, God and matter, that is, two principles:
the soul being of the portion of light, and the body the fashioning of darkness and
matter. The mixture happened in this way. Each of them existed in its own way: the

[30] The Manichee begins by using the third-person-singular imperfect of the verb 'to be'
(*ēn*). It is grammatically odd, because the subject, God and matter, constitute a plural. But
John's representation of the Manichee's words may be significant. Maximos the Confessor, in
a number of places, represents the Manichee position as affirming that 'there was matter',
using the same verb (see *amb.* 10. 40 (PG 91. 1184B)), and argues that this verb can only be
used of God (ibid. 10. 38 (1180 D)). I have argued that this absolute use of *ēn* is a conscious
echo of the first sentence of St John's Gospel, which can be traced back at least to Cyril of
Alexandria (see Louth 1996, 109–10 n. 101). A possibly still earlier example can be found in a
fragment ascribed to Clement of Alexandria (fr. 3, from a commentary on 1 John: GCS
Clement 3, 210, lines 3–6). The verb is not found in any of John's sources for the views of the
Manichee, so it is possible that it reflects a singular Christian use.

good was in one part, the wicked in three. Then the wicked was moved by a dis-
orderly impulse out of its own borders and came to the borders of the good, and
when the good knew this, it emitted from itself a power called the mother of life,
and the mother of life emitted the first human being, and this first human being
I call the five elements, which are air, wind, light, water and fire. Clothed with these,
he went forth and fought against the darkness. The rulers (*archons*) of darkness ate
part of his suit of armour [panoply], that is the soul; they overcame the first man,
and he being in darkness was tortured by them, and cried out to the good, which
emitted another power, called the living spirit. And he came down and gave his right
hand to the first man and led him up. The part that the rulers had eaten, that is the
soul, was left below, and from this portion of the good souls came to be, and from
the substance of wickedness bodies. (*Manich.* 28. 1–22)

John now interrupts the Manichee, beginning by citing the 'divine
Apostle' (an authority for Manichees as well as Christians) and his protest
against the idea of there being any communion of light and darkness (cf.
2 Cor. 6: 14), and continues with a series of rhetorical protests against
dualism, and rhetorical questions addressed to the Manichee, who is
given no chance to respond. Indeed, from this point onwards, the
Manichee's involvement in the dialogue becomes less and less. His next
interjection is to raise against John's insistence on the goodness of the
whole creation the problem of the existence of the devil (*Manich.* 32).
John's reply is that the devil was created good—indeed, he was created to
be the ruler of the cosmos—but he willed to rebel against God. Against
the objection that God knew, since he is omniscient, that the devil would
rebel (*Manich.* 34), John maintains that it is a sign of his exceeding goodness that God created him at all, and later on, when the Manichee raises
the problem again, insists that the devil was created free (*Manich.* 69). John
develops the idea of God's providential ordering of his good creation so
that everything that happens fits with God's good purposes, and in
this context deals with the Manichee's objection to eternal punishment
for the wicked as being incompatible with a good God by maintaining
that

God does not punish anyone in the future, but each one makes himself receptive to
participation in God. Participation in God is delight, and lack of participation is
punishment. Thus God is not punishing, when he allows temptations, but is
educating us and healing us of wickedness, that we may come to know him and turn
to him and obtain his holiness. (*Manich.* 44. 1–6)

The problem of eternal punishment recurs, and John develops various
other ways of seeing this as a consequence of the free ability of creatures
to respond or not to God, eternal punishment of the wicked being not

something arbitrary, but simply part of what is meant by a wicked will finding itself in the eternal presence of the good God:

In this life there is a certain economy and government and ineffable providence that calls sinners to conversion and repentance, but after death there is no longer change, no longer repentance, not because God will not receive repentance—for he cannot deny himself nor can he fail in compassion—but because the soul cannot change. . . . For as the demons after their fall do not repent, nor do the angels now sin, but both are unchangeable, so human beings after death are unchangeable, and the just long for God and possessing him eternally rejoice in him, while sinners long for sin, and not having any matter for sin, are as it were consumed by fire and the worm, and are punished not having any kind of assuagement. For what is punishment, save the privation of what one longs for? According, therefore, to the analogy of desire, those who long for God rejoice, and those who long for sin are punished. And those who obtain what they long for rejoice in accordance with the measure of their longing, and those who fail suffer pain in accordance with the measure of their longing. (*Manich.* 75. 5–9, 13–24)[31]

This distinction between demonic or angelic willing and human willing is something we shall encounter again, when we explore the Damascene's cosmological and anthropological ideas. But here it is part of an attempt to understand the nature of a created order in which creatures have the freedom to rebel against the source of their being. The defence of providence also has to deal with the problem of evil, which John tackles by appealing to two principles developed by earlier Christian thinkers (and indeed before them by their non-Christian predecessors): first, the notion that evil is essentially privation of goodness, and secondly, the notion that the origin of evil lies in the movements of the created rational will (whether demonic or human). The first principle involves demonstrating that there is nothing naturally evil. Even in the case of an undoubted sin such as fornication one has to distinguish: 'fornication, as desire and friendship and union, is good, but as desire for what is not owed, and indeed forbidden, it is wicked' (*Manich.* 59. 1–2). The second raises the question as to why God created free, rational beings if their freedom entailed the possibility of sin. This is discussed in the last passage in which the Manichee is allowed to raise points repeatedly: in chapter 69. The core of John's answer is that virtue is the greatest good, and is possible only for rational beings who are free and unconstrained, a version of the old Stoic justification for the ultimate goodness of a cosmos in which good and evil appear to be mixed.

[31] This doctrine of eternal punishment is essentially that of Maximos the Confessor: see *qu. Thal.* 59 (CCSG 22, 55, lines 160–70).

The nature of John's engagement with Manichaeism in this dialogue is puzzling. The issues discussed—dualism, the origin of evil, the nature of the devil and eternal punishment, the nature of providence—are all issues on which Christians and Manichees disagreed.[32] But the two occasions on which the Manichee is allowed to have his say scarcely contribute to the development of the dialogue, except in very general terms. John never returns to what the Manichee has said, and the agenda of the debate is determined entirely by John. Yet, these two passages are accurate accounts of Manichaean doctrine. They are accurate because they are drawn from good (Christian) sources. The source he follows most closely is the *Acts of Archelaus* by the late fourth-century Hegemonios. This purports to be the account of a public debate in Mesopotamia between a Christian bishop, Archelaus, and an unnamed Manichee. The second speech by the Manichee in John's dialogue is strikingly similar to the beginning of the account of Manichaeism in the *Acts of Archelaus*.[33] But John seems to be aware of other Christian sources, too, including Epiphanios's *Panarion* (chapter 66). One wonders why John went to the trouble of giving an accurate account of Manichaean doctrine in a dialogue that ignores the accurate detail recorded. One might also recall, as noted above, that early on the debate takes a turn that recalls Muslim objections to the Christian doctrine of the Trinity, and further observe that the rest of the issues discussed by John were also of interest to his contemporary Muslims, especially the topic of providence and creaturely free will, which was hotly disputed in Muslim circles under the Umayyads.[34]

In his book on Manichaeism, Samuel Lieu suggests that the anti-Manichaean works of Byzantine theologians (including John of Damascus) should perhaps be interpreted as 'a standard form of rhetorical training for the theologians',[35] given that Manichaeism no longer existed as a religion within the Byzantine Empire after the end of the sixth century. Although, as we have seen, Manichaeism may have had something of a revival in Mesopotamia and Syria under the Umayyads, John's dialogue with a Manichee does not look like a genuine engagement with Manichaean ideas; it is, rather, an opportunity to refute dualism and

[32] These are much the same issues as those covered by the four chapters in *Expos.* (92: 'That God is not the cause of evil'; 93: 'That there are not two principles'; 94: 'Why God created beings, foreknowing that they would sin and not repent'; 95: 'On the law of God and the law of sin').

[33] Cf. *Manich.* 28. 10–20 with Hegemonios, *Arch.* 7 (Beeson, 10, l. 2–11, l. 1).

[34] Le Coz 1992, 136–44. See (d) below, on John's engagement with Islam.

[35] Lieu 1988, 175.

solve the theological problems to which dualism might seem to provide an answer. Given that these are issues that engaged his Muslim contemporaries, and the fact that John at one point seeks to respond to problems raised by the Christian doctrine of the Trinity, one might conjecture that this dialogue was indeed a rhetorical exercise, composed when John was in contact with Muslims, with his ears full of their debates and their taunts against Christianity. If so, we might further conjecture that it is an early work, written when John was still in Damascus. His concern to represent Manichaean doctrine accurately would be an early sign of John's scholarly bent, further evidence for which we shall find in abundance in his later, more mature works. But unlike in those later works, John allows himself to argue here in his own words about dualism and the problem of evil; in his later works, he is much more concerned to keep strictly to the words of the Fathers. If this work does belong to John's time in Damascus, we might also see in it a safe way for John to think through arguments that were hotly contentious among Muslim thinkers, as well as work out a defence against Muslim objections to Christianity in a way that would not attract unwelcome attention. John's defence of human free will might have been thought to align him with the Qadarites (though see below, in the final section on Islam), who asserted the reality of human free will, believing that an absolute determinism was unworthy of God (note how John defends the notion of eternal punishment against the idea that it is unworthy of God). Qadarites were, apparently, to be found in the administration of Damascus, as was John, and were the object of persecution by the Umayyad caliphs, including 'Abd al-Malik, whom John's father served as treasurer.[36] If the *Dialogue against the Manichees* belonged to the early period of John's life when he was in Damascus, this might explain why so few manuscripts of the text survive, as copies of such an early work might well not have formed part of collections of the works of John the monk.

(c) Messalianism

Although John Damascene tells us a great deal about Messalianism— indeed, he is one of our principal sources—his engagement with this heresy is rather different from his engagement with either Manichaeism or Islam. In both the latter cases we see John advancing arguments of his own, whereas in the case of Messalianism, what we have is rather a kind of dossier. Messalianism was the last of the heresies included in

[36] See Le Coz 1992, 141 and n., 142.

Epiphanios's _Panarion_, and John includes the brief section devoted to Messalianism from the _Anakephalaiosis_, which, as we have seen, forms the basis of John's _On Heresies_. But he then adds two lengthy sections, the first called 'Chapters of the impious doctrine of the Massalians, taken from their book', and the second being an extract from Theodoret's _Church History_, in which he tells of the Messalians.[37] These two sections amount to a remarkable dossier, telling us virtually all that we know about this heresy.

Messalians were members of an enthusiastic monastic group that emerged in the fourth century. Their name derives from the Syriac, _Mṣalyane_, meaning 'those who pray', which was transliterated into Greek as _Massalianoi_, or translated as _Euchitai_.[38] Who or what they were is obscure, as most of what we know about them directly comes from their enemies; for, although it now seems likely that there were those in Messalian circles who found some sympathy with Basil the Great and his brother Gregory of Nyssa (though not with Gregory Nazianzen), they were denounced by synods held at Antioch and Side, and finally at the Third Oecumenical Synod held at Ephesus in 431. It is from the propositions taken from the ascetic writings of the Messalians for condemnation by those synods (especially the _Asketikon_, condemned at Ephesus) that we have most of our direct knowledge of Messalianism, and what we have in John is much the fullest extant account of these propositions.

As the name suggests, the Messalians originated in Syria, and it has been maintained with some justice that it was the incursion of theological language of Christian experience at home in the Syriac world into the rather different linguistic world of Greek Christianity that led to misunderstanding and condemnation.[39] Their name also points to the importance they attached to prayer; in the propositions drawn from the _Asketikon_ it appears that they attributed almost exclusive power to prayer. To be saved, all one could do was pray for the descent of the Holy Spirit, which, when granted, was experienced in a palpable way ('as a woman experiences intercourse with her husband': _Haeres._ 80. 22). The sacraments, the episcopal hierarchy, and priestly ministry were of no value. Along with this insistence on prayer, the Messalians depicted the fallen human state in the darkest colours. As a result of Adam's primal sin, sin had become a kind of second nature to human beings, so that inwardly

[37] Theodoret, _h.e._ iv. 11 (Parmentier, 229. 4–231. 20).

[38] 'Messalians' is the term used in English (with similar terms in other western European languages): it is closer to the Syriac, though apparently based on the Greek term.

[39] See Stewart 1991.

they experienced the mingling of good and evil, the presence of evil being due to a demonic presence. Only the Holy Spirit could drive out this demon, and to acquire the Spirit, all one could do was pray.

Another problem posed by Messalianism concerns the relationship of the so-called Macarian Homilies to this movement. Many of the passages of the *Asketikon* condemned as Messalian seem to be drawn from these homilies; indeed, the parallels with the Macarian Homilies are even more striking in the material preserved by John. First noticed in the 1920s, the apparent dependence of the Messalian *Asketikon* on the Macarian Homilies, one of the most influential sources, along with the works of Evagrios, of Byzantine monastic spirituality, has caused heated debate. But it is now coming to be accepted that, although the *Asketikon* draws on the language and ideas of the Macarian Homilies, the author of the homilies is in fact often critical of the more extreme tendencies of Messalianism, and the most recent study of this question, by Klaus Fitschen, comes to the conclusion that 'the Messalians were therefore a group that grew up in the same ascetical milieu as Ps-Makarios, shared his ideas, but radicalized them, and made use of both his writings and oral tradition. Ps-Makarios is no Messalian heresiarch, nor even a Messalian theologian, but an involuntary source of slogans for the movement.'[40]

The 'direct' sources for Messalianism, mentioned above, include, as well as the chapter of John's *On Heresies*, a list put together by Timothy of Constantinople in the late sixth century,[41] and the more nearly contemporary accounts by the fifth-century theologian and church historian Theodoret: the passage from his *Church History* that John reproduces and also a chapter from his *Compendium of Heretical Fables*.[42] All the propositions included in Theodoret are found in Timothy (though Theodoret includes a good deal more narrative detail, including an interview that took place at the Synod of Antioch with one of the Messalian leaders, Adelphios, whom Fitschen conjectures to have been the author of the *Asketikon*), so interest has focused on the relationship between the lists found in Timothy and John. The similarities are striking in both phraseology and content, but the lists are by no means the same: John's is considerably longer, but fewer than half of Timothy's propositions are found in John's list, and only a third of John's propositions occur in Timothy's list. There are various theories to account for this. In his seminal book on the Macarian writings, Hermann Dörries suggested that

[40] Fitschen 1998, 218.
[41] This list can be found in PG 86. 45–52.
[42] *Compendium of Heretical Fables*, PG 83. 429–32.

Timothy's list was based on the dossier prepared for the synod that condemned Messalianism at Constantinople (to which, being in the capital, he had access), while John's list was based on the dossier of the Oecumenical Synod of Ephesus.[43] In his recent book Fitschen suggests that both Timothy and John have a common source, unknown to Theodoret, which may be the synodal letter of the Constantinopolitan synod of 426, or part of it; this Timothy supplements from notes drawn up by Flavian of Antioch and Amphilochios of Iconium for the fourth-century synods, while John supplements it by drawing directly on the *Asketikon*.[44] Whatever the sources for John's summary of Messalian doctrine in this part of *On Heresies* 80 (ll. 5–100), it is clear that it is the fullest extant account of Messalian teaching from the perspective of those who condemned it in the late fourth and early fifth centuries, and John's further inclusion of the chapter from Theodoret's *Church History* means that John has supplemented the note in the *Anakephalaiosis* of the *Panarion* with a remarkably full dossier.

John's chapters from the Messalians' book fall into two groups, the first consisting of relatively short propositions, all beginning *hoti* ('that') and sometimes supplemented by 'they say', the second including longer sections more discursively presented (these are often numbered, though in different ways in different editions). Fitschen suggests that the first group consists of propositions taken word for word from the *Asketikon*, whereas the others are from a summary of Messalian teaching in a report presented to the synod. If we compare John's account with the other lists (something vastly facilitated by the synopsis in Appendix 2 of Columba Stewart's book and Fitschen's presentation of the propositions in his book[45]), it becomes clear that John (or his source) is especially concerned about the threat posed by the teaching of the Messalians to the hierarchical and sacramental structure of the Church. The proposition about the inefficacy of the sacraments, found in both Theodoret and Timothy, is prefaced in John's account by the assertion that even the Apostles were tainted by the indwelling demon, and a recurrent concern in the second group is the Messalian emphasis on spiritual experience which seems to overshadow participation in the sacraments: for instance, it is alleged that 'some of them say that they never participate in the mysteries unless they palpably experience the presence of the Spirit, taking place at that very moment' (*Haeres.* 80. 95–7).

---

[43] Dörries 1941, 425–41.

[44] Fitschen 1998, 60–88.

[45] Stewart 1991, 244–79; Fitschen 1998, 78–87.

Most discussion of John's material on Messalianism is naturally concerned with the information that can be gleaned from it about the historical quasi-monastic movement of the fourth and fifth centuries. But my primary concern here is rather different: why did John add this lengthy section to the brief mention in the *Anakephalaiosis* of the *Panarion*? It is unlikely that John himself made the selection from the synodal account (or accounts) of the heresy; it is much more likely that what we have in *On Heresies* 80 are two already existing sources, one drawn from the Messalians' book, as John says (presumably the *Asketikon*), the other from Theodoret's *Church History*. But the question still stands: why did John give Messalianism such treatment, when he devotes no more than a brief paragraph to most other heresies? The only heresies that get anything like the treatment meted out to Messalianism are Monophysitism, where John seems to have added a section from a Monophysite work by John Philoponos (though it is not included in all manuscripts), and Islam. This would suggest that Messalianism was a contemporary challenge, as were Monophysitism and Islam (though Monothelitism, no less a contemporary challenge to the Palestinian monks, gets no more than a paragraph). Yet all the evidence we have suggests that Messalianism, at any rate in the sense of the movement originating in the fourth century, condemned at Antioch, Side, Constantinople, and Ephesus, died out shortly after its condemnation at Ephesus in 431, though the name 'Messalian', as the name of an already condemned monastic heresy, continued to be used by heresiologists throughout the Byzantine period.[46]

Perhaps the answer lies in its valuing of felt spiritual experience over against sacramental participation: something that we have noticed looms large in John's account. The claim that felt spiritual experience was a necessary prelude to sacramental participation is by no means unknown in Byzantine monasticism. In the eighth letter of the Dionysian corpus, Dionysios, telling the story of the monk Carpos, mentions with approval the fact that he never celebrated the sacred mysteries without first having experienced, during the prayers of preparation, a favourable vision.[47] There are several stories in John Moschos's *Spiritual Meadow* that envisage experience of the descent of the Spirit by the priest celebrating the Eucharist, lack of such experience being a cause for concern.[48] The same idea, not perhaps so dramatically expressed, emerges again in Byzantine monasticism at the turn of the millennium, with St Symeon the New

[46] See Fitschen 1998, 273–341.
[47] Dionysios, *ep.* 8 (PG 3. 1097BC (Ritter, 188. 11–13)).
[48] John Moschos, *prat.* 25, 27, 150 (PG 87. 2870D–2872A, 2873BC, 3013C–3016C).

Theologian's insistence on spiritual experience as a qualification for priestly ministry, as Holl remarked long ago.[49] Symeon also insisted that receiving communion without conscious experience of the grace received is worthless.[50] The long life of Messalianism as a heretical category in Byzantine theology and heresiology is probably due to the persistence of this tradition in Byzantine monasticism, whereby spiritual experience tended to overshadow sacramental efficacy, and the prominence given to Messalianism in John's *On Heresies* is an early index of this. For this we must be grateful, for without John's chapter on Messalianism, our knowledge of that movement would be still further impoverished.

(d) Islam

The final heresy (apart from Christological heresies, which will be dealt with in the next chapter) to which John devotes his attention is Islam.[51] In the surviving works attributed to the Damascene, there are two works that discuss Islam: the final chapter of *On Heresies* and his *Dispute between a Saracen and a Christian*. The authenticity of both these works has been doubted. In the former case this is partly because the version in which *On Heresies* has long been known, that published in Migne's *Patrologia Graeca*,[52] consists of 103 chapters, of which the last but two is on Islam. It has sometimes been suggested that the last three chapters constitute additions by John to an already existing work of 100 chapters,[53] or, contrariwise, that these additional three chapters were added later.[54] Kotter's edition reveals that the original version of *On Heresies*, as we have seen, was a century, and that the chapter on Islam was the final chapter. Part of this demonstration turns on an early manuscript (Mosqu. Synod. gr. 315), from the ninth or tenth century, which closes with chapter 100 on Islam, making it clear that the view, long held, that the chapter on Islam is dependent on the *Treasury of Orthodoxy* by the twelfth- or thirteenth-century Nicetas Choniates can no longer be maintained. The case of the *Dispute* is rather different. It was first explicitly ascribed to John by Robert

---

[49] Holl 1898, 210 n. 1.

[50] e.g., Symeon the New Theologian, *eth.* 10. 758–77 (Darrouzès, ii. 314). Discussed in Krivochéine 1980, 115–19.

[51] For this section, see Le Coz 1992; Sahas 1972, 1992; P. Khoury 1957–8; A.-T. Khoury 1969, 47–82; Hoyland 1997, 480–9.

[52] PG 94. 677–780.

[53] e.g., Chase 1958, p. xxxi.

[54] So Altaner and Stuiber 1978, 527, perhaps based on the epilogue to *Haeres.* in PG 94. 777B, as Le Coz (1992, 184 n. 8) suggests.

Grosseteste, who translated it in the thirteenth century. It was used, however, by the Arab Christian theologian Theodore Abū Qurrah, in the ninth century, so the material in it cannot be much later than John. It has plausibly been suggested that the *Dispute* is based on John's oral teaching, rather than having actually been written down by him.[55]

If these two works are indeed by John Damascene (or even if their arguments can be traced back to him), they constitute the earliest explicit discussions of Islam by a Christian theologian ('explicit', because it is evident that Anastasios of Sinai is aware of Islam and some of the Qur'ānic traditions[56]). They are thus of intrinsic interest. In contrast with John's other works on heresy, it would seem that they contain John's own reflections on the phenomenon of Islam; as we have seen, most of John's engagement with heresy consists of the compilation of earlier 'patristic' material, and even in the dialogue with a Manichee, John seems to have drawn his accounts of Manichaeism from patristic sources. In writing on Islam, however, he was a pioneer. It is not surprising then that both these works manifest oddities from a literary point of view. *On Heresies* 100 starts off defining Islam, situating Muhammad historically, and summarizing his teaching, especially as it bears on Christianity; it then deals with Muslim objections to Christianity, and goes on to discuss various suras from the Qur'ān, the last of which is no more than mentioned, after which there is a brief and rather inconsequential list of Muslim practices. It gives the impression of tailing off, after a fairly coherent beginning. The *Dispute* is also odd, in that the beginning and ending constitute a proper disputation (*Sarac.* 1–4, 11), while the middle section (*Sarac.* 5–10) considers various objections that the Saracen might make to the Christian ('If the Saracen were to ask you, saying . . .'), which supports the view that here we have notes taken from John's teaching.

Both works present Islam as politically dominant: *On Heresies* 100 presents it as 'the religion that leads people astray and prevails up to the present', and both works give the impression that Christians are under pressure from the Saracens to defend their faith. *On Heresies* 100 attempts to give an account of Islam, while the *Dispute* simply goes through a series of topics of disagreement between Muslim and Christian or topics for debate on which the Muslim hopes to catch out the Christian and demonstrate the absurdity of Christian theology.

The final chapter of *On Heresies* begins by identifying its subject as the

[55] See Kotter iv. 420–1. For a more extended discussion of the authenticity of both *Haeres.* 100 and *Sarac.*, see Le Coz 1992, 193–203. See also Sahas 1972, 1992.

[56] See Griffith 1987 and Haldon 1992, 131.

'religion of the Ishmaelites that leads people astray and prevails up to the present', and asserts that it is the 'forerunner of the Antichrist'.[57] The Ishmaelites are also called Hagarenes and Saracens, and John gives an etymology for all these names: 'Ishmaelite' derives from Ishmael, Abraham's elder son by his wife's slave, Hagar, from whom the name 'Hagarenes' derives; the name Saracen is derived from Sarah, who expelled Hagar (see Gen. 16). Ishmael figures in the Qur'ān, along with Abraham, Isaac, and other patriarchs, as a prophet, though Muslims are not called Ishmaelites; but Hagar is not mentioned in the Qur'ān (nor is Sarah mentioned by name). The Damascene's derivation of 'Saracen', etymologically perhaps a term meaning 'Eastern' applied to Arabs, is more fanciful. John's etymologies, however, identify Islam as the religion of the Arabs, which is historically sound for the Umayyad period, though contrary to the portrayal of Islam in the Qur'ān as a universal religion. These people, says John, once worshipped the morning star and Aphrodite. They remained idolaters until the time of the emperor Herakleios, when there appeared a false prophet called Muhammad (in Greek: *Mamed*). He concocted his own heresy, from the Old and New Testaments which he had chanced upon, and from conversation with an Arian monk. He made out that there had been revealed to him a 'scripture from heaven', and from these 'laughable revelations' he taught his followers to worship God.

The essence of Muhammad's teaching is that there is one God, the creator of everything, who himself neither begets nor is begotten. Christ is a word of God and his spirit, created and a slave, born from the Virgin Mary. Christ was not crucified, nor did he die, but was assumed into heaven by God, 'because he loved him'. After this brief account of Muhammad's teaching, John turns to criticism. He criticizes the revelation to Muhammad, because there were no witnesses—he draws an unfavourable comparison with Moses—indeed, the revelation was made to Muhammad in his sleep. John then turns to Muslim attacks on Christians: first, the charge of being 'associators' (*hetairiastai*)—that is, those who associate someone, in this case Christ, with God, and thus derogate from the unique sovereignty of God (this accusation is called *shirk* in Arabic); and secondly, the charge of being 'idolaters', who worship the Cross. John defends Christians against these charges. In the first case, he appeals to the Scriptures, in particular the prophets, who teach that Christ is 'the Son of God and God', and further argues that if

[57] In my account of the Damascene's two treatises on Islam I have made grateful use of Le Coz's 'commentaires': Le Coz 1992, 89–182.

Christ is the word and spirit of God, then to deny that Christ is God is to deny the divinity of the word and spirit of God, as a result of which John calls the Muslims in turn 'mutilators' [of God] (the question of the created or uncreated status of God's word and spirit is discussed at greater length in the *Dispute*). In the second case, he charges Muslims with worshipping the *Ka'ba* at Mecca, and mocks the traditions he alleges are associated with the *Ka'ba*.[58]

It is worth reflecting on the nature of these charges against Christians with which John is familiar. The charge of *shirk* is a standard charge against most non-Muslims, including Christians, in the Qur'ān, but the charge of idolatry because of Christian veneration of the Cross is not.[59] There is, however, in the *ḥadīth* (traditions about Muhammad) a story about a discussion between Muhammad and some Christians, in which he is represented as saying: 'What prevents you from becoming Muslims is your claim that God had a son and your worship of the Cross and eating the flesh of swine.'[60] Such a charge is not surprising, as there is a good deal of evidence that in the seventh century Jews taunted Christians with idolatry for venerating the cross (as well as icons and relics);[61] it may well be that Muslims added this charge to the Qur'ānic accusation of *shirk*.

John then turns to discuss the Qur'ān.[62] He discusses (or mentions) four suras, which he calls 'the woman', 'the camel of God', 'the table', and 'the cow'.[63] Three of these are identifiable: 'The woman' is sura 4 (properly: 'Women'); 'The table', sura 5; 'The cow', sura 2—all lengthy suras, dated by scholars to the later Medinan period of Muhammad's life. The sura called 'The camel of God' does not appear in the Qur'ān. In his discussion of the sura 'Women', John criticizes the Muslim law of marriage and its permitting polygamy and divorce; he also accuses Muhammad of adultery over Zayd. Although there is no sura called 'The camel of God', elements of the story which John tells of the camel occur

[58] Le Coz demonstrates that John is in some confusion here, perhaps associating the sheep slaughtered on the *Ka'ba* during the Hajj with Abraham's sacrifice of Isaac: Le Coz 1992, 117–19. See also Sahas 1972, 86–9.

[59] Sahas 1972, 84; Le Coz 1992, 116.

[60] Quoted in Haleem 1996, 77.

[61] Leontios of Neapolis, Jerome of Jerusalem, Stephen of Bostra, and Isaac of Nineveh all defend the veneration of the Cross against Jewish objections of idolatry, the first three in conjunction with the veneration of icons. See below, Ch. 7 on iconoclasm.

[62] He does not mention the Qur'ān by name, and uses the Greek word *graphē* for both the Qur'an (*Haeres.* 100. 14; though note *biblos* at *Haeres.* 100. 16) and the individual suras (*Haeres.* 100. 96, 114, 149, 152).

[63] John uses the unusual diminutive *boidion*, 'little ox', which is, however, found in Scripture (Jer. 27: 11, LXX).

in the Qur'ān (in suras 7, 11, 17, 26, 54, 91), though there appears to be no
trace of the accompanying story of the 'little camel'. John uses the story to
attack the prophetic authority of Muhammad, and mock his portrayal of
paradise. John's account of the sura 'The table' is very brief, summarizing
accurately enough the passage in which Christ asked God for a table and
was given an incorruptible table. Of the sura 'The cow', John simply says
that it contains some 'ridiculous sayings' which he is going to pass over.
On Heresies 100 closes abruptly with a list of Muslim customs: the practice
of circumcision, even in the case of women, abjuring the sabbath and
baptism, dietary laws that forbid some foods allowed by the Old
Testament and permit some that are forbidden, and finally the absolute
prohibition of wine, all mentioned without comment.

There is no doubt from this that John has a fairly accurate picture of
Islam: he dates Muhammad correctly, and knows about the revelations
that came to form the Qur'ān; he seems to know of the Qur'ān as a book,
and knows certain of the suras, though he appears to be mistaken about
'The camel of God', though much of the story he relates is authentic
enough; his summary of Muslim teaching, especially as it affects Christian
beliefs, is accurate; and his account of the charges Muslims make against
Christians is precisely what one would expect, though John's replies seem
to reveal some misunderstanding of Muslim practice. If On Heresies 100 is
indeed by John, then from his knowledge of the Qur'ān, limited though it
is, one can deduce that he was familiar with parts of the Qur'ān in the
Arabic original, as the earliest Greek translations post-date him.[64] All this
is entirely likely, from what little is known of John's upbringing in
Damascus. But I am tempted to go further, and suggest that it fits in with
the account of the growth of Islam that has been advanced by scholars in
the last few decades. According to this account, associated especially with
Patricia Crone and Michael Cook,[65] Islam was not fully formed by the
time of the death of Muhammad in 632, but was, in part, a reaction to the
success of the Arab conquest of the Middle East in the 630s and 640s.
From a movement inspired by apocalyptic Judaism, emerging Islam distinguished and separated itself from Judaism, and found its identity in the
revelations made to Muhammad. The development of the religion took
some decades, and only towards the end of the seventh century did something recognizable as Islam emerge. John's account, if written about
the turn of the century, would fit with such a picture. The clear sense of
Islam as a (pseudo-)prophetic religion, focusing on the unity and

[64] Le Coz 1992, 191–2.
[65] See Crone and Cook 1977; Crone 1980, 1987. See also Humphreys 1991, 84–5.

transcendence of God, John's understanding of Islam as finding its identity in Ishmael (as opposed to Isaac), his rather fluid awareness of the scriptural status of the revelations made to Muhammad (awareness of written traditions, most, but not all, of which were soon to find their place in the 'book', the Qur'ān): all this fits such a picture. But here is not the place to pursue this topic any further.

If, in the last chapter of *On Heresies*, we have a Christian response to a credible, early Muslim attack on Christianity, in the *Dispute* we find something rather different: a Christian engagement with theological issues at dispute in early Muslim theology. As A.-T. Khoury remarked long ago, 'One fact has attracted the attention of critics: the text is concerned with the central problems that occupied Muslim theological reflection at the beginning, in the eighth century.'[66] So, even though the *Dispute between a Saracen and a Christian*, in its present form, is unlikely to be by John, it is appropriate to discuss it here, for it concerns issues that were live in the Damascene's time, issues to which he certainly devoted attention. We noted above that the *Dispute* falls into two parts: one part with the literary form of a dialogue (*Sarac.* 1–4, 11), the remainder more like Christian notes for a Christian–Muslim disputation. Certainly topics are discussed about which Christians and Muslims might well argue—principally Christological issues, such as the divinity of Christ, and the coherence of the idea of incarnation of a transcendent God—but several times the debate touches on issues that were disputed among early Muslim thinkers, such as the reconciliation of human free will with divine pre-destination, the closely related matter of the nature of creation, and the question about the created or uncreated status of God's word. The first question, about divine providence, is one of the first issues we know to have been discussed in early Muslim speculative theology (*kalām*). The discussion concerned the nature and extent of the divine decree (*qadar*): does this leave room for human free will, or do people act under compulsion? According to M. Abdel Haleem, this dispute gave rise to two groups: the Qadarites, who held that people had *qudrāh* (power) over their actions, some of whom went so far as to deny the pre-existent knowledge of God, and the Jabriyyah, 'who affirmed the divine power and held that one is under compulsion to the extent that God creates one's actions, good or bad, and one is like a feather in the breeze without any power of one's own'.[67] Among the Qadarites were included Ma'bad al-Juanī (d. AD 699) and Ghaylān of Damascus (d. AD 767), and among the Jabriyyah, al-

---

[66] A.-T. Khoury 1969, 71.
[67] Haleem 1996, 79–80. The discussion above is based on Haleem.

Jahm ibn Ṣafwān (d. AD 745): it is evident from their dates that their lives most likely all overlapped that of John. Although it might seem that the doctrine of the Jabriyyah that 'whatever is, is right' (or at least ordained by God) would be attractive to the established power of the Umayyad caliphate, it is not at all clear that the Jabriyyah were 'court theologians', as is sometimes claimed,[68] since both Maʿbad and Jahm rebelled against the Umayyads and were killed by them.[69]

John's discussion in the *Dispute* certainly reflects awareness of the arguments of the Jabriyyah, whom he represents as arguing that God is the cause of everything, both good and evil (*Sarac.* 1. 29–30). John's response pursues a middle way between the Qadarites and the Jabriyyah, arguing that God has foreknowledge, but works with and through his created order, which itself has a relative freedom, not least in the case of beings with free will, such as human beings, so that there is a distinction between what is expressly God's will and what takes place by his consent, tolerance, or long-suffering (*Sarac.* 3. 19–20). One way of putting this is to say that creation is complete, and that what takes place in the universe now is in accordance with God's will, but not evidence for continued creative activity (*Sarac.* 10). John's position here is close to the later Muʿtazilite[70] doctrine of free will, based on an interpretation of the Qurʾānic verse (6: 81) that good comes from God and evil from humanity (*Sarac.* 1. 1–5).[71] It is also worth recalling here, that the doctrine of providence is a principal concern in John Damascene's *Dialogue against the Manichees*, which itself, as we have argued above, may be seen as reflecting the intellectual climate of early Islam, of which John seems to have been thoroughly aware.[72]

The other subject of early Muslim debate that seems to be reflected in the *Dispute* is that concerning the nature of the Qurʾān, whether it is created or uncreated. Dispute about this reached its apogee about a century after the death of the Damascene, in the middle of the ninth century, when the Muʿtazilite doctrine that the Qurʾān was created was opposed by Ibn Ḥanbal, who maintained the orthodox teaching of Islam that the Qurʾān is uncreated, as it is part of God's uncreated attribute of speech.[73] In the *Dispute* there seem to be echoes of this debate. In chapter 5, John defends the divinity of Christ by arguing for the eternity of the attributes of God, such as word and spirit, which he claims are ascribed to Christ in the Qurʾān itself: the Muslim must accept the eternity of these attributes, for the alternative would be that before their creation God was

---

[68] e.g., by Le Coz 1992, 142.

[70] For the Muʿtazilites, see Corbin 1993, 105–12.

[72] For this paragraph, see Le Coz 1992, 136–53, 157–8.

[69] Haleem 1996, 80.

[71] Pavlin 1996, 109.

[73] Pavlin 1996, 106–7.

without his word and spirit (an argument Athanasios had made much of against the Arians[74]). John also remarks that to deny the uncreatedness of God's word and spirit is dire heresy among the Muslims, and those who made such a denial could be in fear for their lives (*Sarac.* 5. 19–22): a remark that Le Coz plausibly argues suggests a date in the last decade of the Umayyad Empire (probably the last decade, too, of the Damascene's earthly life).[75] In chapter 6, the Muslim follows up his argument by pursuing the uncreatedness or not of the 'words' (*logia*) of God, forcing John to make a distinction between the 'personal' (*enypostatos*[76]) Word of God, which is uncreated, and what are properly called 'divine communications' (*rêmata theou*), which are created: John's understanding of the created status of written Scripture seems close to the Mu'tazilite doctrine attacked a century after his death.[77]

In this chapter we have explored John Damascene's engagement with the manifold variety of heresy, suggesting that it reflects a concern to define the nature of Orthodox Christianity in Palestine in the competitive situation for the religions of the Middle East that emerged after the Arab conquest of the former eastern provinces of the Byzantine Empire, but also shows awareness of the emerging structures (especially intellectual structures) of Islam, in the context of which, too, John seeks to define Orthodox Christianity. Such definition is very much by way of marking off a boundary, outside which truth is not to be found. It is, for John, a second preparatory step towards summing up the nature of Christian truth, to which John devoted the third part of his *The Fountain Head of Knowledge*, the century of chapters usually known as *On the Orthodox Faith*, to which we now turn.

---

[74] See, e.g., Athanasios, *decr.* 15. 4 (Opitz, p. 13, lines 11–17).
[75] Le Coz 1992, 161–2.
[76] For the meaning of this word, see below, on Christology.
[77] For this paragraph, see Le Coz 1992, 158–66.

6

Defining the Faith

(a) On the Orthodox Faith

John Damascene's *On the Orthodox Faith*, the third part of his trilogy, *The Fountain Head of Knowledge*, is probably the best known of his works, and certainly, outside the Byzantine world at least, the most influential. By the end of the first millennium, it had been translated into Arabic, for the benefit of John's successors in the Middle East who in the generation after John began to think and express their faith in what had become their vernacular. By that time it had also been translated into Old Slavonic, to provide a clear and concise account of the tenets of Byzantine Christianity for the Slav nations that had begun to embrace the faith of Byzantine Orthodoxy about a century after the death of the Damascene. Early in the next millennium, *On the Orthodox Faith* was translated into Latin, in which guise it provided the principal means of access to the dogmatic tradition of the Greek East for the scholastics of the High Middle Ages.

But, as its influence spread, it underwent modification. Initially, as we have seen, *On the Orthodox Faith* circulated as the second part of '150 chapters', preceded by the shorter form of the *Dialectica*, and even after John had produced the trilogy, the older form remained popular, as the manuscript tradition makes clear. In translation, *On the Orthodox Faith* tended to be separated from the earlier part (or parts). Furthermore, in the Latin tradition, the translation by Burgundio of Pisa was by 1224 divided into four books, corresponding to the division of the *Summae* of the scholastic theologians: book 1, consisting of chapters 1–14, concerning God and the Trinity; book 2, chapters 15–44, on creation and human kind; book 3, consisting of chapters 45–73, on Christology; and book 4, beginning with the chapter on Christ's resurrection (chapter 74) and closing with that on the general resurrection (chapter 100), giving it a broadly eschatological orientation. It is in this division into four books that *On the Orthodox Faith* has been generally known in the West. Such a division both disguises its original form as a century of chapters and suggests something more systematic than John ever intended. Instead of being regarded as a work of monastic provenance, it is taken to be a Byzantine precursor of a systematic, even scholastic, approach to theology.

The division into four books is not, however, wholly arbitrary. In contrast to its closest predecessors in the genre of monastic century, the two *Centuries on Theology and the Incarnate Dispensation* by Maximos the Confessor (where there are some clusters of related chapters, but not much discernible structure), much of John's *On the Orthodox Faith* can be convincingly divided into large groups of consecutive chapters. Chapters 1–14 concern God and the Trinity, and chapters 15–44 the created order and human kind within it, corresponding exactly to the Latin division into books. The next obvious group consists of chapters 45–81, on the incarnate *oikonomia* (or dispensation), eight chapters longer than the third book of the Latin division. The last nineteen chapters, however, are harder to characterize: there are chapters on faith, baptism, and the Cross; on praying towards the East; on the mysteries (or sacraments); on the genealogies of the Lord and the Mother of God; on saints and their relics and icons; on Scripture; then a long discussion of the different ways of speaking of Christ; then four chapters directed against Manichaean views; three chapters against the Jews (if the chapter on virginity is construed thus), or perhaps four, as the chapter on the Antichrist (chapter 99) seems to engage with Jewish positions (though, given the way John describes the 'heresy of the Saracens' in *Haeres.* 100 as the 'forerunner of Antichrist', it may be Islam he is concerned with here); and finally a chapter on the Resurrection (on which Jews, Christians, and Muslims were in agreement). If there is a common theme linking the last nineteen chapters, it would seem to be the *practices* of Christians, and the way these distinguish them from Jews and Muslims, leading to clarification of issues at stake between Christians and their religious opponents in Umayyad Palestine. Baptism, sacraments, and veneration of the Cross; praying towards the East (instead of facing Jerusalem or Mecca); veneration of the Mother of God and the saints, and also relics and icons: all these were practices that distinguished Orthodox Christians in the Middle East from their neighbours. If this perception is right, then the concern of *On the Orthodox Faith* seems clear: it is a century of chapters setting out the Christian world-view, including doctrines about God and his attributes, about the Trinity, about the universe he has created and, within that world, the constitution of human kind, followed by a careful exposition of the nature of the Incarnation, concluding with a clarification of the points, both practical and theoretical, on which Christians differed from their religious neighbours. This is exactly what we would expect if our account of the religious situation of the Orthodox monks of the Holy Land, expounded in earlier chapters, is correct. As a century, *On the Orthodox Faith* is a collection of considerations, or meditations, to help Christians understand and articulate their religious identity, over against those amongst whom they live, who maintain different doctrines and ways of devotion. John is concerned about clarity, but he is not in any serious way systematic.

Before looking more closely at the teaching John expounds in *On the Orthodox Faith*, we need to say a little more about its structure. This involves two considerations: first, the actual ordering of the work, and secondly, how it is constructed in general.

As in the cases of the other components of *The Fountain Head of Knowledge*, *On the Orthodox Faith* survives in two forms, both well attested in the manuscripts. Unlike the *Dialectica* and *On Heresies*, however, in this case it is almost entirely a matter of the order of the chapters. Many manuscripts contain a text of *On the Orthodox Faith* (called by Kotter the *Expositio inversa*, as opposed to the *Expositio ordinata*) in which the chapters are reordered, with the final nineteen chapters inserted between chapters 18 and 19—that is, between the discussion of the invisible creation (angels and demons, chapters 17 and 18) and the discussion of the visible creation (beginning with chapter 19). It is very difficult to see what the point of this could be.[1] It is argued later on that this final section, despite the odd assortment of themes, is held together by the notion of human kind as a nature that unites the visible and invisible realms. It is possible that it is this perception that led to these chapters being inserted between the chapters on invisible creation and those on visible creation. This, however, is an idea that is ingenious rather than convincing. Nevertheless, there seems to be no doubt that the original order was that of the *Expositio ordinata*; it is the order of the earliest manuscripts, which is confirmed decisively by the fact that *Expos.* 87. 3–6 seems to refer back to *Expos.* 56. 2, as it promises to add to what has already been said about the title *Theotokos*.[2] What lay behind the making of the *Expositio inversa* is unclear. The manuscript tradition demonstrates that the changes involved not just reordering but also supplementation (chapter 12, which is mostly a quotation from Dionysios the Areopagite on the naming of God, is followed by another chapter, which contains a more detailed

---

[1] *Pace* Thümmel 1981, 30.   [2] See Kotter iii, p. xxv.

paraphrase of Dionysian doctrine—the numeration is restored, because chapters 9 and 10 have been condensed into chapter 9—and chapter 23, on water, has been supplemented by a section on seas), which suggests that the change in order was deliberate (rather than an early misplacement of pages).[3]

If the ordering of *On the Orthodox Faith* is something of a conundrum, the other general consideration, that of its structure, raises more accessible questions. From what we have seen so far of John's manner of composition, it is to be expected that this work takes the form of something approaching a florilegium. But John has not simply compiled his work from existing patristic sources; it is rather, as I suggested in chapter 2, that John follows an already existing tradition, in which certain Fathers are drawn on for certain theological topics. John's own selection is guided by the tradition within which he worked. In many cases this seems to have been an oral tradition (though it may simply be that earlier examples of this practice have not been preserved in the manuscript tradition). Until very recently it has been thought that the immediate source for much of the first part of *On the Orthodox Faith*, that on the Trinity, can be identified with a work, *On the Holy Trinity*, ascribed to Cyril of Alexandria, though in fact somewhat later in date, since it betrays awareness of the developments in Christology that belong to the seventh century, especially Monothelitism.[4] However, a recent article by Vassa Conticello has demonstrated that it is John's *On the Orthodox Faith* that is one of the sources for Pseudo-Cyril's *On the Holy Trinity*, which is in reality a much later work, compiled in the fourteenth century by the Byzantine thinker Joseph the Philosopher.[5] There was always something odd about the view of John's theological method entailed by the acceptance of Pseudo-Cyril as John's source, since it would only be here that John simply accepts with scarcely a modification someone else's patristic compilation. If Conticello is right (and her arguments seem to me absolutely compelling), then in the early chapters of *On the Orthodox Faith*, as in the later

---

[3] It will be evident that I am unconvinced by Thümmel's arguments (1981) that *Exp. inversa* is part of John's final revision of *The Fountain Head of Knowledge*, to which also belong *Dial. fus.* and the augmented version of *On Heresies* (see above, p. 55). For counter-arguments to Thümmel's arguments in the earlier part of his article, see my contribution to the Festschrift for Julian Chrysostomides (Louth, forthcoming *b*). For Thümmel's resurrection of the idea that *Expos.* is inspired by book 5 of Theodoret's *Hæreticarum fabularum compendium*, see below.

[4] The text of Pseudo-Cyril, *de Sancta Trinitate*, can be found in PG 77. 1120–73 (= *CPG* 5432). The most important study of its theological ideas (which accepts that it is a source of John's *Expos.*) is Fraigneau-Julien 1961.

[5] See Conticello 1995.

chapters, we can trace the way in which John, working within an already existing tradition, built up his own presentation of the doctrine of the Trinity. It follows that much that has in the past been ascribed to the theological genius of the mysterious Pseudo-Cyril is most likely to belong to the known theological genius of John himself.

There is a broader question about the structure of *On the Orthodox Faith*, and that is whence John derived it: God and Trinity–creation and human kind–the incarnate dispensation–baptism, resurrection, etc. It has sometimes been argued that John borrowed this structure from the fifth book of the *Compendium of Heretical Fables* by the fifth-century bishop and theologian Theodoret of Kyrrhos. This was first suggested by the scholar J. Langen,[6] and, from its mention as a possibility by H.-G. Beck in his influential survey of Byzantine ecclesiastical literature,[7] it has gained a certain currency in modern scholarly literature (though it is ignored by Kotter).[8] The fifth book of Theodoret's work can be divided into four sections: chapters 1–3 on the Trinity; 4–10 on creation, matter, aeons, angels, the devil and demons, human kind, and providence; 11–17 on the Incarnation; 18–29, a rag-bag consisting of chapters on baptism, the Resurrection, judgement, the Second Coming, the Antichrist, virginity, marriage, and various other topics. What is striking is not so much the fourfold structure, for God–creation–Incarnation–baptism/resurrection is very much the order of the Creed, but the sequence of the section on creation, and the rag-bag-like nature of the fourth section with its inclusion of topics such as baptism, resurrection, the Antichrist, and virginity. However, apart from this, there is very little to suggest any dependence of John on Theodoret. John's discussion is very different from Theodoret's, even when the order is the same (cf., e.g., the chapters on angels and demons), and, in reality, John's order is very different from Theodoret's, for what is most striking about the Damascene's section on creation is its amazing detail, both about the visible cosmos and about the constitution of human kind, none of which is found in Theodoret. The fact that both Theodoret and John end with a section of miscellanea is not so much a case of parallelism, as a warning against trying to impose on either of them a very definite structure. In short, it would seem that the parallels between Theodoret and John are either commonplace (reflecting the structure of the Creed) or fortuitous: it is quite improbable

---

[6] Langen 1879, 62, referred to by Thümmel (1981, 29 n. 63), who revived his theory.

[7] Beck 1959, 479.

[8] e.g., John's dependence on Theodoret in *Expos.* is stated as a fact by Kazhdan in his article on John Damascene (1991, ii. 1064).

that John based the structure of his *On the Orthodox Faith* on that of the fifth book of Theodoret's *Compendium of Heretical Fables*.[9]

Let us now turn to John's exposition of the tenets of the Orthodox faith, as he discerned it in the tradition of the Church. We shall follow the sequence suggested by his *On the Orthodox Faith*, with sections on God and the Trinity, creation and human kind, the incarnate dispensation, with a final section discussing the miscellaneous topics with which John closes his century. Each section will seek to elucidate John's presentation of Christian doctrine in *On the Orthodox Faith* and his sources, but will also supplement this account from his other works. In the third section, on the incarnate dispensation, this will amount to more than simple supplementation, for John composed a number of substantial polemical treatises, directed against what he deemed to be Christological error, especially what he called Monophysitism.

(b) God and the Trinity

The first fourteen chapters of *On the Orthodox Faith* contain John Damascene's account of the Christian faith in God as Trinity.[10] His account of Trinitarian doctrine is placed in a setting that develops the mysterious nature of God and the limitations of any human thinking or speaking of God. In chapters 1 and 2, John bases what he has to say on a passage from Cyril of Alexandria's *Treasury on the Holy and Consubstantial Trinity* (a passage preserved elsewhere only in the *Doctrina Patrum*[11]). The emphasis on the ineffability of God returns in chapters 9–14, with chapters 10 and 12 drawing very heavily on Dionysios the Areopagite, but also on Gregory Nazianzen, especially his homily 28, the second of the 'Theological Orations', where Gregory waxes eloquent on the incomprehensibility of God. Chapter 13 discusses the fact that God alone is uncircumscribable, and draws from this a series of conclusions that again underline the incomprehensibility of God. The final chapter of this

---

[9] At the Byzantine Congress held in Paris in August 2001, Vassa Conticello suggested that the sequence of the chapters of *On the Orthodox Faith* might be derived from (or at least echo) the structure found in Eucharistic Prayers, or Anaphorae, such as those in the *Apostolic Constitutions* and in the ninth-century Liturgy of St Basil. It is an extremely attractive idea, that fits in well with what we have suggested about the nature of John's theology.

[10] For John's Trinitarian theology, see the still useful Bilz 1909.

[11] *Expos.* 2. 2–6 = *Doct. Patr.* 7. 16–8. 1; *Expos.* 2. 11–15 = *Doct. Patr.* 8. 1–5; *Expos.* 2. 19–23 = *Doct. Patr.* 8. 5–7 (Diekamp). The single passage from Cyril's *Thesaurus*, preserved in the *Doct. Patr.*, has been split into three by John. See Kotter iii, 8–9, apparatus.

section, chapter 14, summarizes much that has already been said under the rubric of the 'characteristics' (*idiomata*) of the divine nature.

John's presentation of the doctrine of the Trinity is, therefore, set between two blocks of material, *On the Orthodox Faith*, 1–4 and 9–14, that raise more general considerations concerning human knowledge of God and its limitations. In what follows we shall deal with these outlying sections first, and then turn to the heart of this section of *On the Orthodox Faith* that deals with the doctrine of the Trinity.[12]

Human Knowledge of God

John begins *On the Orthodox Faith* by quoting the last verse of the Johannine Prologue: 'No one has seen God at any time. The only-begotten Son, who is in the bosom of the Father, he has declared him' (John 1: 18). It follows from this that 'the divine is ineffable and incomprehensible'; yet God is known to himself, and can make himself known. John quotes part of Matthew 11: 27: 'No one knows the Father save the Son, nor the Son save the Father', and alludes to 1 Corinthians 2: 11, where the Apostle Paul speaks of the Holy Spirit knowing the things of God, as the human spirit knows what is in man. John concludes by affirming that 'after the first and blessed nature no one ever knows God, unless by revelation, not only human beings, but also the powers beyond the world, and by them I mean even the Cherubim and the Seraphim'.

Thus John begins his exposition of the Christian faith by confessing God's utter incomprehensibility, but at the same time suggesting the paradox that we know God's incomprehensibility because he has made himself known. The doctrine of the incomprehensibility of the divine nature might lead to human agnosticism, but John is pointing to a more profound incomprehensibility: that of God who makes himself known as Father, Son, and Holy Spirit, as the Holy Trinity. He goes on to say that God has not left us in complete ignorance: knowledge of God can be derived naturally from creation, and God has made himself known, first through the law and the prophets, and then through his only-begotten Son. What has been made known of God has been passed down to us, and we have received it. This has happened because God is good and not envious of his creatures: a Platonic principle that John caps with a quotation from Gregory Nazianzen, 'the Theologian' (a title already current in John's day). In this first chapter, John has marked out the broad

---

[12] Book 1 of the *Hiera*, it will be recalled, was concerned with the doctrine of God; but only a small fragment survives in its original form.

outlines of his theology, his understanding of God: God, incomprehensible in his goodness, has made himself known through his own Trinitarian being, through the Son and the Spirit; this knowledge has been passsed down to us, and this 'tradition' (what has been 'passed down'), rooted in the Godhead itself (it is the only-begotten Son, who has made it known), has been passed down to us by the Fathers, who have laid down 'eternal boundaries' that we should neither alter nor attempt to cross (as John puts it in his last sentence, alluding to Prov. 22: 28).

What we find in this first chapter is a kind of harvest of patristic theology, in its strict sense as knowledge of God. Such stress on God's ineffability had long been traditional; it can be traced back to the Old Testament, and is explicit in Philo the Jew (a contemporary of both Jesus and Paul); it is marked in Christian theologians such as Clement and Origen of Alexandria, and in the great fourth-century thinkers Basil the Great, his friend Gregory Nazianzen, and his younger brother Gregory of Nyssa (the 'Cappadocian Fathers'), and also John Chrysostom. The sense of the incomprehensibility of God of these Fathers was deepened by their opposition to Eunomios, an 'extreme Arian' or 'Anomoean', who maintained, against the confession of Nicaea, that far from the Son being consubstantial with the Father, he was in fact unlike (*anomoios*) the Father, the sole true God, supporting his arguments with an insistence on the clarity and exactness of the human conception of God. Against this, the Cappadocian Fathers and John Chrysostom laid stress on the mysteriousness of the divine being, holding that we have no knowledge of the divine being itself, whom we celebrate principally by epithets that deny the adequacy of our concepts of God: he is not-finite, not-created, not-visible (adjectives that in Greek are formed by the prefix of the alpha-privative). Other distinctions were introduced into theology: we do not know God, but we know 'about' (*peri*) him;[13] we do not know his being or essence, but we know his activity (or energy) or power. A somewhat older distinction is also relevant here: between *theologia* and *oikonomia*, between knowledge of God in himself, which principally entails recognition of the mystery of the divine being (including the mystery of the Trinity), and knowledge of God's revelation of himself through the *oikonomia*, his activity with regard to human kind in and through creation, including his presence among us in the Incarnation. This distinction corresponds largely to the distinction between God's unknowable being and his activity or energy, through which he makes himself known, though even in the realm of

[13] Cf., e.g., Athanasios, *decr.* 22. 1 (Opitz, 18. 24); Gregory of Nyssa, *Maced.* (Mueller, 114. 24).

oikonomia there is much that is unknown to humans, especially in relation to the Incarnation, which involves not just God's activity with regard to us, but his presence among us as Word or Son.

This emphasis on the mysterious reality of God was given further conceptual definition in the early sixth century by the writer who composed his works under the pseudonym 'Dionysios the Areopagite', the Apostle Paul's Athenian convert (cf. Acts 17: 34), and, drawing on the philosophical terminology of late Athenian Neoplatonists such as Proklos (412–85), expressed this paradox of the revelation of the unknowable God by introducing the terms 'apophatic' (negative) and 'kataphatic' (affirmative) theology. In the rest of the chapters that preface John's exposition of the doctrine of the Trinity, all these distinctions are drawn upon. (It is perhaps worth noting that all the above distinctions are drawn together in the theology of Maximos the Confessor, as Savvidis has recently demonstrated.[14])

In chapter 2, John draws on the traditional distinction between *theologia* and *oikonomia*, and asserts that in the case of both *theologia* and *oikonomia* neither is everything knowable or unknowable, nor is everything expressible or inexpressible: even what we know we are not necessarily able to express clearly. John gives an example of this in the way we are compelled to use language drawn from what we are familiar with to describe what transcends us—as when we ascribe sleep or anger to God, or speak of his hands or feet. He then launches into a list of the divine attributes, all either expressing what God is not, through epithets prefaced by an alpha-privative, or expressing his universal transcendence ('all-powerful', 'creator of all creatures', etc.), save for the peerless qualities of being good, just, judge, and supreme authority. There follows a brief summary of Trinitarian doctrine, and of the nature of the Incarnation, expressed in an expanded credal form, 'to which the divine Scripture is witness, and also the choir of the saints'. This leads to reflection on the fact that we do not know what the divine being is, or how (*pôs*) the divine nature is immanent, or how the Trinitarian natures obtain, or how the Incarnation took place, or how the Incarnate One did what he did. In relation to God, in matters concerning both *theologia* and *oikonomia*, we know 'that', we do not know 'what' or 'how': a matter on which St John Chrysostom had waxed eloquent in his homilies on the incomprehensibility of God.[15] And we know 'that' from the Scriptures of the Old and New Testaments.

According to the chapter heading, chapter 3 is concerned to demonstrate that God exists; its content makes clear, however, that John does

---

[14] Savvidis 1997, 23–50.   [15] Cf. esp. *Hom.* 1. 156–64 (Malingrey).

not envisage a 'proof of God's existence' on the basis of natural reason, as later understood. God's existence is demonstrable, first of all, he says, from Scripture, but it is affirmed by most of the pagans (as we should, in this context, translate *Hellenes*, literally 'Greeks'), since it is revealed through nature. Nevertheless, there are those who deny the existence of God, because they have been deceived by the devil, and John goes on to speak of the Apostles demonstrating God's existence through miracles, and being followed in this by 'shepherds and teachers'. He laments that he has not received such gifts of miracles and teaching, and can do no more than discuss considerations that have been handed down.

The first of these considerations concerns the distinction between created and uncreated being. This had become the fundamental onto-logical distinction for Christian metaphysics. Whereas Platonic meta-physics worked with a fundamental distinction between the spiritual and the material, from the fourth century onwards Christian thinkers had asserted the fundamental significance of the divide or gulf between uncreated and created: uncreated being comprising the Holy Trinity (the Son and the Spirit consubstantial with the Father, to use the terminology that in the latter half of the fourth century became the hallmark of Orthodox 'Nicene' theology), all else being created out of nothing. For Gregory of Nyssa and, later, for Maximos the Confessor, this distinction assumed a fundamental significance, which is reflected in the theology of the Damascene. Its relevance here is to provide the premiss for an argu-ment for the necessity of an uncreated creator. The argument develops by equating the distinction between uncreated and created with that between unchangeable and changeable (the idea that created beings were essentially changeable, as their very origin, from nothing, involved a change, is an argument found in the Fathers from at least Athanasios[16]), and then arguing that change stands in need of explanation, which can only be provided by the unchangeable: a variant of Aristotle's argument for an unmoved mover.[17] It might well be thought that the argument conceals its conclusion (the existence of a creator God) in its premiss (the distinction between uncreated and created).

Another consideration concerns the harmony of the created order, which involves a uniting of opposites, that cannot have come about by chance, an argument of Stoic provenance.[18] The establishment of the

[16] See Athanasios, *Ar.* 1. 36 (Bright, 37. 28–30).
[17] See Aristotle, *Ph.* 8. 5 (249B27–250B7), *Metaph.* 4. 8 (1012B22–31), 12. 7 (1072A19–1072B13).
[18] Again a traditional theme, found as early as Clement of Rome (1 *Clem.* 20 (Funk *et al.*, 46–7)) and developed particularly by Athanasios (*gent.* 42–4 (Thomson, 114–22)).

existence of God leads into the next chapter, in which God's unity is demonstrated as a corollary of, and the ultimate reason for, his incomprehensibility. What this incomprehensibility involves is drawn out in a number of ways. John makes use of the observation, mentioned above, that the divine attributes do not describe the being of God, but are 'about' (*peri*) God; he also introduces the language of kataphatic and apophatic theology. Already in this chapter John is beginning to draw on Gregory of Nyssa's presentation of the doctrine of the Trinitarian God in his *Great Catechetical Oration*, to the significance of which we shall return when we discuss the Damascene's understanding of the Trinity.

The central section on the Trinity (chapters 5–8) is followed by chapters in which John again returns to the question of incomprehensibility, and again heightens it. Chapter 9 is concerned with the reconciliation of the manifold divine attributes and the simplicity of God. According to John, when we speak about God, we do not describe what he is in his essence or being (*kat' ousian*); we either say what he is not, or we point to some relationship between God and something else, or something that follows from his nature, or to an activity (*energeia*). John then deals with two names: 'He who is' (*ho ôn*) and 'God' (*theos*). 'He who is' was God's self-designation to Moses at the Burning Bush (Exod. 3: 14, LXX); it is 'the most proper of all the names we give to God . . . for like some limitless and boundless sea of being, he holds all being in himself' (quoting and embellishing Dionysios[19]). In interpreting the name 'God', he follows the two Cappadocian Gregories, for whom the term *theos* describes not the being of God, but his activity, either of running (*theein*), as referring to his providential care, or of burning up (*aithein*) every wickedness (cf. Heb. 12: 29, quoting Deut. 4: 24), or of beholding (*theasthai*) the universe. 'The former [of these names] is expressive of his existence, and not of his essence, the latter of his activity,' John comments; epithets formed with the alpha-privative express what God is not; attributes like good, just, and such like express what follows from his nature, and not the divine being itself; titles like king, lord, creator, shepherd, express a relationship. In chapter 11 John discusses corporeal imagery used of God, in which it is argued, following Dionysios and Gregory Nazianzen, that such bodily imagery, drawn from what is familiar to us, has a 'hidden meaning' that expresses something that transcends us (cf. *Expos.* 2. 6–9), except in the case of the Incarnation, where it describes the physical reality of that event.

Chapter 10 concerns 'divine union and distinction', and summarizes

---

[19] Dionysios the Areopagite, *d.n.* 5. 4 (Suchla, i. 183. 5).

Dionysios's teaching in *Divine Names*, 2, about 'unions' and 'distinctions', or 'names that unify' and 'names that make distinction': names that unify apply to the whole Godhead, while names that make distinction apply either to the members of the Trinity ('Father', 'Son', 'Spirit', 'uncaused', 'caused', 'unbegotten', 'begotten', 'proceeding') or to the Incarnation. None of these names applies to the divine being itself: names of union tell us 'about' the divine being, and names of distinction indicate a relationship between the persons of the Trinity, or a 'mode of existence'. If the teaching is Dionysian, the terminology is not: John is drawing much more closely on the Cappadocian Fathers than on the Areopagite, who expresses the idea that divine attributes do not comprehend the divine essence in other ways than by saying that they are 'about' God.[20] Chapter 12 is an explicit citation from Dionysios (*Divine Names*, 5. 4, somewhat rearranged and supplemented), giving the key to establishing the 'hidden meaning' of expressions used of God. (In *Expos. inversa*, chapter 12 is followed by another chapter, not found in *Expos. ordinata*, the first half of which seems to be a free paraphrase of *Divine Names*, 7.) Chapter 13 is on the 'place' (*topos*) of God,[21] and on the fact that the divine alone is uncircumscribable.[22] It is a chapter that might be described as a set of variations on the fundamental distinction between the uncreated and the created, and closes with a series of assertions about the Trinity, based on what has been established in the central section of the first part. The final chapter of this first section, chapter 14, summarizes the teaching so far, affirming the transcendence of God, the abiding and resting (*monê kai hidrysis*) of the three divine Persons in a way only possible to uncreated nature; the unity, simplicity, and undivided nature of the divine energy, which reaches through all beings without being affected by them.

The setting, then, of the central part of this first section of *On the Orthodox Faith* explores in a host of ways the incomprehensibility and ineffability of God whose nature is utterly simple. This is the context in which John wishes to place his doctrine of the Trinity.

The Doctrine of the Holy Trinity

Chapters 5–8 form the centre-piece of the first part of John's *On the Orthodox Faith*. We shall first look at the presentation of the doctrine of the Trinity in *On the Orthodox Faith*, and then look beyond this text of

[20] Ibid. 2. 8 (Suchla, i. 132–3).

[21] Cf. Exod. 24: 10–11 (LXX).

[22] Cf. Maximos, *ambig.* 10. 38 (PG 91. 1180B–1181A), where it is argued that everything apart from God can be said to exist in a place.

John's to his treatment of the doctrine of the Trinity in his other works. There are, in fact, no works by John that deal directly with the doctrine of the Trinity (even the *Letter on the Thrice-Holy Hymn* is really about Christology, though it insists that the hymn is Trinitarian), for Trinitarian theology was not such a hotly disputed topic in John's day as Christology.

But first it will be useful to provide some historical context for the Trinitarian theology we find in John Damascene. The origins of Christian Trinitarian theology lie in the Trinitarian experience of early Christians, expressed in their Trinitarian forms of worship. Their worship took Trinitarian forms, because, without departing from the monotheism of their Scriptures, not least what they came to call the Old Testament, the Scriptures they shared with the Jews, Christians came to worship as God Jesus, whom they called the 'Lord', and who himself called God 'Father', and experienced this worship in the 'Holy Spirit', whose divinity they consequently came to affirm. In the early centuries, Trinitarian language took the form of speaking of God the Father, together with his Word and his Spirit. The first step towards the more clearly defined Trinitarian theology we find in John Damascene was the first Oecumenical Synod, held at Nicaea in 325, at which the Son was declared to be consubstantial (*homoousios*) with the Father. Perhaps it would be more correct to say that this first step was taken with the recognition, somewhat later than the synod, of the necessity of using such terminology, if the Church's confession of One God, Father, Son, and Holy Spirit, was to be safeguarded. This recognition was seen to be inescapable by various Christian thinkers of the fourth century, especially Athanasios, patriarch of Alexandria from 328 to 373, and the three Cappadocian Fathers.

As a result of their struggles, the Nicene doctrine of the consubstantiality of the Trinity was reaffirmed by the Second Oecumenical Synod, called at Constantinople in 381 to define the Orthodox Christian faith that the emperor Theodosius was to make the official religion of the Roman Empire. Basil and, following him, the two Gregories sought to clarify the language used in relation to the Trinity by confining the word *ousia* (being, essence) to the one Godhead, and using the word *hypostasis* for the three members of the Trinity, Father, Son, and Holy Spirit. Various analogies were used to elucidate this distinction: Basil and Gregory of Nyssa compared the distinction between *ousia* and *hypostasis* to the distinction which Aristotle made in his *Categories* between generic substance and particular or individual substance, as cats share the nature of being a cat (*ousia*), but each individual cat is an instance of a cat (*hypostasis*). They also characterized *hypostasis* as 'mode of existence' (*tropos hyparxeôs*) in contrast to what it was to 'be' (*einai*, from which verb the noun *ousia* is derived), the different 'modes of existence' in the Godhead being identified with unbegottenness in the case of the Father, being begotten in the case of the Son, and proceeding in the case of the Spirit, while all three *hypostaseis* shared the same being, or *ousia*. The mystery of the Trinity, however, remained a mystery: these distinctions were not pressed very far; they simply provided terms in which the oneness of the God-head and the threeness of the Father, Son, and Spirit could be expressed.

The language, settled by the Cappadocians, of *ousia* and *hypostasis* left many puzzles unresolved. The suggestion that the use of *ousia* for the one-ness of the Godhead was analogous to the generic use of *ousia* might seem to imply that divine *ousia* means the kind of being that God (or a god) is a suggestion that the Cappadocian Fathers uniformly resisted. For, as we have seen John expounding already, the divine essence is utterly unknow-able: we do not know what kind of a being God is; we only know what he is not, and how he relates to us through his activity. But this implies that the divine essence is beyond composition, for that is something that we can understand, and if the divine essence is beyond composition, it is one and simple (see John's arguments in *Expos.* 9. 2–6). One way in which Basil makes this clear occurs regularly when he explains that the term *homoousion* does not mean that there is a divine *ousia* that is anterior to the divine persons, or that there is some divine *ousia* underlying them; rather, the divine *ousia* is the Father's *ousia*, which he shares with the Son by begetting him and with the Spirit through procession.[23] Basil, in fact, insists that the term *homoousion* is itself a relational term: to say that the Son is *homoousios* with the Father is to affirm what has been called 'full unbroken continuity of being'[24] between the Father and the Son. To affirm that two beings are consubstantial could not mean that they were brothers (as some of the Arian controversialists sarcastically suggested), for *homoousios* implies a relationship of derivation.[25] The unity of *ousia* which the term *homoousios* safeguards is manifest in the single divine *energeia* that comes from the Father, through the Son, and is received in the Holy Spirit;[26] it is in response to this single divine *energeia* that human worship of God originates in the Holy Spirit, and passes through the Son to the Father.

Cappadocian theology of the Trinity was worked out in opposition to

[23] See Basil, *ep.* 52 (Deferrari, i. 330).
[24] Stead 1974, 249 (quoting, and slightly revising, Robertson 1892, p. xxxii).
[25] Basil, *ep.* 52 (Deferrari, i. 332–4).
[26] See Basil, *Spir.* 8. 19. 42–5; 16. 37. 18–20; 16. 39. 15–16 (Pruche).

Arianism, or, more precisely, in opposition to an anomoean Eunomian-
ism understood by the Cappadocians as a resurgence of Arianism, which
denied that the Son could share the Father's *ousia* in any intelligible way,
and sometimes drew the conclusion—explicitly in the case of Arius himself—that whereas God the Father is uncreated, the Son is created *ex
nihilo*. The Cappadocian response articulated a strong sense of the
mystery of the divine being, a mystery that remained even in speaking of
the consubstantial begetting of the Son and the consubstantial procession of the Holy Spirit. As Gregory Nazianzen remarked, 'What then
is procession? You explain the ingeneracy of the Father and I will give you
a biological account of the Son's begetting and the Spirit's procession—
and let us both go mad the pair of us for prying into God's secrets.'[27]
Nevertheless, differences soon emerged in the way in which the West and
the East conceived the place of the Spirit within the Trinity, with the East
asserting that the Son derived from the Father by begetting, while the
Spirit derived from the Father by procession (the doctrine affirmed in
the so-called Niceno-Constantinopolitan Creed, which scholars now
generally hold was associated with the Oecumenical Synod held in Constantinople in 381, though there is no trace of it until it was cited at the
Synod of Chalcedon in 451),[28] whereas the West tended to say that the
Son derived from the Father alone, and the Spirit from both the Father
and the Son.[29] These differences eventually led to the so-called *Filioque*
controversy, which remains a matter of dispute dividing Eastern and
Western Christianity today, and the beginnings of which are discernible
in John's writings.

After the Cappadocians, at least so far as the East was concerned,
controversy about the Trinity receded into the background, to be
replaced by controversy about Christology. Such controversy raged from
the end of the fourth century, and was a concern of all the Oecumenical
Synods from the time of the Cappadocian Fathers to the time of the
Damascene; we shall discuss it in greater detail below. But controversy
about the doctrine of Christ had repercussions for Trinitarian theology,
especially after the Synod of Chalcedon, which drew on the Cappadocian
distinction between *hypostasis* and *ousia* (which was equated with *physis*,
nature) in its Christological Definition. For the controversy that
Chalcedon unleashed, not least about the meaning of such terms as *ousia*,

---

[27] Gregory Nazianzen, *or.* 31. 8. 16–19 (Gallay; Wickham's trans. 283).

[28] Kelly 1972, 296–332.

[29] e.g., Augustine, *Serm.* 52. 2. 2 (PL 38. 355C), or the so-called Athanasian Creed, *Quicunque
vult*, 22–3 (Kelly 1964, 130).

physis, hypostasis, and *proposon,* clearly had implications for Trinitarian theology, which was itself expressed in this terminology. We are, however, largely in the dark about Trinitarian speculation in the sixth century, tantalizingly so, for we seem to hear echoes of such speculation in the writings of Maximos and John Damascene: but what they are echoes of remains unclear. The principal reason for this is that such speculation seems to have been most intense in circles not regarded as Orthodox, and therefore not preserved by later generations. Among the so-called Monophysites, Trinitarian speculation led to some of them being labelled 'tritheists'. There also seems to have been Trinitarian speculation in Evagrian circles, about which we are even more in the dark.

Tritheist ideas among Monophysites[30] seem to have been philosophical rather than theological in origin, and the philosophical arguments presented by the greatest advocate of 'tritheism' (the term used by their enemies), John Philoponos, have been preserved in their original Greek (rather than in Syriac translation, as is the case with most Monophysite works) by John Damascene himself, in his appendix to *On Heresies* 83 on the Monophysites.[31] In this extract from his *Diaitetes* ('The Arbiter'), which is principally concerned with Christological matters, Philoponos argues that the terms *ousia* and *physis* are synonymous, and are both used in a double way: first, to refer to the common nature or substance, and secondly, to refer to the individual nature or substance. The common nature is realized in the individual nature, and, as realized in that individual nature, is no longer common to any other individual. Not only is it impossible for the common nature to exist apart from the individual, it has no independent existence, and is indeed a construct of the mind, which forms a conception of a common nature by abstracting from individuals. When it comes to the question of the meaning of *hypostasis* (which, as we shall see, the Monophysites held to be identical with *physis* in its Christological use), Philoponos argues that *hypostasis* and *physis* are almost the same, *hypostasis* being distinguished from *physis* in that it comprises not merely the common nature realized in an individual, but the special properties belonging to that individual as well (cf. *Haeres.* 83, addit. 93–5).[32] It follows from this that the Church's confession of the Trinity as existing in three *hypostaseis* and one *ousia* is equivalent to saying that in the

[30] See Ebied *et al.* 1981, 25, and the whole section 20–33, on which I have based my brief account above. See also Chadwick 1987, 54.

[31] The passage from Philoponos's *Diaitetes* is also preserved in *Doct. Patr.* 36 (Diekamp, 272–83).

[32] A distinction not unlike that between *hypostasis* and *prosopon* made by Theodore of Raïthu: see above, p. 52.

Trinity it is proper to speak of three *ousiai* or *physeis*, and that the unity of
nature, affirmed of God, is a purely intellectual unity, an abstraction. This
position, held by Monophysites like John Philoponos, and more extreme
positions that spoke of three Gods or Godheads,[33] were attacked by
fellow Monophysites. For the Orthodox it served as a lesson about the
dangers of philosophy, for the sixth century had seen a great revival of
interest in Aristotle, in which Philoponos played a major role. There is an
echo of such an Orthodox reaction to the danger of a philosophically
inspired tritheism in one of the Damascene's works, in which, attacking
Philoponos's notion of 'particular natures', he makes a scornful reference
to 'your Saint Aristotle' (*Jacob*. 10. 13).

Having painted the background, let us turn to the presentations of
Trinitarian theology we find in John's own writings, dealing first with
the long Trinitarian section in *On the Orthodox Faith*. John begins his
presentation of the doctrine of the Trinity by establishing the unity of
God (*Expos.* 5) and then moves on to consider the Word of God (*Expos.*
6) and the Spirit of God (*Expos.* 7). What is striking about this discussion
is its reliance on the early chapters of Gregory of Nyssa's *Great Catechetical
Oration* (prologue and chapters 1–4). John follows the order of Gregory's
presentation; to begin with, he condenses and paraphrases, but when he
comes to the treatment of the Holy Spirit, he follows Gregory much
more closely. This is an approach that starts from the unity of God
(understood, following the New Testament and much pre-Nicene theology, as God the Father), and then unfolds, as it were, from within this
unity the Word and the Spirit, thus expounding God's simple nature as
Trinitarian.

The unity of God is repeatedly affirmed by a series of quotations from
Scripture: the first of the Ten Commandments (Exod. 20: 2–3); the
affirmation of the oneness of God at the beginning of the *Shema*—'Hear,
O Israel, the Lord your God is one Lord' (Deut. 6: 4); and the affirmation
of the prophet Isaias ('Second Isaias') that 'For I, God, am the first and I
am the last, and apart from me there is no God. Before me there is no God
nor will there be after me, and apart from me there is none' (Isa. 44: 6, 43:
10); and finally, from the New Testament, the beginning of Jesus' high-
priestly prayer—'This is eternal life, that they may know You the only true
God' (John 17: 3). This repeated biblical, and predominantly Old
Testament, witness to the unity and oneness of God is not something
John found in Gregory of Nyssa; it is his own emphasis, and it leads into
the argument with which Gregory closes his prologue that there can

[33] See Ebied *et al.* 1981, 25 n. 79.

be no difference (*diaphora*) in God, and therefore God is one,[34] but the biblical starting-point is John's. It is hard to avoid the thought that John starts with this strong affirmation of biblical monotheism with an eye to Jews, and perhaps especially Muslims; he begins his exposition of the doctrine of the Trinity by making it abundantly clear that this is a doctrine about the one God proclaimed by the Scriptures.

The next chapter argues that God is not without a word (or 'irrational': the Greek *alogos* means both). Gregory goes on to argue that this word is not like the word of a human (for analogy entails both similarity and difference), for 'human nature is corruptible and weak, therefore its life is transient, its power unreal, and its reason (or word) unstable'; but these limitations do not apply to the 'transcendent substance', 'so just as our nature is perishable and has a perishable word (or reason), so that nature which is incorruptible and abides eternally has an eternal and subsisting word'.[35] John reproduces this argument much more concisely, using technical language not found in Gregory:

this God, one and unique, is not *alogos*. But, having a word, he will not have one that is unreal [*anypostatos*, with the implication here of not being a *hypostasis*], nor one that begins to exist or ceases to exist. For there was not, when he was once God without a word [or: an irrational God]. But he has his own word eternally, begotten from himself, not like our word, unreal [*anypostatos*] and dissolving into air, but real [*enypostatos*, with the implication that the word is a *hypostasis*], living, perfect, not existing outside himself, but eternally being in him. (*Expos.* 6. 2–7)

The rest of the chapter elaborates this difference between the human word, not properly distinct from the human mind or subsistent in itself, and the divine word, which shares fully the being of God, as well as being subsistent in itself: much of this section is drawn almost word for word from Gregory's *Catechetical Oration*.[36]

In the next chapter, John extends this analogy, and argues that the Word must have spirit, just as our word is not bereft of breath (*pneuma*: in Greek meaning both breath, or wind, and spirit). Here John follows Gregory of Nyssa very closely, simply embellishing Gregory's language here and there. Gregory himself is following his older brother, Basil, who also developed the analogy of Word and Spirit as God's speech and breath, save that with God speech (or word) and breath (or spirit) have a permanence and a distinctness that human speech and breath do not

---

[34] Gregory of Nyssa, *or. catech.*, prol. (Mühlenberg, 7. 1–8. 9, paraphrased).

[35] Ibid. 1 (9. 1–3, 8–11).

[36] Cf. *Expos.* 6. 11–20 with Gregory of Nyssa, *or. catech.* 1 (Mühlenberg, 11. 12–12. 3).

have.[37] The argument is precisely parallel to that in the previous chapter, and John's modifications of Gregory (though he follows Gregory much more closely than earlier) are similar in nature, amounting to the introduction of more precise language, not least the more precise connotations of the words *anypostatos* (which Gregory does use) and *enypostatos* (which he does not). Into the passage that defines the nature of the Spirit as 'substantial power, itself contemplated as from himself [i.e., God] in its own particular hypostasis, not capable of being separated from God, in whom he is, nor from the Word, whom he accompanies . . .',[38] John inserts a significant phrase: 'proceeding from the Father and resting in the Word and being his manifestation'. This greater precision about the procession of the Spirit and his relationship to the Son is something that will be developed further in the next chapter of *On the Orthodox Faith*, and expresses with precision the nature of the Spirit's procession in language to which John reverts several times in his other writings. The rest of chapter 7 draws its argument from chapters 3 and 4 of Gregory's *Catechetical Oration*, in which Gregory returns to his opening theme (omitted by John) of how Christian Trinitarianism is a middle way between the narrow monotheism of Judaism and the polytheism of paganism ('hellenism'), in which the errors of both are pruned away, and what is true—the Jewish belief in the oneness of the Godhead and the pagan 'simple distinction of *hypostaseis*'—affirmed.

This introduction to the doctrine of the Trinity, in which, following the argument of the first few chapters of Gregory of Nyssa's *Great Catechetical Oration*, the trinity of persons (hypostases) is unfolded within the unity of the Godhead, is followed by a much longer discussion of Trinitarian theology in *On the Orthodox Faith*. But before we move on to this much more technical discussion, it is worth reflecting on what we have found in chapters 5–7. We have already noted that John, in prefacing his paraphrase of Gregory's *Catechetical Oration* with a strong affirmation of the unity of God, may well be displaying some sensitivity towards Jewish and Muslim objections to the Christian doctrine of the Trinity. It seems to me plausible to argue that this is confirmed by his choice of Gregory's presentation of Trinitarian theology in terms of God and his Word and Spirit, for such an approach draws on the understanding of God found in the Old Testament Scriptures that Christians share with Jews and Muslims. In the last chapter we noticed that John, in his account of Islam in *On Heresies* 100, argues against the accusation of Christians being

---

[37] Cf. Basil, *Spir.* 16. 38. 29–36; 18. 46. 1–9 (Pruche).
[38] Gregory of Nyssa, *or. catech.* 2 (Mühlenberg, 13. 5–12); cf. *Expos.* 7. 18–25.

'associators' from the fact that the Qur'ān recognizes that God possesses both Word and Spirit. Drawing on his awareness of the controversy probably already live within Islam about whether God's attributes, especially his Word (and by analogy his Spirit), are to be regarded as uncreated or created, John argues that the Christian doctrine of the Trinity should not, on the evidence of the Qur'ān itself, draw down on Christians the charge of being 'associators'. This suggests that John decided to base the introductory chapters of his doctrine of the Trinity in *On the Orthodox Faith* on Gregory's early chapters of the *Catechetical Oration*, precisely because a presentation in terms of God and his Word and Spirit established common ground with Jews and Muslims, who were critical of Christian Trinitarianism. We shall, when we come to consider iconoclasm, find further evidence for a Christian–Jewish dialogue that sought common ground in the late seventh century.

Chapter 8, one of the longest chapters of *On the Orthodox Faith*, presents a more technical account of Trinitarian doctrine. In this more technical presentation, John draws principally on the Cappadocian Fathers, and also reproduces some of the characteristic emphases of Alexandrian Trinitarian theology, as found in Athanasios, Didymos, and Cyril. But John goes beyond this, partly in dependence on Leontios of Byzantium and Theodore of Raïthu, and uses some of the characteristic language of the Chalcedonian Definition (which is, of course, a *Christological* statement) in the context of Trinitarian theology, thereby introducing further refinements that have since become part of the heritage of Orthodoxy. Chapter 8 falls into four sections. The first of these (*Expos.* 8. 2–95) begins by iterating Christian belief in one God, ineffable and transcendent, and then introduces the notion of the Trinity and begins to expound the doctrine of the Trinity in relation to the Father and the Son, leading into a discussion of the difference between begetting (or generation) and creation. The second section (*Expos.* 8. 96–171) discusses the nature of divine generation (and also procession), using various traditional analogies, especially that of light and fire, and early on making explicit and expounding the distinction between two very similar Greek words, often confused in earlier literature, *agennetos* ('unbegotten') and *agenetos* ('unoriginated', 'uncreated').[39] The third section (*Expos.* 8. 172–222) is on the Holy Spirit and the nature of his procession, and closes by

[39] The distinction *agennetos-agenetos* is discussed again, in a Christological context, in *Expos.* 80. According to Fraigneau-Julien (1961, 198), this distinction was first made explicitly by Pseudo-Cyril; if Conticello is correct, then the introduction of this distinction should be ascribed to John.

arguing that the Trinity is not composed out of (*ek*) the three hypostases, but is a simple *ousia* existing in (*en*) the three hypostases. The final section (*Expos*. 8. 223–97) discusses the nature of the divine unity, and introduces the term *perichoresis* ('coinherence') into Trinitarian theology for the first time.[40]

The first part of *Expos*. 8 begins with a carefully constructed confession of faith in God, beginning with the first four words (in Greek) of the Niceno-Constantinopolitan Creed in its synodal, rather than its liturgical, form (i.e., in the first person plural, rather than the first person singular): 'We believe in one God.' This is followed by a long list of divine attributes: first those with the alpha-privative ('without beginning, uncreated, unbegotten, etc.'), those expressing God's transcendence over everything (generally beginning with 'all', *pantôn*: 'of *all things* visible and invisible creator, holding *all things* together and preserving them, etc.'), then a series expressing God's transcendence by the use of the 'Dionysian' prefix *hyper-* ('beyond being, beyond deity, beyond good, beyond fulness, etc.'). This list then cedes to another prefixed by the term *auto-*, expressing the idea that God is the original source (on the analogy of the Platonic Forms) of these qualities ('light itself, goodness itself, life itself, being itself'); which in turn yields to a series of affirmations of God's oneness ('one being, one Godhead, one power, one will, etc.'), at which point the final clause of the sentence (for this is a single sentence of twenty-five lines) introduces a Trinitarian confession: 'acknowledged in three perfect hypostases and venerated with a single veneration, believed and worshipped by the whole rational creation, as united without confusion and divided without being parted, which is paradoxical' (*Expos*. 8. 23–6). The echoes of the Chalcedonian Definition are unmistakable— 'acknowledged' (*gnôrizomenên*), 'without confusion' (*asygchytôs*)—and suggest the transfer of Christological terminology to Trinitarian theology that finds its apogee in the term, *perichoresis*. The 'three perfect hypostases' are now named—'Father, Son and Holy Spirit'—in whom we are baptized, in accordance with the Lord's command, which is quoted (Matt. 28: 19). This carefully constructed confession of faith recapitulates the teaching about God found earlier in *On the Orthodox Faith*, casting it now in the form of a confession, rather than an argument, so that it almost takes the form of an aretalogy. A. D. Nock once remarked that 'aretalogies give concrete details',[41] insisting thereby on close attention to detail; *mutatis mutandis* the same remark is valid here.

[40] See Fraigneau-Julien 1961, 390, and Prestige 1952, 280–1, 294–5.
[41] Nock 1972, 964.

Faith in the 'One Father' is now confessed, and his names defined: 'principle and source of all things, not begotten by any, alone existing without source and unbegotten, maker of all things, Father by nature of his one and only only-begotten Son, our Lord and God and Saviour, Jesus Christ, and emitter of the all-holy Spirit', the term 'emitter' (*proboleus*) being taken from Gregory Nazianzen.[42] John quickly moves on to the confession of the 'one Son', which he begins by quoting from the Niceno-Constantinopolitan creed. He comments that 'begotten before all ages' means that this begetting is 'timeless and without beginning'. John goes on to list other attributes of the Son, emphasizing the eternal coexistence of Father and Son, and asserting the eternal fertility of God— 'For it is impossible to call God bereft of natural fertility; his fertility is to beget from himself, from his own being, one like by nature' (*Expos.* 8. 48–50)—in this following Athanasios and Cyril. He recalls the anti-Arian arguments of Athanasios that excluded any element of temporality from the begetting of the Son, arguing that to admit such would introduce change into the Father's *hypostasis*. Creation, of course, is not eternal, but this fact does not introduce change into the divine being, for creation is external to the divine being, unlike begetting, which is from the being of God: again, a distinction made much of by Athanasios.[43] There follows a brief discussion of the difference between making and begetting, both human and divine: by an act of will, God creates from nothing creatures that, since they are from nothing, are not coeternal with him, whereas human creation needs pre-existing material, and is a process involving planning and design, then working by hand and undergoing toil, and often failing to bring to completion. God begets his own Word as a perfect being without beginning or end, whereas humans beget in time beings themselves subject to corruption and death, in a process in which male and female have need of each other. With both creation and begetting, there is an underlying difference between human and divine activity, the latter taking place in an eternity outside time, beyond the constraints of need, and former limited by temporal conditions and marked by neediness—a distinction emphasized by Athanasios in his youthful treatise *On the Incarnation*.[44]

The second section begins by recalling the teaching of the Catholic and Apostolic Church that the Father and the Son are coeternal, the only-begotten Son being begotten in a way that is beyond time, flux, passion,

[42] e.g., Gregory Nazianzen, *or.* 29. 2. 15 (Gallay).
[43] See Louth 1989*b*.
[44] Cf. Athanasios, *inc.* 2 (Thomson, 136–8).

or indeed comprehension. This is something of which one can catch a glimpse only by analogies that fall far short of the divine reality. John dwells mostly on the analogy of the coexistence of light and fire, drawing probably on Cyril or perhaps on Basil's *Against Eunomius*,[45] though the analogy is an old one, going back at least to the second-century apologists. Light comes from fire, but simultaneously with the kindling of the fire: so the analogy expresses simultaneous derivation. However, the analogy falls short of divine reality in that light does not have its own *hypostasis* alongside the fire, but is rather a natural property of fire, in contrast to the relation of the Son to the Father (*Expos.* 8. 104–7). The Word is also called 'brightness' and 'character of the Father's *hypostasis*' (*apaugasma* and *charakter.* cf. Heb. 1: 3), which again express the simultaneous derivation from the Father, but not the hypostatic reality of the Son. He is also called 'only-begotten' (cf. John 1: 14, 1 John 4: 9), 'because he alone was only-begotten from the only Father' (*Expos.* 8. 112), which leads John to remark that the Spirit too derives from the Father eternally, 'but not by begetting but by procession' (*Expos.* 8. 115). Begetting and procession are called 'modes of existence' (*tropoi hyparxeôs*), and they are both incomprehensible and unknowable. This notion of *tropos hyparxeôs* is illustrated by the analogy of Adam, Eve, and Seth, all consubstantial, since Eve and Seth were derived from Adam, but with different 'modes of existence', since Adam was unbegotten (being made by God), while Eve proceeded from Adam's side (and was therefore also not begotten), and Seth was begotten (being the son of Adam). This analogy, borrowed from Gregory Nazianzen,[46] illustrates how three consubstantial beings may have different modes of existence. This leads John to discuss the difference between the two Greek words that differ in only a single letter: *agenetos* and *agennetos*. The former means that which has not come into being, and makes a distinction at the level of being; the latter means something that has not been begotten and indicates no difference of being, for in each species of living being there was one that was first and unbegotten, but the beings begotten from it share the same being. The former word applies to each of the persons of the Godhead (and indeed to nothing else), whereas, within the Godhead, the latter word applies solely to the Father. John further remarks that the term 'Father' is not really applied analogically to the divine person, but just the reverse: it applies properly to God the Father, and only derivatively to human fatherhood, a point

---

[45] Cf. Cyril, *thes.* 5 (PG 75. 61BC, 72CD); Basil, *Eun.* 2. 26–9 (Sesboüé).
[46] Gregory Nazianzen, *or.* 31. 11 (Gallay).

already made by Athanasios and Basil,[47] and inspired by Ephesians 3: 14–15, which John quotes.

He goes on to discuss two further issues: what is meant by saying that the Father is the principle or beginning (*archê*) of the Son, and that the Father is 'greater' than the Son (cf. John 14: 28: the latter was to exercise later Byzantine theologians in the first two centuries of the second millennium), and also what is meant by the assertion in Hebrews (1: 2) that 'through him [i.e., the Son] he made the ages' (echoed by the clause of the Creed). Both issues are clarified by reference to the analogy of the fire and the light. The first is settled by reference to the Father's precedence within the Godhead by virtue of being 'source' (*aition*); John does not consider the explanation of the Father's greatness in relation to the Son in terms of the Son's incarnate state. The second issue is clarified by the idea that the Father does not create the ages through the Son, as if the Son were some sort of instrument, for the Son is a natural and real (*enypostatos*) power. This section closes by claiming that no image can be found within the created order for the 'mode of the Holy Triad' (*Expos.* 8. 165–6), because of the utter contrast between the simplicity and serene eternity of the Godhead and the changeable and composite character of creation out of nothing.

The third section begins by recalling the article on the Spirit in the Niceno-Constantinopolitan Creed, to which, however, John makes two (or perhaps three) additions. The opening lines of this section read (with the additions italicized): 'Likewise we believe in *One* Holy Spirit, the Lord and Giver of Life, who proceeds from the Father *and rests in the Son*, who together with the Father and the Son is together worshipped and glorified, *as consubstantial and co-eternal*'. The additions are worth noting: the first simply brings this article into line with the other articles of the Creed that confess *one* God the Father and *one* Lord Jesus Christ; the last makes explicit what has always been held to be implicit in this article of the Creed (ever since the letter to Pope Damasus from the Fathers of the Synod of Constantinople held in 382, explaining the achievements of 381[48]) that the Holy Spirit is *homoousios*, consubstantial, with the Father and the Son.

But most interesting is the middle addition: 'and rests in the Son'. This needs to be taken with what John says a little later on (*Expos.* 8. 289–3) about the procession of the Spirit, where he denies that the Spirit can be said to be 'from the Son' (*ek tou huiou*), even though he is called the 'Spirit of the Son', deriving this latter title from the fact that he is 'made manifest

---

[47] Athanasios, *Ar.* 1. 23 (Bright, 25. 5–9); Basil, *Eun.* 2. 23. 41–9 (Sesboüé).

[48] See the letter of the bishops gathered in Constantinople (Tanner 1990, 28. 19–27, 34–6).

and bestowed on us through the Son'. In support of this, John quotes
Jesus' words to the disciples as he gave them the Holy Spirit on the
Sunday after the Resurrection (John 20: 22). Fraigneau-Julien[49] professes
to find a very close analogy between what he regards as Pseudo-Cyril's
doctrine of the procession of the Spirit here and that advanced by
Maximos in one of his *opuscula*,[50] where he replies to complaints made by
Byzantine theologians about the Western doctrine of the double procession of the Holy Spirit (in the eighth century just beginning to take root
outside Visigothic Spain).[51] Maximos's irenic response to the Byzantine
theologians was that though it is certain that the Spirit proceeds from the
Father and no one else, there was the authority of Cyril of Alexandria for
speaking of the Spirit proceeding from the Father through the Son, and it
was in such a way that the Western way of speaking of the Spirit should be
taken.[52] But John's response is rather different; apart from the denial of
'from the Son' (which may simply be part of his explanation of how the
Spirit could be called Spirit of the Son, as well as of the Father, as the context makes explicit), he seems quite unaware of the *Filioque*, and seems to
be addressing a rather different problem: namely, given that in the Trinity
the Father is the sole principle (*archê*), what is the relationship of the Spirit
to the Son, from whom he does not derive (essentially a problem for
Greek theology)?[53] John's explanation here, with the reference to John
20: 22, suggests that he is making a distinction between what is true in
theologia and what is true in the *oikonomia*: the Spirit proceeds from the
Father, and not from the Son, but in the *oikonomia* he is bestowed by the
Son, and hence called the Spirit of the Son. It has to be said, however, that
the analogy he immediately gives of the sun, its ray, and its brightness
rather tells against this interpretation (*Expos.* 8. 293–6).

In his 'modification' of the credal statement, he speaks of the Spirit
proceeding from the Father and resting in the Son; in the expansion of the
passage from Gregory of Nyssa's *Catechetical Oration* in his earlier chapter

[49] Fraigneau-Julien 1961, 201.

[50] Maximos, *opusc.* 10 (PG 91. 133A–137C: the brief discussion of the double procession is
at 136AB). For a recent discussion of this work see Larchet 1998, 11–75, though I cannot
agree with the whole of Larchet's learned analysis of the issue.

[51] Although Rome did not incorporate the *Filioque* into the Creed until 1014, under
pressure from the Ottonian emperor Henry II (Swete 1876, 225; Vischer 1981, 51), Rome was
clearly concerned about the doctrine of the *Filioque* (which it upheld), as is manifest from the
florilegium on the *Filioque*, held in the papal scrinium by, at the latest, 774/5, when the archetype of Parisinus Graecus 1115 was copied: see Alexakis 1996, 71–85.

[52] Cf. the rather similar suggestion of the Synod of Ferrara-Florence in 1439: Tanner 1990,
526. 31–527.10 (Greek text).

[53] Grégoire (1969, 715) makes a similar point.

on the Spirit he had spoken of the Spirit as 'proceeding from the Father and resting in the Word and being his manifestation, being separated neither from God, in whom he is, nor the Word, whom he accompanies' (*Expos.* 7. 19–22). John here brings together refinements in the understanding of the procession of the Holy Spirit that have been determinative for later Orthodox theology.[54] The idea that the Spirit is in the Son, as the Son is in the Father, can be found in Athanasios and Didymos the Blind.[55] Athanasios has no verb, however, and Didymos (or whoever wrote *On the Trinity*, attributed to him) uses the Johannine verb 'abide'[56] to say that the Spirit 'abides' (*menei*) in the Son. But Didymos also uses the verb 'to rest' (*anapauein*), in a passage commenting on Isaiah 11: 2. José Grégoire has suggested that the idea of the Spirit resting in the Son derives from Alexandrian exegesis of Isaias 11: 1–2, which (according to the LXX text) speaks of a rod or shoot (*rabdos*) growing from the root of Jesse, as well as a flower, upon which the Spirit of God rests.[57] The shoot or flower is the incarnate Word coming from the womb of the Virgin Mother of God. Didymos, in his comment on the passage from Isaiah, says that we see in the Gospel passage (undoubtedly John 1: 32, the Baptist's account of his baptism of Jesus) the Spirit resting on the incarnate Word.[58] Cyril takes up this suggestion, but is concerned to demonstrate that the events of the Baptism reveal the permanent resting of the Spirit on the Son, not something that took place for the first time on that occasion (it is significant that all this grows out of reflection on the account of the Lord's baptism, seen by the Fathers[59] as a revelation of the Trinity).[60] In both these Alexandrians, it is a matter of the Spirit resting on the Son in his incarnate state. John takes this reflection on John 1: 32 in the light of Isaias 11: 2 a step further, and speaks of an eternal resting

[54] See esp. Stăniloae 1981.

[55] Fraigneau-Julien 1961, 198 and n., referring to Régnon 1892–8 '4. 145' (properly, 3. 2. 145–6), who cites Athanasios, *ep. Serap.* 1. 14 (PG 26. 565B2, cf. B10–11) and Didymos (or perhaps Pseudo-Didymos), *Trin.* i. 31 (PG 39. 425A5). One could also add, from Didymos, *Trin.* ii. 5 (540B7–14), ii. 27 (753A9–B2); the former develops the notion from the Johannine notion of the mutual abiding of the Father in the Son, while the latter cites a verse from the Sibylline Oracle.

[56] See John 14: 10, 17; 15: 1–10, and elsewhere in the Johannine writings.

[57] Grégoire 1969, 728–9 n. 2.

[58] Didymos, *Trin.* ii. 7. 9 (PG 39. 596A8).

[59] And the Byzantine liturgy: see the apolytikion for the Feast of the Theophany, celebrating the Baptism of the Lord, which begins, 'As you were baptized in the Jordan, Lord, the worship of the Trinity was made manifest' (Lash 1999, 89).

[60] Cyril, *Is.* ii. 1 (PG 70. 313D3–4), where the verb used is *anapauein*; *Joel* 2 (Pusey, i. 338, 14–19); *Jo.* 2. 1 (Pusey, iii. 175. 1), in both of which cases the verb is *menein*, and Cyril is commenting on John 1: 32.

of the Spirit *in* the Son, manifest in the *oikonomia*, where the Spirit rests or abides *on* the Son. Similarly with the Spirit as the manifestation of the Son: this takes place in the *oikonomia*, but it depends on the eternal self-manifestation of the Son in the Spirit. As Stăniloae puts it:

The accompaniment of the begetting of the Son by the procession of the Spirit is a manifested accompaniment. For, without doubt, it is only if the begetting of the Son by the Father is accompanied by the procession of the Spirit from the Father, that the begetting of the Son can also be accompanied by the manifestation or shining forth of the Spirit. But if the accompaniment of the begetting of the Son by the procession of the Holy Spirit from the same Father is on the one hand the more profound fact, on the other it leaves it possible for us to think in terms of certain parallelism between the two cases. But the accompaniment of the begetting and in general of the Person of the Son by the manifest shining out of the Spirit demonstrates that there is an inner dynamic presence of the Spirit in the Son. That is why it employs the expressions 'through' or 'from' the Son, words which cannot be used of the procession itself. At the same time the shining out of the Spirit through or from the Son constitutes the basis for the shining out of the Spirit through or from the Son to the created world.[61]

John recalls this development of the doctrine of the procession of the Holy Spirit elsewhere in his writings. For instance, in his *Letter on the Thrice-Holy Hymn*, he asserts that 'the Word is a real offspring, and therefore Son. And the Spirit is a real procession and emanation from the Father, of the Son but not from the Son, as breath (*pneuma*) from a mouth, proclaiming God the Word' (*Trisag.* 28. 40–3). Similarly in one of his sermons, he speaks of the Holy Spirit as 'the Holy Spirit of God the Father, as proceeding from him, who is also said to be of the Son, as through him manifest and bestowed on the creation, but not as taking his existence from him' (*Sabbat.* 4. 21–3).[62]

John goes on to list the names or attributes of the Holy Spirit, drawing on Gregory Nazianzen, who himself is indebted to Athanasios the Great and to his friend Basil.[63] He goes on to reaffirm that, although we have been taught that there is a difference between begetting and procession, what this difference is we do not know. The rest of this section is concerned to affirm that Father, Son, and Holy Spirit are three *perfect* hypostases. By this John means (and here he is drawing on Leontios of Byzantium[64]) that the Trinity is not a 'single perfect nature composed

---

[61] Stăniloae 1981, 183.
[62] To which one could add the brief Trinitarian statement in *Manich.* 5. 9–11.
[63] Cf. Gregory Nazianzen, *or.* 31. 29. 14–44 (Gallay).
[64] Leontios of Byzantium, *Nest. et Eut.* (PG 86. 1288B).

of three imperfect elements, but a single simple *ousia* in three perfect *hypostaseis*?' (*Expos.* 8. 204–6). (Again, I think we should recognize here the transfer of Christological language to a Trinitarian context: the Chalcedonian Definition affirmed Christ as existing *in* two natures, not *out of* two natures, and the same distinction between the prepositions *en* and *ek* is utilized here.)

The final section begins by making a distinction between knowing something in reality (*pragmati*) and knowing something in reason and thought (*logôi kai epinoiâi*). Kotter suggests that this distinction is drawn from a passage from Basil's *Ascetica*, preserved in the *Doctrina Patrum*.[65] The parallels between the two passages are very striking: in both the distinction is expressed in the same terms, and in both it is used to express a fundamental distinction between God and created reality—indeed, it would appear that John is simply amplifying and rearranging Basil's text. The distinction between perceiving something in reality and perceiving it simply conceptually recalls the distinction used by Cyril of Alexandria in Christology, whereby the union of natures in Christ can be perceived only by thought (*theoriâi*) and not in reality.[66] This seems to be the context of another source for John's use of this distinction, suggested by Fraigneau-Julien:[67] namely, the *Proparaskeuê* of Theodore of Raïthu, where, in what seems to be a Christological context, Theodore makes the same distinction using slightly different terminology, distinguishing between being united in operation and reality (*ergôi kai pragmati*) and divided in thought (*epinoiâi*), and vice versa.[68] If the passage from Basil in the *Doctrina Patrum* is genuine, then it of course pre-dates Cyril; but even so, it is likely that it was Cyril's use of this distinction in Christology that popularized it, so we have yet another example of John's tendency to transfer theological considerations from the realm of Christology to that of Trinitarian theology.

Whatever its origin, it is employed by John to set out a fundamental distinction between the uncreated Godhead and created reality. We have already seen in *On the Orthodox Faith* several ways in which this difference is exploited: primarily in terms of the contrast between the eternal, changeless nature of uncreated reality that transcends any kind of need, and temporal, shifting, needy, created reality. In the present section the distinction is between the fundamentally simple nature of the uncreated God and the fundamentally composite nature of created reality (it is clear

---

[65] Kotter ii. 28 apparatus, citing *Doct. Patr.* 26 (Diekamp, 188–9).

[66] Cf., e.g., Cyril, *ep.* 44 ad Eulogium (Wickham, 63. 18–64. 4).

[67] Fraigneau-Julien 1961, 391 n. 109.

[68] Theodore of Raïthu, in Diekamp 1938, 215. 20–3.

that this distinction could be regarded as the fundamental reason for the contrasts just mentioned). In created reality, individual *hypostaseis* are just that: individual units, separated from one another in reality. Any communion, any union one with another, is perceived only conceptually. Individual human beings are separate one from another in reality; what they have in common, humanity, is only conceptual.[69] In this, John follows Gregory Nazianzen against his young friend Gregory of Nyssa, who had argued, in *On Not Three Gods,* that it is a misuse of language (*katachrêsis*) to speak of several human beings, since they share a single nature.[70] In contrast, Gregory Nazianzen had argued that the unity represented by our common human nature is only conceptual.[71] It is quite the opposite 'with the holy and incomprehensible Trinity, beyond being and transcending everything':

For there what is one and common is perceived in reality through the coeternity and sameness of being and activity and will and the agreement in judgement and the sameness of authority and power and goodness—I did not say 'likeness', but 'sameness'—and the one thrust of movement; for there is one being, one goodness, one power, one will, one activity, one authority, one and the same, not three similar one to another, but one and the same movement of the three *hypostaseis.* 'For each of them is in entire unity as much with himself as with the partnership',[72] that is that the Father and the Son and the Holy Spirit are one in every respect, save for unbegottenness, being begotten and procession; the division is conceptual. For we know one God, and solely in the properties of fatherhood and sonship and procession, according to cause and being caused[73] and the perfection of the *hypostasis* or the mode of existence do we conceive the difference. (*Expos.* 8. 240–53)[74]

John goes on to say that, since there can be no 'spatial distance, as with us, in the uncircumscribable Godhead', the *hypostaseis* are 'in one another [*en allêlais*], not so as to be confused, but in accordance with the word of the Lord, "I in the Father and the Father in me" (John 14. 10)' (*Expos.* 8. 253–6). This being 'in one another' of the divine *hypostaseis* John explains by using the term *perichoresis,* 'coinherence':[75] they have 'coinherence one in another without any coalescence or mixture' (*Expos.* 8. 263–4). The notion of coinherence of the persons of the Trinity has been implicit from the first paragraph of chapter 8, but the term itself, used in a

[69] Cf. Ch. 4 above.
[70] Gregory of Nyssa, *tres dii* (Mueller 40. 5–42. 3).
[71] Gregory Nazianzen, *or.* 31. 15 (Gallay).
[72] Ibid. 31. 16. 17–18 (Gallay).
[73] Cf. Gregory of Nyssa, *tres dii* (Mueller 56, esp. line 1).
[74] Cf. *Fides,* 48.
[75] For the background of this term, see Prestige 1952, 282–301. See also Twombly 1992.

Trinitarian context, is an innovation of John's. First, the verb had been used to describe the interpenetration of the natures united in Christ; then Maximos used the noun to describe the same thing.[76] Now, with John, in a way that we have come to see as characteristic of him, the term is transferred to the realm of *theologia*. It describes something that is uniquely true of the uncreated reality of the Godhead, where the distinction of *hypostaseis* does not detract from the unity of the Godhead: the *hypostaseis* can be discerned to be distinct in their several 'modes of existence', but in reality they are wholly at one, and that unity between the *hypostaseis* is manifest in their interpenetration or coinherence, *perichoresis*. John goes on to give a picture of this coinherence by using the analogy of three suns with no space between them shining with a single radiance, an analogy has drawn from Gregory Nazianzen whom he is following closely here.[77]

John's understanding of *perichoresis* is relevant to another topic that we have already broached: the nature of *hypostasis*. Earlier we saw that the Christian logic textbooks, of which John's *Dialectica* is an example, seem to move towards defining the term *hypostasis*, which was not in current philosophical use in the same way as the terms *ousia, physis,* etc. were. *Hypostasis*, as a term distinct from *ousia,* had been introduced into Trinitarian theology by Basil. *Hypostasis* was also used—in different ways—in Christology by theologians of both the Antiochene and the Alexandrine traditions, and this use was confirmed by the Fathers of Chalcedon in their Christological Definition. The difference between these terms and others, as we have already seen and will see in greater detail later in this chapter, gave rise to controversy between those who accepted Chalcedon and its assimilation of Christological and Trinitarian terminology in the distinction between *hypostasis/prosopon* and *physis/ousia,* and those who rejected this synod and its definition. Those who rejected this assimilation of terminology (usually called Monophysites) accepted the Cappadocian distinction between *hypostasis* and *ousia,* but could not accept the distinction drawn by Chalcedon between *hypostasis* and *physis* in the realm of Christology. This was partly because they made a distinction between *physis* and *ousia* (and saw *hypostasis* as more or less equivalent to *physis,* at least in some contexts), and partly because they drew a line between *theologia* and *oikonomia,* a distinction that had a long history, especially in the tradition of Alexandrine theology.

Seen in this light, what John is doing with the concept of *hypostasis* takes

[76] Maximos the Confessor, *opusc.* 7 (PG 91. 88A).

[77] *Expos.* 8. 265–74 = Gregory Nazianzen, *or.* 31. 14. 7–13 (Gallay), with some slight supplementation.

on a particular interest. It is a central term in John's Christian ontology: reality is primarily hypostatic. Following earlier theologians such as Leontios of Byzantium and, especially, Maximos the Confessor, John applies what might be called a 'Chalcedonian logic'[78] consistently in both *theologia* and *oikonomia*; we shall find further evidence for this when we come to discuss his Christology. In accordance with this logic, he distinguishes between the level of nature or being, *physis* or *ousia*, at which level beings are defined by their *logos tês ousias*, the principle or meaning of their being, and the level of existence, where beings have concrete existence as *hypostaseis*, persons, individuals, in accordance with their 'mode of existence', *tropos hyparxeôs*. In the Incarnation, the *hypostasis* of the Son can assume human nature, for the mode of filial existence can take both a divine and a human form. For the most part, however, John defines his logical concepts in terms of creaturely reality. Although the distinction between *hypostasis* and *ousia* was first made to elucidate Trinitarian theology, John, in common with his sixth- and seventh-century predecessors, defines this distinction in creaturely terms. One might have thought that the fact that person or *hypostasis* first emerged as a term in Trinitarian theology and then led to a deepening sense of what is meant by human personal reality suggests some kind of analogy between the Trinity and human personal relationships, in which the notion of human personhood finds its origin, and indeed its resources, in the perfect communion of persons in the Trinity. But, however attractive such an idea might seem to many modern theologians, it is not one that John himself is prepared to entertain. Even though he adopts a uniform 'Chalcedonian logic', applying it equally in *theologia* and *oikonomia*, the reality to which this logic is applied is not uniform; it does not even have any kind of analogical continuity. In fact, it is improper to think of reality as divided into uncreated and created reality, for there is no common reality to be thus divided. Uncreated reality is utterly unlike created reality. We use the same terms, *hypostasis, ousia*, etc., of both God and created being, but the reality they map on to is quite different: one uncreated and utterly simple, so that the divine Persons are coinherent one in another, the other created, occupying space and time, which entails genuine separation, and prevents any genuine coinherence. The distinction between *theologia* and *oikonomia* is reasserted; the application of Chalcedonian logic to both is not allowed to encroach on the ultimate ineffability and incomprehensibility of the divine.

John Damascene's doctrine of the Trinity is a deeply considered

[78] Cf. Louth 1996, 49–51.

synthesis of patristic *theologia*. He draws on developments in Christo-logical reflection to secure a Trinitarian theology against the logical abstraction, and consequent inchoate tritheism, that the increasing impact of logical definition on Christian theology was in danger of fostering.[79] His use of the term *perichoresis* is a symbol of this, but the cross-over from Christology to Trinitarian theology accomplished by John is more far-reaching. John reverts to this in the last chapter of the first section of *On the Orthodox Faith*, when he affirms 'the rest and abiding of the *hypostaseis* one in another' (*Expos.* 14. 11).

But chapter 8 of *On the Orthodox Faith* does not exhaust John Damascene's Trinitarian theology. Elsewhere there are hints, but only hints, of other traditions of Trinitarian theology. We have already seen that John on occasion attacks the incipient tritheism he detected in his Monophysite opponents: in the longest attack on the Monophysites, *Against the Jacobites*, he argues against the idea, found in Philoponos, that the Trinitarian *hypostaseis* are to be regarded as 'particular natures', alleging that it entails either Arianism, or tritheism, or, even worse, tetratheism. In other places John seems to be arguing against the heresy that emerges if one holds that the *ousia* of the Godhead is purely abstract; for instance, in *Against the Akephaloi* 5 he argues that to reject the notion of *ousia enypostatos* entails tritheism. But the context of all these arguments is really Christo-logical—John just draws out the Trinitarian heresy inherent in Mono-physite ideas for good measure. For this reason, the arguments involving the term *enypostatos* will be left to the later section on Christology.

Basil Studer, in his pioneering study of the theological method of the Damascene, remarks that John's vision of the Trinity 'does not disclose an authentic Trinitarian mysticism; the name Trinity rather stands simply for God or Godhead'.[80] I am not quite clear what Studer means by 'authentic Trinitarian mysticism', but it is true that John in *On the Orthodox Faith* generally uses the term *trias* to refer to the Godhead. But we also find a use of *trias* that seems more complex, involving the coupling of *monas* and *trias*. Gregory Nazianzen seems to be the first to use the phrase *monas kai trias* of God; it occurs again in Dionysios the Areopagite and also in Maximos. The background of this usage is obscure: Dionysios seems to be arguing that the phrase expresses the idea that God

[79] See Fraigneau-Julien 1961, 390, and Prestige 1952, 296–9.

[80] Studer 1956, 41. He gives a series of references to Evagrios and Maximos, who resemble John in this: Evagrios, *cap. pract.* 3 (Guillaumont, 500. 1); Maximos, *cap. carit.* i. 86, 94, 97, ii. 21, iv. 47 (Ceresa-Gastaldo, 82, 86, 86, 100, 212). The same is true of Dionysios the Areopagite: see, e.g., *d.n.* 3. 1 (Suchla, i. 138. 1–12).

transcends number,[81] and the same seems to be true of Maximos.[82] The idea that the Trinity transcends enumeration is an old idea going back at least to Basil's *On the Holy Spirit*.[83] What is not clear is what the opinions were that Dionysios and Maximos were seeking to refute by their arguments. For John Damascene seems to use these terms in a slightly different way, and if we had more idea of the kind of ideas entertained about God as *monas kai trias*, we might be able to make more of the little he says. In *On Right Thinking*, John expresses his Trinitarian faith by confessing 'Father, Son and Spirit, consubstantial Triad and trihypostatic Monad',[84] a formulation that recalls Maximos's first *Difficulty*.[85] More interesting, however, is a remark in *Letter on the Thrice-Holy Hymn* (which is principally concerned with Christology):

The monad [or unit] is without quantity, the dyad is the beginning of number, and the triad a complete number. But it is not because of number that the Godhead is in a triad, but because the Godhead is in a triad that the number three is complete. For 'the monad is moved from the beginning towards the dyad until it reaches the triad'. (*Trisag.* 28. 11–14)

That last quotation is from Gregory Nazianzen,[86] and was such a source of puzzlement to Maximos that he commented on it at least three times.[87] What Gregory meant by it is clear from the words that precede it: 'though there is numerical distinction there is no division in being' (something true only of uncreated reality). John Damascene seems to go beyond that and suggest that the fact that three is a perfect number is a reflection of the Trinity. The idea that three is the first complete number is an old Pythagorean idea that was the cause of much reflection among the sixth-century Aristotelian commentators.[88] It is likely that the quotation from Gregory (which seems to have been itself a quotation in the original sermon) is a reflection of this idea, and John's remark above seems to be a rebuttal of any suggestion that number theory provides a clue to the Trinitarian mystery, which is perhaps only a different way of saying, with Dionysios and Maximos, that the Trinitarian Godhead transcends number.

[81] Dionysios the Areopagite, *d.n.* 13. 3 (Suchla, i. 229. 6–10).
[82] See Savvidis 1997, 56–8.
[83] Basil, *Spir.* 17. 41–3 (Pruche).
[84] *Rect.* 1 (PG 94. 1421B).
[85] Maximos, *ambig.* 1 (PG 91. 1036BC).
[86] Gregory Nazianzen, *or.* 29. 2. 13–14 (Gallay).
[87] Maximos, *ambig.* 1 (PG 91. 1033D–1036C), 10. 43 (1193C–1196C), and 23 (1257C–1261C).
[88] See Roueché 2002, 108.

(c) Creation and Human Kind

The next section of *On the Orthodox Faith* is concerned with the created order. After an introductory couple of chapters on aeon (age or eternity) and creation, there follow sections on the invisible creation, angels and demons (chapters 17–18), and the visible creation leading from heaven to paradise and displaying on the way a good deal of astronomical, cosmological, and geographical learning (chapters 19–25). The section on paradise, created as a human habitat, leads into the third group of chapters on human nature: first a lengthy analysis of the human being as both spiritual and corporeal, created in God's image and likeness to fulfil the role of 'bond of creation', together with an elaborate analysis of the human constitution as a psychosomatic unity (chapter 26), followed by a lengthy psychological analysis of the human person (chapters 27–36). Next there is an analysis of human action and freedom (chapters 37–42), which leads naturally into a discussion of divine providence (chapter 43), and finally a chapter on divine foreknowledge and predetermination, which ends with a discussion of the fall of human beings (chapter 44).[89]

The mere fact of this lengthy section is worthy of comment. For John Damascene and the Greek tradition he follows, the creation is not simply a backdrop for the drama of Fall and Redemption, set in place and then more or less ignored; the whole created order—the invisible creation, the visible heavens, the earth, the human person in whom the extremities of creation meet (as Maximos had put it[90]), and the whole mystery of human nature—is explored in careful detail. Only at the end of this section does John recount the Fall, seen as already within God's providential plan for humanity. It is not that John plays down the Fall (the demons are, of course, fallen), or that he devotes his energies to an account of an ideal creation. His account of creation is of creation as it is, open to distortion by human (and demonic) wickedness. None the less, creation is fundamentally good, and everything created has a proper function, given to it by God. This is very much the vision of Maximos the Confessor, whose approach to the created order John clearly knows (as will emerge in the course of our exposition). Nevertheless, a striking element of the Maximian vision is missing, for John makes no mention of Maximos's

[89] As stated above, the chapters of *Expos.* are being enumerated as a century, as in the Greek manuscripts, and not as four books, as in Migne and the available English translations, which follow the later Latin division. This second section corresponds to book 2 of this division.

[90] See Maximos, *ambig.* 41 (PG 91. 1304D–1316A).

notion of the *logoi* of creation, the inviolable principles that underlie the created order, the fulfilment of which manifests the deification of the whole of the cosmos.

In this section, John draws on a variety of sources. For the invisible and visible creation, he draws especially on Basil's homilies *On the Six Days of Creation*, the related homilies on human creation by either Basil himself or his brother, Gregory of Nyssa's own *On Human Creation*, several homilies by Gregory Nazianzen, especially homilies 38 and 45, and the popular sermons on cosmogony by Severian of Gabala, one of John Chrysostom's more determined opponents, who adopted a literalist interpretation of biblical cosmogony (ironically these sermons were often preserved under the pseudonym of Chrysostom). On human nature and providence, John relies heavily on a remarkable work by Nemesios, a fourth-century bishop of Emesa, *On Human Nature*, a learned discussion of (especially) the psychological constitution of human nature, the final purpose of which was apologetic, to demonstrate God's providential care for creation and, within it, the human race. In his use of Nemesios, as we shall see, John makes the same selection as Maximos the Confessor, though he reproduces Nemesios's words more exactly than the Confessor, who tends to paraphrase.[91] This suggests, I think, that John stands in a tradition of the use of Nemesios that goes back at least to Maximos; whether this was an oral tradition of 'reading the Fathers' (in the sense suggested in Chapter 2), or whether John was inspired by Maximos's writings to seek out his sources, seems to me an open question.

Creation

John prefaces his discussion of the created order with a chapter each on the meaning of *aion* (aeon) and on creation. There are probably two reasons for the preliminary chapter on *aion*. First, in Platonic and Neoplatonic usage *aion* belongs before creation, creation being based on an eternal model (the word *aion* can be translated either 'eternity' or 'age'), time itself being a 'moving image of eternity'.[92] Against this John asserts the transcendence of the Christian God, 'who exists before the ages', and indeed is their creator (*Expos.* 15. 2). Secondly, he comments on the different ways in which *aion* is used, and puts forward what he regards as its true metaphysical meaning. He thus lists some of these ways: of a

[91] For evidence for this assertion see Louth 1996, 204–11, nn. 5, 6, 93, 94, 95, 99, 100, 110, 112, 114, 115, 117, 118, 121, and the text (*ambig.* 10) to which they refer.

[92] Plato, *Ti.* 37D5. For a concise account of Neoplatonic ideas on time and eternity, see Dodds 1963, 227–30.

human life, a millennium, the present age, the age to come being 'that age without end after the resurrection' (*Expos.* 15. 8–9). He mentions the notion of the seven ages of the universe, the eighth being that which is to come. But the most important use of *aion* is in distinction from time (*chronos*): the latter is measured by the course of the sun, by days and nights, whereas *aion* is a 'kind of temporal movement and extension that embraces everlasting (*aidiois*) beings; what time is for those subject to time, *aion* is for everlasting beings' (*Expos.* 15. 11–13). This was the 'time' before creation, and so God can be called *aiōnios*, but he can also be called *proaiōnios*, 'pre-eternal', for he transcends the *aion*, which he created. But *aion* is also the 'time' after this age has passed away: it is 'eschatological time', the time without end that characterizes the age to come, where there is no measuring of time by days and nights, but 'rather there is one day without evening where the sun of justice shines brightly on the just, while for sinners there is a deep interminable night' (*Expos.* 15. 33–5). But the fundamental point that John wants to make is that *aion*, or eternity, belongs to the created order, distinct from time by virtue of being beyond measure, but 'of all the ages God is the one creator, who fashioned the universe, who exists before the ages' (*Expos.* 15. 36–8). This teaching on eternity is very similar to that found in earlier Christian theologians, such as Dionysios[93] and Maximos,[94] save that Maximos tends to reserve the term *aidios* (translated above as 'everlasting') for God himself.[95]

The second chapter deals with creation itself, and asserts, largely in the words of Gregory Nazianzen,[96] though he could have quoted any one of a long list of Fathers, that God created everything, invisible and visible, including humans who unite both visible and invisible, out of nothing, and did this because he was not content to contemplate himself in lonely splendour but, out of his goodness, wanted to bring into being creatures to whom he could do good, and who could participate in his goodness. We have already seen something of the significance for John of the doctrine of creation out of nothing, a doctrine that had long been a touchstone of Christian theology.[97] Here John does no more than briefly affirm the essentials of the doctrine. The last sentence of this chapter is puzzling, however, probably because John has severely truncated his source. Gregory says (in nearly identical words in both homilies 38 and 45) that

---

[93] Dionysios the Areopagite, *d.n.* 10. 3 (Suchla, i. 216. 2–217. 4).

[94] Maximos the Confessor, *ambig.* 10. 31 (PG 91. 1164A–D).

[95] See, e.g., Maximos the Confessor, *cap. theol.* i. 5–6 (PG 90. 1085AB).

[96] Gregory Nazianzen, *or.* 38. 9. 1–6 (Moreschini), and 45. 5 (PG 36. 629AB): the two passages are nearly doublets.

[97] See May 1994.

'first he thought to make the angelic and heavenly powers, and what he thought (*ennoêma*) was a work fulfilled by the Word and accomplished by the Spirit' (language that recalls Irenaeus's account of creation). In the next chapter, John quotes this passage to support the view that the angels were created first (that is, before heaven itself: *Expos.* 17. 75–9). But here his truncated citation appears to refer to the whole created order: 'He created by thought, and what he thought came to subsist as a work through the fulfilment of the Word and the accomplishment of the Spirit' (*Expos.* 16. 6–8).

The Invisible Creation: Angels and Demons

Belief in an invisible world, mediating between the divine and the human realms, was a widely held belief in Antiquity. In Hellenistic Jewish writings, notably the Septuagint, an inhabitant of this invisible world is generally called *angelos*, angel, 'messenger'. In the classical world, the word used was *daimon*. Philo, for instance, regarded the two words as inter-changeable: 'it is the custom of Moses [i.e., the practice of Scripture] to give the name of angels to those whom other philosophers call daimons'.[98] This, however, was a bit ingenuous, for although angels in Jewish sources and daimons in classical sources could be either good or evil, already in the Septuagint there is a tendency to use *angelos* for God's messengers (who are generally good) and *daimon* (or, more accurately, the diminutive *daimonion*) for malevolent denizens of the invisible world. It is this use that is familiar from the Gospels, and that has imposed itself on those languages nurtured by the Christian tradition, so that, in English for example, 'angels' are generally good, and 'demons' invariably wicked. The reason for this is most likely the tendency of Jewish apologetic (already felt in the Septuagint) to identify the pagan gods, worshipped as idols, with malevolent invisible beings, called, following the Greek custom, *daimones* (or *daimonia*).

In the Christian centuries before John, the concepts of both angels and demons underwent considerable development. Angels were particularly associated with Christian worship, in which the Church on earth joined with the angelic hosts in their continual praise of God as holy. The different words in Scripture used of these celestial beings—seraphim, cherubim (always thus, in the Hebrew plural form), powers, authorities, principalities, thrones, archangels—are found in various rankings, and certain of them are designated roles as guardian spirits, of both nations

---

[98] Philo, *gig.* 6 (Colson and Whitaker, 448).

and individuals. In the context of the Anomoean controversy, the Cappadocian Fathers and John Chrysostom pointed to their mysterious character, although created, as a way of deepening the sense of the incomprehensibility of God: for, if God is incomprehensible to these beings, which, though created, transcend human minds immeasurably, how incomprehensible must God be to mere human minds? This argument was pressed notably by Gregory Nazianzen at the end of his second Theological Oration (*or.* 28), and at length in John Chrysostom's homilies on the incomprehensibility of God; these sermons, therefore, are valuable sources for the development of angelology at the end of the fourth century.[99] But the most important contributor to the development of patristic angelology was Dionysios the Areopagite.[100] In his *Celestial Hierarchy* he presented a vision of the angelic beings in three ranks of three: first, seraphim, cherubim, thrones; secondly, dominions, powers, authorities; third, principalities, archangels, angels. Dionysios's vision of these beings, together with their role in raising the created order to deification through purification, illumination, and union, profoundly influenced the later Christian tradition, in both the East and the West.[101]

The development of the doctrine of demons was, by contrast, strangely uneven: in certain circles there was great interest in the nature and activity of demons, in others they are scarcely mentioned (though their existence is not denied so much as taken for granted). Interest in demons was most intense in ascetic circles. It is well known that the stories of the Desert Fathers are full of the exploits of demons. Evagrios, the great theorist of Egyptian desert monasticism, classifies the demons according to their activities, relating them to the eight principal thoughts or temptations that the monk must learn to overcome—greed, fornication, avarice, grief, anger, listlessness, vainglory, and pride.[102] But elsewhere interest in demons was much more muted. For instance, Basil the Great, in his ascetic writings, had very little to say about demons. This contrast in attitude to demons is perhaps most acute in Athanasios, who has much to say about demons in his *Life of Antony*, but elsewhere hardly mentions them.

John Damascene is principally concerned with the nature of angels and demons, rather than with their activity for good or ill; neither here, in his

---

[99] See esp. Daniélou's introduction to Malingrey's edition of these sermons of Chrysostom: SC 28*bis*, esp. 40–50. See also, for the development of patristic angelology, Daniélou 1952.

[100] See Louth 1989*a*, 33–51, with the literature cited there.

[101] For a brief account of this influence, see Louth 1989*a*, 111–29.

[102] On demons, see the Guillaumonts' article 'démon' in *DS* iii. 129–212.

discussion of demons, nor later, in his discussion of human nature and its propensities, does he make use of the ascetic literature just mentioned, which is deeply concerned with both these issues. In his discussion of angels, John spells out what is entailed by the angelic nature, created but immaterial, transcending rational beings that have corporeal natures, but infinitely transcended by God. The angelic nature is an incorporeal nature created in God's own image. Here John affirms this without equivocation; elsewhere he distinguishes between the way in which angels and humans are in the image of God, though he does not go so far as Athanasios, who denies outright that angels possess the divine image.[103] In his work against the Monothelites, for instance, John twice draws a distinction between the divine image in humans and that in angels. Angels and human souls share being in the image of God by virtue of possessing life, understanding, and will, but the soul also manifests the divine image in its relationship to its body: in its 'governing the body and granting it life and movement and freely, in accordance with its own appetite or will, leading the body and its irrational appetite, desire and aggression and instinctive movement, and naturally ruling its own body as its own servant. Therefore, more than the angels is the human being said to be in the image' (*Volunt.* 16. 5–10). Later on in the same treatise, John again affirms that in virtue of being rational, intellectual, and free, angels and humans are alike in the image, but that, because the whole of creation finds its unity both in God and in human kind, the divine image is also manifest in the human role of being the 'bond of intellectual and sensible creation', 'which the Son of God was to become; for he did not become an angel, but a human being' (*Volunt.* 30. 9–11). The former distinction, according to which humans, more than angels, manifest the divine image, because they give life to the body, is found again, later in the patristic tradition, in St Gregory Palamas.[104]

Angels are said to be bodiless and immaterial, but only in comparison with humans, for in comparison with God all beings 'have a certain density and materiality, for God alone is truly immaterial and incorporeal' (*Expos.* 17. 11–14). They are capable of change, for only God is changeless. They are not immortal by nature, but by grace. They are spiritual radiances, but receive their radiance from God. They have no need of tongue or hearing, for they communicate directly by thought. They are circumscribed, John says, picking up a theme he introduced in chapter 13,

---

[103] Athanasios, *inc.* 13. 29 (Thomson).
[104] Gregory Palamas, *cap.* 38–9 (Sinkewicz, 124–6; trans. also in *Philokalia* 1979 ff., iv. 362–4).

according to which only God is beyond space; for when they are on earth, they are not in heaven. Yet, when they are on earth, they are not confined by walls and doors, but are unbounded (*aoristos*), which also implies that they are not bound by any particular form, but appear in different forms to different people. Nevertheless, only the uncreated God is by nature unbounded. Angels are holy by grace, and also prophesy by grace; they do not marry, for they are not mortal. Being intellects, they do not occupy places bodily, as they are uncircumscribable, but they are present and act intellectually; they cannot be in different places at the same time. John professes not to know whether angels are equal in essence, but they do differ in radiance and standing, and higher angelic beings illuminate lower ones.

John affirms the lapidary way in which they execute the divine will, and speaks of their being set over places and nations, and their directing our affairs and helping us (though he does not mention guardian angels). It is with difficulty that they are moved to evil, but they are not immovable. Now, however, they can no longer be moved to evil; but this state of affairs is the result of grace, and not natural. Contemplation of God is their nourishment. Though they are not affected by bodily passions, they are not dispassionate (*apathes*), for God alone is *apathes*. They dwell in heaven, where their one task is to praise God and serve the divine will. John then introduces the Dionysian ordering of the ranks of the celestial hierarchies, and discusses the passage from Gregory Nazianzen, already referred to, about the creation of the heavenly beings, arguing that angels were created first, though admitting that others maintain that angels were created after the creation of the first heaven, but before the human race. Finally, he affirms that the idea that angels can create is a suggestion of the devil.

John now turns to the demons. The devil was one of the angelic beings, created good, and entrusted with custody of the earth. By his free will, he turned from what was natural (*kata physin*) to what was unnatural (*para physin*), and rebelled against God, becoming the first to abandon good and become evil. John does not speculate as to why this happened (though others did, many holding that the devil rebelled against God out of envy (cf. Wisd. 2: 24) of the splendour of God's last creation, Adam, who had been entrusted to his care[105]), but asserts that evil has no substantial existence of its own, but is simply a privation of the good. With this first angel, a boundless multitude of other angelic beings followed him. Their power over other beings is dependent on God's permission, but once they have

---

[105] See Gregory of Nyssa, *or. catech.* 6 (Mühlenberg, 22. 18–23. 8).

that permission, they can turn themselves into whatever form they wish. John then remarks that neither angels nor demons know the future; nevertheless, they can foretell it: the angels, when God reveals it to them, and the demons, sometimes by being far-sighted, and sometimes by guesswork. The demons can attack humans through inspiring passions, but they cannot force humans to sin.

The distinction between angels (or demons) and human beings that leads John to argue that humans are more 'in the image of God' than angels (because human beings have bodies) has other consequences. Angels, he says, cannot repent, 'because they are bodiless; for human kind has the chance of repentance because of the weakness of the body' (*Expos.* 17. 20–1). As we have already seen, it is difficult to move angels to evil, but they are not immovable, 'though now they are immovable, though not by nature, but by grace and their assiduous attention to the good' (*Expos.* 17. 58–9). Finally, John asserts, 'it is necessary to know that what death is to humans, the Fall was to angels; after the Fall repentance is not open to them, just as it is not open to humans after death' (*Expos.* 18. 35–7).[106] Of these three assertions, the first and last are from Nemesios of Emesa, who argues that human beings have two unique prerogatives: only human beings can gain forgiveness through repentance, and only the human body, though mortal, can attain immortality, the soul's privilege being for the body's sake, and the body's privilege being for the soul's sake. Angels and demons cannot repent, if they sin, for being purely spiritual beings they have no reason for turning from the good, and therefore no excuse if they do. Human beings are not simply rational spiritual beings; they are also living beings, subject to distraction by their needs and passions. For this reason, either angels are (immediately) confirmed in the good or they fall, whereas human beings have a whole lifetime to make their fundamental choice either for or against God: thus the fall is to angels what death is to human beings.[107] The second assertion is drawn from Gregory Nazianzen, though John goes further than Gregory (influenced, doubtless, by his reading of Nemesios) in saying that angels are now immovable: Gregory says he would like to affirm that, but can go no further than saying that they are difficult to move.[108]

John's presentation of what is essentially Nemesios's teaching was destined to be very influential. The problems with which it is grappling

---

[106] Cf. also *Expos.* 44. 52–6.

[107] Nemesios, *nat. hom.* 1 (Morani, 9. 22–10. 21).

[108] Gregory Nazianzen, *or.* 38. 9. 10–18 (Moreschini) = *or.* 45. 5 (PG 36. 629B).

can only be divined, but would seem to be bound up with the legacy of Origenism. Origen, as is well known, held that all intellects, or rational beings (*logikoi*), were created equal, contemplating God through the Logos. These beings experienced satiety (*koros*) in the vision of God, their attention faltered, and they fell. As a result of their fall, the material cosmos came into being, providing bodies that arrested the fall of the rational beings (who in their descent had cooled from being intellects to being souls, an idea based on the derivation of the Greek word for soul, *psychē*, from the word, *psychesthai*, to grow cool) and, through the irksome necessities of bodily existence, furnishing them with the stimulus to struggle to regain their lost life of contemplation. Not all rational beings fell equally (indeed one *logikos*, which was to become the soul of Christ, remained in unfaltering contemplation of God): those whose attention had wavered but slightly became angelic beings, those whose distraction was moderate became human beings, while those who had rejected God more completely became demons. But this hierarchy of angels, humans, and demons was provisional: rational beings rise and fall, throughout the ages, in accordance with their diligence in seeking to regain a state of contemplation. 'Angels', 'human beings', and 'demons' are names given to *logikoi* at different levels of remove from God. But 'demons' may rise, and indeed finally regain contemplation, whereas 'angels' may fall: there is no stable hierarchy. For a host of reasons this whole scenario was thought intolerable from the fourth century on (save for continuing 'Origenists'), and Nemesios's solution is a strikingly effective alternative, preserving, as it does, the stability of the angelic hierarchy,[109] the possibility of human repentance in this life (but no later), as well as the eternal perdition of the fallen angels, or demons, though it seems to have been forgotten until John rescued it three and a half centuries later.[110]

The Visible Creation: Heaven to Paradise

John now turns to the visible creation, and gives an account of what is known of it, beginning with the celestial spheres, then treating in turn each of the four elements, fire, air, water, and earth, and ending with an account of paradise, which God created for human beings to dwell in.[111]

[109] Also affirmed by Gregory of Nyssa: *hom.* 15 *in Cant.* (Langerbeck, 446. 2–10).

[110] See also Telfer's long note in his translation of Nemesios: Telfer 1955, 245 f. n. 2. The idea that angels are moved with difficulty towards evil is found in Ps-Cyril, *Trin.* 16 (PG 77. 1153D), but it is not developed.

[111] For a general account of Greek patristic views of the visible creation on which John draws, see Wallace-Hadrill 1968.

It is evident from this summary that John is drawing not only on Scripture, but also on the science of his day. In this he is following Basil the Great's exposition of the created order in his *On the Six Days of Creation*, where he expounds Scripture in a universe of discourse provided largely by Plato's *Timaeus*, perhaps the most influential cosmological text in Antiquity and Late Antiquity. Neither John nor Basil displays any anxiety over apparent conflicts between the scriptural account and what for them was the scientific (or at least philosophical) approach of Plato. This is partly, at least, because John is very ready to accept the limitations of human knowledge of the created order; frequently, he gives alternative accounts, or simply admits his ignorance. His theological certitude, provided ultimately by Scripture, is manifest in his repeated insistence that the created order is indeed creaturely, and also in his stress on divine providence and human free will (especially in his rejection of the claims of astrology).

First, in *On the Orthodox Faith* 19, John repeats the doctrine of creation out of nothing in cosmological terms: heaven and the four elements were created *ex nihilo* by God; other things—animals, plants, and seeds—were fashioned out of these created elements. The next chapter is concerned with heaven (*ouranos*, which, as in most languages, can also mean 'sky'). This consists of a summary of the traditional astronomical wisdom of the ancient world, something John makes explicit by his reference to 'those learned in matters external [i.e. to the faith]' (*hoi tôn exô sophoi*), a variant on the already traditional distinction between 'outer wisdom' (i.e., classical science and philosophy) and 'inner wisdom' (i.e., the teaching of Scripture). Heaven, he says, is the circumference of all things visible and invisible, within which are enclosed 'the intellectual powers of the angels [presumably present in the "intellectual" way described above] and all things perceived by the senses' (*Expos.* 20. 3–4). But only God is strictly uncircumscribed, transcending everything and creating everything. When Scripture talks of 'heaven' and the 'heaven of heaven' and the 'heavens of heavens', and even the 'third heaven', John is happy to interpret this as the 'starless sphere' of Greek astronomy. Scripture also speaks of the heaven as the 'firmament' (*stereôma*: Gen. 1: 8), fashioned, according to Basil, from something 'subtle, like smoke', but fashioned, according to others, of the four elements, or of the 'fifth element'—all ideas mentioned by John. Within the circumference of heaven, some see four zones, corresponding to each of the elements, compressed by the revolution of heaven itself; others consider that there are seven zones, corresponding to each of the seven planetary bodies then known—that is, the sun, the moon, Jupiter, Mercury, Mars, Venus, and Saturn, called planets because of their 'wandering' motion (the Greek verb *planaô* means 'to wander'), which is opposite to that of the fixed stars (west to east, rather than east to west). These ideas, all perfectly acceptable to John, put the earth at the centre of the celestial sphere, with the stars and planets revolving round it. But there are those, says John, who imagine that heaven is stretched over the (flat) earth like a hemispherical dome (referring here to Severian of Gabala).[112] Whatever is the case, concludes John, it has been made and established by God in accordance with his divine will. Furthermore, everything that has been created from nothing, even heaven itself, is subject to corruption, and is only preserved by God's grace. Heaven greatly transcends the earth, and consequently its nature is unknown to us. Nevertheless, the heavens and the stars are not living beings; they are lifeless and insensible. John thus firmly rejects an idea popular in the ancient world, an idea given credence by Origen,[113] and apparently implied by some scriptural texts, which John discusses (Pss. 95: 11; 113: 3, 5–6; 18: 2).

John now leads us on a tour of the realm beneath heaven, dealing with each of the four elements, one by one. Fire is the first of the elements, created on the first day of creation, when God created light (Gen. 1: 3). Some say it is the same as light, others posit a cosmic fire above the air, which they call *aithêr*. Darkness is simply absence of light, which is why day is mentioned first in the Genesis narrative, so that night follows day. John supports this by citing Genesis 1: 5, 'and there was evening and morning one day', a formula repeated throughout the creation narrative (at Gen. 1: 8, 13, 19, 23, 31), which with its repeated placing of evening *before* morning seems to suggest the opposite. For the first three days of creation, the alternation of light and darkness was brought about by God's release and retention of light, but from the creation of the sun on the fourth day, the alternation of light and darkness has been determined by the revolution of the sun. The moon and the stars were made to illuminate the night (Gen. 1: 16–18), but that does not mean, John assures us, that the moon and the stars are not shining during the day, simply that during the day their radiance is outshone by the sun.

John now undertakes a survey of celestial phenomena, drawing on traditional astronomy (and astrology, terms not distinguished until much later). He gives the names (and astrological signs) of the seven 'planets',

---

[112] The same idea is found in Cosmas Indicopleustes' *Christian Topography*: see Wolska 1962, and her edition of Cosmas (SC 141, 159, 197 (1968–73)).

[113] See Scott 1991.

and lists them in their correct order of descending distance, according to the Ptolemaic system of the cosmos: Saturn, the most remote, Jupiter, Mars, the sun, Venus, Mercury, the moon (John, of course, gives them their Greek names: Kronos, Zeus, Ares, Helios, Aphrodite, Hermes, Selene). John then tells us that the four seasons of the year are determined by the 'turnings' (*tropai*) of the sun, or the solstices. The spring solstice (or equinox) ushers in spring, for it was then that God created the world; summer solstice ushers in summer; the autumn equinox autumn; and the winter solstice winter. These seasons are characterized by the two oppositions, warm–cold, moist–dry, spring being warm and moist, summer being warm and dry, autumn being cold and dry, winter being cold and wet. The gradual progression of the seasons, whereby only one of these factors changes at a time, is a sign of God's providence, since more dramatic changes of climate would promote ill health. John gives the dates of the turnings of the sun (spring, 21 March; summer, 24 June; autumn, 24 September; winter, 25 December), and tells us that each of the seasons promotes the growth of one of the four humours (*chymoi*), which are also characterized by the oppositions warm–cold, moist–dry, the balance of which controls the health of living beings (see *Expos.* 26. 62–70): spring promoting the growth of blood; summer, yellow bile; autumn, black bile; and winter, phlegm. John then gives the signs of the zodiac and the months during which the sun passes through each. According to the 'Greeks', everything to do with us is governed by the rising, setting, and conjunction of the stars. John rejects this, and asserts that the signs of the heavens may give indications of rain and drought, cold and heat, periods of moisture and dryness, the prevailing direction of the winds, and so forth; but of our own deeds they tell us nothing, for we have been created with free will (*autexousioi*: with control over our actions). The condition of the atmosphere, determined by celestial movements, may favour various temperaments, habits, or dispositions, but habits at least are under our control, for we can break them or cultivate them.

Various bits of astronomical information follow. Comets, John admits, may be the signs of the death of kings: they are not part of the original constitution of the heavens, but are created when needed by the divine command and dissolve again. The same is true of the star that led the Magi to Bethlehem. The moon's light is reflected from the sun. Eclipses demonstrate that the celestial bodies are subject to change and variation, and are caused by the moon blocking the light of the sun (in a solar eclipse) or the moon finding itself in the shadow of the earth cast by the sun (in a lunar eclipse). There follows a curious piece of astronomical calculation, intended to elucidate the discrepancies between the solar and lunar cycles. The moon was created perfect—that is, full. The sun, we know, was created, like the moon, on the fourth day of creation. But since the moon is full on the fifteenth day of the lunar month, 'eleven' days of the first lunar month had already 'elapsed' before the first day of creation, which is why the lunar year (of twelve lunar months adding up 354 days) is eleven days shorter than the solar year of 365 days (*Expos.* 21. 171–86). Though we know that the celestial bodies are composite and corruptible, we do not know their nature. The chapter concludes with further astrological information about the 'houses of the planets'.

The next element is air, which is both moist and warm, heavier than fire but lighter than water or earth, colourless, clear, and transparent, receptive of light, but with no light of its own. Winds are movements of air. Some manuscripts add a paragraph to this chapter giving the names of the winds.

Then follows a discussion of the element water, 'a most fair creation of God'. It is moist and cold, heavy with tendency to descend, and fluid. According to Genesis, God divided the water, placing part above the firmament and part on the earth (Gen. 1: 7). John follows Basil in suggesting that the water above the firmament was to cool it down because of the burning heat of the sun. The creation narrative also speaks of the lower waters being 'gathered together' (*mian synagogen*; Gen. 1: 9). This does not mean, John says, that the lower water was gathered together in one place, for the gatherings together of the water are called 'seas' (Gen. 1: 10). John goes on to talk of the seas, mentioning the two seas that enclose Egypt (presumably the Red Sea and the Mediterranean), and also the Indian Ocean and the Caspian Sea. There is then (as in Homer) a sea that encircles the whole earth, which John identifies with the 'river that flowed out of Paradise', which was divided into four 'heads or rivers' (Gen. 2: 10): Phison (English Bibles: Pison or Pishon), identified as the Ganges in India; Geon (Gihon), that is, the Nile; the Tigris, and the Euphrates. There are many other rivers, and also springs. The water that flows from paradise is sweet and drinkable, but after standing in the seas it can become bitter or salty. Water is drawn up by the sun and waterspouts to form clouds, a process that filters the water, which then falls as rain. God's command to the water to bring forth life (Gen. 1: 20) was, as Basil had said, a prefiguration of the renewal of human kind in baptism through water and the Holy Spirit, who had moved over the waters in the beginning (Gen. 1: 2). John concludes by saying that 'water is a more fair element, with many uses, cleansing from dirt, not only the bodily kind,

but that which attaches to souls, if there is added the grace of the Spirit'
(*Expos*. 23. 58–60). In some manuscripts there follows a more detailed
section on seas. It is perhaps not surprising that someone whose nearest
major sea was the Mediterranean should say nothing about tides; they are
mentioned, however, in Pseudo-Aristotle's *On the Cosmos*, which presents
a picture of the cosmos in many ways very similar to that of John.[114]

Finally, John comes to earth, 'dry and cold, heavy and inert, brought
into being by God from nothing on the first day' (*Expos*. 24. 3–4). How
the earth is established, whether in itself, or on air or water, or even on
nothing, we do not know, save that, like everything created, it is sustained
and held together by the power of the Creator. Originally empty, and
covered with water, there were brought into being dry places and even
mountains, covered by trees and plants, where came to dwell every kind
of animal. All this was created to satisfy human needs in one way or
another, and everything was subject to human control. It was because of
this that the devil tempted the man and woman to sin. Human sin upset
the order of creation, though there are still signs of the original harmony
even in the fallen cosmos. John then discusses the shape of the earth,
whether spherical or conical, 'lower than the heaven and much smaller,
hanging like a point at its middle' (*Expos*. 24. 57–9). It will pass away and
be changed. The earth that the meek will inherit as a blessing (cf. Matt. 5:
4), the earth that will receive the saints, will, however, be immortal. John
ends with an exclamation of wonder and thanks for the bounty of the
Creator. In some manuscripts there follows a section on the provinces
and satrapies of the earth.

John's presentation of the visible creation is a remarkable fusion of
biblical and classical learning. It is possible to assign the information
given to one or another source, but, as John presents it, it forms a single
whole. In this, John is, of course, following his predecessors: notably,
Basil in his homilies *On the Six Days of Creation*. But it is not simply a
matter of the fusion of 'inner' and 'outer' wisdom; what we find in John is
a rounded view of the created order in which astronomical/astrological,
meteorological, geographical, and medical knowledge (already hinted at,
and to be developed further in his account of the human constitution) all
belong together. It is this that is perhaps most odd from a present-day
point of view: these are now all separate specialisms that have little
relationship one to another. But with his sense of the unity of knowledge
John was simply a man of his time: the picture of the development of the
cosmos in Plato's *Timaeus* shows the same kind of unity of knowledge,

---

[114] Ps-Aristotle, *Mu*. 396a26–8. See the following note.

something even more evident in a work, *On the Cosmos*, popular in Late Antiquity when it was wrongly ascribed to Aristotle, which parallels much of John's discussion, though John seems independent of it.[115] Perhaps the last work in which this interrelationship is evident is Robert Burton's *Anatomy of Melancholy*.

John ends his treatment of the visible creation with paradise, which was created by God as the original habitat for the human race, where human beings would, as kings and rulers in a kind of kingdom, live 'a blessed and truly happy life' (*Expos.* 25. 5).

> This divine paradise, planted by God's hands in Eden, is a treasure-house of all gladness and rejoicing. For Eden means delight. Set in the East, and higher than all the earth, temperate, and radiant with a light and most pure air, decked about with plants always in bloom, full of fragrance, flooded with light, surpassing any conception of perceptible fairness and beauty, it is a truly divine region and a worthy dwelling-place for one in the image of God, in which none of the irrational beings dwelt, but only human kind, the fashioning of divine hands. (*Expos.* 25. 6–13)

This delectable place was to be the human home; it was to be a place without care or anxiety, where human beings could live a life free from passions (a life of *apatheia*), and devote themselves together with the angels, to singing God's praises and rejoicing in contemplating him. But that did not happen: humans sinned and were expelled from Paradise, and outside their intended dwelling-place they found a life of care and anxiety, prey to passions and disordered desires. Much of what John has to say about paradise takes the form of reflection on the meaning of the trees planted there: the tree of life and the tree of knowledge (some manuscripts have a further paragraph that continues these reflections). In what he says, he is, as we would expect, drawing on earlier thinkers, especially the Cappadocian Fathers, but he is not following closely anyone in particular. As he speaks of the two trees, they often seem to merge with each other, and this may relate to another feature of his reflections in this chapter: his insistence on the double nature of paradise, corresponding to the double nature of human kind, with both body and soul. For one problem facing any exegete of Genesis was whether paradise was to be taken literally or not. Some argued that the story could not be taken literally; Gregory of Nyssa, for instance, argued that because *two* trees are

---

[115] *On the Cosmos* treats of heaven, the stars, the zodiac, planets, the fiery ether, and air with winds, clouds, rain, etc. (*Mu.* 391b–392b), the earth, its plants and animals, geography, islands, seas, etc. (*Mu.* 392b–394a), different kinds of weather and their causes (394a–396a), the cosmos as a harmony of opposites (*Mu.* 396a–397b), and the divine ordering of the cosmos (*Mu.* 397b–401a).

said to be in the centre of the garden, and two trees could not occupy the same place, the story must be taken figuratively.[116] The fusion of the trees in John's account may reflect knowledge of that objection. However, even if one did take the story literally (as most of the Fathers did[117]), it could not be regarded as simply a matter-of-fact narrative: the story clearly had a meaning, which was to be sought on another level—hence John's insistence on the twofold nature of paradise. In his repeated attempts to fathom the meaning of the tree (whether of life or of knowledge), John comes back to his insight that what the tree offered was something good in itself (it could hardly be evil in itself, given John's doctrine of the parasitic nature of evil), but something that Adam was not yet ready for: so Adam falls by overreaching himself, so to speak. Three times he comes back to this insight in the form that what the tree offered was knowledge of one's own nature (*Expos.* 25. 17 ff., 55 ff., 68 ff.): knowledge that is 'too wonderful' for the newly made Adam, either because it reveals his bodily side, with its propensity for bodily pleasure (*Expos.* 25. 58–62), or because it might turn Adam's head to know how wonderfully he is made (*Expos.* 25. 70–1). Alongside this insight is his notion of the twofold nature of paradise:

Just as the human being was created at once sensible and intellectual, so his most sacred precinct had a double significance, both sensible and intellectual; for as he dwelt in his body in a most divine and fair place, as we have recounted, so in his soul he lived in a transcendent and incomparably beautiful place, having the indwelling God as his house and wearing him as a most noble garment, wrapped about with his grace, delighting in the sole most sweet fruit, that is, divine contemplation, like one of the angels, and nourished by it. This is worthily called the tree of life; for the sweetness of divine participation communicates a life never cut short by death to those who partake of it. (*Expos.* 25. 42–51).

But paradise was only a temporary dwelling-place for human kind.

It is worth reflecting on what is missing from this account of paradise: there is nothing about Eve (this might seem typical of a male monk; on the other hand, it means that Eve is not blamed for the Fall, as is often the case with the Fathers); consequently there is nothing about the relationship between Adam and Eve (though John elsewhere endorses the tradition, more or less universal in the East, that saw in Adam and Eve a virginal couple: 'in paradise the way of life was virginity' (*Expos.* 97. 7)) Neither is there anything about Adam's naming of the animals (Gen. 2: 20, though cf. *Expos.* 23–4); indeed, John states, contrary to what this

---

[116] Gregory of Nyssa, *hom. in Cant. prol.* (Langerbeck, 10. 12–11. 7).
[117] See Louth 1995.

biblical verse suggests, that there were no irrational animals in Eden (*Expos.* 25. 12). For John, paradise was a passing experience, almost immediately denied human kind by the Fall.

Human Kind

Chapter 26 of *On the Orthodox Faith* is a moving epitome of the patristic doctrine on human kind, drawing especially on Gregory Nazianzen and Nemesios of Emesa.[118] The central theme is that the human person is a being that mediates between the extremes of creation, uniting the invisible and spiritual to the visible and material: he is a being on the frontier, as it were, linking what is separate. John begins by drawing a contrast between the intellectual being, that of the angels and the celestial orders, and material being, that of the heaven and earth and what lies between them, stating that intellectual being is 'akin' (*oikeion*) to God, whereas material being is far beneath him. He goes on to quote Gregory Nazianzen to the effect that it was necessary (if there were to be a coherent cosmos) that the human be created, as a 'mixture of both' and as 'a kind of bond between visible and invisible nature' (*Expos.* 26. 9, 11–12). So the human being was made, by the very hands of God, from visible and invisible nature, his body from the earth, his rational and intellectual soul by God's own inbreathing and in his image and likeness: that which is 'in the image' (*kat' eikona*) indicating his free intellectual nature (*noeron, autexousion*), and that which is 'in the likeness' indicating assimilation to God by virtue as far as is possible. Body and soul were created together, not one after the other 'in accordance with Origen's ravings' (*Expos.* 26. 23). John sums up this view of human kind with a passage drawn almost entirely from Gregory Nazianzen:[119]

God therefore made human kind free of evil, upright, virtuous, free from grief and anxiety, adorned with every virtue, decked in everything good, a kind of second cosmos, little in great, another angel, a worshipper of mixed parts, contemplator of the visible creation, initiate of the intelligible, king of those on earth, ruled over from above, earthly and heavenly, passing away and immortal, visible and intelligible, a mean between greatness and lowliness, the same both spirit and flesh, flesh on account of pride, spirit on account of grace, the one that he might suffer and when suffering remember and be chastened, the other that he might abide and glorify his benefactor, aspiring to greatness, a living being guided in this life and transformed in the age to come, and—the furthest reach of mystery—by his

[118] Book 2 of the *Hiera* was concerned with human nature; all that survives of the original form, however, are the preface, index, and some excerpts (PG 86. 2017–2100).
[119] Gregory Nazianzen, *or.* 38. 11. 13–24 (Moreschini) = *or.* 45. 7 (PG 36. 632AB).

inclination to God deified: deified, however, by participation in the divine radiance and not transformed into the divine being. (*Expos.* 26. 24–36).

John goes on to add that the human being was created with a sinless nature and a free will, not that he was sinless by nature (which is true only of God); but 'he had the power to remain and advance in the good by the co-operation of divine grace, just as he could change from the good towards evil through his free will, with God's permission; for virtue cannot be forced' (*Expos.* 26. 40–3).

John now turns to examine the human constitution. First, he deals with the soul, simple and incorporeal, rational and intellectual, using the body as an instrument, having an intellect not as something distinct from itself, but as its purest part, free, willing, and active, and changeable (like all creatures): all this received by the grace of the Creator. Then follows a brief reminder of the relative nature of creaturely incorporeality, a point with which we are already familiar. Already John is beginning to draw on Nemesios, who will increasingly become his guide to the intricacies of human nature and also the nature of providence, into which his discussion of human nature leads.

Bodies exist in three dimensions, they are formed of the four elements, and the bodies of living beings are formed of the four humours. The four elements and the four humours manifest themselves as pairs of the two opposites warm–cold and moist–dry, that we have already met in connection with the seasons. Human kind, John continues, has something in common with inanimate beings, shares in the life of irrational beings, and also participates in the intellectual activity of rational beings. With inanimate beings, it shares body and the blending of the four elements; with plants it shares the faculties of nourishment, growth, and propagation; with irrational beings, not only these, but appetite, sense (there are five senses, John goes on to clarify), and instinctive movement; with rational beings, the capacity to think, understand, judge, and pursue the virtues and exercise piety. For all these reasons human kind is called a 'little cosmos' (*mikros kosmos*: *Expos.* 26. 84–5).

The body can be subject to section, flux, and change (i.e., it can be divided up, emptied out, and thus need replenishment—hence hunger and thirst—and change in quality, e.g., become warmer or cooler). The soul's properties are piety and understanding, to which are often added the virtues, but these the soul properly shares with the body, through which they are exercised. The rational by nature rules the irrational, we are told, and this leads into an analysis of the powers of the soul. The fundamental division is between the rational and irrational powers, the latter being divided into those that are biddable to reason and those that are not. The former include desire (*epithymia*) and aggression (if we may thus translate *thymos*), and also instinctive motion: all these can be subjected to reason. The latter include the faculties of life: generation, nourishment, and growth. This is a much more complex account of the faculties of the soul than the tripartite view we find in Plato (with *nous* ruling desire and aggression), though it is an elaboration of it, owing something to Aristotle, though drawn immediately from Nemesios. John then goes on to analyse how the human being responds to its perceptions of the world, where it perceives some things that are good and others that are bad. These can be experienced as either present or anticipated. To anticipate good things is desire (*epithymia*), to have good things present is pleasure (*hêdonê*), to anticipate evil is fear (*phobos*), and to have evil things present brings grief or pain (*lypê*). This analysis is of Stoic origin, though drawn immediately from Nemesios. With these analyses of the human constitution and its relation to the surrounding world, John embarks on a more elaborate analysis of human psychology.

Before we go any further, it may be worth asking why John is undertaking this elaborate analysis. Here, as elsewhere, he often introduces pieces of information with the rubric 'it is necessary to know' (*chrê eidenai*). Why, and for whom, is it necessary to know? Here I think the answer is bound up with his emphasis in the chapter on paradise on the ambivalent nature of self-knowledge: necessary, but potentially disastrous for those not ready for it. For John, it is necessary to know something of the finite complexity of human nature; without this knowledge, we shall only misunderstand ourselves, mistaking what is natural for what is wrong, or vice versa, or realizing only one aspect of human nature, and thus being dangerously elated, or equally dangerously downcast. The Damascene is here close to Pascal with his insistence on our grasping both the *misère* and the *grandeur* of human kind.[120]

There are perhaps also more immediate reasons for this 'necessity to know'. In this chapter, and in many of the immediately following chapters, we are confronted by many lists. We have already noted John's penchant for lists in connection with his presentation of heresy. There, as here, lists are reassuring: they tame the potentially uncontrollable nature of reality. Both when he looked at the religious scene of his day, and when, as a monk during long hours of prayer, he looked within himself, he saw a bewildering and threatening scene. In both cases, lists gave him some assurance of being in control, or at least of *someone* being in control.

[120] See Pascal, *Pensées* §§ 151–5 (Sellier 1976, 83–5).

The analysis of human psychology that follows relies for the most part on philosophical sources (mediated by Christian thinkers, principally Nemesios), but the discussions of pleasures and anger, fear, the imagination, and memory are all topics of ascetic theology, and it is probably in that context that his definitions would have been used, as an aid to understanding the nature of human beings as they strive to overcome the propensities of fallen nature and purify themselves to draw near to God.

Human Psychology

The chapters on human psychology are drawn almost entirely, and with little alteration, from Nemesios's *On Human Nature*. Here, we are able not only to identify John's sources, but also to identify the prior use of these sources. For in his discussion of human psychology (and also providence), John adopts the selection from Nemesios already made by Maximos (notably in his tenth *Difficulty*[121]). However, although John uses the same passages from Nemesios as Maximos did, he seems to have gone directly to Nemesios, since Maximos paraphrases his borrowings from Nemesios, while John quotes him much more exactly. The psychology which John (and Maximos) adopt from Nemesios is rather more elaborate than one usually finds in the Greek Fathers. The Byzantine ascetic tradition tends to adopt the tripartite analysis of the soul, into the intellect and the aggressive and desiring parts, that we find in Plato, which was commonplace in the broadly Platonic philosophical tradition popular in Late Antiquity. This tripartite analysis lies behind Evagrios's analysis of the 'thoughts' (*logismoi*) that afflict the soul (especially in prayer) of greed, fornication, avarice, anger, grief, listlessness (*akedia*, 'accidie'), vainglory, and pride, an analysis also adopted by Maximos, though supplemented by other 'thoughts' such as those of envy and resentment. The most likely reason for Maximos's supplementation of Evagrios's almost canonical list is that, whereas Evagrios was writing for hermits, Maximos was writing for coenobitic monks (and indeed for devout laymen, too) who were likely to be afflicted by thoughts, or temptations, involving other people, like envy and resentment. Nemesios's more elaborate analysis enabled him to explore these refinements.

John begins his account of human psychology by discussing pleasures. There are two kinds of pleasure: of the soul alone, such as learning and

---

[121] See Maximos's analysis of the passionate part of the soul in *ambig.* 10. 44 (PG 91. 1196C–1197D).

contemplation, and of the soul and body in fellowship, such as food and sexual intercourse. Of the body alone apart from the soul, there are obviously none. Of the pleasures that involve the body there are three kinds: first, those that are natural and necessary, such as food and necessary clothing; secondly, those that are natural and not necessary, such as lawful sexual intercourse; and thirdly, those that are neither lawful nor necessary, such as drunkenness, lustful behaviour, etc. One who lives a life *kata theon* pursues the first kind of pleasures, gives second place to the second kind, and renounces the third. Good pleasures are not mixed with grief, nor do they lead to repentance or harm; they are moderate, do not draw us from devout works, or enslave us. John goes on to discuss grief (or pain, *lypē*), fear, and anger. The four kinds of grief are anguish or distress (*achos*), which renders one speechless; sorrow (*achthos*), which weighs one down; envy (*phthonos*), grief at another's good fortune; and mercy (*eleos*), grief at another's ill fortune. The six kinds of fear are alarm (*oknos*), fear at the approach of something; shame (*aidōs*), fear in expectation of blame (the best form of the passion of fear, John remarks); disgrace (*aischynē*), fear of something shameful done; consternation (*kataplēxis*), at the imagination of something great; panic (*ekplēxis*), at the imagination of something unexpected; and anxiety (*agonia*), fear of failure. Anger (*thymos*) is 'heating-up of blood around the heart as a result of the boiling or thickening of the bile'; it is also called bitterness (*cholē*) and revenge (*cholos*). There are three kinds of anger: rage (*orgē*); wrath (*mēnis*), which includes resentment (*mnēsikakia*); and rancour (*kotos*). Anger is said to be the bodyguard (*doryphorikon*) of reason, and the avenger of desire, since a thwarted desire, of which we rationally approve, gives rise to anger. (The rest of the chapter on anger (*Expos*. 30. 17–32) seems to continue the discussion of human nature in *Expos*. 26, where Le Quien in his edition, followed by Migne, placed it, probably correctly.[122])

There follow chapters (31–5), drawn from Nemesios, on the imagination, on sensation and the five senses, on the faculty of thinking, on memory, on inward reason and its expression in speech (*endiathetos* and *prophorikos logos*), in which John affirms the rational humanity of those dumb from birth or those who have lost their power of speech. These chapters express conventional wisdom, and include location of these faculties in various parts of the brain. Chapter 36 begins with an analysis of passion (*pathos*) and activity (*energeia*), based on Nemesios, but then moves on to analyse the way in which human beings make rational

---

[122] See PG 94. 928D–929B, and the note at the bottom of col. 928, together with Kotter's note: ii. 82.

choices, and introduces (and defines) the terminology that enabled the
Orthodox to defend and understand the doctrine that Christ had, along
with his two natures, divine and human, two wills (this is made explicit).
This analysis is drawn from various passages in Maximos the Confessor.

The discussion of passion and activity is long and elaborate. The basic
framework is Stoic, and the discussion becomes a little clearer if one
reflects that the Greek terms involved express, more directly than in
English, the idea that passion is what happens to one (the 'movement of
something caused by something else'), whereas activity derives from oneself (an 'active movement, that is, moved from oneself': *Expos.* 36.
14–15). Anger is both a passion and an activity, as it is certainly an action,
albeit caused by something that has afflicted the soul. However, not
everything that affects the soul can be called a passion, for some things are
too slight to have any effect. Passions disturb the soul. So another distinction between passion and activity is put forward: passion is a movement contrary to nature (*para physin*), whereas activity is a movement in
accordance with nature (*kata physin*) (*Expos.* 36. 19–20), which is the
definition generally found in ascetic literature, where passions are bad
because they are unnatural. This brief discussion really brings to a conclusion John's descriptive psychology, and underlines a constant factor in
his analysis—what one might call the integrity of the natural: everything
that is natural is good; what is evil is a distortion of the natural.

This affirmation, in fact, is a good starting-point for what follows in
chapter 36, the analysis of human free activity; for, behind Maximos's
understanding of human free will, both in itself and in relation to Christ,
was a similar emphasis on the integrity of the natural. There was in
Christ's human experience everything that was natural in human willing,
and nothing of what is unnatural. The analysis John presents is fundamentally that found in Maximos, worked out especially in his polemical
Christological *opuscula*.[123] First, a distinction between willing (*thelêsis*)
and wishing (*boulêsis*) is posited:[124] willing is 'natural and rational desire
(*orexis*)', whereas wishing is such willing directed towards a particular end.
Wishing concerns the end, not the means, the means (*tropos*) to that end
being something determined upon (*bouleuton*). To find this means
involves inquiry (*zêtêsis*) and consideration (*skepsis*), which lead to counsel
(*boulê*) or deliberation (*bouleusis*). Deliberation leads to judgment (*krisis*),
which issues in inclination (*gnômê*) and disposition (*diathesis*). Following

---

[123] For an analysis of Maximos's doctrine of human willing, see Gauthier 1954.
[124] Greek has a much richer vocabulary even than English—which is my excuse for the
awkwardness of the English equivalents to the Greek terms here.

inclination and disposition involves choice (*proairesis*) or selection (*epilogê*), leading to an impulse (*hormê*) to enjoy what is desired, which is called use (*chrêsis*). After use, the desire ceases. The process of human willing can be set out like this:

willing → wishing → enquiry and consideration → counsel and deliberation → judgement → inclination/disposition → choice/selection → impulse → use

John now goes on to consider how this analysis of willed action applies in the case of God, and, in particular, in the case of Christ. Although we do speak of wishing in relation to God, we cannot really speak of choice or deliberation or counsel, for all these imply ignorance on God's part: God does not need to work out or deliberate how to bring about his will. Nor is this the case with the soul of the Lord. In the case of Christ's willing, there is no deliberative will (*gnômikon thelêma*), there is just a natural simple willing (*physike haplê thelêsis*), such as is found in all human beings. John then draws in other considerations advanced by Maximos (which are presented quite abruptly, in a way that is potentially confusing). For instance, corresponding to the distinction between *hypostasis* and *ousia* or *physis* is a distinction between willing (corresponding to nature) and *gnômê* (corresponding to *hypostasis*), so that in the case of Christ there is both human and divine willing (corresponding to the two natures), but a single inclination (corresponding to the one *hypostasis*), to the one object of both Christ's divine will and his human will. This analysis is followed by a series of definitions of the various terms employed—willing, wishing, the object of will (*thelêton*), the capacity to will (*thelêtikon*), and the one willing—after which John makes a distinction between the two ways in which the word *thelêma*, the usual Greek word for will, may be used: to mean willing (*thelêsis*) or the power of willing, in which case it is called the 'natural will', or to mean the object of willing (*thelêton*), in which case it is called the 'gnomic' (or inclining)[125] will. In Christ there are two natural wills, but only one gnomic will. This distinction helps to clarify Maximos's difficult distinction between natural and gnomic will, though Maximos generally uses the term 'gnomic will' to indicate a deliberative will, which is not present in God or the incarnate Son at all.

After this brief Christological interlude (he returns to these issues later on in *On the Orthodox Faith*[126]), John returns to his dependence on Nemesios, and discusses the terms and concepts involved in understanding how free will operates in a world guided by divine providence. First is a chapter on activity (*energeia*) and its relation to the related term *dynamis*,

---

[125] *Iterum sit venia verbis!*   [126] Cf. *Expos.* 58–9.

power (or potentiality). In some senses, power and energy are almost interchangeable: the 'powers' of the soul already mentioned are *energeiai*, for activity can be defined as the 'natural power and movement of each being'. This definition underlines the fact that activity belongs to nature: crucial to the Orthodox Christology, in which two *energeiai* correspond to two natures. John then elucidates the distinction, Aristotelian in origin, between being *dynamei*, in potentiality, and *energeiâi*, in act—activity being understood as realizing a potentiality. Having presented this analysis of activity from Nemesios, John interjects that 'independent, that is rational and free, life, constitutive of our race is a first, only and true act of nature; if anyone denies this of the Lord, I do not know how they can say that he who is God became human' (*Expos.* 37. 26–9).

Then follow a series of chapters on the reality and constraints on our freedom. So far as our actions are concerned, some are voluntary, and others are not; those that are not are either constrained by force or due to ignorance. But we act in a world of events, some of which are within our power (*to eph' hēmin*: an Aristotelian term designating the area of the exercise of our free will), and others are not. The reason for free will is that freedom is, for John, a corollary of the possession of reason: both are involved in what it is to be in the image of God (as he has already explained). What is not in our power is subject to God. However, some things not in our power have their origin in what is in our power. The most striking example of this is death, which has its origin not in God but in human disobedience, though death itself is not in our power but subject to God's providence. This chapter ends with the assertion that 'our creation is due to God's creative power, our continuance to his sustaining power, and government to his providential power' (*Expos.* 42. 9–11).

Providence

The section on creation and human nature closes with chapters on providence (*Expos.* 43) and foreknowledge and predetermination (*Expos.* 44). They form an appropriate close to this section, but the more immediate reason for their occurrence after John's discussion of human psychology lies in his principal source for this section, Nemesios's *On Human Nature*, which is, as already mentioned, an apologetic work that builds up to a defence of divine providence.[127] Providence was a subject much dwelt on by Greeks in Late Antiquity and the Byzantine period. E. R. Dodds remarked that 'the topic of *pronoia* bulks almost as large in

---

[127] For Nemesios on providence, see Sharples 1983.

Neoplatonism as does that of predestination and grace in the Christian theology of the period'.[128] The truth is, rather, that Greeks, both Christian and non-Christian ('Neoplatonic' in Dodds's sense), were equally exercised about providence. In the Christian Byzantine context, this is manifest both in the frequency with which the topic of providence comes up in general theological treatises, such as Maximos's *Difficulties* and Photios's *Amphilochia*, and in a particular genre of treatises 'On predestined terms of life' (that is, on whether the precise moment of death is determined), beginning with those by the seventh-century historian Theophylact Simocatta and the eighth-century patriarch Germanos.[129] The reason for this common interest in providence is an aspect of the affinity which Christian thinkers felt for Platonism. For Plato, denial of the gods' providence was a blasphemy meriting banishment from the ideal state,[130] an affirmation of the importance of providence (not least religious) that Christians found most congenial in the context of other philosophical systems of Late Antiquity that either denied providence altogether (Epicureanism), merged it with Fate and thus robbed humans of their freedom (Stoicism), or confined it to the realm above the moon ('Aristotle', according to the Fathers[131]). But it was not just in relation to philosophical schools that Christians had to defend the doctrine of providence: the gnostics, and especially the Manichees, also rejected providence, and made the apparent unfairness of earthly existence a premiss for their rejection of divine providence in their arguments with Christianity (as we have already seen in John's *Dialogue against the Manichees*). Also, as we have seen, providence was an issue among the earliest Islamic theologians, some—the Jabriyyah—holding to such a strict doctrine of providence as to exclude the reality of human freedom.

John's brief account of providence begins by repeating the two definitions given by Nemesios: 'providence is the care God shows for existing beings' and 'providence is that purpose of God, by which every-

[128] Dodds 1963, 263.
[129] Both edited by C. Garton and L. G. Westerink, Arethusa Monographs, 6, 7 (Buffalo, NY: Department of Classics, 1978, 1979).
[130] Plato, *Lg.* 10. 899D ff.
[131] In the extant works of Aristotle (the Andronican corpus), the idea of providence being confined to the superlunary world is not found; rather, all providential activity on behalf of the highest god is precluded (see Aristotle, *Metaph.* 12. 1074B15–1075A10). The idea of superlunary providence is, however, found in *De Mundo*, ascribed to Aristotle, and it has commonly been maintained that this is the source of the Fathers' ascription of the notion to Aristotle; it is possible—indeed likely—that the idea that providence was confined to the superlunary realm was maintained by the early Aristotle, who was better known to the Fathers than to us (see Runia 1989, 19, and the works cited in n. 40).

thing that is finds its most appropriate outcome' (*Expos.* 43. 2, 3–4). Providence is a corollary of creation, by which the Creator brings about what is good for what he has created. The goodness of providence follows from the goodness and wisdom of the Creator. 'It is necessary, therefore, that those who understand these things should wonder at everything, praise everything, and accept unconditionally all the works of providence, and if some things appear to many to be unjust, it is because of the unknowability and incomprehensibility of God's providence.' John adds, however, that 'when I say all things, I mean those things that do not depend on us (*ta ouk eph' hēmin*); for that which does depend on us is not a matter for providence, but for our own free will' (*Expos.* 43. 21–5). This would provide a potentially massive exception to the remit of divine providence, and it is not clear to me that it is an exception that could be carried through without effectively denying God's providential care over human affairs. The paragraphs that follow, however, return to a closer dependence on Nemesios, and seem to qualify this stark exception.

John introduces a distinction between what happens by God's good pleasure (*kat' eudokian*) and what happens by his permission (*kata sygchorēsin*). What happens by God's good pleasure is unequivocally good; but he permits misfortunes, and even plainly evil things, to test human virtue or make it manifest, or to bring about some greater good, as in the case of the Cross. God appears to abandon people for various reasons: for the instruction of others, 'for we are naturally humbled, seeing the suffering of others' (*Expos.* 43. 37–8); for the glory of another, as with the man born blind for the glory of the Son of Man (John 9: 3). Someone may even be allowed to fall into sin for the purpose of correction: John gives the example, common in ascetic literature, of ascetic pride being corrected by falling into sexual sin. As well as such corrective abandonment, there is also the final abandonment of eternal perdition. Yet God 'principally wills all to be saved and attain to his kingdom: he did not create us for punishment, but, because he is good, to share in his goodness' (*Expos.* 43. 67–9). In his justice, however, he does wish to punish sinners.

John sums this up by asserting that there is therefore a first and a second (or primary and secondary) will in God: the first is his 'principal will and good pleasure, that is from himself', the second 'a consequent will and concession, caused by us'. This second, consequent will is two-fold: primarily, ordering things and educating towards salvation; secondarily, a forlorn abandonment to final punishment. The good things that depend on us he principally wills and approves; those which are wicked and genuinely bad he wills neither principally nor consequently: they are a concession to free will (cf. *Expos.* 43. 71–8). This seems to me a much more subtle doctrine than John's earlier exclusion from providence of what depends on us: rather, providence works through human beings for good, not overriding free will, but supporting its efforts towards the good. This recalls something the poet Rilke said to a young friend: 'one must gradually learn that what we call fate does not come upon humans from outside, but emerges from within'.[132] For all John's lack of ultimate clarity, it is clear that his doctrine of providence does not exclude human freedom, and he rejects any notion of predestination, whereby God creates some for glory and others for reprobation.

The final chapter, before John embarks on the doctrine of Christ, concerns foreknowledge (*prognôsis*) and predetermination (*proorismos*). As it develops, it becomes apparent that one of John's concerns here is how the fall of humans fits into his doctrine of God's providence. His basic principle (something 'necessary to know') is that 'while God foreknows everything, he does not predetermine everything; for he foreknows those things that depend on us (*ta eph' hêmin*), but does not predetermine them' (*Expos.* 44. 2–3). The next thing 'necessary to know', which John expounds at some length, is that virtue is natural (*kata physin*), while vice is unnatural (*para physin*): there is no ontological dualism between good and evil, for evil is a privation of good. John then goes on to give a brief account of the fall of human kind (referring back to chapter 25 on paradise, for more detail). According to John, man was originally created male, entrusted by the Creator, in whose image he was created, with the government of all earthly things, including the naming of the animals. In seeing the original, unfallen human creation as male, John adopts one of the views found among the Fathers. It is not that of Maximos (or of the Cappadocians), for whom sexual differentiation, as such, was introduced with a view to the Fall, the original human creation transcending sex altogether.[133] But, foreseeing the Fall, God created woman, to be a companion, with whom the man would have children and thus perpetuate the human race through a succession of generations, now made necessary by death. John is so laconic here that he passes over the fact that generation, of some kind, was to have taken place in paradise, quite apart from the Fall (cf. Gen. 1: 28). The account here needs to be supplemented by the

---

[132] Rilke, letter to Franz Xaver Kappus, 12 Aug. 1904, in *Briefe* (Frankfurt am Main: Insel Verlag, 1950), 96.

[133] See Gregory of Nyssa, *hom. opif.* 16 (PG 44. 181AB); Maximos, *ambig.* 41 (PG 91.

later chapter on virginity, where John depicts the virginal life intended for paradise, and, like most of the Fathers, maintains that human kind would have increased and multiplied in paradise in 'another way' than through 'married intercourse' (*Expos.* 97. 18–19). John then concludes his discussion of foreknowledge and predetermination by relating the nature of the fall of human kind in terms we are already familiar with from his chapter on paradise.

(d) The Incarnate *Oikonomia*

The longest section of *On the Orthodox Faith*, whether in terms of number of chapters (37) or pages (74 in Kotter's edition), is concerned with the Person of Christ. It was also the theological issue most disputed in John Damascene's own day, since Christians were divided mainly over matters of Christology: this was true of the divisions between the Orthodox (Dyophysites), Monophysites, Monothelites, and Nestorians, and even Manichees, as we have seen, were regarded by Christians as embracing a Christological heresy, that of docetism. It is not surprising, therefore, that virtually all John's polemical works were concerned with refuting Christological heretics: Monophysites (Jacobites, *acephali*), Monothelites, Nestorians. In this section, then, we are able to develop a much fuller account of John's theology, for we can supplement the picture presented in summary form in *On the Orthodox Faith* with the more detailed account that emerges from his polemical writings. Polemical works, however, have their own limitations: they are not so much concerned with contemplation of Christ, which Keetje Rozemond rightly regards as central to John's Christology,[134] as with preventing a distorted understanding of Christ that hinders or precludes such contemplation. John's own contemplation of Christ is better represented in his sermons and liturgical poetry, which we shall discuss in the third part of this book. Our discussion here of the chapters in *On the Orthodox Faith* and the polemical works, therefore, remains to be complemented by our later examination of his sermons and poems.

By John's time, the philosophical terminology in which the mystery of the Incarnation of the Son of God was expressed had developed a forbidding complexity. It is striking, then, that John begins the Christological section of *On the Orthodox Faith* by placing the Incarnation in the context of the biblical history of salvation, the divine *oikonomia*. Leading on from the account of the Fall at the end of chapter 44, chapter 45 begins

[134] Rozemond 1959, *passim*, but esp. 62–3, 104–5.

by describing the human fallen state: stripped of grace and deprived of the open converse (*parrhesia*) with God that they had known in paradise, humans were clothed with the 'roughness of a wretched life' (symbolized by fig-leaves), their bodies became mortal and coarse (symbolized by the garments of skin), and they were excluded from Paradise, condemned to death, and subject to corruption. But God, in his compassion, did not abandon human beings in their fallenness; on the contrary, he endeavoured in many ways to educate them and call them to conversion: by their life of groaning and trembling, by the Flood, by the confusion of tongues at Babel, 'by the care of angels, by the conflagration of cities, by prefigurative theophanies, by wars, by victories, by defeats, by signs and wonders and various miracles, by the Law, by prophets' (*Expos.* 45. 14–16). In this way John characterizes the saving history of the Old Testament, all of which was intended 'to destroy sin in its many forms . . . and to restore human kind to a state of well-being' (*Expos.* 45. 16–19). Since human sin had brought about death, 'it was necessary for the one who was to redeem human kind to be sinless and thus not subject to the death of sin, and also for human nature to be strengthened and renewed and by his example educated and taught the way of virtue, that turns away from corruption and leads to eternal life' (*Expos.* 45. 20–4). This carefully worded statement demands attentive reading: what was needed was not simply the conquering of death, but at the same time the education of human kind so as to benefit from this redemption: in this John echoes the same dual emphasis we find in Athanasios, when he says, 'for in two ways the Saviour showed his love for human kind through the Incarnation, because he both rid us of death, and renewed us'.[135] With this, John introduces the Incarnation itself: 'at last, the great ocean of his loving kindness towards human kind was manifest. For the creator and Lord himself took up the struggle on behalf of his own creation and became a teacher in deed' (*Expos.* 45. 24–7). In this God demonstrated his goodness, wisdom, justice, and power: goodness in his compassion; justice by making human nature victor over the one who had enslaved it, so saving 'like by like' (*Expos.* 45. 35: a kind of divine homeopathy we encounter again in *Expos.* 62. 10); and wisdom in finding a most fitting solution.

By the good pleasure of God the Father, the only-begotten Son and Word of God and God, who is in the bosom of the Father, consubstantial with the Father and the Holy Spirit, before eternity, without beginning, who is in the beginning, and is with God the Father, and is God, he who is in the form of God inclined the heavens and came down, that is he lowered, without lowering, his inalienable exaltedness, and

---

[135] Athanasios, *inc.* 16. 21–3 (Thomson).

descended to be among his slaves in an ineffable and incomprehensible descent (for that is what descent means), and being perfect God he became perfectly human and accomplished the newest of all new things, the only new thing under the sun. (*Expos.* 45. 36–45)

'The newest of all new things, the only new thing under the sun': thus John characterizes the radical innovation of the Incarnation. God as human became the mediator between God and human kind, and in his human life 'he became obedient to the Father and healed our disobedience by that which is ours and from us, and became an example to us of that obedience, without which there is no salvation' (*Expos.* 45. 51–3).

The next chapter returns to the history of salvation, giving an account of the Annunciation to the Holy Virgin, following this with a careful statement of the virginal conception and the Incarnation. Once the Virgin had given her consent,

the Holy Spirit came upon her . . . purified her, and gave her at once the power to receive the Godhead of the Word and to beget. Then the subsistent (*enypostatos*) Wisdom and Word of God Most High, the Son of God, consubstantial with the Father, overshadowed her and, in the manner of a divine seed, from her chaste and most pure blood compacted for himself flesh animated with a rational and intellectual soul, the first-fruits of our compound nature, not by seed, but by creation through the Holy Spirit, the form not being put together bit by bit, but perfected all at once. The Word of God himself became the *hypostasis* of the flesh. . . . So there was at once flesh, at once the flesh of God the Word, at once animate, rational and intellectual flesh, at once the animate, rational and intellectual flesh of God the Word. Therefore we do not speak of a deified human being, but of God become human; for, being by nature perfect God, the same became by nature a perfect human being, not changing his nature nor simply appearing to be incarnate, but being hypostatically united without confusion, change or division to the rationally and intellectually animated flesh assumed from the Virgin, which possesses its existence in him, neither changing his divine nature into the substance of flesh, nor changing the substance of his flesh into his divine nature, nor bringing about one composite nature out of his divine nature and the human nature he had assumed. (*Expos.* 46. 16–42)

Such passages in these two chapters bristle with technical language, which John goes on to elucidate in the chapters that follow. This language had a history, and that history we should now recount, at least in its essential outlines.

Historical Background to John's Christology

John stands at the end of centuries of controversy over the Person of Christ. Although the roots of this controversy can be traced back to the New Testament, for our purposes we may start with the first Oecumenical Synod, which took place in Nicaea in 325. Famously, that synod decreed that the Son or Word of God was to be understood as *homoousios*, consubstantial, with the Father. This led to the classic formulation of the doctrine of the Trinity, as has already been related, but it also had profound implications for how Christians understood the mystery of Christ. For the doctrine of the *homoousion* entailed that the divinity of Christ, the Son of God incarnate, was no diminished divinity, but Godhead in the full sense of the word, equal to that of God the Father. The problem of how to reconcile in one being undiminished divinity and the evident humanity of the Christ of the Gospels became acute. Earlier attempts to make sense of the ascription of both divinity and humanity to Christ by understanding Christ to be some sort of intermediate being were no longer viable. There were various ways of solving this problem, but among them there emerged two strikingly different approaches.

The first, which had by far the widest acceptance, solved the problem by affirming in unqualified terms the paradox of the mystery of Christ, fully God and fully man. Christ was to be understood as God (or, precisely, the Son of God) living a fully human life; the Christ of the Gospels was the Word of God living a human life. The paradox of the union of divinity and humanity was a paradox of divine love: in his incomprehensible love for human kind God had become one of us. The unity of Christ, based on the Word as the single subject of the Incarnation, was unconditionally affirmed. Everything that Christ did, everything that he suffered, was to be ascribed to the Word of God in human form. The nature of the union, however, was a mystery. Analogies could be offered—for instance, the union of soul and body in a human person, or of iron plunged into fire. These gave but hints of the nature of the incomprehensible union found in Christ. Attempts to work out the nature of this union quickly met with disaster. Apollinaris, a friend of Athanasios, the earliest famous advocate of this approach to the Incarnation, found that he could only make sense of the Incarnation unequivocally, and distinguish it from the obviously inadequate union between the Spirit of God and human nature that occurred in the case of a prophet, by asserting that the Word of God had taken the place of the soul, or the intellect, in Christ. This view was quickly condemned as heresy, for, as Gregory Nazianzen put it: 'the unassumed is the unhealed, it is that which is united to the Godhead that is saved'.[136] The suspicion remained, however, that this approach to the mystery of Christ could only make sense if room were made for the Word of God (so to speak) by denying that the highest part of what it was to be human was present in Christ.

The other approach, sharply different from this, began by preserving the fundamental integrity of both divinity and humanity in Christ by keeping them separate. Inspired, probably, by hermeneutical principles, this approach distinguished clearly between what Christ did as God and what he did as man by distinguishing two different *prosopa* ('persons', *personae*: characters as in the *dramatis personae* of a play) in the Gospels. This distinction made possible an assertion of the full humanity of Christ, necessary if Christ were to fulfil his redemptive role. For human kind fell by a moral failing, and could be restored only through correction of this moral failing by a human life of complete moral obedience to God, something possible only for a fully human being. The problem with this approach was clearly that, although it safeguarded Christ's full humanity, it was difficult to see how such a Christ could be regarded as genuinely one. Those who adopted this approach thought rather in terms of the divine presence in Christ making possible a life of complete moral obedience to God, but they had difficulty explaining how their view of Christ differed fundamentally from that of a particularly inspired prophet.

These two approaches, the former conventionally associated with Alexandria, the latter with Antioch (the convention is not very accurate geographically), were well developed by the beginning of the fifth century, and those who embraced them were already suspicious of each other, the Antiochenes regarding all Alexandrians as potential Apollinarians, the Alexandrians fearing that the Antiochenes either reduced the Incarnation to some kind of prophetic inspiration or failed to affirm in any coherent sense the unity of Christ. This mutual suspicion developed into full-blown controversy at the end of the 420s, when Nestorios, a priest from Antioch, was appointed patriarch of Constantinople. The controversy was heightened by the growing rivalry between the see of Constantinople and that of Alexandria, the pre-eminence of which in the eastern Mediterranean was threatened by the growing ecclesiastical importance of the new capital of the Roman Empire. Nestorios's opponent was Cyril, patriarch of Alexandria, a redoubtable theologian and consummate politician. The ostensible issue

[136] Gregory Nazianzen, *ep.* 101. 32 (Gallay).

was the Virgin Mary's title, *Theotokos* ('one who gave birth to God', or, more simply, Mother of God), which for Cyril was a touchstone of correct Christological doctrine (for, if the Incarnate One was God living a human life, then the one who had given birth to him had given birth to God), but which Nestorios could accept only with qualification. At the Synod of Ephesus, held in 431, Nestorios was deposed, and Cyril's doctrine upheld. Most of Nestorios's supporters accepted this decision, subject to a clarificatory statement, called the 'Formula of Reunion', agreed between Cyril and the patriarch of Antioch, John, in 433.[137] This formula affirmed the unity of subject in Christ and the title *Theotokos* for the Virgin Mary, but it also affirmed the integrity of the two natures in Christ, stating that the divine nature was consubstantial with the Father (as Nicaea had affirmed) and also that the human nature was 'consubstantial with us'. Those followers of Nestorios who did not accept the decisions of Ephesus eventually made their way to the Persian Empire, where they continued to flourish.

Controversy welled up again fifteen years later, when an elderly and respected archimandrite (a senior monk responsible to the patriarch for the monks in the city) called Eutyches taught that the correct teaching about Christ was that he had 'one nature after the union', and that that nature was not consubstantial with us. In this he claimed that he was simply repeating the teaching of Cyril; but to Flavian, his patriarch, he was in breach of the 'Formula of Reunion' that had kept theological peace for fifteen years. Eutyches was condemned at the home synod in Constantinople, but he appealed to Dioscoros, the patriarch of Alexandria who had succeeded Cyril in 444, and who sought to emulate his predecessor by holding a synod, which vindicated Eutyches and condemned Flavian at Ephesus in 449. Flavian was so roughly handled at the synod that he died shortly afterwards. However, before setting out for Ephesus, he had secured the support of the Roman pope, Leo, whose letter to Flavian, the so-called *Tome of Leo*, set out the pope's understanding of Christological doctrine and condemned Eutyches. (Nestorios, who heard of Leo's *Tome* in his exile at the Great Oasis, claimed that it vindicated him.[138]) Dioscoros had the support of the Emperor, Theodosius II, but Leo had the ear of his sister, Pulcheria. When Theodosius died in 450, Pulcheria effectively took over the reins of power by marrying a military officer, Marcian, who succeeded Theodosius as emperor. So, in 451, another synod was held, this time at Chalcedon, on the Asian shore

[137] For the decisions of Ephesus, see Tanner 1990, 40–69; for the 'Formula of Reunion', see ibid., 69–70.   [138] Nestorios, *Heracl.* ii. 2 (Nau, 298).

opposite Constantinople, which vindicated the deceased—indeed martyred—Flavian, condemned Eutyches, and deposed Dioscoros (the latter, strictly speaking, not for heresy, but for contumaciously refusing to appear before the synod). The synod also produced a Christological Definition, based on the 'Formula of Reunion'. The papal legates, however, insisted on the incorporation into this definition of the teaching of Leo's *Tome* (which was received at Chalcedon, along with some of Cyril's letters), so that the final version differed from the draft in stating that Christ was recognized 'in two natures' rather than 'out of two natures'. The difference of one letter ('n' instead of 'k') was fateful.[139]

For the Synod of Chalcedon was received very differently in the eastern and western parts of the Empire. In the West, it was received as Leo's synod, and the Definition read as confirming Leo's teaching. In the East, however, if it was received at all, it was received as confirming the teaching of Cyril. It is impossible to understand the attitude of the East to Chalcedon, or the later Christological controversy in the East, without appreciating the immense regard in which Cyril was held (save for a few surviving Antiochenes, such as Theodoret of Kyrrhos); he was soon known as 'the Seal of the Fathers'.[140] Many did not accept Chalcedon, for they regarded the Definition as a betrayal of Cyril: these are the people later known as 'monophysites' (a misleading label, though one established by John's time: they were not followers of Eutyche, whom they all condemned, for they held that Christ's single nature was certainly consubstantial with us, just as much as it was consubstantial with the Father). They were, in fact, Christians who insisted on sticking to the Christological language and concepts of Cyril. One of Cyril's favourite expressions for the Incarnation (which he believed, wrongly, had been used by Athanasios; in reality, it was a coinage of Apollinaris) was the formula 'one incarnate nature of God the Word' (*mia physis to Theou Logou sesarkomenē*). On the face of it, this was in stark contradiction to Chalcedon, which spoke of Christ as having two natures, united in a single *hypostasis* and *prosopon*. In fact, the contrast was more apparent than real, for the distinction between *hypostasis* and *physis* or *ousia*, which Basil and the Cappadocians had made in their Trinitarian theology, was not customary in Christological doctrine; Chalcedon was unusual in using this distinction in this context. For Cyril, at least in Christology, there was no sharp distinction between *hypostasis* and *physis*, and he explained what

---

[139] For the decisions of Chalcedon, see Tanner 1990, 77–103.

[140] First attested in the late seventh century: Anastasios of Sinai, *hod.* 7. 1. 101 (Uthemann, 107). On Cyril, see most recently Russell 2000.

he meant by the formula 'one incarnate nature of God the Word' in ways that make clear that in this context he meant by nature what the synod later meant by *hypostasis*. None the less, he valued the *mia physis* formula for its uncompromising emphasis on the unity of Christ, maintaining that the two natures in Christ could not be distinguished in reality, but only discerned by the intellect.[141] Furthermore, the distinction between *theologia* (in the strict sense of the doctrine of God as Trinity and the divine attributes) and *oikonomia* was a firmly established distinction, especially in Alexandrian theology: one would not expect the same terminology to apply in both areas. It was the blurring of this distinction that underlay Arianism,[142] and one should not underestimate the long shadow cast over Alexandrian theology by Athanasios's opposition to Arianism.

The immediate fate of Chalcedon was uncertain. The West supported it, but many in the East rejected it. Thirty years on, imperial policy sought to bury it. A statement of union, called the *Henotikon*, issued by the emperor Zeno in 482, affirmed the teaching of the first three Oecumenical Synods, but remained equivocal over Chalcedon, condemning those who taught differently from the *Henotikon*, 'either in Chalcedon or in any synod whatever'.[143] The *Henotikon* secured a certain union in the East, though at the expense of union with Rome and the West; but those who refused to accept anything less than unequivocal condemnation of Chalcedon remained in schism. As all the Eastern patriarchs accepted the *Henotikon*, those who rejected it were called (and thereafter continued to be called) *acephali* (or *akephaloi*: 'headless ones'). Their leader, the most noted theologian in the wake of Chalcedon, was Severos ('of Antioch', where he was patriarch from 512 to 518). Severos is the single most important figure from the time of the *Henotikon* to the 530s; it was the uncompromising clarity of his Christological position, together with its evident faithfulness to Cyril of Alexandria, that made the running in this period, though it was his Chalcedonian opponents who actually *did* the running, since, as Henry Chadwick has sardonically remarked: 'I do not feel sure that one can really call a "movement" a group which showed less and less inclination to move.'[144]

With the accession as emperor in 518 of Justin I, the uncle of Justinian who succeeded him in 527, the tide turned for Chalcedon, and a

---

[141] For both these points, the equivalence of the one nature of Christ to what Chalcedon called *hypostasis* and that the two united natures of Christ could be distinguished only by mental consideration, see Cyril, *ep.* 45. 7 (to Succensus) (Wickham, 76).

[142] See Alexander of Alexandria, *ep. Alex.* 4 (Opitz, 20. 5–11).

[143] For an English translation of the text of the *Henotikon* see Coleman-Norton 1966, 527.

[144] Chadwick 1987, 50.

determined attempt was made to read the Chalcedonian Definition in the light of the theology of Cyril.[145] This movement is generally known as 'Neo-Chalcedonianism', though, more recently, a preferable term 'Cyrilline Chalcedonianism' has come to be used. This interpretation of Chalcedon is based on three premisses. First, the one hypostasis of the incarnate Christ is understood to be 'one of the Trinity', the Second Person of the Trinity, the Son of God; this is not explicit in the Definition, though it is a natural interpretation of it (it was affirmed in the *Henotikon*). Secondly, Cyril's favourite formula for the Incarnation, 'one incarnate nature of God the Word', is affirmed as being acceptable, the point being made that the adjective 'incarnate' makes it clear that the divine nature has been joined to human nature in Christ (a further feature of this aspect of Cyrilline Chalcedonianism is the tendency to supplement Chalcedon's 'in two natures' by the 'out of two natures' of the original draft). Thirdly, the so-called theopaschite formula—'One of the Trinity suffered in the flesh'—is affirmed. This last formula had been proposed by a group of Scythian monks at the beginning of Justin's reign, as a way of achieving unity between those who accepted Chalcedon and those who rejected it. At the time, they made little impact, but their proposal became part of Justinian's attempt to achieve reconciliation.[146] Not all Chalcedonian theologians accepted Cyrilline Chalcedonianism; notable among those who did not was Leontios of Byzantium, whose refutations of Mono-physitism had considerable influence, not least on John Damascene. But Cyrilline Chalcedonianism became the basis on which Justinian sought to re-establish unity in the Empire. In 532, conversations were held in Constantinople between those who supported Chalcedon and those who condemned it, at which these clarifications of Chalcedon were advanced. No agreement was reached, more because of vested ecclesiastical interests than theology.[147] Cyrilline Chalcedonianism was endorsed, however, by the Fifth Oecumenical Synod, called by Justinian in 553.[148] But by this time the schism between the Orthodox and the Monophysites was established, for in 542 Jacob Baradaeus was consecrated bishop of Edessa, and he spent the rest of his life (he died in 578) clandestinely ordaining clergy who rejected Chalcedon, thus setting up a rival hierarchy of 'Monophysite' bishops (called 'Jacobites', after him, by the Orthodox).

The attempt to interpret Chalcedon in the light of Cyril, and thus, it was

[145] See Coleman-Norton 1966, 549, 550.
[146] On the Scythian monks, see Chadwick 1981, 185–90; see also Coleman-Norton 1966, 636, 645.   [147] See Brock 1980.
[148] For the decision of Constantinople II, see Tanner 1990, 107–22.

hoped, in a way that Monophysites would find acceptable, turned on
the meaning of the terms that the Chalcedonian Definition had made
canonical: nature, person, *hypostasis*, for the Monophysites were adamant
that to distinguish between nature and person was incoherent, and that to
affirm two natures therefore meant two persons. This definition was
assisted by contemporary developments in Aristotelian logic, principally
in Alexandria, though the influence of such technical philosophy was
very uneven. But there were theological issues, too, behind Monophysitism: the fear of blurring the distinction between *theologia* and
oikonomia that we have already seen, and also an anxiety that too sharp
a definition of terms would lead to an abstractness in theological terminology far removed from the immediate impact of Cyril's own language,
and incapable of expressing the real, even palpable involvement of
God himself in rescuing fallen humanity. The theopaschite formula, in
particular, was aimed at that fear.

 Theological language and sensibility were also affected in the sixth
century by the amazingly swift spread of influence of a small body of
writings ascribed to Dionysios the Areopagite. These writings drew
together themes already prominent in the Fathers: the ineffability and
incomprehensibility of God, a sense of the cosmic vastness of the
Christian Gospel, a delight in mysterious and endlessly self-qualifying
language as a way of expressing these mysteries, a conviction that we
come close to God in the liturgy, in its praises of God and its sacramental
rites, and in the inward assimilation of truth unfolded by the glittering
ranks of the celestial hierarchies and also within 'our hierarchy'. The
extraordinary combination of boldness and awe conveyed by these
writings had a profound effect on theological sensibility. Dionysios made
one of his rare ventures into the realm of theological definition with his
phrase 'a certain new theandric [divine–human] energy', referring to the
activity of the Incarnate One.[149] This phrase, misquoted (or maybe not[150])
by the Monophysites as 'a single theandric energy', became a formula that
everyone wanted to make their own. Initially the Monophysites used it to
demonstrate the validity of their position: one energy implies one nature,
a theandric one. But in the next century, Dionysios's phrase became,
along with the clarifications of Cyrilline Chalcedonianism, part of one of
the most celebrated 'ecumenical' ventures of the early Byzantine period:

[149] Dionysios the Areopagite, *ep.* 4 (Ritter, ii. 161, 9).
[150] All the Greek manuscripts of Dionysios go back to an edition by John, a sixth-century
bishop of Scythopolis, who was no friend to Monophysitism. On John see Rorem and
Lamoreaux 1998.

Monenergism, the doctrine that though Christ had, as Chalcedon affirmed, two natures and one person, yet in his activity there was a seamless unity—he had one theandric energy. This was the emperor Herakleios's bid to unite the Empire he had just rescued from the Persian invasions of the early seventh century, which had exposed in the territories that fell to Persia (Syria, Palestine, and Egypt) the dangerous divisions between Monophysite and Dyophysite (i.e., Orthodox). In 633, Monenergism healed the schism in Egypt that had lasted for nearly two centuries.[151] The protesting voice of Sophronios, soon to become patriarch of Jerusalem in 634, was not welcome. Monenergism was further refined as Monothelitism (the doctrine that there is in Christ but one will, his divine will), which became imperial policy in Herakleios's *Ekthesis* of 638.[152] Monothelitism drew forth the opposition of the greatest theologian of the day, Maximos the Confessor, who wrote ceaselessly against this heresy, and secured the support of Rome, where Monothelitism was condemned at a synod held at the Lateran in 649. Both Maximos and the pope, Martin, paid for their opposition to the imperial will with their lives. Nevertheless, within twenty years of Maximos's death (in 662), Monenergism and Monothelitism were condemned at a synod in Constantinople, the Sixth Oecumenical Synod, 680–1.[153]

Opposition to Monothelitism took Christological controversy into even deeper waters; for now, not only was it necessary to be clear about nature, person, and *hypostasis*, the notions of energy (or activity) and will needed clarifying, and with them the nature of human willing. As if that were not enough, it soon became clear that, since human willing as we know it is bound up with the consequences of the Fall, which makes a free choice of the good well nigh impossible, it would be necessary to form some concept of what unfallen experience of free will would be like, if one were not to misconstrue the moral experience of the Incarnate One (who, according to the Chalcedonian Definition, echoing Heb. 4: 15, is 'like us in all respects save sin').

Such is the historical background to the Christological controversies in which John engaged. Before turning to John, it remains to reflect on how this affected Christianity in the Near East under the early caliphs.

[151] The Pact of Union (the Nine Chapters) that the patriarch of Alexandria and Augustal prefect Cyrus of Phasi used to secure unity in Egypt in 633 is conveniently available in Hahn 1897, item 232; critical edition in *ACO*, ser. 2, ii. 2, 594–602.
[152] The *Ekthesis* is conveniently available in Hahn 1897, item 234; critical edition in *ACO*, ser. 2, i. 156–62.
[153] Decisions of Constantinople III in Tanner 1990, 124–30.

Herakleios's various Christological nostrums were of no avail; he had barely begun to see how far Monenergism could heal the wounds of centuries in the lands which he had recovered from Persia, when the recovered territories fell victim to a quite unexpected, and much more serious, foe: Arabs. The Arabian victories of the 630s and 640s brought about not only the collapse of the eastern provinces of the Byzantine Empire, but also the complete collapse of the Persian Empire, all of which was incorporated into a new Arab Empire, which altered for ever the political geography of the Near East.[154] The religious situation there under the new religion, Islam, became one in which the various forms of Christianity, and indeed other religions that could claim to be 'of the Book', were all equally tolerated. We have already seen that this may have led to a revival of Manichaeism in its original homeland, Mesopotamia. It certainly also meant that Nestorianism, from being in the sixth-century Byzantine Empire a 'traditional' heresy though not an active threat (because of the migration of most Nestorians to Persia), became in the Umayyad Empire one form of Christianity, vying not only with Dyophysite Orthodoxy, but also with Monophysitism and Monothelitism. It also meant that there was pressure for controversy about Christology to be genuine: the Orthodox were no longer attacking their opponents from a position of political power; they needed to convince their opponents by the cogency of their arguments and the genuine weight of scriptural and patristic support. All this is relevant to understanding John's own presentation of Christology.

John's Polemical Writings

The fullest account of John's Christology is to be found in his polemical treatises, which are directed against all three kinds of what he regarded as Christological heresy: Nestorianism, Monophysitism, and Monothelitism. From these works we can form a picture, not just of the arguments and terminology of Christology, but of what John thought the issues were. We shall trace first his engagement with these heretical positions, rather than following the presentation of Christology in *On the Orthodox Faith*. For, although the chapters of *On the Orthodox Faith* might appear to present a systematic account of John's Christology, in reality, what we have for the most part is simply a summary of the refutations of Christological heresy (as he occasionally makes clear: cf. *Expos.* 47. 39–40). This is hardly surprising, for, as the above summary of the historical background has made clear, Christological doctrine did not

---

[154] For stimulating reflections on these changes see Fowden 1993.

develop on its own, but as a response to a series of misunderstandings of what faith in Christ entailed. What we have called above, following Keetje Rozemond, the 'contemplation of Christ' was something that took place not at synods themselves, but rather in the prayer and worship of ordinary Christians. The synods, in their definitions, simply sought to preserve the integrity of such prayer and worship by ruling out misunderstanding. We shall look, therefore, directly at John's engagement with heresy. In the case of Monophysitism, we can explore the nature of the controversy still more deeply, for there survives a Monophysite attack on Orthodox Christology that takes issue with John himself; here we are not only reliant on John's sensitivity to the Monophysite position, but can form some idea of what it was that drove the Monophysites to reject even Cyrilline Chalcedonianism, promoted by Justinian and endorsed by later Byzantine theology.

There are six polemical treatises by John on Christological topics: *Against the Jacobites, On the Two Wills in Christ, On the Faith, against the Nestorians, Against the Nestorians, Letter on the Thrice-Holy Hymn,* and *On the Composite Nature, against the Acephali.* There are thus three directed against the Monophysites, one against the Monothelites, and two against the Nestorians. For most of these treatises there is no indication of date or occasion. *Against the Jacobites,* however, was addressed to Peter II of Damascus, who was martyred under the caliph Walid II in 743, so it must be earlier than that date. John also refers to Peter as his bishop, which may indicate that the treatise belongs to his period in Damascus, before he became a monk; but such a conclusion is by no means certain, as John may simply be referring to him as his former bishop.[155] The *Letter on the Thrice-Holy Hymn* is addressed to an abbot named Jordanes. In the course of the letter John Damascene mentions Patriarch John of Jerusalem (presumably John V) as his mentor, and also claims that he knew him better than anyone else (*Trisag.* 26. 13–15); he goes on to refer to this patriarch as a 'celebrated [sacrificial] calf', which suggests that John had suffered for his faith. If so, this letter was written after John's death in 735.[156] *Against the Jacobites* ends with a florilegium; the *Letter on the Thrice-Holy Hymn* is a reply to a florilegium; and some other treatises betray the use of florilegia. We have already seen something of the importance of florilegia for John's style of theology, and we shall see that John makes significant use of them in his opposition to iconoclasm.

---

[155] *On Right Thinking* is also addressed to Peter of Damascus.

[156] See Kotter iv. 291–2. Rozemond's suggestion (1984) that the reference is to John Moschos seems far-fetched.

John's Defence of Orthodox Christology

If we look back at the preliminary statements of Christological doctrine
that John draws out of his presentation of the saving history of the Bible,
we can now see, in the light of the account just given of the development
of Christology from Nicaea to John, that John stands firmly within the so-
called Cyrilline Chalcedonian tradition. His statements carefully affirm
the full integrity of the natures: the divine nature which the Word of God
possessed from eternity and the human nature he assumed in time for our
salvation. They also make clear the unity of the person, or *hypostasis*, of
Christ, which is explicitly affirmed to be the *hypostasis* of the Word or
Son of God. We can see here what has been called a 'Chalcedonian
logic', which is also manifest in his definition of the relevant terms in
the *Dialectica*: both Trinitarian theology and Christology are expressed
in terms of the same distinction of terms, that between *ousia* or nature
(or form), on the one hand, and person, *hypostasis*, or individual, on the
other (see *Dial.* 31, 40–4). A further feature of John's preliminary
Christological affirmations, is what Fr. Georges Florovsky called an
'asymmetrical Christology', in that the Christological affirmations do not
manifest the symmetry between divinity and humanity which the
Chalcedonian Definition seems at pains to make clear; rather, it is
asserted that the union takes place from the side of the divine Word,
which exists eternally and assumes humanity in the Incarnation.[157]

The succeeding chapters of *On the Orthodox Faith* clarify the principles
of Christological doctrine. We shall proceed, however, by looking at
John's engagement with what he regarded as Christological heresy. In
taking this approach, we shall find ourselves recapitulating in greater
detail the history of Christology since Ephesus and Chalcedon.

Monophysitism

In his work *On Heresies* John has a chapter on the Monophysites. It
begins thus: 'Egyptians, also called schematics[158] or Monophysites, who,
on the pretext of the document, the *Tome*, agreed at Chalcedon, have

---

[157] Florovsky 1987, 297. Florovsky sees asymmetry in the Chalcedonian Definition itself.
It can certainly be read in that way, but it seems to me that Chalcedon was more concerned to
stress symmetry.
[158] What this means is puzzling, and clearly puzzled ancient copyists, as the variant reading
'schismatic' is found (see Kotter, *ad loc.*). Lampe suggests 'one who believes that Christ's
humanity is only in appearance', i.e. docetist (Lampe 1961, 1359, *s.v.*); but see the following
note.

separated themselves from the Orthodox Church. They have been called Egyptians, because it was the Egyptians who began this form of thought[159] under the Emperors Marcian and Valentinian; but in every other respect they are orthodox' (*Haeres.* 83. 1–5). The 'Tome' is presumably that of Leo (Leo's *Tome* was certainly unacceptable to the Monophysites), though it could perhaps refer to the Chalcedonian Definition itself. But, from the way John puts it, he seems to be suggesting that their separation from the Church was more a matter of geography than some fundamental doctrinal disagreement.[160] This statement of John's was cited by the Greek Orthodox theologian Karmiris at a meeting held in the 1960s between the Orthodox and the Oriental Orthodox (as the 'Monophysites' should properly be called), as an appropriate starting-point for a series of discussions that reached the conclusion that there were no fundamental Christological differences between these two groups of Churches.[161] Such a conclusion seems to be borne out in John's engagement with the Monophysites, where he generally takes a quite irenic line. Of the three treatises directed against the Monophysites, the most significant is *Against the Jacobites*, the others being concerned with particular issues: the Monophysite interpretation of the *Trisagion* and the Monophysite designation of Christ as 'one composite nature'.

In *Against the Jacobites* John presents Orthodox doctrine as a middle way, or, more precisely, as 'the royal middle way' (*Jacob.* 3.4), developing an image that goes back at least to Gregory of Nyssa, who uses it in relation to Trinitarian theology.[162] The first objection from the Monophysite side that John meets is the fundamental one that there is one account (*logos*) for the holy Godhead and another for the divine economy. As mentioned earlier, this fundamental distinction between *theologia* and *oikonomia* was particularly characteristic of the Alexandrian theological tradition, and it is one that John himself embraces. This distinction is the reason advanced by the Monophysites for being prepared to use *physis* to refer to the one Godhead (following the example of Athanasios),[163] thus assimilating *physis* to *ousia* in the realm of *theologia*, but remaining unwilling to make a similar assimilation in the realm of *oikonomia*, unlike the defenders of Chalcedon who had come to identify the distinction

[159] Greek *schēma*: perhaps 'schematic' is derived from this. See previous note.
[160] For a rather different interpretation of John's treatment of the Monophysites in *On Heresies*, see Larchet 2000, 66–9. It seems to me, however, that the tenor of John's overall attitude to the Monophysites bears out my interpretation, as given above.
[161] J. N. Karmiris, in Gregorios *et al.* 1981, 30–1.
[162] Gregory of Nyssa, *or. catech.* 3 (Mühlenberg, 14. 1).
[163] See, e.g., Athanasios, *Ar.* 3. 4. 7 (Bright, 157).

made by St Basil in the realm of *theologia* between *hypostasis* and *ousia* with the distinction the Fathers of Chalcedon had made in Christology (that is, in the realm of *oikonomia*) between *hypostasis* and *physis*.

This rejection of 'Chalcedonian logic', as we have called it, is for John the fundamental error of the Monophysites.[164] He meets it in various ways. Immediately in *Against the Jacobites* he subjects it to ridicule by pressing the consequences for Trinitarian theology of failing to make such a distinction (here he seems to have John Philoponos in mind, and scoffs that none of these problems would have arisen had the Monophysites not introduced 'St Aristotle' as the 'thirteenth apostle': *Jacob.* 10. 13). But he quickly gets to the heart of the Monophysite case, which turns on their denying that there is, or could be, a *physis anypostatos*, or any *ousia aprosopos*, or again any *anousios hypostasis te kai prosopon*.[165] The Monophysite argument is a kind of *reductio ad absurdum*: if nature and *hypostasis* are distinct, then there must be a 'nature without any concrete reality', 'essence without a person', or '*hypostasis* or person that is not really something' (to translate into English the phrases quoted above); but because *anypostatos* and *anousios* may both have the meaning 'unreal',[166] the implication is the even more absurd idea that to separate nature and *hypostasis* entails an unreal nature or *hypostasis*. John, following Leontios of Byzantium, agrees with the Monophysites that there can be no *ousia anypostatos* or *hypostasis anousios*, arguing instead that every *ousia* is *enypostatos*, and every *hypostasis* is *enousios*. In John's presentation of the argument, *ousia* and *physis* are treated as equivalent, an equivalence that Severos of Antioch and most Monophysites would certainly have denied. The one Monophysite, however, whom John quotes at length, John Philoponos (whom he seems to have in mind in *Against the Jacobites*, as we have just noted), himself accepted the identity of the terms *ousia* and *physis*, not just in *theologia*, but in *oikonomia* too.[167] By insisting that every *ousia* is *enypostatos*, and every *hypostasis* is *enousios*, John means that no essence exists without having a concrete form (*enypostatos*), and that there is no particular thing that does not manifest some essence (*enousios*). It is therefore possible to distinguish between nature and *hypostasis*, even though in reality it is not possible to have one without the other; for there is a distinction between the kind of thing that something is (its essence or nature, *ousia* or *physis*) and a

---

[164] The charge is repeated in *Expos.* 47. 39–40.

[165] *Jacob.* 11; he meets the same charge in *Expos.* 53.

[166] 'Being in no way at all or non-existent' is the first definition of *anypostatos* given in *Dial.* 46.

[167] See *Haeres.* 83, addit. 33 (in the long passage from Philoponos's *Diaitetes*, quoted as an appendix to his chapter on the Monophysites in *On Heresies*).

concrete or particular instance of some kind of thing (individual, 'person', or *hypostasis*).

Armed with this distinction, John proceeds to apply it in the case of the hypostatic union manifest, according to Chalcedon, in the Incarnation. Although the Incarnation is unique (a point on which the Monophysites and John agreed), it is not unparalleled. There are analogies, two of which John cites frequently: the union of soul and body in a human being and the flame of a candle. In the case of the union of soul and body in a human being, neither soul nor body on its own is the human *hypostasis*, for neither on its own is a human being; it is only as the soul informs the body, and the body is animated by the soul, that we have a human being—each achieves human reality (is *enypostatos*) in conjunction with the other. In the case of the flame of a candle, the candle and its wick are concrete things, they are *hypostaseis*, while the flame exists only in relation to the wick: it is real (*enypostatos*), but depends on the wick for its reality. Both these analogies are imperfect. The soul–body analogy suffers because soul and body come together to make another nature, a human nature, a compound nature, whereas in the case of Christ, divinity and humanity do not come together to make another nature, for Christ is perfectly human and perfectly divine.[168] The flame in the wick analogy suffers from being material: though the flame is dependent on the wick for its reality, it is distinct from the wick; whereas in the case of Christ, there is a perfect coinherence (*perichoresis*) of natures.

John's Christology, and the nature of his response to Monophysitism has, however, long been the subject of misunderstanding, a misunderstanding created by Friedrich Loofs (following on from the presentation of Christology by certain Protestant scholastic theologians), and popularized in the English-speaking world by Maurice Relton.[169] This misunderstanding is the doctrine of *enhypostasia*,[170] the notion that the human nature of Christ is 'anhypostatic', and finds its *hypostasis* in that of the assuming Word, so that the Word, in becoming incarnate, accomplishes an ontological process known as 'enhypostatization'. The error underlying this is very simple, and also typical of the etymologizing style of theology of the first half of the twentieth century, according to which words, and their supposed etymologies, had a kind of life of their own. But in fact, as Brian Daley has argued, the adjective *enypostatos* is not

---

[168] See the argument in *Jacob.* 24, and cf. *Expos.* 51.

[169] See Loofs 1887 and Relton 1934.

[170] I include the 'h', because *enhypostasia* is not, in fact, a transliteration of any Greek word found in the Fathers.

formed from the preposition *en* plus an adjective formed from *hypostasis* (suggesting the idea of being inward to a *hypostasis*); it is rather the simple adjective from *hypostasis*, the prefix *en* affirming the quality designated by the root, in contrast to the prefix *an*, which denies it (cf. *emphonos/aphonos, enylos/anylos, entimos/atimos*): *enypostatos*, therefore, means 'real', and *anypostatos* 'unreal', or sometimes, more precisely, possessing (or not) concrete reality.[171] There is no mysterious process of 'enhypostatization'.

There is a good deal more in *Against the Jacobites* than John's defence of Chalcedonian logic against the Monophysite insistence on the identity of *physis* and *hypostasis*, but this defence is the heart of the matter. It is striking, however, that John seems to regard the Monophysite assertion here as *potentially* heretical, rather than actually so. At several points, he appeals to the Jacobites as sharing a common faith, rather than as heretics who undermine the faith. 'It is confessed by all the holy Fathers that the union has come to be from divinity and humanity, and that there is one Christ, perfect in divinity and the same perfect and lacking nothing in humanity'—and adds, significantly: 'Tell us: do these things also appear thus to you? You are making a common confession with us, so it seems to me' (*Jacob*. 14. 1–4).

Much of John's argument is not that the Monophysites are wrong, and the Orthodox right, but that the words they use mean the same thing. He argues that to use the genuinely Cyrilline phrase 'out of two natures' implies the Chalcedonian form 'in two natures', for they could not become something other than divinity and humanity (*Jacob*. 14. 15–28). Like the Monophysites, he regards the nature of the union in Christ as ineffable, so he does not seek to explain it, but rather points out that union cannot mean union in every respect, so it must be possible to make distinctions, and distinction does not itself entail division (*Jacob*. 23). He does, indeed, reject the Monophysite formula of 'one composite nature', as we have seen, arguing that this applies in the case of a human being who is one composite nature, composed of body and soul, since the human being is neither soul nor body, but a composition, whereas Christ is wholly God and wholly human, not something else (*Jacob*. 24). He deals with another Monophysite argument, this time one in which the

---

[171] Brian Daley argued this in a paper presented to the Eighth International Conference on Patristic Studies in Oxford, 1979 (not 1983, as Grillmeier states (1995, 187 n. 14)), 'The Christology of Leontius of Byzantium: Personalism or Dialectics', which has never been published (but which Daley has kindly let me see in typescript). Daley's arguments have been accepted by Grillmeier, who expounds his position in Grillmeier 1995, 193–8. Uwe Lang's (1998) criticisms of Daley are not convincing: the different meanings of *enypostatos* he attests seem to me simply to reflect different philosophical ideas as to what constitutes reality.

Monophysites applied to Christology an argument already rehearsed in Trinitarian theology. Basil had argued against the idea that you can count the Persons of the Trinity, for this seemed to dissolve the unity of the Godhead.[172] The Monophysites similarly argued against counting the natures of Christ: against this, John argues that number does not divide or unite, it simply counts (*Jacob.* 50. 19–22).

Again, when John turns to the Christological formula most precious to the Monophysites, he affirms: 'You confess one incarnate nature of God the Word, and this is something held in common by you and us; for it is a saying of the Fathers.' But he goes on to suggest, first, that the adjective 'incarnate' is used in vain if it does not indicate the human nature joined to the divine, and then maintains that 'nature' was not used by Athanasios (John accepted the ascription of the formula to him) and Cyril in its proper sense, for nature is not normally used to indicate an individual, and to say that the nature of the Word became incarnate would be misleading, for the nature of the Word is the one divine nature, and no one thinks that the Father and the Holy Spirit became incarnate as well. John introduces here the idea of *hypostasis* as mode of existence (*tropos tēs hyparxeôs*), asserting that incarnation is 'a mode of second existence naturally appropriate to the only-begotten Son and Word, since the property (*idiotēs*) remains the same' (*Jacob.* 52. 57–8). This last enigmatic remark is clarified in *On the Orthodox Faith*, where John says that in the Incarnation the property of sonship is not changed but preserved; for in the Incarnation the Son of God became the Son of man, and the filial mode of existence is maintained (*Expos.* 77. 5–6).

In John's presentation of the Incarnation in *Against the Jacobites* there is a striking emphasis on its asymmetry, in Florovsky's sense:[173]

Incarnation is to partake in flesh and what belongs to the flesh. The real *hypostasis* of God the Word, that is, God the Word, was made flesh and assumed density and became *hypostasis* to the flesh, and first being God later became flesh or human, and is called one composite *hypostasis* of two natures, and in it the two natures of divinity and humanity are united through the incarnation and coinhere in each other. The coinherence (*perichoresis*) comes about from the divinity; for it bestows on the flesh its own glory and radiance, and does not partake of the passions of the flesh. Therefore the nature of the flesh is deified, but the nature of the Word is not incarnate; for the worse derives advantage from the better. The better is not damaged by the worse. (*Jacob.* 52. 29–41)

Such an asymmetrical Christology makes common ground with Monophysite Christology, so it is significant that John emphasizes this in

---

his engagement with Monophysitism.[174] The rest of *Against the Jacobites* introduces no fresh points: there are a series of challenges to the Monophysites, followed by a long summary of what John has demonstrated, before he closes with a brief florilegium of relevant patristic texts (*Jacob.* 89–129). Just before introducing the florilegium, John mentions the question of the thrice-holy hymn (*Jacob.* 85–7), which is the subject of a separate letter.

The *Trisagion*, or thrice-holy hymn, means in this context, not the hymn of the seraphim from Isaiah 6: 3 (in its slightly altered liturgical form), but an expansion of this that became part of the Eastern liturgy in the fifth century: 'Holy God, Holy Strong, Holy Immortal, have mercy on us.' (It is a useful convention to call the liturgical hymn of the seraphim the *Sanctus* and this thrice-holy hymn the *Trisagion*, though it not a universally observed convention, nor is there any such distinction in the Greek Fathers.) It became a bone of contention between Orthodox and Monophysite because of a misunderstanding, at least to begin with. Both the *Sanctus* and the *Trisagion* are addressed to God, and the threefold repetition of 'holy' recalls the doctrine of the Trinity. But are these hymns addressed to God the Trinity, or to God the Father, or God the Son, or even God the Holy Spirit? In the case of the *Sanctus* one can tell by looking at the Eucharistic Prayer, or Anaphora, in which it is embedded, and on the basis of that evidence it is clear that there are different traditions, all equally ancient. The predominant tradition sees the *Sanctus* as addressed to the Trinity, but other traditions regard it as addressed to the Father, and some (especially in Syria) as addressed to the Son.[175] There were similarly divergent interpretations of the *Trisagion*, which emerges in the first half of the fifth century, according to tradition (to which John refers: *Jacob.* 86. 1–6; *Expos.* 54. 37–43) revealed miraculously to a child in Constantinople, during the patriarchate of Proklos (434/7–446/7). In Syria, it was understood as addressed to God the Son, and so, to underline the fact that it was the Son of God, 'one of the Trinity', who became incarnate and suffered for us in the flesh, there was added to the *Trisagion* towards the end of the fifth century the clause 'who was crucified for us'. To those, including the Christians of Constantinople, who addressed the *Trisagion* to the Trinity, such an addition was heresy, as it ascribed suffering to the divine nature. To those, especially Syrians, many of whom were Monophysites, who addressed the *Trisagion* to the Son, rejection of

---

[174] On *perichoresis* in Christology, see Twombly 1992, 82–152; also Wolfson 1970, 418–28. For the concept of *perichoresis* in a Christological sense in Maximos, see Thunberg 1995, 21–48.

[175] See Louth 1998.

the 'theopaschite addition' seemed to reject doubt as to whether it was 'one of the Trinity' who became incarnate and suffered for us. The stakes were therefore very high, Monophysites regarding the theopaschite addition as a precious token of orthodoxy, the Orthodox of Constantinople regarding it as an insidious mark of direst heresy. In Constantinople, where there were plenty of Syrian monks, as well as native Byzantines, the disagreement provoked a riot in the reign of the emperor Anastasios, a Monophysite sympathizer who reigned 491–518. In Gibbon's words:

> The Trisagion, with and without this obnoxious addition, was chaunted in the cathedral by two adverse choirs, and, when their lungs were exhausted, they had recourse to the more solid arguments of sticks and stones: the aggressors were punished by the emperor, and defended by the patriarch; and the crown and mitre were staked on the event of this momentous quarrel.[176]

It was all very unfortunate, since the Orthodox could (at a pinch) have accepted the theopaschite addition, had they understood that the hymn was addressed to the Son, and the Monophysites would certainly have execrated it, had they thought that it was being addressed to the Trinity.

John's discussions of this hymn are uncompromising—it is striking how different his attitude is over a matter of worship, in contrast to his irenic attitude to theological formulae. He argues that the hymns (both the *Sanctus* and the *Trisagion*) must be addressed to the Trinity, because of the threefold repetition, and cites liturgical evidence (e.g., *Trisag.* 27), though broader liturgical knowledge would have revealed a more complex picture. He also argues, though everyone accepted this point, that the original form of the *Trisagion* was without the addition (and it is striking that all the early accounts of the hymn remark that no additions were ever to be made to it[177]).

John's other treatise against the Monophysites, *On the Composite Nature, against the Acephali*, adds little to what we have already discovered. John defends the Orthodox meaning of the formula 'one incarnate nature of God the Word', adducing Cyril's letter to Successus in support of his interpretation of this phrase. He dismisses the contention that to enumerate the natures of Christ is to divide them. And we find the same response to the Monophysite argument that there is no *ousia anypostatos* or *physis aprosopos*. That is true, John concedes, but it does not mean that there is no difference between *ousia* or *physis* and *hypostasis* or *prosopon*— that way lies Trinitarian heresy, either Sabellianism or tritheism—for the

---

[176] Gibbon, *History*, ch. 47 (Womersley, ii. 966).   [177] See Louth 2002.

correct conclusion from the Monophysite premiss is that *ousia* is always *enypostatos*, and *hypostasis* is always *enousios*.

> For both *hypostasis* and *enypostatos* are spoken of in a double way. For *hypostasis* is both manifest in simple existence, in so far as what is indicated does not indicate being simply but also the accident, but is also manifest in the individual or the person, which in relation to itself is called an *hypostasis*, such as Peter, Paul, this horse, and such-like. *Enypostatos* both indicates being when it is beheld in a particular thing (*hypostasis*) and is self-existent, and also each of these things that come together in the composition of a single *hypostasis*, as in the case of soul and body. The divinity and the humanity of Christ are *enypostatos*; for each possesses the one common composite *hypostasis*, the divinity from before the ages and eternally, and the animate and intellectual flesh, assumed by it at the end of the ages and existing in it and having it as a *hypostasis*. (*Aceph*. 6. 3–15)

But what of the Monophysite response to John? As remarked above, a letter survives in Syriac from a certain Elias to the Chalcedonian bishop of Harran's *synkellos* (or private secretary), who was called Leo. Elias had converted from Chalcedonian Orthodoxy to Monophysitism, and in this letter he defends his decision on theological grounds. We know nothing about either Elias or Leo. Van Roey, in an article introducing the letter (of which he later made a critical edition), advanced various considerations as to who they might be, excluding the possibility that Elias might be the famous patriarch of Antioch, who died in 723, on the grounds that he cites *The Fountain Head of Knowledge*, which Van Roey believed to be later than 743. In fact, Elias cites the early form of *The Fountain Head of Knowledge*, which he calls '150 chapters' (that is, the short form of the *Dialectica* plus *On the Orthodox Faith*), which may well have been in circulation as early as 723. He also knows *Against the Jacobites*, which he refers to as 'against us, written in the name of Peter, his bishop'. It is possible that both these works were written before 723, so our Elias may be the famous patriarch. In his letter, he makes three charges against the Chalcedonians: first, that the union of the natures is only a union of accidents, and that the Chalcedonians understand by *hypostasis* nothing more than a bundle of characteristics (or accidents); secondly, that the Chalcedonians only affirm one *hypostasis* of Christ, because they admit a confusion within it; and thirdly, that, for the Chalcedonians, the two natures in Christ are not really united but separated, and are, in fact, *hypostaseis*. Two points emerge from these accusations. First, as Van Roey puts it, 'here is the whole reason for Elias' conversion: for him the norm of orthodoxy is the teaching of St Cyril of Alexandria';[178] for him, everything the Chalcedonians say

[178] Van Roey 1944, 37 n. 139.

leads away from Cyril's teaching, rather than developing it. What this means comes out especially in the first objection listed above, which might be paraphrased as an objection to the abstract terms in which Chalcedonian Christology had come to be expressed. In Elias's eyes, the Chalcedonian use of *hypostasis* means 'the characteristics rather than the thing itself they characterized'.[179] I am not sure how valid a charge this is, though it is certainly my impression that John seems closer to the sixth century, in which such abstraction is rife, than to Maximos. The real answer will be found in the rest of this chapter. But it is a charge with which many scholars would agree (as we have seen above, in relation to Trinitarian theology), and it is one that Van Roey endorsed: 'one cannot rid oneself of the idea that the dyophysite doctrine had more or less abandoned the great tradition of the Fathers, still represented by Elias, and had allowed itself to be carried away by the pure speculations of a decadent philosophy'.[180]

Monothelitism

The longest of John's Christological works, and one of the most popular, judging by the manuscript tradition, was his treatise *On the Two Wills in Christ*, directed against the Monothelites. As we saw above, Monothelitism was a refinement of Monenergism, devised by the theologians of the Byzantine capital (taking up a suggestion in Pope Honorius's reply to a letter from Patriarch Sergios informing him about Patriarch Kyros's ecumenical success in Alexandria in 633) in a further attempt to heal the long-standing schism between Monophysite and Orthodox in the East. In that regard it seems to have had little success, but there were supporters of Chalcedon in the eastern provinces who embraced it: namely, the Maronites of the Lebanon. They were unimpressed by the decision of the Oecumenical Synod held in Constantinople in 680–1 and as, by then, they were beyond the reach of the Byzantine Emperor, they continued unhindered in their adherence to Monothelitism. (At the time of the Crusades, they accepted papal authority, though it seems that many Maronites continued in their adherence to Monothelitism even as late as the fifteenth century.[181])

[179] Van Roey 1944, 30.

[180] Ibid. 51–2.

[182] On the Maronites and Monothelitism, see Suermann 1998, 159–237, and also, though less satisfactory, Atiya 1968, 75–8, 394–403 (who, probably in the interests of simplicity, assimilates Monenergism and Monothelitism). Suermann (1998, 259–67) discusses John's treatment of the Maronites in *Rect.* and *Trisag.*

John's treatise exists in two slightly different forms in the manuscript tradition. The two forms amount to a slight reordering of the early chapters and seem, so Kotter argues, to go back to a very early revision of the treatise, possibly by John himself. In this lengthy treatise John explains carefully the necessity of confessing two wills in Christ. The treatise begins, in a fashion with which we are now familiar, by presenting the Chalcedonian logic of *hypostasis* and nature, demonstrating how it operates in both Trinitarian theology and Christology. John then moves on to expound in outline his doctrine of human nature, in which, as we have noticed earlier, he develops his doctrine of the angelic state, a purely spiritual state, by way of contrast with the human state, in which the spiritual and the material are united. His account of human nature follows closely the account we have already traced in his presentation in *On the Orthodox Faith*. All the functions of human nature, whether active or passive (*energeiai* or *pathê*), are innocent; there is nothing natural that is opposed to God the Creator. However, the spiritual being is created rational and free, and, by the free inclination (*gnômê*) or choice of its will, can be good or evil.

The errors of Christological heresy arise from the confusion of these terms: either confusion between the definitions of nature and person (both Monophysites and Nestorians confuse these terms, and argue either that one person implies one nature, or that two natures imply two persons), or confusion over the natural will and the hypostatic (or personal) or 'gnomic' will, in the case of the Monothelites (*Volunt.* 20). John now goes on to clarify the nature of the will (following the same analysis as we have earlier traced in his discussion of human psychology): will (*thelêma*) is an ambiguous term; it can mean either the process of willing (*thelêsis*), or the thing or action willed (*thelêton*). The process of willing is a matter of nature; only a being with a free rational nature can will. But the act of willing a particular thing or action is hypostatic, or personal, and in the case of human willing, as we know it, it involves a process of deliberation, leading to inclination (*gnômê*). Persons will, and will in a particular way—indeed, they will particular things. But they are only able to will because they have a nature that is free. It is confusion over the nature of the will that leads to the heresy of Monothelitism. Monothelites confuse the different senses of will, and conclude that because Christ wills as a single person, it must follow that he has a single natural will. On the contrary, Christ wills both humanly and divinely; there is no opposition of wills in Christ, for nothing natural is opposed to the divine will of the Creator; the two natural wills are always united in being directed to a single goal. John supports his account by listing definitions of natural will as essentially 'rational desire', which is naturally directed towards the good, drawn from the Fathers, especially Irenaeus and Clement of Alexandria. These definitions come immediately from Maximos's Christological *opuscula*, and it has been argued that it is unlikely that any of these definitions is genuine;[182] they demonstrate, nevertheless, John's dependence on the Confessor.

Central to the Confessor's defence of the notion that in Christ there are two wills, one divine and one human, is that in Christ there is no deliberative (or 'gnomic') will, for that would make it impossible for the two wills to be united, as there could be no discursive process of deliberation in the divine will. That John concurs with this, we have already seen in our account of his human psychology. The idea that Christ did not deliberate seems very strange to us post-Enlightenment (and especially post-Kantian) westerners, since deliberating between different options is what we are accustomed to think that free will is all about. In the course of her criticism of current trends in moral philosophy in the *The Sovereignty of Good*, Iris Murdoch at one point observed that 'freedom is not strictly exercise of the will, but rather the experience of accurate vision which, when this becomes appropriate, occasions action'.[183] From this point of view, deliberation is what we fall back on when our vision is clouded or confused: it is a measure of our *lack* of freedom, not the signal exercise of freedom. That Murdoch may help us to understand the Maximian picture of Christ that John expounds is not perhaps surprising. Earlier on in the book, she maintains that 'one of the main problems of moral philosophy might be formulated thus: are there any techniques for the purification and reorientiation of an energy which is naturally selfish, in such a way that when moments of choice arrive we shall be sure of acting rightly?'[184] This is close to the approach of Byzantine ascetic theology, save that in that tradition selfishness is not strictly natural, but rather the normal experience of fallen rational beings. The bridge between ascetic and dogmatic theology is explicit; for John's discussion of Christ's willing in *On the Orthodox Faith* is part of his presentation of human psychology, which, as we have argued, serves an essentially ascetic purpose.

John moves on from his exposition of the correct use of terms to a more theological argument (though the implicit argument of the above, that God in the Incarnation respects the integrity of the natural is a theological argument, too) that Monothelitism jeopardizes human salvation in the same way as Apollinarianism did.

---

[182] Madden 1982.   [183] Murdoch 1970, 67.   [184] Ibid. 54.

If he did not assume a human will, he did not become perfectly human. If he did not assume a human will, he did not heal that which first suffered in us. For the unassumed is unhealed, as the theologian Gregory said. For what was it that fell save the will? What was it that sinned save the will? (*Volunt.* 28. 34–7)

Later on in *On the Two Wills*, John waxes eloquent about the thoroughly human experience of Christ. Citing scriptural support at every step, he argues Christ's possession of a human soul, a body, the arrangement of his bodily members, 'the mouth that bestows the Holy Spirit', teeth and throat, stomach, liver, muscles and nerves which, exercised, lead to tiredness, a foreskin that was circumcized, buttocks with which he sat on a donkey, a back that was scourged, cheeks that were slapped, and a face that was spat on. That he had the activities and passions (*energeiai* and *pathê*) of the soul is clear from his weeping over Jerusalem and at the death of Lazarus, his tasting the bitterness of gall mixed with wine, his touching the leper, his physical nourishment and growth, his hunger, his thirst, his anger, his producing sweat, saliva, saving blood, and water (much of this expressed by John in contemporary medical terms). John concludes:

For he felt and used all these, not as subject to passion (*empathôs*), but naturally, and he was nourished not in accordance with passionate pleasure, but for the replenishment of what had flowed away. For if his all-holy body did not know corruption, it naturally endured section and flux; for corruption is dissolution into that of which the body is composed. And before everything else there is life itself, which is the first activity of the living being, bestowed by the soul on the body. (*Volunt.* 36. 38–43)[185]

This eloquent account of the complete humanity of Christ is odd, perhaps, in that there is no account of the prayer of the Agony in the Garden, to which Maximos the Confessor returned again and again in his polemic against the Monothelites. Not every human faculty is present in Christ, however:

He did not have the seed-producing and generative faculty; for the distinguishing characteristics of the divine *hypostaseis* are unalterable, and it is impossible for the Father or the Spirit to become the Son. Therefore, no one became the Son of man, except the Son of God, that the distinguishing characteristic might remain unaltered. So then, an individual has intercourse with an individual of the same kind. For the only-begotten Son is one, alone from the Father alone, and alone from his mother alone, Son of God and Son of man, God and man, Jesus Christ the Son

---

[185] On the distinction between *diaphthora*, 'corruption' in this passage, and *phthora*, the corruption or decay that is the result of human frailty, see *Expos.* 72, according to which Christ's body was subject to the latter, but not to the former.

of God. For even if intercourse for the propagation of the human race is natural, it is not necessary. For it is possible for a human being to live and be human without intercourse, and many have delivered themselves from this passion. (*Volunt.* 37)

There seem to be two points underlying what John is saying here, and we have met both of them in different contexts. The first is that the Son of God became incarnate, for it involved no change in his distinguishing characteristic of sonship. The consequence of this, John argues, is that he cannot then become a father, for that would be to take on the distinguishing characteristic of the Father. But secondly, for John, as we have seen, sexual differentiation (and therefore sexual intercourse) is not natural to humanity; it is a kind of providential supplement, to provide for the state of human fallenness. John seems to be saying (as did Maximos and many of the Fathers) that God assumed unfallen humanity: he assumed what was natural to humanity, and the Fall is not natural. Elsewhere, however, even in *On the Two Natures*, John seems to suggest otherwise. For instance, the passage quoted above, in which he cites Gregory Nazianzen, continues: 'Therefore, that which had fallen, that which sinned, it was this rather that needed healing. If then you say that he did not assume a sinning nature, he did not assume a nature that had sinned and was sick. If he did not assume this, he did not assume human nature; for it was the same that had sinned' (*Volunt.* 28. 38–41). Clearly what John means here is that God assumed a humanity that was *capable* of sinning, by virtue of having a mind and a will, in contrast to what the Monothelites maintained, that the assumed humanity lacked a human will, and therefore was not capable of sinning. Whether that entails that God assumed a fallen human nature is not made clear. A similar ambivalence is found in *On the Orthodox Faith* 64, where John insists that Christ assumed 'every natural and blameless passion' (*panta physika kai adiableta pathe*).

But John's discussions of the passions elsewhere point in different directions: sometimes (e.g., *Expos.* 36) he seems to suggest that *pathe* are the lot of created, rather than fallen, beings (even angels are not *apathoi*: *Expos.* 17. 60–2), so that, by assuming natural and blameless passions, Christ is entering into the human created condition, rather than the human fallen condition; but on the other hand, *apatheia* was characteristic of human life in paradise (*Expos.* 25. 25–38), which would suggest that *pathe* are part of the human fallen lot. This assumption of natural and blameless passion is for John an entailment of his understanding of Hebrews 4: 15, that Christ was like us in every respect, save sin. In passing, it is interesting to note that this is in general how the Fathers read this verse; and it is certainly how the Chalcedonian Definition takes it. But

Hebrews 4: 15 makes a bolder claim: that Christ was *tempted* like us in every respect; if that assertion is taken seriously, it is difficult to see how Christ's humanity was wholly free from the effects of the Fall.

John goes to some length to maintain that the human wisdom retains its integrity, and even its capacity to develop, in Christ, who, in virtue of his divine nature, possesses perfect divine wisdom:

The body itself does not have its own activity, save for section and flux, which are passions, not activities; all the rest are clearly activities of the soul using a body, not of the divinity: being troubled—'now' he says, 'is my soul troubled'; sorrow and distress—'he began to be sorrowful and distressed', and 'my soul is very sorrowful, even to death'; fear of death—'Father,' he says, 'if it is possible, let this cup pass from me'; death. None of these are of the divinity—for the divine is beyond passion and eternally living and immortal—but of a living being, that is of an animate and feeling being. And from a rational and intellectual soul comes wisdom. 'He advanced in wisdom and stature.' For he did not advance in divine wisdom; for from the first moment of his conception there came about a perfect union and entire concord and there was no increase of a certain divine power, but he advanced in human wisdom. For according to the measure of his bodily stature human wisdom is manifest in him; for just as he became a perfect foetus at the moment of conception, and not gradually as the body took form and shape, as Basil the Great says in his sermon on the Nativity,[186] so also he came to be perfect in human and divine wisdom from the moment of conception, clearly as a human, for as God he did not come to be perfect in divine wisdom, since he was that eternally, but the manifestation in him of perfect human wisdom in accordance with the increase of the stature of his body was reckoned as advance. And if he had human wisdom, of necessity he had an intellect; for wisdom is the product and power of intellect. . . . And the holy fathers, to whose testimony we submit, understand being in the image as referring to the intellect. If therefore he assumed humanity fashioned in accordance with his image, that is the nature of humanity, then clearly he assumed an intellectual and rational nature. He therefore assumed a self-determining will. For just as he assumed irrational desire subject to reason, so he assumed rational desire [= will]; for he did not assume a nature without intellect or reason. For if he had assumed a nature without intellect or reason, he would not have assumed humanity, but something irrational. For human kind is an intellectual and rational nature. (*Volunt.* 38)

The two natures, divine and human, come together in a genuine union, in which they work together, as John expresses it in a paraphrase of Dionysios's fourth letter:

For he did not do divine deeds divinely—for he did not work miracles as naked

---

[186] See Basil, *hom. in s. Christi generationem* 4 (PG 31. 1465A), a homily of doubtful authenticity: see *CPG* 2913.

God but through touch and stretching out his hands—nor did he work human deeds humanly—for it was not as a mere human being that he endured the passion that saved the world—, but being God and having become human he manifested a certain new and strange theandric activity, divine but working through the human, human but assisted by the divine, and showing the signs of the divinity coexistent with it. (*Volunt.* 42. 27–33)[187]

We find here an assertion of the strange newness of the actions of the Incarnate Word, difficult to reconcile with the sharp separation between the activities of the Word and the flesh maintained by Leo in his *Tome*.[188] Indeed, John's gloss on Dionysios is very close to Severos's interpretation of the activity of the Incarnate Word, which was certainly an implicit attack on Leo's *Tome*.[189]

John's difference from Monothelitism is sharper than his difference from Monophysitism, which might seem surprising, since Monothelitism accepted Chalcedon and was intended as a compromise between Monophysitism and Chalcedonian orthodoxy. Perhaps this only goes to show the danger of compromise in ecumenical dialogue. But the reason for John's position is clear: in his eyes, the Monophysites are simply muddled, whereas the Monothelites base their heresy on the denial of a human will in Christ, which in John's eyes is tantamount to a denial of human salvation.[190]

Nestorianism

The two treatises which John wrote against Nestorianism are brief and tersely expressed. They are not really independent works: *Against the Nestorians* is a reworking of *On the Faith, against the Nestorians* as a dialogue. To judge from the manuscript tradition, *Against the Nestorians* was the more popular work. It is not clear whether John is engaged in a paper debate, or whether he has in mind real Nestorians whom he wishes to

[187] Cf. Dionysios, *ep.* 4 (Ritter, ii. 161. 8–10), and also Maximos's comment on this: *ambig.* 5 (PG 91. 1056B–1060C).

[188] Cf. Leo, *tom.* agit enim utraque forma cum alterius communione quod proprium est, verbo scilicet operante quod verbi est, et carne exequenti quod carnis est. Unum horum coruscat miraculis, aliud succumbit iniuriis (Tanner 1990, 79, col. 2, ll. 3–7).

[189] See Severos's interpretation of the Lord's walking on the water in *ep.* 1 to Sergios, in Torrance 1988, 154.

[190] John's estimate of Monothelitism is therefore in sharp contrast with much Roman Catholic scholarship, which, perhaps partly because of the encouragement given by Pope Honorius to the evolution of the doctrine, has often tended to argue that Monothelitism is a matter more of words than doctrine: see Jugie 1926–35, ii. 669; Léthel 1979, 26–7, endorsed by M.-J. Le Guillou in his introduction (ibid. 10).

convert to Orthodoxy. As mentioned above, although most Byzantine attacks on Nestorians are simply rehearsals of an old debate, and perhaps intended (as it has been suggested with works against the Manichees) as a kind of theological exercise, it is possible that John envisages real Nestorians, as the incorporation of the former Persian Empire into the Umayyad Empire would have meant that the Chalcedonian Orthodox were once again under the same political regime as the Nestorians. Nevertheless, as their name suggests, the Church of the East (as the Nestorians are properly called) made its mark further east, rather than in the former provinces of the Byzantine Empire.[191]

John's works against the Nestorians do not, however, give much impression of genuine engagement—certainly not in comparison with his works against Monophysites and Monothelites. Although he begins *On the Faith* by putting forward his conciliatory analogy of Orthodoxy as a royal middle way (*Fides* 1. 10–11), his way with the Nestorians is quite terse, presenting brief syllogistic arguments in refutation of their position. Much of his effort is spent seeking clarity on the technical terms of Christological debate, as with the Monophysites and the Monothelites. He agrees with the Nestorians in their insistence on the immutability of the divine (*Nestor.* 2), but argues that their failure to distinguish properly between *hypostasis* and nature renders their position open to all sorts of errors: only personal (hypostatic) union makes it possible to affirm the incarnation of the Word, without making the Father and the Spirit incarnate as well (*Nestor.* 21). In his presentation he defends the legitimacy of the Virgin's title *Theotokos*, as we would expect, and expounds what one might call the doctrine of the 'two births':

We must say that the Virgin bore God the Word and that the Son and Word of God was not born of a woman. For we know two births of the only-Begotten Son and Word of God, one from before the ages, immaterially and divinely, from the Father alone, according to which birth he was not born of a woman and is motherless, and the other, in the last days from a mother alone in the flesh in accordance with the divine economy and for our salvation, according to which birth he is fatherless. According to the first birth, he was not born of a woman; according to the second birth, he was born of a woman. For he does not have the beginning and principle of his divine existence from a woman, but from the Father alone, but the beginning of his incarnation and becoming human is from the Holy Spirit and the Virgin Mary. (*Fides.* 49. 1–11)

John goes on to say that such apparent contradictions are commonplace, and simply need careful attention.

[191] See Atiya 1968, 239–302, esp. 257–66.

Conclusion

The picture of Christ that we have traced so far from the polemical writings is simply a fuller picture of what we find in *On the Orthodox Faith*; there is very little else to be found there. After his initial presentation of the Incarnation in the context of the saving history recorded in the Scriptures, John's account in *On the Orthodox Faith* simply deals with a series of problems—the problems thrown up by the errors of the heretics. It remains, however, sum up the picture presented above.

One feature that runs through almost every attempt by John to expound the Orthodox doctrine of Christ is his insistence on the complementarity of Trinitarian theology and Christology. The same distinction between, on the one hand, nature, being (or essence), and form, and, on the other, person, *hypostasis*, and individual, applies equally in Trinitarian theology and the doctrine of Christ. In the Trinity, there are three Persons and one nature, in Christ there is one Person and two natures; and the one Person of Christ is 'one of the Trinity'. 'Chalcedonian logic' applies universally. In this John is simply following the development of Byzantine theology since Chalcedon, through the theologians of the sixth century, to Maximos. In John, as we have seen, Trinitarian theology and Christology constantly borrow from each other; there is a process of mutual information. There are limits to this, however. The divine Persons are not individuals; they are not separate one from another; they mutually coinhere. But the incarnate Person of the Word is, like a created *hypostasis*, separate and distinct from other human persons. The distinction between *theologia* and *oikonomia*, so precious to Byzantine theologians, is not breached by the universal application of Chalcedonian logic: uncreated being and created being are fundamentally different, even if we can describe them using the same terms. John marks this difference through the notion of *perichoresis*, coinherence, which means that the divine Persons mutually interpenetrate one another, and in this way manifest their essential unity.

Perichoresis, we noted, was a concept first used in Christology to denote the mutual interpenetration of the natures of Christ, John apparently being the first to use the notion in Trinitarian theology. The coinherence of the natures of Christ is a subject on which John dwells a good deal. The way he treats it highlights the 'asymmetrical' character of John's Christology. For instance, he says,

it must be known that, although we say that the natures of the Lord coinhere in each other, we know that this coinherence takes place from the divine nature. For this nature naturally pervades and coinheres with everything, but nothing pervades it. For it bestows its own spendours on the flesh, while remaining itself beyond passion, and does not partake of the passions of the flesh. For if the sun bestows on us its own energy but does not partake of ours, how much more must this be so with the Creator and Lord of the sun? (*Expos.* 51. 57–63)

This asymmetrical coinherence leads John to argue that the Virgin Mary is called *Theotokos* not simply because she gave birth to God in human form, but also because the humanity of Christ was deified by the union (cf. *Expos.* 56. 60–2). The same asymmetry is found in his treatment of the unction, or anointing, implicit in Christ's very name, which in Greek is, of course, simply an adjective meaning 'anointed': 'we say that Christ is the name of the *hypostasis*, not spoken of in one way, but meaning something for both of the natures. For he anointed himself, anointing as God the body with his divinity, and being anointed as human; for he is both the former and the latter. Unction (*chrisis*) is the godhead of the humanity.'[192] It is a consequence of this deification or unction that, although human nature is naturally limited in its knowledge, the soul of the Lord was 'enriched, because of the identity of *hypostasis* and the unbroken union, with knowledge of the future and other miraculous powers' (*Expos.* 65. 6–8). It is also because of this deification that the flesh of Christ is life-giving, not something natural to human nature; in this context, John is most likely thinking of the life-giving Body of Christ received in the Eucharist.

John's understanding of coinherence is remote from most modern approaches to Christology, and he has been criticized even by theologians of impeccable orthodoxy, such as Richard Swinburne.[193] On the face of it, Swinburne's charge that, in John's account, Christ's humanity is swamped by his divinity seems justified. It is true, also, that John makes little of the kenotic dimension of Christology: the idea, inspired by Philippians 2: 5–11, that in the Incarnation God 'emptied himself' (*ekenôsen*: Phil. 2: 7); Kotter's detailed analytic indices to volume ii (containing *On the Orthodox Faith*) and volume iv (containing the polemical treatises) of his edition do not list *kenôo* or its derivatives, despite the popularity of the term with theologians he respected, such as Cyril of Alexandria. However, Swinburne's account of Christ seems to involve some kind of 'divided mind' in Christ, which is scarcely more credible. It is not clear to me, either, that what to modern theologians appear to be objectionable features of John's Christology are simply due to his understanding of the hypostatic union. The Fathers generally (not just those

---

[192] *Expos.* 47. 21–5; cf. *Expos.* 79.   [193] Swinburne 1994, 209–12.

who follow Cyril) are quite reluctant to admit any limitations in Christ (and indeed the Gospels give them little encouragement to do so). It seems to me that, here as elsewhere, interpretation of the Fathers involves more than an accurate reading of what they say. Perhaps the greatest problem lies in too confident an idea of what it might mean to be God in human form (both Swinburne and even the Damascene seem fairly confident of this). But John is quite clear elsewhere that the nature of God is a profound mystery, best approached through disclaimers of any understanding. The rigorous logic of John's Christology is perhaps deceptive: as we have seen above, it is better honed to excise error than to plumb the depths of the mystery of Christ. John's Christology may be more apophatic than it appears to be on the surface.

Nowhere, perhaps, does John make clearer his understanding of the Incarnate Word's accommodation (*oikeiôsis*) to the human condition— the nearest he gets to the notion of *kenosis*—than in his brief chapter on the prayer of the Lord (*Expos.* 68). 'Prayer is an ascent of the intellect to God or a request to God for things appropriate': so John defines prayer in traditional terms.[194] But why, then, did the Lord pray, given that his intellect was united with God, so had no need to ascend? John takes as examples his prayer at the raising of Lazarus, and the prayers of the Passion: in Gethsemane and on the Cross. The Evangelist's account of the raising of Lazarus gives John his lead, for the Evangelist himself makes it clear that Jesus did not pray because he needed to, but 'on account of the people standing by' (John 11: 42). In his prayer, then, Jesus accommodated himself to the human condition: he did what we would need to do, but which he did not. This is because part of the point of the Incarnation is to teach us the way back to God (cf. *Expos.* 45. 23), to enable us to make that ascent to God which is prayer: he teaches us by his example. So, in the case of the prayer of Gethsemane, John has this to say:

When he said, 'Father, if it be possible, let this cup pass from me; but not as I will, but as you', is it not clear to everyone that he is teaching us in temptations to ask for help from God alone and to prefer the divine to our will, and that he is showing us, as he truly accommodated himself to our nature, that in truth he possessed two natural wills, corresponding to his two natures, but not opposed to each other? 'Father,' he said as consubstantial, 'if it be possible', not in ignorance—for what is impossible to God?—but teaching us to prefer the divine will to ours; for this alone is impossible, what God does not wish or allow. 'But not as I will, but as you': as God, having the same end in view as the Father, as human, he manifests the

---

[194] The first part of the definition is found in identical words in Evagrios, *or.* 36 (*Philokalia* 1782, 158; *Philokalia* 1979, i. 60).

natural will of his humanity; for this naturally seeks to avoid death. (*Expos.* 68. 19–30)

This is far more superficial than the kind of treatment of the Agony in the Garden we find in Maximos, who returns again and again to meditation on the Lord's prayer of Agony, as we have already had occasion to remark.[195] Similarly, the cry of dereliction on the Cross is the result of the Lord's accommodating himself to human estrangement from God (*Expos.* 68. 31–6).

The next chapter treats directly the notion of accommodation, and distinguishes, following Maximos,[196] between natural accommodation, which is the assumption of human nature by the Word in the Incarnation, and relative accommodation (or 'prosopic', playing a role?), in which the Incarnate Word speaks words on our behalf, which do not concern himself. Other examples of such relative accommodation are the Lord's taking on himself our curse (cf. Gal. 3: 13) and the cry of dereliction (on the Cross). Reading this, one cannot avoid making a sharp contrast between natural and relative accommodation, thereby robbing the latter of any deep significance. But perhaps we should see relative accommodation as an extension of natural accommodation, rather than something opposed to it.

John's treatment of the prayer of the Lord as accommodation to our human condition must seem inadequate: what of the stress in the Gospels of Jesus' spending whole nights in prayer, something that is particularly emphasized in St Luke's Gospel (cf. Luke 4: 42, 5: 16, 6: 12, 9: 18, 11: 1; note also 3: 21 (the Baptism), and 9: 28–9 (the Transfiguration))? This would seem to be a more intimate part of Jesus' life than the Damascene's notion of accommodation would suggest. Perhaps prayer itself should be understood as implicated in the Son's 'distinguishing characteristic' of filiality, and therefore something that is at the very heart of the Word's incarnate life as the Son of man. Such an idea, which suggests some sort of *kenosis* in the very life of the Godhead itself, is taken up later by Russian Orthodox theologians in the nineteenth and twentieth centuries, such as Philaret of Moscow and Sergii Bulgakov, but it is not something that can claim much of a precedent in the tradition of Byzantine theology as represented by John Damascene.

There is one final matter to raise: namely, the purpose of the Incarnation. To a Western theologian, that might take the more specific

[195] For translations into English of two of Maximos's meditations on the Lord's agony, see Louth 1996, 186–7 (*opusc.* 7), 194 (*opusc.* 3).

[196] Maximos, *opusc.* 19 (PG 91. 220BC).

form: what of John's doctrine of the Atonement? But the truth, it seems to me, is that John is more concerned about the person of Christ, than his work, to use the later Protestant distinction; it is the person that determines the work, rather than vice versa. His summary accounts of the purpose and achievement of the Incarnation are largely traditional:

He assumed the punishments due to the first transgression, that, having on our behalf laid aside the penalty that was our due, he might free us from condemnation. (*Volunt.* 44. 16–18)

Since through sin death had entered into the world as a wild and savage beast, causing great harm to human life, it was necessary for the one who was to redeem human kind to be sinless and thus not subject to the death of sin, and also for human nature to be strengthened and renewed and by his example educated and taught the way of virtue, that turns away from corruption and leads to eternal life. (*Expos.* 45. 19–24)

For the Incarnation of God the Word took place for this reason, that that very nature, sinning and falling and being subject to corruption, might conquer the deceiving tyrant and thus be set free from corruption, as the divine Apostle said, 'Since by man came death, by man came also the resurrection of the dead' (1 Cor. 15: 12). If the former truly, then also the latter. (*Expos.* 56. 15–19)

The compassionate God in his love for human kind, wishing to show that the one who had fallen had conquered, became human that he might restore like by like. (*Expos.* 62. 8–10)

For the Son of God became human that he might give back to humanity the state it had when he made it. For he made it in his own image intelligent and free, and in his likeness perfect in virtues, so far as it is possible for human nature. For these are the characteristics of the divine nature: freedom from care and distraction, innocence, goodness, wisdom, justice, freedom from every vice. Therefore, he established human kind in communion with himself ('for he made him for incorruption'), and through communion with himself he led him to incorruption. Since through the transgression of the commandment we obscured and obliterated the marks of the divine image and, entering into wickedness, were stripped of divine communion ('for what communion has light with darkness?'), and finding ourselves outside life we succumbed to the corruption of death, since he bestowed on us what was better and we did not keep it, he partook of what was worse, I mean our nature, that through himself he might renew in himself that which is in the image and likeness, and teach us a virtuous way of life and make this easy for us through himself, and by communion in life free us from corruption, becoming the first-fruits of our resurrection and renewing the worthless and worn-out vessel, that he might redeem us from the devil's tyranny and, calling us to knowledge of God, train us and steel us through patience and humility to overthrow the tyrant. (*Expos.* 77. 9–28)

The Incarnation restores human kind to its original destiny: to bring to full likeness the human creation according to the image, a process which brings about assimilation to God, or deification. John himself does not use the language of deification very much, although he does regard the deification of human kind as the 'ultimate mystery' (*Expos.* 26. 34–6). When he does speak of deification, it is often in relation to Christ's human nature; none the less, he sees the restored state of humanity in terms that other Fathers (not least Maximos, whom he so often follows) would describe as deification. This restoration takes place as a result of the Incarnation, in which there is a 'wonderful exchange' between God and human kind. John makes it very clear that the Incarnation opens up again to human beings a way of asceticism whereby, in answer to the divine Word's assumption of humanity, we gain the splendours of divinity. All this is expressed in metaphor that gestures towards the incomprehensible mystery of our transfiguration in Christ. In all this, however, John simply displays his affinity with the patristic tradition, the harvest of which he is reaping, for it is characteristic of the patristic tradition to focus on the person, rather than the work, of Christ, to be concerned less with the precise nature of the mysterious exchange wrought in the Incarnation than with contemplation of the Person of the Word made flesh.

(e) Concluding Chapters

The last nineteen chapters of *On the Orthodox Faith* seem, at first sight, an odd assortment: there are chapters on faith, baptism, the Cross, worship facing East, and the sacraments, relics, icons, Scripture, with two groups of chapters, one against dualism, the other against the Jews, raising questions about the sabbath, virginity, and circumcision, a final two chapters on the Antichrist and the Resurrection, with two interspersed chapters recalling the themes of the third section: one on the genealogy of Christ and the holy Mother of God (chapter 87) and the other on the different ways in which things may be asserted of Christ (chapter 91). It has already been noted that all these chapters concern matters that marked Christians out from the other religions of the Middle East: principally, distinctive religious practices. There is, perhaps, another unifying factor that, in fact, is present the whole of *On the Orthodox Faith*, and that is the idea of Christianity as a middle way, a way of mediation. We have already noted that John picks up Gregory of Nyssa's idea of Trinitarian theology as a middle way between monotheism and polytheism (*Expos.* 7. 28–32). In his presentation of Christology, John not infrequently presents Chalcedonian Orthodoxy as a 'royal middle way' between Monophysitism and Nestorianism (*Jacob.* 3. 4; *Fides* 1. 10–11). Central to his long discussion of creation is the notion of human kind as a middle being between spiritual and material reality, a microcosm in which the extremities of the cosmos are united (*Expos.* 12. 9, 26). When he comes to discuss worship facing East, he begins by making the point that since human beings are composed of visible and invisible substance, we therefore offer a 'double worship' to God, just as we are baptized in water and the Spirit, and are united with the Lord in a twofold way, by partaking of the mysteries and by the grace of the Spirit. Because human kind exists on the border between spiritual and material reality, this is reflected in human religion, the human relationship to the Creator: this is the theme that runs through these final chapters. All religious practices that distinguish Christianity from other religions exemplify this fundamental truth: Christianity is both material and spiritual, with the corollary that objections to Christianity often come from a misguided desire to see all religion in purely spiritual terms. This distinction between material and spiritual does not entail any kind of dualism, however, on the contrary, hence the chapters against dualism (chapters 92–5). Christianity holds the material and the spiritual together; it is not simply attached to the material, which is seen as the danger of Judaism, which is addressed in chapters 96–8. The Antichrist is an appropriate penultimate subject on any reckoning, but John recalls what Christians believe about the Antichrist to exclude (by not mentioning) the idea of a millennial rule, subsequent to the defeat of the Antichrist, which Christians for generations had rejected on the grounds of materialism (see, e.g., Eusebios's account of Dionysios of Alexandria's discussion with millennialists in his *Church History*[197]). The resurrection of the body is not only an appropriate final topic, but also one that affirms unconditionally the complementarity of the spiritual and the material.

Baptism

This emphasis on the twofold nature of Christianity is introduced in the first of these final chapters, that on baptism, for baptism is by water and the Spirit, and also because being baptized in Christ means both believing in him and being baptized, or, equally, faith in the Trinity and being baptized in the name of the Trinity. The complementarity of water and the Spirit has another significance, in that water indicates cleansing and

---

[197] Eusebios, *h.e.* 7. 24 (Schwartz, 684. 21–690. 8).

destruction of what is opposed to God, while the Spirit is the pledge of life. John develops a little the typology of baptism in the Old Testament, referring to Noah and the many cleansings prescribed by the Law, and pointing to the hidden meaning behind the symbols of the Law. John then produces a list (drawn largely from Gregory Nazianzen's thirty-ninth homily, for the Theophany, which commemorated the baptism of Christ[198]) of eight different types of baptism: the Flood, 'through the sea and the cloud' (Exodus and the wilderness), the cleansings of the Law, the baptism of John, Christ's (which is ours), through repentance and tears, the martyr's baptism 'through blood and bearing witness', and the final baptism, in which sin is destroyed in eternal punishment, 'which is not saving' (*Expos.* 82. 67–92). As well as water, oil (*elaion*) is used in baptism, 'to show our anointing and make us christs' (*Expos.* 82. 99–100; though the oil used for anointing is a blended (and scented) oil, different from olive oil, called *myron*); it also proclaims God's mercy (*eleon*).

Faith and the Cross

Faith, discussed in the next chapter (83), is likewise twofold: both 'coming from hearing', which is a matter of our own inclination, and 'the substance of things hoped for', which is a gift of the Spirit. The chapter on faith leads naturally on to that on the Cross, for the Cross is a pre-eminent sign of how the ways of God transcend human categories (John quotes 1 Cor. 1: 18):

Every work and miracle of Christ is most great and divine and most wonderful, but more wonderful than anything is his precious cross. For through nothing else has death been abolished, ancestral sin loosed, hell despoiled, resurrection bestowed, the power of despising things present and death itself given to us, the way back to pristine blessedness made straight, the gates of paradise opened, our nature set down at the right hand of God, and we become children of God and heirs, save through the cross of our Lord Jesus Christ. (*Expos.* 83. 21–9)

John goes on to evoke the idea of the cosmic Cross, an idea familiar to Christian since Irenaeus:[199] 'just as the four arms of the Cross have been made firm and bound closely together at the middle, so through the power of God height and depth, length and breadth, that is, all creation both visible and invisible, has been secured' (*Expos.* 83. 36–9). John then extols the sign of the cross:

[198] Gregory Nazianzen, *or.* 39. 17 (Gallay).
[199] Cf. Irenæus, *hær.* V. 17. 4 (Harvey, ii. 372).

It is a shield and weapon and trophy against the devil. It is a seal, lest the destroyer touch us, as Scripture says. It is the resurrection of the fallen, a support for those who stand, a staff for the weak, a rod for the shepherded, leading by the hand those who turn back, the perfecting of those making progress, salvation for both soul and body, a talisman against every evil, a promoter of everything good, the destruction of sin, the plant of resurrection, the tree of eternal life. (*Expos.* 83. 42–8)

Because Christ was offered as a sacrifice on it, and because it was in contact with his sacred Body and Blood, the 'precious and truly august cross' is to be venerated, and not only the Cross itself, but the 'nails, the lance, his garments, and such sacred resting places of his as the manger, the cave [of the nativity], saving Golgotha, the life-giving tomb, Sion the citadel of the churches, and such places. . . . For if the house and the bed and clothing of those we love are dear to us, how much more those of our God and Saviour, through which we have been saved' (*Expos.* 83. 51–4, 58–60). We hear the voice of a monk of Jerusalem, proud of the Holy Places among which he lives.

'We also venerate the figure (*typos*) of the Cross, and if it is made out of some other matter, we do not honour matter as such, but the figure as a symbol of Christ' (*Expos.* 84. 61–3). The principle is: 'we venerate everything that is dedicated to God, though it is to Him that we offer our worship (*sebas*)' (*Expos.* 84. 72–3). John ends the chapter with some Old Testament examples of the typology of the Cross. These examples are perhaps not simply intended for Christians, but may also be directed to the Jews, showing that veneration of the sign of the Cross is implicit in the Scriptures recognized by the Jews. One reason for thinking this is that the earliest attacks on veneration of the Cross (together with veneration of relics and icons of the saints) seem to have come from Jews in the seventh century. We shall look at this more closely in the next chapter, on the iconoclast controversy.

Prayer Facing East

The next chapter concerns worshipping towards the East. The direction adopted when praying would have been one of the clearest marks distinguishing Christian from Jew, Jew from Muslim, and Muslim from Christian in John's time: Jews turned towards Jerusalem, Muslims towards Mecca, and Christians turned to face East. As we have seen, John defends this, first, on the grounds that worship is not simply a matter of intellectual recognition, but involves the body. He then goes on to justify facing East. Christ is called the 'sun of justice' (Mal. 4: 2) and the 'East' (Zach. 3: 8, LXX): both of which suggest the appropriateness of facing

East to pray to him. Similarly, paradise is towards the East (Gen. 2: 8); so it is looking towards our 'ancient fatherland', to use Basil the Great's phrase,[200] that we pray. John gives various other justifications, drawn mostly from the Old Testament (perhaps, therefore, directed to the Jews), before concluding by asserting, again following Basil, that this is one of the 'unwritten traditions' of the Apostles.[201]

The Eucharistic Mystery

The chapter that follows on the sacraments, or mysteries (*mysteria*) places them in the context of the whole divine economy. God, because of his exceeding goodness, was not content that his goodness should not be shared. He therefore brought into being the creation: first, spiritual and heavenly beings, and then human kind, which is both spiritual and material. Part of the goodness of rational beings is to share in goodness and be united with God freely. Alas, human kind fell; but, even so, God did not desert humanity, but assumed our human nature in order to restore to us what we had lost through disobedience. He was not content, however, that only the first-fruits of our nature (that is, the humanity of Christ) should share in the benefits of the Incarnation; so he provided a second spiritual birth and spiritual food, so that fallen human beings 'born from Him might be assimilated to Him and become heirs of his incorruption and blessing and glory' (*Expos.* 86. 37–9). Both this spiritual birth and this spiritual food are twofold, meeting the needs of both soul and body. (John's argument that the sacraments are necessary in order for humans other than Christ to benefit from his saving work would seem to make it quite clear that John himself, whatever may be the case with others of the Fathers, does not believe that Christ's humanity was some sort of Platonic concrete universal, such that all humans shared, by being human, in his victory. I am not at all sure that such an idea is maintained by any of the Fathers, but it certainly is not held by the Damascene.)

After giving an account of the institution of the Eucharist, he goes on to affirm the reality of the transformation of the Eucharistic bread and wine into the pure Body and precious Blood of Christ, first, by referring to the creative power of the Word of God, who both created everything at the beginning and also formed for himself a humanity from the human nature of the Mother of God, and secondly, by invoking 'the over-shadowing power of the Holy Spirit' (*Expos.* 86. 75). The creative Word and the power of the Spirit are sufficient explanation: 'I tell you, the Holy

---

[200] Basil, *Spir.* 27. 66. 61–3 (Pruche).   [201] See the whole of ibid. 66.

Spirit comes down and does these things that are beyond reason and understanding' (*Expos.* 86. 82–3). The use of bread and wine in the Eucharist is a concession to human weakness; as with all sacramental actions, God takes what we are used to—bread, wine, water, oil—'so that through what we are familiar with and in accordance with nature we might come to those things that are above nature' (*Expos.* 86. 92–3). The Eucharistic body is 'the body truly united to divinity, that which came from the holy Virgin, not that the body that was taken up comes down from heaven, but that the bread itself and the wine are changed into the Body and Blood of God' (*Expos.* 86. 94–6). We cannot know how this change takes place, but he gives an analogy (drawn from Gregory of Nyssa's *Catechetical Oration*, which he is following closely here) of the way in which food and drink are changed into a human body by the process of digestion, 'so the bread of the offering and the wine and water are changed in a way beyond nature through the invocation and descent of the Holy Spirit into the Body and Blood of Christ' (*Expos.* 86. 104–6).[202]

John goes on to reject the idea (that was to be dear to the iconoclasts) that the Eucharistic bread and wine are a *typos* of the Body and Blood of Christ: they are the 'deified body of the Lord itself' (*Expos.* 86. 115). Similarly, if the sacred elements are spoken of as 'antitypes', this is so only before the consecration (*Expos.* 86. 163–6). The Eucharist is also called 'participation' (*metalēpsis*), because through it we participate in the divinity of Christ, and 'communion' (*koinōnia*), because 'through it we have communion with Christ and partake in his flesh and his divinity, and have communion and are united with one another through it. For since we partake of one bread, we all become one body and one blood of Christ and members of each other, having become con-corporate with Christ' (*Expos.* 86. 168–72).

Because of this, we should approach communion in Christ's Body and Blood with awe and wonder:

Therefore, let us approach with all fear and a pure conscience and faith free from doubt, and it will certainly be for us as we believe without doubting. Let us honour it with all purity, of soul as well as body; for it is twofold. Let us approach it with burning desire, and forming our palms crosswise let us receive the Body of the Crucified and lifting up our eyes and lips and forehead let us receive the divine coal, that the fire of our desire, increased by the burning of the coal, may burn up our sins and enlighten our hearts and we ourselves may be burned and deified by participation in the divine fire. (*Expos.* 86. 121–9)

---

[202] Cf. Gregory of Nyssa, *or. catech.* 37 (Mühlenberg, 96–7).

This follows the ancient practice of receiving the Body of Christ in the hands placed crosswise, to which Cyril of Jerusalem bore witness in the fourth century.[203] It had also been enjoined by the Quinisext (or Trullan) Synod in 691–2, which further commented that the sacrament was to be received in the hands, and not from sacred vessels, 'thus preferring subordinate and inanimate matter to the image of God'.[204] But the reference to the 'divine coal' (the coal that touched the lips of the prophet Isaias (6: 6), as John makes explicit in the next line) seems to foreshadow the practice, soon to be introduced, of the reception of communion by the laity in a spoon, called a *labis*, the 'tongs' with which one of the Seraphim picked up the burning coal.

Relics and Icons of the Saints

Chapters 88 and 89 concern the veneration of saints and their relics and icons. It is not clear whether chapter 89 (on icons) was written before the Byzantine iconoclast controversy or not (the gentle tone of the chapter does not seem to me to rule out a later date, as *On the Orthodox Faith* is not intended to be polemical; but neither does the reference to 'those who find fault with us' entail a date after the beginning of Byzantine iconoclasm, as we know that Jews had already found fault with Christians for venerating icons in the seventh century). But, whatever the date, it is the longer-standing attack by Jews on the veneration of relics or icons of saints as idolatry that John seems to have in mind. This is suggested, it seems to me, by the amount of material drawn from the Old Testament in support of such practices, in which John draws on defences of Christian practice in these matters already formulated by seventh-century Christians. First, John defends veneration of the saints themselves: they are to be honoured 'as friends of Christ and children and heirs of God' (*Expos.* 88. 2–3). Further, they have become 'God's treasuries and pure abodes' (*Expos.* 88. 22), and this divine presence remains in their bodies after their death, so that they are 'fountains of good, flowing with fragrant oil' (*Expos.* 88. 37). John answers the charge that, according to the Law of the Old Testament, corpses were to be regarded as unclean, by claiming that 'they are not dead'; rather, they have 'fallen asleep in the hope of the resurrection and in faith in Him', for dead bodies could not work miracles (cf. *Expos.* 88. 42–6). Such as these we properly honour by setting up images of them and, best of all, by becoming living images of them by

---

[203] Cyril of Jerusalem, *catech.* 23. 21 (Cross, 38).
[204] Canon 101 of the Trullan Synod, in Joannou 1962, 238.

imitation of their virtue (*Expos.* 88. 61–2). John then recounts the saints of the Christian Church: the Mother of God, John the Forerunner, the Apostles, the martyrs, and 'our venerable fathers, the God-bearing ascetics', as well as the prophets, patriarchs, and just men who were 'before grace' (*Expos.* 88. 79–80).

We shall discuss at greater length in the next chapter John's defence of the holy icons against the Byzantine iconoclasts. But let us note the principal points of John's defence in *On the Orthodox Faith*. First and foremost, John defends icons on the basis that human kind is created in God's own image, or icon (the Greek word is *eikôn*). Therefore we honour one another as images of God, for the 'honour shown to the image passes to the model', quoting the phrase of Basil's that became the favourite patristic citation of the defenders of the icons.[205] John goes on to cite Old Testament evidence in support of veneration of images in worship, and distinguishes this from idolatry, which is worshipping the creature instead of the Creator, rather than honouring the creature for the sake of the Creator. The reason for the prohibition making images of God in the Old Testament is that God is uncircumscribable; but this was changed by the Incarnation (which was already foreshadowed in the theophanies of the Old Testament). John also appeals to apostolic unwritten traditions, as in the case of prayer facing East, and also to the story about the Mandylion, the cloth in which the Lord himself impressed his features for King Abgar of Edessa.

Scripture

There follows a chapter on the Scriptures (90). It begins by emphasizing the twofold nature of Scripture, with the two Testaments, the Old and the New. It ends by listing the books of the Old and New Testaments. The Old Testament list does not represent the actual canon of the Byzantine Church, in that it does not include the two books of Wisdom—the Wisdom of Solomon and the Wisdom of Jesus the son of Sirach—probably because John is here basing himself on Epiphanios's *On Weights and Measures*;[206] the New Testament list places the Catholic Epistles before the Pauline ones (as is the custom in Syriac and Slavonic), and includes the Apostolic Canons, ascribed to Clement of Rome (an oddity, although the Trullan Synod accepted their authority as canons).[207] The heart of the

---

[205] Basil, *Spir.* 18. 45. 19–20 (Pruche).
[206] Epiphanios, *mens.* (PG 43. 244A–C).
[207] Canon 2 of the Trullan Synod, in Joannou 1962, 120–1.

chapter concerns the pre-eminent value of the Scriptures, expressed in terms that echo the very first chapter of *The Fountain Head of Knowledge*:

'Every scripture inspired by God is certainly profitable.' So it is very good and most profitable for the soul to search the divine scriptures. For, like 'a tree planted by streams of waters', so the soul, watered by divine scripture, is enriched and produces seasonal fruit, the orthodox faith, and is arrayed with evergreen leaves, I mean actions pleasing to God. Thus by the holy scriptures we are attuned to virtuous activity and untroubled contemplation. For in these we find encouragement to every virtue and aversion from every vice. If therefore we are lovers of learning, we shall be rich in learning, for by care and toil and the grace of the one who gives it, all things are achieved. 'For who asks receives, who seeks finds, and to the one who knocks it shall be opened.' Let us knock then at the most beautiful paradise of the scriptures, the fragrant, the most sweet, the most fair, resounding and filling our ears with all the songs of spiritual, God-bearing birds, which touches our heart, comforting it when sorrowful, calming it when angered, and filling it with eternal joy, and which lifts our mind on to the back of the divine dove, gleaming with gold and dazzling with radiance, which bears us with its most bright wings to the only-begotten Son and heir of the gardener of the spiritual vineyard and through him to the Father of lights. Let us not knock casually, but rather eagerly and persistently. Let us not lose heart while knocking. Thus it will be opened to us. If we read once or twice and do not understand what we have read, let us not lose heart, but let us persist, let us meditate and enquire. (*Expos.* 90. 12–34)

Dualism

The four chapters against dualism, 92–5, do not really add anything to what we have already seen when considering John's lengthy attack on Manichaeism. Their presence in *On the Orthodox Faith* raises the same historical question as did *Against the Manichees*: namely, whether John knew any Manichees, or whether his rebuttal of dualism (for there is no trace in *On the Orthodox Faith* of any characteristic Manichaean beliefs, as there is in *Against the Manichees*) is simply a patristic echo, or whether indeed John had heard of the earliest Paulicians. But these brief chapters give no inkling of an answer.

Against the Jews

The next three chapters, 96–8, seem to be directed against the Jews. Elsewhere in John there is less evidence of anti-Jewish polemic than one might have expected, given that the latter half of the seventh century witnessed a revival of Jewish–Christian polemic, save for the treatises against iconoclasm, especially the second, which bases the justification of the veneration of icons on a shrill supersessionism. As suggested above, these chapters fit here as attacking Jewish 'literalism' or 'materialism'. The question of the sabbath (chapter 96) gives John an opportunity to paint it as an example of divine pedagogy, intended to lead the Jews from their 'grossness, sensuality and propensity towards material things' (*Expos.* 96. 11), an argument of which John will make some use in his defence of icons. A corollary of this argument is that the institution of the sabbath has spiritual significance. The chapter on virginity begins by bewailing the carnality and propensity for pleasure of those who decry virginity and appeal to the Law in support: a group by no means limited to the Jews. John advances his defence of virginity using the examples of the Lord and the Mother of God, of paradise, of Noah (during the Flood), of the prophets Elias and Eliseus (Elijah and Elisha), of Daniel, and of the angels. Marriage is good, in the sense that it is not bad; but virginity is better. Circumcision, the subject of chapter 98, is again interpreted figuratively: it symbolizes baptism and the cutting off of sin.

Christological Echoes

In this survey of the last chapters of *On the Orthodox Faith*, we have passed over two chapters: that on the genealogy of Christ and on the Mother of God (87), and that on the different ways of speaking of Christ (91). They are, in a way, echoes of the Christological section. They occur among these last chapters, perhaps, because they address difficult issues for Christians trying to defend their faith against non-Christians. Chapter 87 deals with problems associated with the virginal conception of Christ: problems about what it meant, in response to which John defends the perpetual virginity of the Mother of God—that is, her virginity before, during, and after the birth of Christ—against accusations that the birth of Jesus was not so much miraculous as illegitimate; and problems associated with the apparently conflicting genealogies of Christ in the Gospels of Matthew and Luke (problems that had long troubled Christians: see Eusebios's account of Africanus's solution to this problem in his *Church History*, an account largely followed by John[208]). Chapter 91, on the ways of speaking about Christ sets out a kind of table of different ways of speaking about Christ, the point being that many of the paradoxes about Christ are solved if one pays attention to the different contexts in which he is described. It largely summarizes points already discussed in the section on Christology above.

[208] Eusebios, *h.e.* 1. 7 (Schwartz, 52. 21–62. 17).

Eschatology

The topics of the final two chapters seem quite natural: the Antichrist and the Resurrection. We have seen that anticipation of the coming of the Antichrist was very much alive in the decades following the Arab conquest of the eastern provinces of the Byzantine Empire: John regarded the 'religion of the Saracens' as the 'forerunner of Antichrist'. There is nothing so specific in *On the Orthodox Faith*—simply a summary of scriptural teaching on the Antichrist, who, John assures his readers, is bound to come. The final chapter on the Resurrection affirms at length the Christian teaching about the general resurrection at the close of the ages, a conviction that Jew, Christian, and Muslim had in common.

PART III

Faith and Images

7

Against the Iconoclasts

The synthesis of Orthodox theology and worship that the Palestinian monks had developed in the century after the Arab conquest of the Middle East was soon put to the test. In 726 the Byzantine emperor Leo III issued a ban on Christian religious imagery and its veneration, thus initiating the policy of iconoclasm.[1] The precise sequence of events and the reasons behind the policy are both unclear. The chronicler Theophanes links the inauguration of iconoclasm with a volcanic eruption in the Cyclades which threw up a new island between the islands of Thera and Therasia, themselves of volcanic origin, and says that Leo's initial act of iconoclasm was to order the removal of the icon of Christ from above the Chalke, the bronze gate at the entrance to the palace.[2] The removal of the Chalke icon, Theophanes alleges, caused a riot, and many protesters were severely punished: the beginning of the persecution of those who resisted the imperial edict, the iconodules or iconophiles. In 730, when another edict was issued, the patriarch Germanos refused to endorse it, and was deposed and exiled to his family estate at Platanion, outside Constantinople, where he spent his remaining years writing. Iconoclasm soon became settled policy, and was to hold sway in the Byzantine Empire for more than a century: until the death of the last iconoclast emperor, Theophilos, in 842, apart from a period when the icons were restored between 787 and 815.

The period of iconoclasm was critical for the Byzantine Empire. It can be seen as the last of the religious reactions to the loss of the eastern provinces in the early seventh century, first to the Persians, and then,

[1] The date of the beginning of iconoclasm is disputed. The year 726 seems to me most likely (see Anastos 1968); the chronology of John's treatises against the iconoclasts would seem to support 726 over against 730 (see below). The bibliography on iconoclasm is vast; relatively up-to-date accounts of iconoclasm, with bibliographical references, can be found in Hussey 1986, 30–68, and (by Gilbert Dagron) in Dagron *et al.* 1993, 93–165.

[2] Whether there was an icon of Christ over the Chalke in 726 has recently been called into question by Marie-France Auzépy (1990).

permanently, to the Arabs. First, Monothelitism offered the possibility of healing the divisions between Christians that had weakened the eastern provinces, where such divisions were rife, and then with iconoclasm the Byzantines seemed to turn the blame upon themselves, seeing in their plight God's punishment for the idolatry implicit in the veneration of icons. As such, iconoclasm is one of a number of measures by which the Byzantines responded to the spectre of defeat, measures that swept away much of the administrative and military system they had inherited from the Roman Empire, to replace it with a centralized bureaucracy, permanently located in the capital city, Constantinople, combined with the organization of the rest of the Empire into areas known as 'themes', governed by a military commander.

The final defeat of iconoclasm in the ninth century was heralded as the 'Triumph of Orthodoxy', and was celebrated by a public ceremony in which the *Synodikon of Orthodoxy* was proclaimed. This *Synodikon* was issued by the synod held in 843 under the presidency of the patriarch Methodios, and reaffirmed the decrees of the Seventh Oecumenical Synod, held in Nicaea in 787, and the oecumenicity of that synod. The *Synodikon of Orthodoxy* was proclaimed in a special supplementary service for the first Sunday of Lent in 843 and succeeding years: a ceremony that involved the proclamation of Orthodox doctrine—not least the orthodoxy of the veneration of icons—and the condemnation of heresy (by no means limited to iconoclasm), with public acclamations that implicated the whole populace of the capital in an annual assertion of the Orthodox identity of the Byzantine people. This celebration of Orthodoxy on the first Sunday of Lent became part of the regular liturgy everywhere where Byzantine Christianity was embraced: in the other cities of the Byzantine Empire and soon, among the other nations, principally Slav, that came to accept Byzantine Christianity from the ninth century onwards. It is still part of the liturgy of the Eastern Orthodox Church today, though celebrated more in the breach than the observance, save in a very truncated form.

Here is perhaps a good place to remark that by 'icons' or images (*eikōn* is the Greek for image) is meant any representation of Christ, the Mother of God, or the saints (and also angels), or of the Cross 'made of colours, pebbles, or any other material that is fit, set in the holy churches of God, on holy utensils and vestments, on walls and boards, in houses and in streets', as the Definition of the Seventh Oecumenical Synod put it.[3] The term 'icon' is not, in the context of Byzantine iconography, to be

[3] Mansi 13. 377D.

restricted to panel icons (as in current art-historical usage), but includes mosaics, frescos, manuscript illustrations, images woven into cloth, engraved on metal, carved in ivory or wood, and probably also statues, though there is little evidence for religious statues in Byzantium (note, however, the fine Byzantine ivory statue of the Mother of God in the Victoria and Albert Museum[4]).

Theologically, the heart of the iconoclast controversy was a matter of tradition. Did the veneration of icons belong to the tradition of the Church that went back to the Apostles? Or was it an innovation (and therefore a corruption, the conclusion all sides would have drawn)? Modern scholarly discussion has all too readily conceded the iconoclast case that the veneration of icons was an innovation; a recent book on the background to the iconoclast controversy begins with the blunt statement that 'the early Christian community grew out of the picture-free Synagogue (*bildlosen Synagoge*), the Old Testament with its prohibition of pictures remaining for it a lasting possession'.[5] It is odd that such a statement can still (1992) be made, since twentieth-century archaeology has made clear that the early synagogue, not least in Palestine, was far from being 'bildlose'. Dura Europos, with its richly decorated synogogue and church, dating from no later than 256, when Dura Europos fell to the Persians, is but one example among many.[6] The traditional scholarly interpretation of the literary evidence from the early Fathers, which sees it as unyieldingly hostile to religious pictorial art, has been questioned in an article, strangely neglected by Byzantine scholars, by Mary Charles Murray, who argues that opposition to idolatry (that is, images of pagan gods) is what we find in the Fathers, rather than opposition to religious imagery as such:[7] precisely the argument the iconodules used about the Old Testament prohibition of image making. Sister Charles Murray's claim has been developed more recently, and supplemented by archaeological evidence, by Paul Corby Finney.[8] The idea that early Christianity was opposed to the use of religious pictorial imagery must be laid to rest.

Nevertheless, it seems probable that the use of religious imagery assumed a more prominent role in the religious devotion, both public and private, of Christians as the centuries passed, especially in the East, and that the sixth century, in particular, saw a marked increase in devotion to

[4] Buckton 1994, item 156.
[5] Thümmel 1992, 23. The standard version of this account is Kitzinger 1954.
[6] See, most recently, Levine 1999.
[7] See Murray 1977.
[8] Finney 1994.

icons. Popular religious literature begins to tell of wonder-working icons,[9] but it is clear too that Christian icons came to play a role in imperial ceremonial in the latter half of the sixth century.[10] By the turn of the century, icons of saints assume the role of protector of cities, the most striking examples being St Demetrios's defence of Thessaloniki against the Slavs and the Avars,[11] and the Virgin's defence of Constantinople, especially in the Avar-Persian siege of 626.[12] The first ecclesiastical canon to concern itself with icons was issued by the so-called Quinisext Synod (the Synod in *Trullo* of 691–2), which supplemented the doctrinal decrees of the fifth and sixth Oecumenical Synods with an extensive recapitulation and consolidation of the canons by which the Church was governed. Canon 82 concerned itself with the depiction of Christ in icons, and decreed that, instead of being depicted as a lamb (the 'lamb of God who takes away the sin of the world', as John the Baptist pointed him out in John 1: 29), he was henceforth to be depicted in human form:

Embracing the ancient figures and shadows that have been received by the Church as symbols and prefigurations of the truth, we prefer to honour grace and truth, receiving this as the fulfilment of the law. Since therefore it is the perfect that should be set down in coloured depictions before the eyes of all, we decree that the lamb that takes away the sin of the world, Christ our God, is henceforth to be set forth in icons in accordance with his human form, in place of the old lamb, through which, grasping the depth of the humility of God the Word, we may be led to the memory of his life in the flesh, of his passion and saving death, and the redemption that was thus brought about for the world.[13]

The outbreak of iconoclasm at the beginning of the eighth century was, therefore, an attack on a religious practice long established among Christians, one that had become part of the fabric of religious devotion, both public and private.

Much of the history of the iconoclast controversy is beyond the scope of this book, which is simply concerned with John Damascene, who witnessed only the first few years of iconoclasm, and those from the safe vantage-point of Arab Palestine. There, however, he would have experienced a local Palestinian variety of iconoclasm that seems to have

---

[9] See esp. *Life of St Theodore of Sykeon*, in Festugière 1970, partial English trans. Dawes and Baynes 1948, 88–192. For a good discussion of the evidence it provides for the veneration of icons, see Cormack 1985, 17–49.

[10] See Cameron 1979.

[11] See Lemerle 1979, 1981, and Cormack 1985, 50–94.

[12] See the account in the *Chronicon Paschale* for AD 626 (Dindorf, 715–26); Eng. trans.: Whitby and Whitby, 168–81, with valuable notes.

[13] Quinisext Synod, canon 82, in Joannou 1962, 219–20.

occurred during his lifetime, and probably during his time in the neigh-
bourhood of Jerusalem (the earliest evidence dates from the 720s, though
there are difficulties about connecting it exclusively, if at all, with the
notorious edict of Caliph Yazīd II). Archaeological evidence makes clear
that such iconoclasm involved the disfiguring of images of living beings,
animal and human, hence probably inspired by Muslim beliefs, though
the care with which much of the obliteration of living images was carried
out suggests that it was done by Christians to prevent more extensive
destruction.[14] John's attacks on iconoclasm seem, as we shall see, to have
been directed against Imperial Byzantine iconoclasm; an awareness of
local iconoclasm is to be found only, if at all, in some of the sources from
which he drew his arguments.

Yet John was quickly recognized as one of the doughtiest opponents
of iconoclasm. In 754, under Constantine V, Leo's son and successor, a
synod was held at the palace at Hiereia, an Asiatic suburb of Constantinople, to condemn the veneration of icons. John was anathematized, along with Patriarch Germanos and George, archbishop of Cyprus
(about whom we know little). Germanos and George merited one line
each, but John's anathema ran to four lines, and he was condemned, not
by his monastic name, but by his secular Arab name, Mansur:

To Mansur, the one with a vile-sounding name and of Saracen opinion, anathema!
To the worshipper of icons and writer of falsehoods, Mansur, anathema!
To the insulter of Christ and conspirator against the Empire, Mansur, anathema!
To the teacher of impiety and misinterpreter of the Holy Scripture, Mansur,
    anathema![15]

This suggests that John's defence of icons profoundly riled Constantine
V and the iconoclasts: something confirmed by the story told by
Theophanes that Constantine made a play on John's name, calling him
'Manzeros' (Hebrew for 'bastard').[16] Despite this, there is little evidence
that John's arguments were known in the Byzantine Empire, among
either the iconoclasts or the iconodules. The definition of the Synod of
Hiereia does not make any attempt to counter John's arguments; and
what we can glean of Constantine V's 'position paper' on iconoclasm, the
Peuseis, or 'Inquiries', from the attacks on it by Nikephoros, the patriarch
deposed in 815, suggests that Constantine did not know much about
John's treatises.[17] Even the iconodule theologians of the second period of

---

[14] See Schick 1995, 180–219; on the connection or not with Yazīd II's edict, see 215–18.
[15] Mansi 13. 356CD. Trans. in Sahas 1986, 168–9 (modified).
[16] Theophanes, *chron.* A.M. 6234 (de Boor, 417; Mango and Scott, 578 (and 579 n. 7)).
[17] For the fragments from the *Peuseis*, see Hennephof 1969, 140–87.

iconoclasm, such as Nikephoros and Theodore, abbot of the Stoudios monastery, seem to have very little knowledge of John's defence of the icons.[18] This is, perhaps, less surprising than it might seem at first sight. John was writing outside the Byzantine Empire, and for most of the first century after his death and his condemnation in 754, possession of his books would have been a capital offence in the Byzantine Empire (though the Empire did not have the resources to impose such a policy with the ruthlessness of a modern police state). In the world in which John lived, where books were expensive, and travel, difficult at the best of times, was further disrupted by the divisions in the eastern Mediterranean between the Byzantine and Umayyad empires, books and ideas travelled slowly and with difficulty, and only at all if there were readers who wanted to read them and were interested in the ideas they expressed. It seems that it was, at the earliest, sometime in the ninth century before John found such readers in the Byzantine capital.[19] In the case of the treatises against iconoclasm, the interests of the iconodule theologians had moved on, partly because in the second period it was icon veneration that was attacked, rather than the making of icons, so that John's defence was less relevant to their position.

(a) The *Three Treatises against those who Attack the Holy Icons*

John's three treatises *On the Divine Images*, as they are usually known in English, are perhaps today the best known of his works.[20] This interest in them is long-standing: the sixteenth century saw nine editions of the treatises, mainly in Latin, but including one French translation, and this interest continued in the succeeding centuries, with further translations into Church Slavonic and Russian, Serbian, German, Italian, and other modern languages. The reason for this interest in the modern period is not far to seek. The iconoclasm of the Calvinists and the Puritans called forth defences of religious art that turned to the Damascene for arguments. Similarly embattled Orthodox, especially in Russia, defended the place of icons in their religious culture by appealing to him (it is significant

[18] See Louth 1997, 334–5.

[19] *Expos.* was translated into Slavonic in the tenth century, which suggests that it was known in Byzantium by the end of the ninth. But Photios makes no mention of John, though part of *Amphilochia* 80 seems to be a close paraphrase of *Expos.* 36.

[20] Though both the translations into English, an older one by Mary Allies (1899) and a revision of that by David Anderson (1980), are little more than selective paraphrase, and omit much of the third treatise. For a complete translation of the treatises, see Louth 2003*b*.

that the first appearance of two of the Damascene's treatises in Church Slavonic accompanied a Church Slavonic translation of Peter Mogila's *Confession*, published in 1696[21]). The ready availability of translations in modern languages has doubtless something to do with the interest in icons shown by many Western Christians who feel that the tradition of icons represents something they have lost in their own tradition. The manuscript tradition of the treatises against iconoclasm suggests that this interest was not present in the 800 years or so after the Damascene's death. Kotter, in his edition, lists only twenty-eight manuscripts, and only one of these contains all three treatises.[22] This possibly reflects the fact that after 843 (or perhaps later, in the 860s) icons had become such an accepted part of the religious culture of Byzantine Christianity that no one had much interest in defending them; something perhaps confirmed by the fact that the only medieval translations were into Arabic and Georgian, in both cases for Christians who either lived under Muslim rule or had close dealings with Muslims. If so, it was the very success of the cause that John promoted that led to the neglect of his treatises.

But there is another reason why the manuscripts hardly ever contain all three treatises, and that is the way John composed them. Comparison of the three treatises makes it abundantly clear that they were composed in the order by which they are known nowadays (though, according to Kotter's text and apparatus, it is only the second treatise that is numbered), for John plagiarized himself when he composed the second and third treatises. So absolutely is this the case that Kotter, in his edition, prints the texts of the three treatises as a kind of synopsis, in parallel columns, merging into one where the parallel texts are identical. (The parallels are actually closer than Kotter's edition indicates, since Kotter's method enables him to display only parallels that are in sequence. But the fact that so many of the parallels *are* in sequence is further evidence of John's self-plagiarism.[23]) The explanation of this odd state of affairs is probably to be found in the fact, already noted at the end of the first

---

[21] See Kotter iii. 41–2 and n. 75. Peter Mogila (1596–1646) was metropolitan of Kiev from 1632. His *Confession* (written in Greek in 1638) is a comprehensive survey of Orthodox doctrine, composed in opposition to the Calvinist presentation of Orthodoxy by Cyril Lucar (1570–1638), several times briefly patriarch of Constantinople.

[22] A manuscript now in Naples: Neapol. 54 (II b 16). See Kotter iii. 36–7.

[23] Kotter's edition makes it very easy to compare the relationships among the treatises, but it also makes it more difficult to grasp the coherence of each treatise. For that purpose, they are more easily read in Matsoukas's edition (1988), which gives Kotter's text for each treatise separately, with a modern Greek translation *en face*.

chapter, that what we have in these treatises is not really three treatises, but three versions of the same defence of the veneration of icons against Byzantine iconoclasm. The second, written a little after the first, was composed as a simplified version of the argument, and the third (perhaps much later) as a more systematic presentation of the argument. Each version went into circulation in the Palestinian monasteries as soon as it was written, with the result that we now have the treatise in its original form, with the two subsequent revisions. Most of the manuscripts, in fact, contain *Against the Iconoclasts* i. 1–27 and iii. 16–42—that is, the whole of the first treatise and the systematic section of the third treatise, omitting in both cases the florilegia (which are preserved in only three manuscripts). We shall see that there is much to be said for this choice, if all one wants to do is to preserve the kernel of John's argument (and no medieval scribe would have wanted to do more).

First Treatise

The first treatise begins with a profession of unworthiness, in which John insists that it is only the extreme seriousness of the challenge to Christian truth that has led him to write this treatise. He then begins the substance of his defence of icons by recalling the Old Testament prohibitions of idolatry, as well as two verses from the New Testament, one of which contrasts God's revelation in the prophets with that in Christ explicitly (Heb. 1: 1), the other implicitly, by adding Christ to the one true God, knowledge of whom is eternal life (John 17: 3). He then gives a quasi-credal confession of faith, into which he inserts his protest that in worshipping the Son of God incarnate, he is both worshipping God and acknowledging his loving dispensation in the Incarnation. There follows an assertion of the Orthodox position that it is impossible to depict God in himself, but that it is not only possible, but necessary, to depict him as incarnate. John then turns to the arguments of the iconoclasts, which were evidently based on the Old Testament prohibition of idolatry (Leo's edict does not survive, but the reactions of both Patriarch Germanos and John himself make it clear that the reason for iconoclasm at this stage was that icons were regarded as idols). John's first response is to insist that that is precisely what the Old Testament commandment means: a prohibition of idolatry, which is worshipping the creature instead of the Creator. He then introduces a theme that he is later to make much of: namely, that the Old Testament makes so much of the danger of idolatry because the Jews were prone to it.

Now John comes to the heart of this, the first, treatise. The issue is images and their veneration; we must therefore be clear about these two notions. John distinguishes five kinds of image: the way in which the Son is an image of the Father; images as God's (future) intentions for his created world (something very like Plato's Ideas); images as visible pictures of invisible things as a kind of pedagogy; images as types of future fulfilment; and images, whether written or in pictures, that remind us of things and people past. As regards veneration, he distinguishes between veneration that is worship of God, and another kind of veneration that is a sign of respect or honour, for people or places. The word translated 'veneration' (following the normal convention among Orthodox who use English) really has a quite concrete meaning: bowing down, either a kind of deep bow or the actual act of prostration (the Greek word is *proskynēsis*, the etymology of which possibly suggests touching with the mouth or lips, in which case it is etymologically close to the Latin *adoratio*, but which to a Byzantine would suggest prostration, either in a religious context, or to the Emperor). The word for worship, *latreia*, originally meant hired service, and in classical use was also applied to service of the gods; in the Septuagint it exclusively means worship due to God (though in its verbal form it is most commonly used to describe the *forbidden* worship given to idols)—and that is the sense it had for John. What John means, then, is that bowing down may either express the kind of total devotion that we call worship, due to God alone, or it may be a sign of respect (for which he produces Old Testament examples, such as veneration of the tabernacle, or Jacob's bowing down before his brother Esau). It is this latter veneration of honour that we offer to images, whether of God or of the saints. It is a way of expressing our worship of God, for veneration is addressed to people and places that are dear to God, and images of such people provide a stimulus and occasion for such veneration.

John then goes back to the question of the two Testaments, arguing that it is the same God in both, and that under the Old Covenant there were material images—the tabernacle and all its accoutrements, including the gilded images of the cherubim—made by hand, that were venerated. To reject such veneration of material things really implies, John suggests, that matter is evil, a view John associates with Manichaeism. But the mention of two Testaments leads John in another direction, which stresses their difference. For whereas God could not be depicted under the Old Covenant, because he is invisible and incomprehensible, under the New Covenant he has become human and lived among human kind;

he has, in fact, united himself with matter. This leads to one of John's most striking confessions:

> I do not venerate matter, I venerate the fashioner of matter, who became matter for my sake and accepted to dwell in matter and through matter worked my salvation, and I will not cease from reverencing matter, through which my salvation was worked. (*Imag.* 1. 16. 4–9)

Matter, as created by God and united to God in the humanity he assumed, is therefore not something to be despised, but something holy: 'therefore I reverence the rest of matter and hold in respect that through which my salvation came, because it is filled with divine energy and grace' (*Imag.* 1. 16. 17). John goes on to show how this is wholly consistent with the worship decreed in the Old Testament. Material images are perceived through the senses, and the chief of these is sight (John here states a philosophical commonplace, affirmed by both Plato and Aristotle). He immediately claims that images are books for the illiterate, but the context suggests not that images are a concession to the illiterate, but rather that images appeal to the highest of the human senses, that of sight.

John now takes up a claim (merely mentioned here, and it is difficult to see who might have made it) that images of Christ and the Mother of God are acceptable, but not those of the saints. He replies that Christ is not to be deprived of his army, the saints, and goes on to introduce a further contrast with the Old Testament, in which death was not yet seen in the light of the Resurrection, so that the dead were not honoured, and corpses were regarded as unclean. But all this has changed. Whereas Jews decorate their Temple with animals and birds and plants, Christians decorate their churches with images of Christ and the saints, who are not dead, but alive. The first treatise closes with two further points. First, the veneration of images is based on unwritten, not written, tradition, and he cites the classic passage from Basil the Great on the necessity of following both written and unwritten traditions.[24] Secondly, he addresses the iconoclast appeal to Epiphanios, which he rejects by arguing that the text cited might well be forged, that Epiphanios's own church in Cyprus is decorated with images 'to the present day', and that even if Epiphanios did say what is claimed, 'one swallow does not make a spring' (as the Greek proverb has it, the contrast with the English proverb reflecting a warmer climate!).

What is impressive about the first treatise is the coherence, and theological depth, of John's defence of icons. John knows straightaway what

---

[24] Basil, *Spir.* 27. 66. 1–9 (Pruche).

there is to say in defence of icons, and where they fit in the Christian scheme of things. This is even more striking, if it is the case, as I shall shortly argue, that the first treatise was an immediate response to the iconoclast controversy, written shortly after 726. But it is all here: his clarity that the veneration of icons is not idolatry, which is what the Old Testament prohibition was about; the crucial difference made by the Incarnation (which, alas, John develops in the second treatise into a shrilly supersessionist account of the superiority of Christians over idolatrous Jews); the necessity to be clear about the meaning of terms such as 'image' and 'veneration'; the dignity of matter; the importance of unwritten tradition. Where he drew these arguments from, we shall discuss in the next section of this chapter.

Second Treatise

The second treatise is very different from the first, even though, towards the end, there is a long passage where John borrows from the first with only minor modification. John again begins by begging his audience to believe that this, his second treatise,[25] has been composed not for his own glory, but because of the seriousness of the threat of iconoclasm (though he admits that he has a 'talent of eloquence', which he must not bury). He also says that some have asked him to make his arguments clearer this time! The argument is certainly simplified. After the introductory chapter, the next ten chapters develop a single argument: that idolatry is the work of the devil, and that the devil was especially successful with the Jews, for which reason Moses forbade the making of images, but that with Christians it is different, for they are grown up, unlike the childish Jews, and may make images without the danger of falling into idolatry; iconoclasm is a further ruse by the devil to undermine the Christian faith in the Incarnation. Even the key to this argument in the first treatise, that in the Incarnation God made himself visible, is mentioned only in passing. Passages from the New Testament (especially from Hebrews), the primary meaning of which is the fulfilment of the Old in the New (which is the way the argument is put in canon 82 of the Quinisext Synod), are quoted in such a way as to degrade what the Old Testament revealed, and present the religion of the New Covenant in a starkly supersessionist way. This anti-Judaic aspect of iconophile theology proved to be enduring; Kathleen Corrigan's study of ninth-century marginal psalters has

---

[25] That it is the second treatise is stated in the body of the text, not just in the inscription: *Imag.* II. 1. 26–7.

demonstrated the importance of anti-Judaism as a theme in the definition of Orthodox belief among the monks whose illustrations in those psalters celebrated iconophile feeling in the wake of the triumph of Orthodoxy.[26]

Chapter 12 introduces the other principal theme of this second treatise: an uncompromising attack on the Emperor for meddling in the affairs of the Church by promoting iconoclasm, an interference that John bluntly calls 'piracy'. Briefly, John develops the traditional Byzantine understanding of the division of powers in the Empire between *basileia* and *hierateuma* (or *hierosynê*), imperial rule and priesthood, that had been affirmed by earlier Greek Fathers such as Athanasios (against Constantius), Basil (against Valens), and Maximos (against Constans II), and would later be affirmed again by Theodore of Stoudios (against Leo V). Leo III's own view of this matter may perhaps be gleaned from the preface to the brief law code, the *Ecloga*, he issued in about 726, in which he applied the Lord's words to Peter, 'Feed my sheep', to himself, as Emperor,[27] which suggests some blurring of the distinction between imperial authority and priesthood, though he goes on to characterize his role in terms that are conventional enough. This is perhaps too slender a basis for attributing to Leo a theocratic view of the Emperor's power.[28] Despite the widely held view that the Byzantine Empire was 'caesaropapist', emperors generally governed the Church through canons issued by synods of bishops, even if they were not disinclined to deal roughly with clerics who opposed them.[29] In this case, it was not until 754 that Leo's son, Constantine, secured formal synodical approval for iconoclasm; but Leo would not have had far to look for precedents for an emperor acting directly with the support of compliant clergy, or securing such (e.g., Justinian's deposition of patriarch Eutychios in 565, when he turned to aphthartodocetism, or Herakleios's promotion of Monothelitism in the *Ekthesis* of 638 with the compliance of patriarch Sergios and Pope Honorius; Philippikos, however, had convened a synod to reintroduce Monothelitism in 712). But, however Leo himself saw his imperial office, John's response is in the tradition of Byzantine churchmen. In this chapter John also mentions the deposition of Germanos from the patriarchal throne, and his exile, as well as the persecution of 'many other bishops and fathers, whose names we do not know' (*Imag.* 11.

---

[26] See Corrigan 1992, esp. 43–61.

[27] See the extract from the *Ecloga* given in Barker 1957, 84–5.

[28] As McGuckin does (1993, 44–5), though without citing the passage from the *Ecloga*.

[29] For imperial acceptance from the beginning of government of the Church by synods of bishops, see T. D. Barnes 1993, 165–75.

12. 29–30). Despite this attack on the Emperor's 'piratical' attack on the customs of the Church, John is at pains to protest the loyalty that Christians owe to the Emperor in all proper matters (such as taxes: *Imag.* II. 12. 38–40).[30] This is conventional: from the beginning, Christians overwhelmingly professed their loyalty to the Emperor (cf. Rom. 13: 1–7; 1 Pet. 2: 13–17). But in John's mouth it raises an interesting question, for his political overlord was not the Byzantine emperor, but the Umayyad Caliph. Who did John think he was: a Byzantine subject in exile, or a subject of the Caliph? The whole tenor of this chapter points to the Byzantine churchman, firm in his loyalty to the Byzantine emperor, but clear about the privileges of the Church and its clergy. After nearly a century of Arab rule, John still seems to have regarded it as a passing phase.[31]

The rest of the treatise follows another simple argument: namely, that iconoclasm, by despising matter, shows itself to be fundamentally Manichee. But the attack on the Emperor continues with the passage from the first treatise (there following on from the idea that icons of Christ and his Mother are acceptable, but not icons of saints) that, in attacking icons, the Emperor is depriving Christ of his army (*Imag.* II. 15; cf. I. 21), but with greater force here, echoing the condemnation of the Emperor in chapter 12. The next chapter introduces the argument from unwritten tradition, but gives it a more populist twist: the long quotation from Basil is omitted, and instead Leo is taunted with composing a 'Gospel of Leo', just as the Manichees composed a 'Gospel of Thomas' (in fact an apocryphal gospel older than Manichaeism, but which had become part of the Manichee canon). John follows this taunt by listing other emperors who 'called themselves Christians and persecuted the

30 Though John follows this profession of loyalty with a protest against any 'altering the ancient boundaries, set in place by the fathers', alluding to one of his favourite biblical verses (Prov. 22: 28). He would have appreciated the chancel screen in the church of Low Ham, Somerset, built by royalists in the seventeenth century, and completed in thanksgiving for the restoration of the monarchy, which bears the verse: 'Fear God and the King, and meddle not with them that are given to change' (Prov. 24: 21).

31 The whole question of Byzantine 'caesaro-papism' is too large an issue to discuss here. Our concern is not even Leo III's understanding of his imperial office, but simply John's understanding of the duties of the priesthood and its relationship to the imperial office. The most recent discussion of the issue is Dagron 1996 (for his conclusion on the question of the relation of priesthood and sovereignty in Byzantium see pp. 303–15). He discusses Leo III in chapter 5, though he seems to me to make too much of the saying attributed to Leo, 'I am emperor and priest' (which he admits cannot be shown to be authentic: Dagron 1996, 167). John's extreme opposition of the New to the Old Testament does not really give us any sure clue as to how the iconoclasts regarded the Old Testament.

Orthodox faith': Valens, the opponent of Basil; Zeno and Anastasios, who tried to set Chalcedon on one side; Herakleios, Constans II ('Constantine of Sicily', where he died), and Philippikos, all of whom promoted Monothelitism. In much of this, John is following his first treatise, and so comes to its response to the appeal to Epiphanios, which is again much simplified; but he now knows of the destruction of the icons in Epiphanios's church in Cyprus 'by the wild and savage Leo' (playing on Leo's name, which means 'lion': *Imag.* II. 18. 30–5). It is striking how all these themes from the first treatise are given an anti-imperial twist in the second. John ends this treatise with a lengthy series of quotations from Hebrews, which underlines the supersessionist theme with which he began. The combination of these two broad concerns, John's supersessionist treatment of the relationship between the Old and New Covenants and his sharp criticism of imperial involvement in matters of doctrine, recalls vividly the starting-point of Dagron's investigation of the relationship between emperor and priest, already alluded to, which is the opposition between Old Testament support for some kind of sacred kingship and the implicit rejection of any such notion by a Christian church founded on the New Testament.[32] Dagron, however, seems to assume that the idea that the New Covenant *supersedes* the Old is the only way in which Christian theology can understand their relationship. That is by no means the case, but it is certainly striking that in John's arguments against the iconoclasts a supersessionist account of the relationship between the Testaments relates so closely to his denial of any sacred office on the part of the Emperor.

This second treatise does, however, introduce a couple of significant new points. The first rebuts the argument that veneration of icons entails the veneration of matter. John argues that this is evidently not so, for if the image on the icon is defaced, it ceases to be an icon, and so may be destroyed by fire without any sacrilege (*Imag.* II. 19. 10–13). The second puts forward a fundamental argument for icons: namely, that 'God himself first made an image and shows us images', by making human kind in the image of God,[33] and further by manifesting himself in the Old Testament in theophanies, which are images of God rather than manifestations of the very being of God himself (*Imag.* II. 20. 15–26). Neither of these arguments appears in the first treatise. The first does not appear in the third treatise either; but the second argument is thoroughly

---

[32] Dagron 1996, 21.

[33] Precisely the argument that the second-century apologists used against Greek pagan art: see Finney 1994, 42 (Minucius Felix), 51 (Clement of Alexandria).

integrated into the long, systematic second part of the third (*Imag.* III. 20, 26).

These are not much more than asides; in this second treatise the argument is essentially reduced to three themes: an anti-Judaic one, another opposed to the Emperor, and the third anti-Manichee. But it also has more specific historical references than we find in the first treatise.

Third Treatise

The third treatise is different from both the preceding treatises, even though it incorporates a good deal from them. To begin with, it dispenses with any *captatio benevolentiae* and simply launches into the argument. The first ten chapters reproduce the first part of the second treatise (*Imag.* II. 2–11) with its stark supersessionist message; this is supplemented in a couple of places with passages from the first treatise missing from the second that deal in more detail with the argument from the Old Testament. The rest of the treatise is freshly composed, though much of it is a development of the theological themes of the first treatise omitted in the second. But in between these two sections there are three transitional chapters, the central theme of which is what we found in the concluding chapters of *On the Orthodox Faith*: namely, that Christianity is a religion with a twofold character, mediating between the material and the spiritual, answering to the twofold nature of human beings.

For since we are twofold, fashioned of soul and body, and our soul is not naked, but, as it were, covered with a veil, it is impossible for us to go to the spiritual (*ta noēta*) apart from the bodily. So just as we hear with our bodily ears audible words and understand something spiritual, so through bodily sight we come to spiritual contemplation. For this reason Christ assumed body and soul, since human beings have body and soul; therefore also baptism is twofold, of water and the Spirit; as well as communion and prayer and psalmody, all of them twofold, bodily and spiritual, and offerings of light and incense.[34] (*Imag.* III. 12. 23–35)

This is followed by a story from the *Spiritual Meadow*, ascribed to Sophronios, as is usual with Byzantine writers, rather than John Moschos, about a demon who promises to stop tormenting a monk with the thought of fornication if he will stop venerating an icon of the Mother of God: the point being that the demon regarded fornication as a lighter matter than venerating an icon. Thereafter follows a systematic discussion of the nature of an image and the nature of veneration, a much

---

[34] Cf. Ps. 140: 1 ('Let my prayer rise up like incense before you')? *Re* 'light and incense' offered to icons, see the Definition of Nicaea II (Mansi 13. 377E).

more elaborate version of what we found in the first treatise. We shall discuss this at some length later on, when we analyse John's doctrine of the
image.

Conclusions

The contrast between the first two treatises and the third is heightened if
we take into account the patristic florilegia that were appended to these
treatises. The florilegia attached to the first two treatises are fundamentally the same, the second simply adding a few further sections to the
first. The florilegium attached to the third is quite different: although
there are some overlaps, and probably borrowings, the florilegium has
been compiled afresh, to the extent that even when the same work is
quoted in both the first two florilegia and the third, it is sometimes
quoted in what is evidently a different form (the most notable example
being the quotations from Leontios of Neapolis). What are we to make of
these differences? The precise historical references of the second treatise
to the deposition of Germanos and the despoliation of the church in
Cyprus, as well as its indignant tone, suggests that it was written shortly
after 730. This in turn suggests a date for the first treatise in the later 720s,
after the beginning of iconoclasm, but before the deposition of
Germanos and the spread of imperial iconoclasm to Cyprus (though this
latter piece of evidence is difficult to use, as we know nothing about what
happened on Cyprus from any other source). The third treatise seems to
me to be less a response to immediate historical events than a considered
presentation of the case for the veneration of icons, for which John prepared a new, and much more extensive, florilegium. It could thus be
much later, perhaps in the 740s, a period during which, after the death
of Leo and the revolt of Artabasdos, although iconoclasm remained
imperial policy, the iconodules were perhaps less harassed than in the preceding or succeeding decades (this is the impression given by
Theophanes, though his account is so patchy that such an impression can
hardly be relied on). This is the position reached, by a slightly different
route, by the Damascene's editor, Bonifatius Kotter.[35]

<hr>

[35] Kotter iii. 5–7, 23–4. Recently Speck has argued for a much later date for these treatises,
after the Synod of Hiereia in 754, awareness of which Speck finds in the treatises (1981,
179–243). Speck's arguments seem to me far-fetched, and to raise more problems than they
begin to solve, not least the fact that Hiereia anathematizes John so vehemently, and seems to
think he is dead.

(b) The Florilegia and the Source of John's Arguments

If what has been suggested above is correct, and the first treatise is to be seen as an immediate response to the challenge of imperial iconoclasm, then the question arises as to where John drew his arguments from, for he is very clear about the validity of the making and veneration of icons, and also clear about how icons fit into the Christian scheme of things. Here the florilegia are very revealing, for they lay bare the patristic foundation that John had to hand for his defence of the veneration of icons. This patristic foundation is more considered than is always realized. It is some- times suggested, for instance, that the quotations from the Fathers used in the controversy are taken out of context—perhaps the most obvious example of this being the renowned quotation from Basil's *On the Holy Spirit*, about the honour offered to the image passing to the archetype. In context, Basil is speaking of the Son as an image of the Father, so that honour paid to the Son passes to the Father; Basil's point is that worship of the Father and the Son (and the Spirit) are not independent acts of worship, because the Son's being an image of the Father means that worship offered to him is offered to the Father as well: there is one worship offered to the three members of the Holy Trinity. It is not unlikely that the popularity of this text among the iconodules provoked the counter-argument of the iconoclasts that an image must be consub- stantial with that of which it is the image, as in the case of the Son in relation to the Father, but manifestly not in the case of a material image of Christ.[36] However, in the florilegium, this quotation is put in its context, suggesting that the iconodule argument may be more subtle; for the example Basil gave of an image in *On the Holy Spirit* was the image of the Emperor: veneration of the Emperor's image is veneration of the Emperor, the image is not venerated separately; nor does it possess any glory separate from that of the Emperor.[37] The context, therefore, justifies the iconodule appeal, and makes one wonder if the iconodule quotation of the text did not contain an implicit allusion to a form of veneration that the iconoclasts themselves accepted: veneration of the imperial image, about which surprisingly little is said explicitly in the con- troversy.[38] This concern to put quotations from the Fathers in context is something that marks appeal to the Fathers in the seventh and eighth

---

[36] See Constantine V's *Peuseis*: Hennephof 1969, 142.

[37] Basil, *Spir.* 18. 45. 15–17 (Pruche).

[38] Though note Germanos, *ep. ad Ioh. episc. Synnadensem* (PG 98. 157B).

centuries. It is so manifest in the *Acta* of the Sixth Oecumenical Synod
that Harnack was moved to call it a 'Council of antiquarians and palaeo-
graphers'.[39]

If we look at the other excerpts (restricting ourselves to the florilegium
to the first treatise), there are some, notably from Dionysios the
Areopagite, that develop further the idea of the image as providing access
to what it images, as in the quotation from Basil. Others document the
widespread practice of veneration of icons, drawing on sermons (some of
which are perhaps speaking of rhetorical images rather than actual visual
ones) and hagiography (e.g., the role of the icon of the Mother of God
above the entrance to the Church of the Cross in the conversion of Mary
of Egypt). These support the line John takes that images are venerated
not for themselves, but as providing access to what they image forth,
and also provide evidence for the contention that there is an unwritten
tradition about the veneration of icons embodied in the devotional
practice of the Church.

But more striking than all this is a series of four extracts from a 'treatise
against the Jews on the veneration of the Cross of Christ and the images
of the saints, and on the relics of the saints' by Leontios, bishop of
Neapolis in Cyprus (*Imag.* 1. 54–7). Leontios is otherwise known as a
hagiographer (the author of *vitae* of John the Merciful, patriarch of
Alexandria; Simon the Fool, of Emesa; and Spyridon, bishop of
Trimuthis in Cyprus). This treatise against the Jews is preserved only in
fragments in iconodule florilegia such as John's. In these extracts we find
set out most of the arguments that John uses in the first treatise: all the
examples (and indeed more) from the Old Testament demonstrating that
veneration of people and places was not thought of as idolatry, but is
recorded without comment (e.g., Abraham bowing before those from
whom he bought the cave for a sepulchre, Jacob bowing to Esau);
evidence that God works miracles through matter (e.g., Eliseus's staff,
Moses' staff, Aaron's rod), and reference to the material accoutrements of
the tabernacle, on which such devotion was lavished; the importance of
visible memorials for recalling the mighty deeds of God in the past; the
distinction between veneration as a way of showing honour and veneration of God, which entails worship (though Leontios does not articulate
so clearly John's distinction between *proskynêsis* and *latreia*).

Here we have most of the points made by John—the difference
between icons and idols, the evidence of the Old Testament for veneration of people and places, the dignity of matter, the difference between

veneration and worship—and frequently the same arguments. But there is a striking difference between John and Leontios (to judge from the passages John cites, an impression not altered by the longer extracts in the florilegium to the third treatise, or that produced at the Seventh Oecumenical Synod). Leontios makes no mention of the Incarnation as introducing a new era marked by the making and veneration of images. He also presses the argument from the Old Testament further than John does. Having pointed to all the evidence of the veneration of the material objects used in the worship of the Old Covenant, he responds to what appears to be a Jewish counter-argument maintaining that only what was specifically ordered by God could be treated in this way, by arguing that in Solomon's temple there were many cultic objects not mentioned in the Law, but that Solomon was not condemned for this (*Imag.* 1. 56. 36–43). The point of Leontios's argument is clear: to establish a general principle from the Old Testament to justify Christian cultic objects, like the Cross and icons. Leontios does not mark a sharp difference between Jew and Christian; he does not accuse the Jews of a propensity to idolatry that had to be kept in check by the second commandment. There is not a trace of supersessionism in his argument; rather, he justifies, on the basis of the Old Testament, Christian veneration of the Cross and icons. On the matter of relics, he does not, like John, make a sharp distinction between the Old Testament abhorrence of the dead as unclean and a Christian treasuring of the relics of the saints; rather, he argues from the Old Testament itself that the bones of good men are to be reverenced, point- ing to the bones of Jacob and Joseph that were taken from Egypt to Palestine for burial.[40]

The reason for the difference between Leontios and John in this respect is not far to seek: Leontios was seeking to convince the Jews with whom he was arguing, whereas John was seeking to tar Christian icono- clasts with the reproach of being Judaizers. But what the evidence of these extracts makes clear is that the source for most of John's arguments in defence of icons is to be found in Jewish–Christian polemic of the seventh century,[41] a polemic in which Christians sought to argue with their fellow Jews on common ground and convince them, rather than assert their superiority, as John did. There is another significant difference between John's arguments and those of Leontios, and that is that Leontios had to defend veneration of both the Cross and icons of Christ

[40] *Imag.* 1. 56. 21–4. Cf. Gen. 50: 4–14, 24–6.
[41] On which see Cameron 1996. For a selection of texts from this seventh-century Jewish–Christian polemic relevant to icons, see Thümmel 1992, 340–67.

and the saints, whereas John is concerned primarily with icons. The reason for this lies in the difference between the Jewish and Byzantine iconoclast objections to Christian veneration of icons. For the Cross, presumably as part of the imperial cult, remained an object of veneration for the Byzantine iconoclasts, a fact which enables John to argue from veneration of the Cross to veneration of the one depicted on the Cross: 'If I venerate the image of the Cross, made of whatever wood, shall I not venerate the image of the crucified one, showing the saving cross?' (*Imag.* II. 19. 7–9).

The more systematic florilegium of the third treatise adds further examples of Christian defence of icons in the context of seventh-century Jewish–Christian dialogue: brief extracts from Jerome of Jerusalem (*Imag.* III. 125) and Stephen of Bostra (*Imag.* III. 72–3), who makes explicit, as John does, the difference between veneration as expressing honour and that expressing worship. Neither of these seventh-century apologists, any more than Leontios, appeals to the Incarnation in his defence of Christian veneration of images. However, John's appeal to the Incarnation as justifying the making of icons is not altogether original. It is implicit in the argument of canon 82 of the Quinisext Synod, and is found independently of John in Germanos,[42] though it has to be confessed that John makes the argument from the Incarnation much more central.[43]

The florilegia appended to John's treatises against the iconoclasts raise many problems that cannot be aired here. They are preserved in only three manuscripts, all of which belong to the thirteenth century,[44] which lends plausibility to suggestions that they might have been interpolated. Both Speck and Chrysostomides have argued for such interpolations.[45]

[42] See Germanos, *ep. ad Ioh. episc. Synnadensem* (PG 98. 157CD), *ep. ad Thom. episc. Claudiopoleos* (ibid. 178B), and also the letter from Pope Gregory II to Germanos (ibid. 152A, which follows on from a citation of canon 82), if, as Gouillard argues, this letter belongs to Germanos: Gouillard 1968, 244–53. On Germanos's theology of the icon, see Lange 1969, 85–105.

[43] There has been much argument as to whether the iconoclast controversy was, from the beginning, a matter of Christology (see, most recently, Henry 1976 and Noble 1987). There seems to me a distinction to be drawn between seeing the question of icons as Christological (and therefore involving arguments that seek to align veneration of icons either with heretical Christologies, such as Monophysitism or Nestorianism, or with Chalcedonian Orthodoxy) and seeing it as based on the Incarnation. The latter argument is already broached in the canon of the Quinisext Synod, but it would appear that John makes more of it than anyone earlier. The more strictly Christological argument, as found in Constantine V's *Peuseis* and later iconoclasm, may be a response to the appeal to the Incarnation; it provoked the more Christological arguments of later iconodules, such as Theodore of Stoudios.

[44] Kotter's A, D, and F (iii. 34–6).

[45] Speck 1989 (an interpolation in *Imag.* I. 67/II. 70); Chrysostomides in Munitiz *et al.* 1997,

More broadly, there is the question of the relationship between John's florilegia and other iconophile florilegia, not least that drawn up for the Seventh Oecumenical Synod in 787. Van den Ven argued long ago that John's florilegia were not used in drawing up the synod's florilegium, partly because of discrepancies between John's quotations and those of the synod, but partly, too, because the synod itself insisted on all quotations from the Fathers being made from complete codices, not from written-down extracts.[46] Most recently, this whole question has been the subject of thorough, and brilliant, analysis by Alexander Alexakis, who has thrown light on the complex interrelationships between the various iconophile florilegia that were in existence both in the East and in Rome in the eighth century, and has also demonstrated that John's florilegia were behind the florilegium of the Seventh Oecumenical Synod, but indirectly, as the source of the iconophile florilegium (Alexakis's F), which, he argues, remained in the papal scrinium in Rome after its compilation in about 770. Alexakis further argues, very persuasively, that both a florilegium and codices of the Fathers were used at the synod, the quotations in the florilegium being checked against the codices (a procedure that raised few problems, since the quotations in F are very reliable).[47] If John's influence on the Seventh Oecumenical Synod was thus indirect, then we can see how John's learning was in fact influential for the synod's deliberations, even though that synod seems to show little awareness of the scope and power of his defence of the icons.

(c) John's Doctrine of the Icon

It remains to explore a little more John's doctrine of the icon, expressed in his defence of icons and their veneration in the treatises against the iconoclasts.[48] The making of icons and their veneration rests for John on two principles: first, what one might call the architectonic significance of the image in the created order, and secondly, on the Incarnation, in which the source of everything, including images, himself beyond image, takes

28–32 (arguing that the accounts of the Edessene *acheiropoietos* icon of Christ's face, given by him to King Abgar, in *Expos.* 89 and *Imag.* I. 33/II. 29, are interpolations. It is certainly odd that the story is not included in the florilegium to the third treatise.)

[46] 'La concile n'a fait usage d'aucun florilège, fût-il de S. Jean Damascène': Van den Ven 1955–7, 360.

[47] Alexakis 1996, *passim*, but for the above summary see esp. 227–33 and 360 (a possible stemma of iconophile florilegia).

[48] As well as literature already referred to, see Lange 1969, 106–40.

on a form, the human form, of which there can be images: in the
Incarnation, as Maximos put it, the Lord 'became a type and symbol of
Himself'.[49] Corresponding to the far-reaching concept of the image,
there is the notion of veneration; as the image bodies forth a higher reality, so it calls forth a response of veneration: acknowledgement, acceptance, and devotion. The germ of this is present in the first treatise, but it
is presented in a systematic form in the latter part of the third treatise, in
which, having established the profound import of the Incarnation, John
teases out the many-layered significance of both image and veneration.
What needs to be clarified here is set out in the two chapters that follow
the transition from the first part concerning the significance of the
Incarnation for the question of images, both as being the fulcrum
between the Old and New Testaments, and also as putting God's own
seal on the dignity of matter (*Imag.* III. 1–10). That transition, as we have
seen above, lays stress on the twofold nature of humanity, and therefore
of the human approach to the divine (*Imag.* III. 11–13). These two
chapters set out the plan for the rest of the treatise, which we will follow:

First, what an image is;
Secondly, the purpose of the image;
Thirdly, the different kinds of image;
Fourthly, what can be depicted in an image and what cannot be depicted;
Fifthly, who first made images?

Then, concerning veneration:

First, what veneration is;
Secondly, the different kinds of veneration;
Thirdly, what the different objects of veneration are in the Scripture;
Fourthly, that all veneration takes place for the sake of God who is naturally
worthy of veneration;[50]
Fifthly, that the honour offered to the image passes to the archetype.[51] (*Imag.* III.
14–15)

Most of this we have already encountered, though not arranged so
systematically. This care about the meanings of words and concepts, and
the danger of being led astray by failing to take enough care, is something
for which we have found plenty of evidence in John already: the very

[49] Maximos the Confessor, *ambig.* 10 (PG 91. 1165D; Eng. trans.: Louth 1996, 132).
[50] This expression, *ton physei proskynêton theon* is probably an allusion to Gal. 4: 8, which refers to *tois physei mê ousin theois*.
[51] These last two topics are discussed together, with no explicit reference back to the topics as listed here, in *Imag.* III. 41 (*pace* Kotter, note to *Imag.* III. 15. 8–9).

existence of the *Dialectica* is evidence of this, though perhaps the most striking example we have encountered so far is the importance John attached to 'Chalcedonian logic' for both Trinitarian theology and Christology. The meaning of veneration is perhaps most immediate: iconoclasm under Leo III was based on the conviction that veneration of icons was idolatry, and John's defence turned on the different ways in which veneration may be offered. There is the veneration due to God alone, which he called (following Stephen of Bostra) worship, *latreia*; but there is another form of veneration that does not imply the absolute devotion of worship, but is simply a sign of honour and respect. John's analysis of the different valencies of veneration in this third treatise makes explicit something that had earlier been implicit: that all true veneration is ultimately an entailment of that worship which is due to God alone. It is not just that veneration as worship and veneration as honour are different; for John the latter is implicit in the former. For all honour derives from the one we worship ('the One naturally worthy of venera-tion'): both the authentic honour or worth of those who are his friends, the saints, and the honour we owe to kings and rulers who are set over us, which does not depend on their intrinsic worth, but their place in God's providential ordering of the world (see *Imag.* III. 41). Veneration is our response to God's *philanthrôpia*, expressed both in providence and in the divine love manifest in the Incarnation and the Redemption: it is an expression of wonder, of thanksgiving, of hope based on need, of repentance and confession (*Imag.* III. 29–32), all ultimately given meaning by that worship we owe to God alone (*Imag.* III. 28).

More far-reaching, however, is John's analysis of the significance of the image.[52] An image is 'a likeness and paradigm and expression of something, showing in itself what is depicted in the image'; it is never completely like its model, otherwise there would be identity (*Imag.* III. 16). The purpose of an image is 'the manifestation and display of the hidden', hidden because either invisible or not present, whether in place or time: the image leads us to this hidden reality (*Imag.* III. 17).[53] But the heart of John's exposition turns on different meanings of the word 'image'. He distinguishes six meanings, adding to the five listed in the first treatise the way in which the human is an image of the divine. These six meanings are: first, the natural image, as a son is an image of the father (and, more particularly, as the Son of God is the image of God the Father); secondly,

[52] On the theology of the image, see Špidlík 1989.
[53] Cf. the whole context of Maximos's idea that the Lord becomes a 'type and symbol of Himself', cited above n. 49.

the images or paradigms (or predeterminations, as Dionysios calls them) within God of what is to be; thirdly, human kind as created in the image of God, manifest both in the Trinitarian structure of the human soul as intellect, reason, and spirit, and in human free will and human rule over the rest of creation; fourthly, there are images that use bodily forms to represent the spiritual world, necessary for human beings, composed of body and soul, if they are to form some conception of the spiritual; fifthly, there are images in the Old Testament that prefigure the realities of the New—the Burning Bush as a figure of the virginity of the Mother of God, or water as a figure of baptism; finally, there are images that recall the past, either in written form or in pictures (*Imag.* III. 18–23).

This is not just a list; it is an evocation of the multitude of ways in which reality echoes reality, from the Father imaging forth the Son and the Son the Spirit in the life of the Trinitarian God, through the patterns of providence, humanity as an image of God, the way in which the visible world finds its reality in the spiritual world and images it forth, the images that shadow the relationship between the Old and the New Testaments, to the images that remind us of the past, of the 'rock from which we were hewn' (cf. Isa. 51: 1). It is a picture of the ways in which images establish relationships between realities: within the Trinity, between God and the providential ordering of the universe, between God and the inner reality of the human soul, between visible and invisible, between the past and the future, and the present and the past. The image, in its different forms, is always mediating, always holding together in harmony. Images in the form of pictorial icons fit into this pattern, in a quite humble way. But to deny the icon is to threaten the whole fabric of harmony and mediation based on the image. At the heart of all this is human kind as the image of God: it is humanity in the image of God, as we know from John's anthropology in *On the Orthodox Faith*, that is the microcosm, the little universe, the bond of the cosmos. This world of signs was created by God, who first made images, when he created human kind in his image, and manifested himself in the Old Testament in theophanies that took the form of images: Adam hearing the sound of the Lord God walking in the garden in the cool of the day, Jacob fighting with God, Moses seeing God's behind, Isaias seeing him as a man seated on a throne, Daniel seeing the likeness of man, and as Son of man, coming to the Ancient of Days (*Imag.* III. 26). And creating human kind in his image, he created him to make images. What John is saying here seems to me well summed up in this quotation from the Anglo-Welsh artist and poet David Jones:

A man can not only smell roses (some beasts may do that, for lavender is said to be appreciated in the Lion House) but he can and does and ought to pluck roses and he can predicate of roses such and such. He can make a *signum* of roses. He can make attar of roses. He can garland them and make anathemata of them. Which is, presumably, the *kind* of thing he is meant to do. Anyway, there's no one else can do it. Angels can't nor can the beasts. No wonder then that Theology regards the body as a unique good. Without body: without sacrament. Angels only: no sacrament. Beasts only: no sacrament. Man: sacrament at every turn and all levels of the 'profane' and 'sacred', in the trivial and in the profound, no escape from sacrament.[54]

Nor from image, icon, the Damascene would add (since David Jones's notion of sacrament includes any use of image or sign[55]).

John finds authority for this idea of a world of mutually reflecting reality, in which signs and images trace its interrelationships and are the means by which human kind, which is both spiritual and bodily, moves through material reality to grasp invisible, spiritual reality, in the writings of Dionysios the Areopagite. Quotations from the Areopagite stand at the head of all the florilegia (though probably because John, accepting Dionysios's claim to be a disciple of the Apostle Paul, takes them to be his earliest witness). He also quotes several times (though he does not include it in the florilegia) a passage from Gregory Nazianzen's second Theological Oration, in which Gregory says that the intellect, tiring of attempting to get beyond the material, either falls into idolatry or treats material things as signs and symbols pointing beyond them to God.[56] This (perhaps rather reluctant) acknowledgement of the human, embodied condition has further consequences for John. We noted, when looking at John's presentation of human progress towards the truth in the early chapters of the *Dialectica*, that John rejects an oversimplified Platonism, and sees the soul as attaining transcendent reality *through* the senses, rather than by abandoning them.[57] John's approach also involves a positive attitude towards the imagination, something unusual in the Byzantine ascetic tradition, and in the Platonic tradition to which it is indebted; for it is the imagination that receives images in the human mind (*Imag.* I. 11).[58] This

---

[54] Jones 1959, 166–7.

[55] Jones goes on to remark: 'but no sooner does he put a rose in his buttonhole but what he is already in the trip-wire of sign, and he is deep in an entanglement of signs if he sends that rose to his sweetheart': ibid. 167.

[56] Gregory Nazianzen, *or.* 28. 13. 22 (Gallay), cited at *Imag.* I. 11. 20–1; II. 5. 13–14; III. 21. 18–20.

[57] *Dial.* 1, and see commentary above in Ch. 4.

[58] Payton (1996) barely notices this, in a study devoted to the Damascene's understanding of human cognition in his argument against the iconoclasts.

appreciation of the imagination remained part of iconophile theology. In one of his letters, Theodore of Stoudios includes a defence of the imagination as part of his defence of images. 'To speak Dionysiacly' (*Dionysiakôs eipein*), he says, it is by images that we 'ascend to intellectual contemplations', and continues:

imagination is then one of the five faculties of the soul, and imagination itself seems to be a kind of image; for they are both manifestations. The image is not unprofitable, therefore, since it is a help to the imagination. If the image were unprofitable, then the imagination which depends on it and coexists with it would be even more useless, and if it is useless, then so too would be the faculties that coexist with it—the senses, opinion, understanding, the intellect.[59]

Ultimately, for both John and Theodore, defence of icons entailed an acknowledgement of the integrity of embodied human nature.

But this understanding of the whole of reality as constituted by, and finding its meaning in, signs is both undergirded by, and finds its highest expression in, the truth of the Incarnation, of God the Word embracing human life and reality. As we have seen, appeal to the Incarnation in defence of icons is something more developed in John than in his predecessors or contemporaries; it is also a legacy that he bequeathed to all later understanding of the icon in Orthodox theology. The two aspects of John's defence of the icons—the role of images and the truth of the Incarnation—are not unrelated. When God became incarnate, and even more when at the Last Supper he gave his disciples bread and wine as his Body and Blood, 'he placed himself in the order of signs', to use the words of Maurice de la Taille,[60] which David Jones used as a motto for his collection of essays *Epoch and Artist*. It is signs and images that relate, and human beings, beings placed on the border between different kinds of reality—visible and invisible, material and spiritual—that can interpret them. That these signs make sense at all is because God has placed himself in the borders where humans live—and indeed, bridged the border between the uncreated and the created, thus opening up to men and women the destiny of deification—thereby restoring to human kind the role of microcosm, bond of the cosmos, that they have failed to fulfil. It is this intimate link between sign or sacrament or icon, the Incarnation, and the very possibility of human understanding that lies at the heart of

---

[59] Theodore of Stoudios, *ep*. 380. 167–73 (translation somewhat paraphrased in the interests of intelligibility). See also Gervase Mathew's discussion of the role of *phantasia* in iconophile theology (including a reference to this passage from Theodore): 1963, 117–19.

[60] de la Taille 1934, 212. De la Taille's discussion, to which this phrase belongs, emphasizes the ecclesial dimension of such human use of signs.

John's defence of icons. Nor is this a matter of theory at any level: Incarnation means taking on the forces of untruth and brutal deception that threaten to fracture all relationships to the point of unmeaning. Images, icons, disclose the world of God's creating, the deified realm of the saints, only to those who look with pure eyes and pure hearts; and that purity of human understanding is the fruit of a simple openness to God's gift and grace that demands a life of sacrificial striving to love. The defence of the icon, of the image, is not a matter of mere aesthetics; it is concerned with preserving and making possible a world in which meaning is mediated by reconciling love.

(d) John's Place in Iconophile Theology

John's defence of icons and their veneration is both far-reaching and fundamental: it makes the icon part of the fundamental fabric of Christian belief, and argues that iconoclasm is more than simply an objection to an isolated devotional practice, but threatens to undermine Christianity itself. In this his defence of icons and their veneration is like Irenaeus's defence of Christianity against gnosticism or Athanasios's defence of the divinity of Christ against Arians, or, to come closer to John's time, Maximos's defence of the integrity of Christ's humanity against the Monothelites: all these oppose heresy not as an incidental error, but as something that undermines the whole faith. This emphasis on the fundamental character of the veneration of icons continues in Byzantine Orthodoxy, but none of the later iconophiles placed icons on such a broad theological canvas.

This is partly because of the way in which iconoclasm itself changed. The iconoclast argument shifted from the crude charge of idolatry to the more subtle accusation of Christological error: to depict the humanity of Christ entails either separating it from his divinity (which implies Nestorianism) or fusing it with his divinity (which implies Monophysitism).[61] To this the iconophiles responded with their own subtleties, especially the claim that what is depicted in an icon is not an abstraction such as human or divine nature, but the concrete reality of a person, or *hypostasis*: a profound idea that influenced the very way in which an icon was perceived.[62] These subtleties, rooted in Christology, go beyond any-

[61] See the Definition of the Synod of Hiereia: Hennephof 1969, 222–3.
[62] See Theodore of Stoudios, *antirr.* 3. 1. 15–21 (PG 99. 396C–400C). The sharp contrast between John's defence of icons based on the holiness of matter and Theodore of Stoudios's defence based on the fact that it is the person that the icon depicts was one of the principal

thing we find in John's defence of icons. Another characteristic of
later iconophile theology, the clarification of the nature of veneration
developed using the Aristotelian category of relation (*schesis*), is perhaps
not so original.[63] It is true (and perhaps surprising, given John's knowledge of logic) that the term 'relative veneration'—that is, veneration
given to something by virtue of its relation to something else—as
opposed to absolute veneration, offered to the object venerated, is not
found in John. But the idea that all veneration, apart from veneration
offered to God, is relative to that offered naturally to God is expounded
with some clarity in John's third treatise, though without using the term
'relation' (*Imag.* III. 41).

The later defence of the Christian use of icons was not restricted to
Byzantium, however. In Palestine, pressure on Christians over their use
of icons increased as the years of Islamic rule passed (we have already
noted the upsurge of local Palestinian iconoclasm from the 720s). Less
than 100 years after John wrote his first treatise in defence of icons
(probably in the first decade of the ninth century), an Arab Christian,
Theodore Abū Qurrah, bishop of Ḥarran, also wrote in defence of the
Christian practice of veneration of icons.[64] We have already met
Theodore Abū Qurrah in connection with John's views on Islam, for one
of Theodore's works claims to contain John's oral teaching on Islam.
Both men are associated with the great monastery of Mar Saba in the
Judaean desert, though the evidence for Theodore having been a monk
there is stronger than for John.[65] He can never have known him, however, even if John had been a monk there, since he was born round about
the time of John's death. Theodore was very much John's intellectual
heir, nevertheless. In their faith, they were at one—like John, Theodore
was a Chalcedonian in Christology—but the situation in which they lived
out their faith was different. Whereas John was clearly a Byzantine
churchman, Theodore, as clearly, was a subject of the Muslim caliph;
whereas John's theological language is Greek (though he certainly knew
Arabic, and could translate from the Qur'ān into Greek), Theodore's theological language is Arabic (though he certainly knew Greek, and perhaps

contentions of Christoph von Schönborn's book on the Icon of Christ (Schönborn 1976),
modified later in Schönborn 1982, in which he recognizes that Theodore's defence is adum-
brated in John.

   [63] This is a key element in what Alexander called the 'scholastic' theory of images, characteristic of later iconophile theology: 1958, 189–213

   [64] Griffith 1997, 21. (Griffith 1997, 1–28, gives a biography of Theodore, and introduces
his work in defence of icons.)

   [65] Ibid. 12–15.

translated Greek theological, and maybe even philosophical, works into Arabic).[66]

These similarities and differences are manifest when one compares their defences of the veneration of icons. All Theodore's arguments are found in John, or are developments of them. But the focus is narrower. Theodore's approach is much closer to that in John's second treatise, with its emphasis on arguments from the Old Testament, arguments that often have an anti-Jewish colouring.[67] There is nothing much on the nature of the image, and hardly anything on John's principle that humans are made in God's image (chapter 21 answers the objection that if one venerates images, one should venerate human beings; Theodore responds that it is only humans in whom the image is manifest—that is, saints—whom we should venerate); even the argument from the Incarnation is turned round: from being a principle on which the making of icons is based, Theodore argues that Christians should not give up veneration of icons because of the ridicule it attracts from others, for the Incarnation itself scarcely attracts any less ridicule (chapter 2). There is also evidence of the influence on Theodore of John's other works: for instance, there is something of the same ambivalence to miracles that we find in John (cf. chapter 6 with *Expos.* 3; chapter 16 takes a rather different tack). But the context of Theodore's arguments seems quite different. John is defending an article of faith; Theodore is meeting the problems faced by Christians in an Islamic country who want to continue the traditional, and public, cultic act of veneration of icons (see especially chapter 2). Furthermore, by using Arabic, the nature of Theodore's argument is subtly altered. This is not so much a matter of references from time to time to the Qur'ān (though there are such references). It is more a matter of his adopting the style of argument of his fellow Arab-speaking contemporaries. One example comes in his explanation of what is meant by veneration or prostration (chapter 11), in which, as Sidney Griffith points out, Theodore takes over an element of the Muslim explanation of what is involved in the formal ritual of prostration, *ṣalāt*: the importance attached to intention as part of the act of prostration. Elsewhere, he defends Christians who, to Muslim eyes, 'add' to the act of prostration by kissing or touching the icon (chapter 11, p. 59). He also defends Christians against what was to become the basic Islamic objection to making images, based on a saying of the Prophet, that those who make

---

[66] Ibid. 15–16.
[67] *Pace* Griffith (1997, 26), it does not seem to me that Theodore's anti-Jewishness is 'considerably heightened' compared with John's.

images, on the day of the Resurrection, will be required to breathe life into them (chapter 10). But beyond all these details, what is striking is the way in which Theodore's method of arguing conforms to the traditions of Muslim *kalām*, particularly the way in which his presentation always takes the form of argument with an adversary (rather than systematic exposition, which John uses as well), and addresses a series of theses in the forms of objections or questions. In expressing his theological argument in Arabic, Theodore found himself assuming the predominant form of Arabic theological argument, which served Islam, even though his faith was different from that embraced by Muslim theologians.

John's defence of icons and their veneration remained unique in the broad sweep of its theological awareness. There can scarcely be any doubt that Theodore knew John's treatises (and more), though his own arguments operate on a much narrower front. With John's Byzantine successors in the second phase of Byzantine iconoclasm, the case is different. There, it seems to me, there is considerable doubt as to how extensive their awareness of John's arguments was, though we may suspect that, even had they known John's work in greater detail, it would have had little effect on the use they made of him, as the issues were now defined differently. It may be only now that the real force of John's arguments is finding the acknowledgement they deserve.

Χρυσορρόας ('flowing with gold'): John the Preacher

John's defence of images against the iconoclasts was, as we have seen, more than simply a defence of the veneration of icons. It was, more widely, a defence of the place of images in Christian theology. We noted earlier, in our discussion of John's doctrine of God, the stress he lays on the incomprehensibility and ineffability of God. Images and the apophatic are complementary. Dionysios the Areopagite says that 'God is known in all things and apart from all things': everything points to him, everything can be an image of him, but he transcends everything. As the modern Greek philosopher Christos Yannaras has said: 'The apophatic attitude leads Christian theology to use the language of poetry and images for the interpretation of dogmas much more than the language of conventional logic and schematic concepts'.[1] In the case of John Damascene, it is rather the case that he uses *both* the language of poetry and images *and* the language of conventional logic and schematic concepts, equally. We have already seen something of the way John uses imagery and rhetoric in theology (for instance, in the first chapter of the *Dialectica* and in *Expos.* 90 on Scripture, which, significantly perhaps, follows immediately the chapter on icons); we have also caught glimpses of the way in which John can use the 'language of conventional logic and schematic concepts' so as to produce a kind of abstract and exhilarating poetry (for instance, the first paragraph of *Expos.* 8, on the Trinity). But it is above all in his homilies (or some of them) and in his liturgical poetry that John expresses his faith in terms of imagery, though, as we shall see, this is not at the expense of precise conceptual terminology; rather, the two forms of expression complement each other. This has long been recognized. Basil Studer, in his monograph on John's theological method, remarked that 'not only his songs, but also his sermons, particularly those on the feasts

[1] Yannaras 1991, 17.

of the Transfiguration and the Dormition of the Mother of God, give eloquent witness of his poetical powers, even if there are models for these sermons'.[2]

In this chapter, we shall first look at the nature of John's preaching, and then follow the hint given by Studer, and look in some detail at his homilies for the Transfiguration and the Dormition of the Mother of God.

(a) The Nature of John's Preaching

It is clear from the references to John Damascene in Theophanes' *Chronicle* that, in his time, John had acquired a substantial reputation as a preacher. First, Theophanes always calls him John *Chrysorrhoas*, and explains the epithet ('flowing with gold') as referring to his fame as a preacher (the same epiphet is used, as a variant of the more usual *chrysostomos*, of John Chrysostom himself).[3] Further, Theophanes mentions that John delivered eulogies for Peter, of Maiuma, who was martyred for cursing Muhammad in 743.[4] This stress on John's renown as a preacher may seem surprising, for relatively few of his homilies have come down to us. Not only that, but a glance at Kotter's description of the more than 400 manuscripts used in his edition[5] reveals that the Damascene's homilies were not transmitted as a collection, but individually, or in small groups (even the three homilies on the Dormition, which clearly belong together, were often separated in transmission), often in a manuscript (e.g., a menologion) intended for liturgical use. As we shall see, all John's homilies were delivered in a specific liturgical context; and it seems that it was to enable them to continue to fulfil this function that they were preserved. Despite the impression given by Theophanes, therefore, John does not seem to have been sufficiently highly regarded as a preacher by posterity for his homilies to have been preserved as a collection, although they were apparently valued individually for their liturgical use, and preserved for this purpose.

Before we look at John's homilies, we should perhaps attempt to place him in the history of Christian preaching.[6] The evidence of the first five

[2] Studer 1956, 15.

[3] Theophanes, *chron.* A.M. 6221 (de Boor, 408; Mango and Scott, 565); 6234 (de Boor, 417; Mango and Scott, 578); 6245 (de Boor, 428; Mango and Scott, 592). For the use of *chrysorrhoas*, see Lampe 1961, 1535.

[4] Theophanes, *chron.* A.M. 6234 (de Boor, 417; Mango and Scott, 577–8).

[5] Kotter v. 3–55.

[6] See the papers collected in Cunningham and Allen 1998.

or six centuries of Christianity makes clear the importance that Christians attached to preaching. The ministry of Jesus is presented in the Gospels as a ministry of preaching and healing, and a similar picture of the apostolic mission emerges from the Acts of the Apostles. There we see the Apostles preaching both in synagogues and also in specifically Christian gatherings, as well as in public places. Justin Martyr makes it clear that in the middle of the second century the president of the Eucharistic assembly preached after readings from the Prophets and the Apostles.[7] The works of the Fathers bear witness to the importance of preaching. In the third century, Origen, though only a presbyter, preached, and many of his homilies have survived. From the fourth and fifth centuries, very many Christian homilies survive, both ordinary homilies for Sundays, and even weekdays, and special homilies for dedication festivals (the earliest extant perhaps being Eusebios's homily at the dedication of the new basilica in Tyre, built after the end of the Great Persecution, preserved in his *Church History*, x. 4), for saints' days (especially for the translation of their relics), and those preached to catechumens (notably those of Cyril of Jerusalem, Ambrose, John Chrysostom, and Theodore of Mopsuestia). In many cases homilies constitute the principal genre through which the Fathers expressed their theology; this is the case with John Chrysostom (who composed little else), Augustine (whose extant homilies bulk larger in his corpus than the better-known treatises), and Gregory Nazianzen (whose verse, however, rivals his homilies in quantity). Many of the great patristic preachers had been highly trained as secular rhetors, and carried their classical training over to this new genre. It is clear that it was normal for such homilies to be delivered *ex tempore*, though the texts that survive have usually been prepared for publication by their authors from versions taken down in shorthand.

As time passed, the homily seems to have become more formalized (though it may simply be that everyday homilies from later centuries have not been preserved, their significance fading before the great homilies of the likes of Chrysostom and Nazianzen; it is striking that later homilies that have survived tend to be for feasts and saints' days introduced after the time of the great patristic preachers). The late fifth and early sixth centuries saw the introduction of the kontakion, a verse sermon that is unlikely to have been delivered *ex tempore*. The kontakion, once composed, was repeated yearly as the feast for which it had been prepared returned year by year. Later sermons, like John's, seem to have been com-

[7] Justin Martyr, *1 Apol.* 67. 4 (Blunt, 100).

posed in a high, poetic style,[8] and preserved for repeated liturgical use. Such formalization of the homily in the Byzantine world, turning it from a free composition into a liturgical or quasi-liturgical text, finds later historical confirmation in the opposition which the eleventh–twelfth-century Cypriot saint Neophytos of Paphos encountered, when he dared to preach in his own words.[9]

What homilies of John's do we now possess? Volume 5 of Kotter's edition, containing 'opera homiletica et hagiographica', prints fifteen items, five of which he judges spurious. This leaves the following ten authentic homilies: a homily on the fig-tree and the parable of the vineyard, a homily for Holy Saturday, the passion of the great martyr Artemios, the praise of the martyr St Barbara, a homily on the Nativity of the Lord, the praise of St John Chrysostom, a homily on the Transfiguration of our Saviour Jesus Christ, and three homilies on the Dormition of Mary the Mother of God. (Kotter's objections to the homily on the Nativity of the Mother of God included by P. Voulet[10] and P. Nellas[11] in their editions of John's Marian homilies do not seem to me absolutely conclusive.)

All these homilies are preserved in Greek, and were presumably delivered in Greek. But from what has already been gleaned about the Damascene's life, it seems almost certain that he spoke Arabic as well as Greek. This raises the interesting question as to whether John ever preached in Arabic.[12] If he did, such homilies have not been preserved, and the impression that John gives in all his surviving works is that of a Byzantine churchman—albeit a Byzantine churchman with a genuine knowledge of Islam. If John had ever used Arabic, whether in homilies or in more formal treatises, it is difficult to see why they would not have been preserved, since within a few decades of his death we witness the beginnings of Arabic Christianity in Palestine, as we have already seen.

There is hardly any evidence from the homilies themselves as to where they were preached, save what can be gleaned from the nature of the audience, and there is scarcely any more evidence as to when they were preached, except in terms of liturgical time. We have already noted that in the second homily on the Dormition John indicates that he is an old man.[13] But this does not help us to determine any historical sequence in

---

[8] e.g., those of Andrew of Crete, on whom see Cunningham's article in Cunningham and Allen 1998, 267–93.   [9] See Englezakis 1995, 111.

[10] Voulet 1961.

[11] Nellas 1995.

[12] For John in Arabic translation, see Nasrallah and Haddad 1996, 152–5.

[13] *Dorm.* II. 1. 30 f.: referred to in Ch. 1 above.

the homilies, for if John was born when Kotter thought he was, in 650,[14] as a monk he was always an old man; if a more plausible date for his birth is taken (say, 675), that would still mean that he was an old man for much of his monastic life. Remarks in the homilies that could be taken as evidence of opposition to iconoclasm (see below) may mean that these homilies are later than 726 or 730, though that conclusion is by no means certain.

If John was indeed a hieromonk in Palestine, the presumption is that these homilies were delivered as part of the monastic round of services. This presumption, however, begs questions to which one would like more concrete answers. Just who did preach at services in eighth-century monasteries in general, and those in Palestine in particular? There is both earlier and later evidence that preaching and monastic catechizing were part of the task of the abbot (e.g., Dorotheos of Gaza in the sixth century and Theodore of Stoudios, at the end of the eighth and beginning of the ninth), but there is no evidence that John was an abbot. It might be thought that preaching was assigned to monks (especially hieromonks) who were thought to be good at it, but I know of no relevant evidence. John's epiphet, *chrysorrhoas*, suggests that he was highly valued as a preacher, though the Christmas homily, at least, suggests that John did not always live up to expectations, unless eighth-century Palestinian monks had very odd homiletic tastes.

One of the strangest features of John's homilies is the way in which he incorporates sometimes quite substantial extracts from other literary sources (including other writings of his own). From this it would appear that John wrote his homilies down beforehand, and read them out (whether this was an odd practice, we have not the evidence to judge, but one would have thought it unusual; it is certainly contrary to traditional rhetorical practice). But this practice raises other questions. The homilies on the Nativity and on St Artemios share the oddity of incorporating wholesale passages from literary works. The former has a long passage taken from the late sixth-century *Religious Conversation at the Sasanid Court*,[15] and concludes with a recital of the whole of Judges 19, supposedly illustrative of Rachel's weeping for her children (cf. Matt. 2: 18); it begins with a passage in praise of spring that seems to rework themes from a homily falsely ascribed to Chrysostom and Gregory Nazianzen's homily 44 ('On New Sunday', the Sunday after Easter). The homily on St Artemios is expressly compiled from various Church historians: John lists Eusebius, Socrates, Philostorgius, Theodoret, and adds that he has used 'many

---

[14] So Kotter 1988, 127.   [15] Bratke 1899.

others' (*Artem.* 4). The passages from Philostorgius are of considerable interest, and include an account of Julian the Apostate's attempt to help the Jews to rebuild Jerusalem, which was thwarted by an earthquake and 'fire from the disturbed foundations' (*Artem.* 68). This homily is also exceptionally long: none the less, it contains evidence that it was delivered, as he addresses his audience (*Artem.* 3). All the homilies, especially in passages of theological exposition, draw on the Damascene's theological treatises, especially *On the Orthodox Faith*. The case of the homilies on the Nativity and St Artemios are clearly very odd: it makes them very literary pieces. In the case of the latter, an explanation could be advanced along the lines that, although originally delivered as a homily, what we have now is more of a hagiographical treatise on St Artemios, composed by someone with a scholarly bent, who has used the opportunity to give an account of the saint's 'times' from a wide range of sources. That John was of a scholarly bent is unquestionable, and that he was keen on accurate presentation of his sources is a feature of John's attitude to tradition already noted.[16] I cannot, however, think of any similar justification for the Christmas homily.

On the use of his *On the Orthodox Faith* in the dogmatic sections of his homilies, to which Kotter draws attention in his apparatus, two remarks can be made. First, what is striking about these sections is not word-for-word quotation (which is rare), but rather the pursuit of a line of thought precisely parallel to what we find in *On the Orthodox Faith*, with the same scriptural and patristic quotations. A good example is *Sabbat.* 12, for which Kotter refers us to *Expos.* 50. 17–36. Both passages expound the union of perfect Godhead and perfect manhood in the Incarnation, and there are lots of parallels. But what is most striking is the way in which the same two quotations are used—Colossians 2: 9 and the famous clause from Gregory Nazianzen's *ep.* 101 ('the unassumed is the unhealed'). It is not, perhaps, surprising that John recalls his own classic treatment in the summary account he gives in his homily. But a second point I would make concerns the nature of *On the Orthodox Faith* itself: in Lionel Wickham's sardonical remark, quoted in an earlier chapter, 'patristic theology may be said to aspire to the condition of the florilegium and in its last representative John of Damascus, whose *De Fide Orthodoxa* is a mosaic of quotations, attains its goal'.[17] Precisely because it is a mosaic of quotations, one might well expect John to remember what he found memorable, and echo what he said in *On the Orthodox Faith* when he covers the same ground in his homilies.

---

[16] See above, especially on *Expos.*   [17] In Laga *et al.* 1985, 117.

So far we have approached John's homilies from the perspective of John himself and his life as a hieromonk in Palestine, where it is presumed he delivered them. But do the homilies tell us anything about those to whom he preached, or about their concerns? He sometimes addresses his congregation in terms that could apply to any Christian: for example, in biblically resonant language as 'brethren, we who have received the name of faith, and are counted worthy both to be called and to be the people of Christ' (*Ficus* 6. 1); as 'longed-for bride of Christ' (ibid. 7. 1), and as 'the divine and sacred flock of the great shepherd and priest and victim, a chosen people, a royal priesthood' (*Sabbat.* 36. 3). Sometimes he uses language that suggests something more formally monastic: 'community beloved of God' (*Transfig.* 1. 1; cf. *Dorm.* III. 1. 5); 'O community lovingly obedient to the divine words' (*Dorm.* II. 1. 18), and 'beloved fathers and brothers' (*Dorm.* I. 4. 1; II. 18. 1), 'best and most dear-to-God shepherds' (*Dorm.* II. 1. 9), which perhaps also include monks visiting the monastery for the great feast of the Dormition. But all this tells us no more than we would expect.

One might hope to pick up something of the nature of his audience from the kind of polemic he indulges in, perhaps even from the way he interprets Scripture, and the kind of ethical conclusions he draws. So far as polemic is concerned, there seems to me to be relatively little that is direct. The story of the Jew who tried to touch the bier of the Mother of God (*Dorm.* II. 13) is part of the traditional account: it was polemical in its original context, and also in John. The account of the attempt to rebuild the temple in the homily on St Artemios is also anti-Jewish polemic (*Artem.* 68), as is John's exegesis of the parable of the vineyard in the homily on Holy Saturday (*Sabbat.* 4 f.). John's accounts of Christian doctrine, especially of the doctrine of the Trinity and the Incarnation, also clearly mark off Orthodox teaching from heresy, but they do not seem to be especially polemical. There is polemic against Apollinarianism (equated with Monothelitism?) in the homily on the fig-tree (*Ficus* 1. 38 f.), and Origenism is explicitly condemned in the homily on Holy Saturday (*Sabbat.* 6. 5–7). It might be argued that the much more extended treatment of the heresy of Monothelitism in that homily (*Sabbat.* 17) indicates that this was a live heresy again in John's day (as it was); but it is not polemical like Maximos's impassioned polemic against the Monothelites in his Christological *opuscula*. There are a few places where I think it might be the case that John is conscious of Muslim objections to Christianity, and keen to counter them, albeit indirectly. Twice he defends Christianity against the charge of idolatry, where his specific point is that, in honouring Mary as Mother of God, we are not venerating her as a 'goddess' (*Barb.* 4 and *Dorm.* ii. 15). More interestingly, in the homily for Holy Saturday we read: 'Anyone who says that Christ was a slave, we close our ears to him . . . and we should bear his reproach as a diadem of glory' (*Sabbat.* 37. 2–5). Jesus is regarded by Muslims as a good Muslim, i.e. slave of God (see, e.g., Qur'ān 4: 172). I wonder if this is what John has in mind here: more traditional adoptionist heresy regarded Jesus as a man, not a slave, and John's words here seem to envisage an actual situation in which Christians would hear Jesus called (to them, blasphemed as) a slave. There are also several places in the homilies where it might be thought that there is implicit polemic against the iconoclasts (e.g., *Nativ. D.* ii. 8–15), where the Magi have a picture made of the child Jesus and his Mother, and *Artem.* 57. 17–27, where there is mention of the statue of Christ set up by the woman with the issue of blood at Paneas, or Caesarea Philippi, and allegedly destroyed by the Hellenists under Julian, which became part of the anti-iconoclast arsenal (cf. *Imag.* iii. 68)).

John is fond of quoting Scripture, and keen to explain difficulties. His explanations are often quite ingenious. One sometimes wonders whether John was much aware of the difference between a homily and a treatise. He seems to take for granted a theologically literate audience, who could pick up his allusions, not just to Scripture, but to the Fathers. He often makes quite significant theological points without dwelling on them.

There is invented dialogue, and such-like, in the hagiographies and the homily on the Nativity, but in all such cases John is reproducing what is in his sources, not making it up himself. To a theologically literate audience, I suspect that John's homilies would be fairly comprehensible, though I am not sure what they would have made of the homily on the Nativity, with the long citation from Judges (though in itself it is, I suppose, unpleasantly racy), and the long history lesson in the context of which the story of Artemios is set.

So far as the ethical conclusions John draws, these are very general, though often very moving. For example, at the end of the homily on the fig-tree, after addressing his congregation as the 'longed-for bride of Christ', he continues: 'Long worthily for the one who longs for you. Open to him wholly the inner chamber of your heart, that he may dwell in you wholly, together with the Father and the Spirit' (*Ficus* 7. 2 f.). It seems to me that John draws a response from his congregation by presenting the mysteries of the faith as powerfully attractive. He is also capable of making his point 'doctrinally', as when in the same homily he argues for the necessity of both faith and works (*Ficus* 6). Again, all this presupposes a theologically literate, though not specifically monastic, audience.

Matters of genre and rhetoric might be expected to reveal something about either the preacher or his audience or both, but there is comparatively little to go on, and I am not sure that more is revealed than what we might presume anyway. So far as genre is concerned, the homilies on St Barbara and St John Chrysostom are both described as *enkômia*, which they are; the homily on St Artemios is described as a *hypomnêma*; and the rest are called *logia* (except for *Dorm.* ii, which in most manuscripts is not described at all). Of those described as *logoi*, the homilies on the fig-tree and for Holy Saturday are mainly straightforward exegetical homilies, though they contain passages of theological exposition, often in the form of encomia (e.g., *Ficus* i, an encomium of the Word who has moved John to speak, which contains a brief exposition of Creation–Fall–Redemption through the Incarnation, or *Sabbat.* 2, an encomium of revelation, and *Sabbat.* 5, an encomium of creation); the homily on the Transfiguration has a similar combination of exegesis and theological encomia; *Dorm.* iii and parts of the other homilies on the Dormition also take the form of encomia.

All John's homilies have a conventional rhetorical structure, whatever their content. They begin with a *captatio benevolentiae*, in which a common *topos* is the impossibility of expressing divine mysteries in human language, and close with a doxology. John is familiar with, and uses effectively, rhetorical devices such as antithesis, anaphora, homoioteleuton, apostrophe, and prosopopoeia. He is particularly fond of anaphora, which he regularly uses as a way of drawing out the doctrinal significance of the event that is being celebrated liturgically, and makes great use of a kind of rhythmical antithesis (often incorporating anaphora), which he uses to great effect in passages of theological exposition, especially on the doctrine of the Incarnation and on Mariology, which, of course, lend themselves very readily to such antithetical treatment. But all this seems to me commonplace in patristic homilies, even if John is capable of using such devices very effectively.

What is most revealing, however, about John's homilies—which, as the manuscript tradition reveals, is why they have been preserved—is that they all relate to liturgical time: all the extant homilies of the Damascene were preached on particular liturgical occasions. Three of the homilies are expositions (or contain expositions) of liturgical Gospels. The homily on the fig-tree and the parable of the vineyard comments on Matthew 21: 18–22:14, the Gospel for matins for the Monday of Holy

Week, and the homily for Holy Saturday on Matthew 27: 62–6, the Gospel for matins for Holy Saturday.[18] The homily on the Transfiguration is not limited to the liturgical Gospels for the feast (Matt. 17: 1–9 for the Eucharist, Luke 9: 28–36 for matins),[19] but also comments on Mark's account, and the differences between all three, notably whether the Transfiguration took place after six or eight days (Matt. 17: 1 and Mark 9: 2 against Luke 9: 28: *Transfig.* 8). This raises the interesting question as to when preaching normally took place. There is certainly evidence that, even outside a monastic context, there were homilies at services other than the Eucharist (both John Chrysostom and Severos of Antioch could be cited: for vespers and for matins, respectively), at any rate earlier on. My suspicion (but based on what?) is that preaching at matins is likely to have been (or become) more of a monastic practice. If so, then John's homilies would fit, where we expect them, into the round of a specifically monastic office.

The homilies on the Dormition were originally a trio of homilies, given in the course of an all-night vigil (John speaks of *pannychoi staseis*): the first homily was given while 'the rays of light were fading' (*Dorm.* I. 4. 5); in the second he speaks of honouring the Mother of God with 'all-night stations' (*Dorm.* II. 16. 2); in the third he is looking forward to breakfast (*Dorm.* III. 1. 6 f.)! By the time of the Damascene, there were two forms of vigil service known in the Church, one essentially monastic and the other a feature of the so-called Cathedral Office, in great city churches, notably the Great Church of Hagia Sophia in Constantinople.[20] They had somewhat different forms, but quickly influenced each other, especially in city monasteries. Such vigil services took place on the eve of Sundays and great feasts, starting either the evening before or at midnight. Monastic vigils were probably more frequent. In John's day the form of the vigil was still in the process of development, and we have no real idea what part preaching played in it: these three homilies are isolated evidence for three occasions for preaching in the course of an extended vigil.

The other homilies have less definite evidence of liturgical occasion.

---

[18] According to the current *Triodion* (see *Triodion* 829, 977); according to the tenth-century typikon of the Great Church, there was no Gospel at matins on Monday of Great and Holy Week, or on Holy Saturday (see Mateos 1962, ii. 69 and n. 1, 83). However, according to the fifth-century lectionary of the Church of Jerusalem, preserved in Armenian, Matt. 27: 62–6 was read at matins on Holy Saturday already in the fifth century (see Wilkinson 1981, 270).

[19] According to the current rite, and also according to the tenth-century typikon of the Great Church: see Mateos 1962, i. 360. 28–362. 2 (for the Liturgy), and ii. 184. 26–7 (for Matins).

[20] On the vigil service and the evidence for it in its various forms, see Taft 1986, 165–213.

The Christmas homily has many oddities. It opens with remarks about the arrival of spring, and compares the Incarnation with the renewal that accompanies spring. It is not clearly on any particular Gospel passage, but draws on both the Infancy narratives (Matt. 1: 18–2: 23 and Luke 2). The three hagiographical homilies were presumably intended for the celebration (*panêgyris*) of the individual saints: St Artemios on 20 October, St Barbara on 4 December (normally: some local calendars observe 3 or 11 Dec.), St John Chrysostom on 27 January.[21] But our texts help us to no closer identification of their occasion.

How does all this affect their content and structure? The effect on content is evident: John's homilies are about the saint or mystery celebrated. On structure: it seems to me significant that the homilies on the Dormition appear to take account of the rigours of an all-night vigil. The first homily, though it is not the longest, is the most dense theologically, and concentrates on the Incarnation and Mary's place in it. The second, the longest, tells the traditional story of the Assumption of the Mother of God, and dwells on its significance, both theologically and for our devotion to the Mother of God. The third homily is quite brief, and presents its message in colourful imagery, already introduced in the first two homilies, much of which recalls the titles ascribed to the Mother of God in Byzantine hymnography, not least the Akathist Hymn.

Four of the homilies seem to me to stand out: the homily on the Transfiguration and the trio of homilies on the Dormition. They do so because, in them John develops something that is parallel to his liturgical poetry: all four of them explore the meaning of the feast by a kind of re-creation of the liturgical event. All of them merit close attention, and beg comparison with the liturgical poetry of the feast involved. In the rest of this chapter, we shall look at them in some detail. In the case of the homily on the Transfiguration, we find ourselves on a path that leads from Origen via the Macarian Homilies and Maximos to one of the central themes of later hesychasm; with the homilies on the Dormition, we shall find ourselves tracing something of the development of devotion to Mary among the Orthodox Christians of Palestine. The comparison with the liturgical poetry of the Damascene we shall leave to the next and final chapter, devoted to his poetry.

---

[21] Kotter specifies this date, the date of the translation of his relics (Kotter v. 351): I do not see why it could not have been intended for the date to which the celebration of his death is transferred, 13 Nov.

(b) The Homily on the Transfiguration of the Lord

John's homily on the Transfiguration takes its place in a long tradition of interpretation of the Gospel mystery.[22] From the very beginning the Fathers were fascinated by this mystery: Irenaeus's famous assertion— *Gloria enim Dei vivens homo, vita autem hominis visio Dei*, 'the glory of God is a live human being, and a truly human life is the vision of God'[23]—occurs in a chapter in which, without explicitly mentioning the Transfiguration, Irenaeus draws together all the themes brought into focus in that mystery: the unknowability of God, his manifestation in the Incarnation, and the transformation of the bodily seen there and offered to those who acknowledge the manifested glory. It is already apparent that, as they seek to understand the Transfiguration, the Fathers are not talking about an event confined to the life of Jesus, but about an experience known and experienced in the life of the Church. So we read in the late-fourth-century Macarian Homilies: 'as the body of the Lord was glorified, when He went up into the mountain and was transfigured in the divine glory and the infinite light, so are the bodies of the saints glorified and shine like lightning'.[24]

    In the Greek tradition, it was Origen who established the pattern of interpretation of the Transfiguration. For him, certain features of the Gospel account were significant.[25] Jesus is said to have been transfigured 'before' the three disciples he took with him up the mountain (tradition-ally, Mount Tabor): why before? why only three disciples? Origen answered these questions by seeing in the Transfiguration an example of what was, for him, a principle: namely, that in the Incarnation Jesus appeared in different forms to different people according to their spiritual aptitude. This, the clearest manifestation of his divine glory, demanded the greatest receptivity, hence it was granted only to the inner three among the disciples. The Transfiguration was seen, then, as the summit of Christian experience of Christ, and the Apostles could provide clues as to the qualities required. Then there is the assertion that it took place after

---

[22] See Coune 1985, for a collection of texts in French translation illustrating the history of the interpretation of the Transfiguration; McGuckin 1986 contains a wide selection of texts translated into English on the Transfiguration. There is a French translation of John's homily in Rozemond 1959, 93–103 (also included in Coune 1985, 187–207).

[23] Irenaeus, *haer.* IV. 20. 7 (Harvey, ii. 219).

[24] Makarios, *hom.* 15. 38 (Dörries *et al.* 149).

[25] The following is based on Origen's interpretation of the Transfiguration in his *comm. in Matt.* 12. 31–43 (Klostermann and Benz, 136. 20–170. 17).

six days (so Matthew and Mark) or eight (so Luke). Here a contradiction needed to be reconciled, both historically and, more important, spiritually. The discrepancy was generally resolved at the historical level by pointing to the difference between inclusive and exclusive counting. But contradictions in Scripture were, according to Origen, signs to seek a deeper meaning, which he duly did: six days indicated the six days of creation, and therefore the world perceived through the senses; eight days go beyond the limit of six (a perfect number, too, Origen points out), so the suggestion is that the Transfiguration takes place to those who have passed beyond the created order. Again this points to the idea of the Transfiguration as a lofty spiritual experience. The face of Jesus, 'altered' (Luke) or 'shining like the sun' (Matthew), and his garments, radiantly white, all beg for interpretation: the shining face indicates that the trans-figured Lord appears only to 'the children of light', while the whitened garments indicate the transparency of the Scriptures to those of deep enough spiritual experience. The presence of Moses and Elias points to the harmony between the Old Testament (the Law and the Prophets) and the New Testament of the Lord. Peter's words to Jesus—'it is good for us to be here, let us make three tabernacles . . .'—Origen interprets as an attempt by Peter to deter Jesus from his mission, parallel to the words after his confession of faith, when he sought to dissuade Jesus from the passion and death he had prophesied (Matt. 16: 22–3), explaining that before the Resurrection, the disciples were far from being perfect. Such a negative interpretation had few echoes in subsequent tradition. The cloud descends: the cloud of the divine presence, the Shekinah. The disciples fall to the ground in awe and confusion, and when they raise their eyes, they see 'Jesus alone' (Matt. 17: 8).

Origen's interpretation of the Transfiguration provided a basis for later interpretations. But these could take very different forms. Eusebios of Cæsarea, the Church historian, appealed to the Transfiguration in responding to a request from the Emperor Constantine's sister, Constantia, for a picture of the Lord. This, he says, is not possible, for Christ is now risen, so his bodily form is now transfigured, and even the disciples could not bear to look at the transfigured Lord.[26] Such an interpretation was probably unusual, but the letter became part of the arsenal of the iconoclasts (probably later, as John seems not to have known of it). A rather different development of the Origenist interpreta-tion of the Transfiguration is found in Maximos the Confessor, who uses Dionysios's language of apophatic and cataphatic theology to interpret

[26] Hennephof 1969, 110.

the mystery. The light irradiating his body and his clothes, so that the human aspect of Christ becomes transparent to the divine nature, speaks to Maximos of the transparence and limpidity of Scripture and creation to those whose understanding has been purified and attuned to Christ. That is the cataphatic side, as Maximos puts it, the affirmative side of the Transfiguration. But the face, the face altered and shining like the sun: that draws us into a mystery beyond anything we can understand, into the mystery of the person of Christ, the divine Person who assumed our human nature. The face of Christ—face and person being the same word in Greek: *prosôpon*—speaks of the 'characteristic hiddenness of his [divine] being'.[27] This is the face-to-face encounter with Christ, it is that to which all the radiance draws us, but it is an unfathomable mystery. We simply gaze, and are struck with awe at the ineffable personal encounter that lies behind all that is revealed in the radiance flowing from his body and his clothes. What we find here in Maximos is a fusing together of a mysticism of darkness and a mysticism of light, an assimilation of the two mountains of divine revelation: Sinai and Tabor. The light of the Godhead irradiates the created humanity of Christ, and draws us into a state where the whole cosmos is revealed as shot through with the light of the Godhead; but the light itself, because it is the light of the uncreated Godhead, and therefore itself uncreated, cannot be grasped by our human faculties.

This is the background for John's interpretation of the Transfiguration in his homily. In this homily John displays his skills both rhetorical and theological. It is addressed to what seems to be a monastic congregation (*philotheon systêma*: *Transfig.* 1. 1), and is punctuated by appeals to them to celebrate the mystery of the Transfiguration and meditate on its meaning. Where John excels is in his theological meditations, principally on the Trinity and Christology. His theology is expressed with precision, much as we find it in *On the Orthodox Faith*. If we think that such precision belongs to a theological treatise, rather than a homily, we should perhaps recall that even Byzantine liturgical poetry, written to be sung, delights in language of similar precision. Compare, for instance, this passage from the beginning of the sermon:

For whom is this feast and celebration? For whom this gladness and rejoicing? For those who fear the Lord, who worship the Trinity, who reverence the Father, the Son and the coeternal Spirit, who confess with soul and mind and mouth one

[27] Maximos, *qu. dub.* 191. 48 (Declerck, 134). The Transfiguration is also interpreted by Maximos in his *cap. theol.* ii. 13–18 (PG 90. 1129C–1133B), and in *ambig.* 10. 17, 31 (PG 91. 1125D–1128D, 1160B–1169B).

Godhead, acknowledged undividedly in three Persons, who know and say that Christ is acknowledged to be the Son of God and God, one person in two undivided and unconfused natures with their natural properties. (*Transfig.* 1. 4–10)

with a Theotokion (a liturgical verse, or troparion, addressed to, or concerning, the Mother of God) for Saturday evening vespers:

Who does not bless you, all-holy Virgin? Who does not hymn your giving birth without travail? For the only-begotten Son, who shines out timelessly from the Father, the same went forth, incarnate ineffably from your pure blood, being God by nature, and becoming by nature human for our sake; not separated into two persons, but acknowledged unconfusedly in two natures. Beseech him, august all-blessed one, to have mercy on our souls.[28]

The homily begins with a repeated invitation to celebrate the feast: 'Come, let us celebrate, O God-loving assembly! Come, let us feast together with the heavenly powers that love to feast! . . . Come, let us cry out loudly with our lips, accompanied by well-sounding cymbals! Come, let us dance in the spirit!' (*Transfig.* 1. 1–4) He then defines who should join in this celebration: those who rightly confess the Trinity and Christ (see the passage quoted above).

The celebration then begins (*Transfig.* 2). The subject of the celebration is recalled in an anaphora, beginning 'Today'. We are in liturgical time; we are present with the disciples on the Mount of the Transfiguration:

Today, the abyss of unapproachable light. Today, a limitless out-pouring of divine radiance is clearly seen by the apostles on Mount Tabor. Today, Jesus Christ is recognized as Master of the Old and New Testaments. . . . Today, the exarch of the Old, Moses, the divine lawgiver, is present with Christ, the granter of the Law, as with his master, on Mount Tabor and discerns clearly His dispensation, into which of old he was initiated figuratively—this, I might say, was when he saw the behind of God—and sees plainly the glory of the Godhead that he once beheld from a hole in the rock, as Scripture says. And the rock was Christ, God, Word and Lord made flesh. . . . Today, the supreme leader of the New Testament, who confessed Christ the Son of God most plainly with the words, 'You are the Christ the Son of the Living God', sees the exarch of the Old, present with the one who granted the Law to them both and talking to him clearly. (*Transfig.* 2. 1–19)

This recollection of where we are and whom we are among on this day of the Transfiguration closes with the claim: 'Today the virgin of the Old [Elias] proclaims to the virgin of the New [John] the Virgin from the Virgin' (*Transfig.* 2. 23–5). John then turns to his audience: 'Today therefore, persuaded by the prophet David, "Let us sing psalms, let us sing

---

[28] Theotokion for vespers on Saturday of the second plagal tone: *Paraklitiki*, 597–8.

psalms to our God, let us sing psalms to our King" ' (*Transfig.* 2. 26–7), an exhortation that closes:

Let us also sing psalms in the Spirit that searches all things, even the ineffable depths of God, seeing the unapproachable light, the Son of God, in the light of the Father by the Spirit that enlightens everything. Now things beyond beholding have been seen by human eyes, an earthly body shining forth divine radiance, a mortal body the source of the glory of the Godhead. (*Transfig.* 2. 31–5)

John moves on to make his first theological point: 'O marvel surpassing all understanding! The glory does not come from outside the body, but from within from the Godhead of the transcendently divine Word of God, united to it hypostatically in an ineffable manner' (*Transfig.* 2. 38–40), a marvel to be understood thus: 'What was human became divine, and what was divine human by the mode of exchange and unconfused mutual coinherence and the strictest hypostatic union. For that which was eternally and this which became later were one' (*Transfig.* 2. 47–50).

John continues introducing the circumstances of the Transfiguration (*Transfig.* 3). The name of the mountain, Tabor, recalls the verse of the psalm: 'Tabor and Hermon shall rejoice in your name' (Ps. 88: 13). The verse is interpreted as if Hermon witnessed the first time Jesus was called 'beloved Son' by the Father in the presence of the Spirit (in the form of a dove) at his baptism, whereas Tabor witnessed the second occasion, at the Transfiguration: 'Whence [Tabor] skipped and rejoiced and imitated the leapings of lambs, having heard the same witness to sonship from the cloud, that is the Spirit, that the Father addressed to Christ, the giver of life' (*Transfig.* 3. 30–3). This can hardly be meant literally, since Hermon is about 100 miles north of where Jesus was baptized. 'Hermon' might, as the source of the river Jordan in which Jesus was baptized, be a metonymy for 'Jordan'. A further possibility, suggested to me by my colleague Crispin Fletcher-Louis, is that John might here betray awareness of a tradition of the cultic identity of Lebanon-Hermon and Jerusalem.[29] The joy of Tabor leads to a repeated apostrophe: 'O, rejoicing beyond understanding given to us! O, this blessedness beyond hope! O, the gifts of God conquering longing!' (*Transfig.* 3. 38–44).

There follows a contrast between Sinai, the mountain of revelation in the Old Testament, and Tabor, the mountain of revelation in the New: the one wreathed in smoke and darkness, the other filled with light and radiance. In the description of what happened on Tabor that follows, John lays stress on how the Incarnation transcends the original creation (*Transfig.* 4).

[29] See his article, Fletcher–Louis 2001, 267–71.

John turns again to his congregation, and calls on them to follow the disciples on to Tabor, which is presented as the mountain of virtues (*Transfig.* 5). He now comes closer to his exegetical task. First, we are taken to Caesarea Philippi (which he says is the same as Paneas, though he does not say that it is at the foot of Mount Hermon, something he can hardly have been ignorant of, as Hermon lies between Damascus and Paneas), to Peter's confession, which leads to an encomium of Peter (*Transfig.* 6. 29–34). Then John turns to Matthew 16: 28 (= Mark 9: 1 = Luke 9: 27), which immediately precedes the account of the Transfiguration (*Transfig.* 7).[30] This is the verse in which Jesus prophesies that 'there are those standing here, who will not taste death, until they see the Son of man coming in his kingdom'. John's treatment is tantalizing. What he draws out of it is that not all are equal, that some are chosen for higher revelations. The three chosen for the Transfiguration are the same three who will witness Gethsemane, their number being a symbol of the Trinity. John curiously suggests that, had Andrew been included in the inner group, Judas might have felt excluded and made that an excuse for his betrayal; but, because Andrew was not included, Judas could have no ground for feeling excluded! But he does not make at all explicit what relationship he sees between this verse and the account of the Transfiguration; he does not seem to follow the Latin tradition in seeing the Transfiguration as the fulfilment of this prophecy.

The next verse says that the Transfiguration took place after six or eight days, as we have seen. John's commentary (*Transfig.* 8) is a reworking of Origen's: six is a perfect number (he explains why: its factors, 1, 2, and 3 add up to 6 itself), which is why creation took six days, but the perfect are promised the vision of divine glory, which is beyond everything. Eight is a figure of the age to come, this life consisting of seven ages. And on Tabor the final vision of God was anticipated. In support of this exegesis, John cites Gregory Nazianzen and Dionysios the Areopagite.[31]

The three apostles are now introduced (*Transfig.* 9): Peter, the one to whom the Father revealed his confession of Christ; James, the first martyr; and John, the 'virgin of theology' (*Transfig.* 9. 7–8). He does not,

---

[30] John is unusual in this, in the Greek tradition, which generally sees the Transfiguration narrative as beginning with the next verse, Matt. 16. 29 (= Mark 9: 2 = Luke 9: 28) (though cf. Origen, *comm. in Matt.* 12. 31 (Klostermann and Benz, 136. 20–138. 4)). The Latin tradition, by contrast, regularly begins with this verse, seeing the Transfiguration as its fulfilment: see Ambrose, *Luc.* 7. 1–6 (Schenkl, 281–4); Jerome, *Matt.* 3. 16. 28–17. 2 (Hurst and Adriaen, 146–7); Augustine, *Serm.* 78 (PL 38. 490BC).

[31] *Transfig.* 8. 22–9, referring to Gregory Nazianzen, *or.* 44. 5 (PG 36. 612C); Dionysios the Areopagite, *d.n.* 1. 4 (Suchla, i. 114. 7–11).

however, allegorize them, as, for instance, Maximos did.[32] Then the mountain itself (*Transfig.* 10): the idea already broached of the mountain as a symbol of the virtues is reintroduced, for 'love has been constituted as the summit and citadel (*akropolis*) of the virtues' (*Transfig.* 10. 2–3). In Luke's account, it is remarked that the Transfiguration took place while Jesus was at prayer. John picks this up now, prayer being implicit in the virtuous life that leads to the vision of God:

For the one, who has come to the pinnacle of love, goes out of himself in a certain way and beholds the invisible, and flying beyond the intervening darkness of the bodily cloud, he comes into the clear air of the soul, and reaches out more distinctly to the sun of righteousness, although he is not able to be filled with the vision, going aside by himself to pray; for quietness is the mother of prayer, and prayer the manifestation of divine glory. For when we lull the senses to sleep and hold converse with ourselves and God and, freed from the turmoil of the world outside, we enter within ourselves, then clearly within ourselves we shall see the kingdom of God. (*Transfig.* 10. 11–20)

Notice how John uses the metaphors of going out of oneself and entering into oneself in a complementary way. But the prayer of the Lord cannot be quite the same as our experience of prayer, and he deals with this, drawing on the same ideas he put forward in *On the Orthodox Faith (Expos.* 68). He concludes this discussion with an example of the contrast between Moses' and Jesus' experience of the divine glory: 'What happens to the one who beholds [God] in prayer recalls the radiant face of the glorified Moses. But Moses was glorified with a glory that came to him from outside, while the Lord Jesus does not have an acquired brightness of glory, it comes from the implanted radiance of the divine glory' (*Transfig.* 10. 39–43). This leads into further Christological meditation (*Transfig.* 11), which in turn leads to the Transfiguration itself, and the meaning of Christ being transfigured 'before them' (Matt. 17: 2 = Mark 9: 2). John's treatment of this (*Transfig.* 12) is very different from that of Origen, for whom, as we have seen, it refers to the way in which the Incarnate Word appeared in different ways to different people. John's interpretation, on the contrary, is that the Transfiguration involved no change in Christ: what happened was that the disciples came to see the enduring truth about the Incarnate Word. Both allow that Jesus appeared to people differently, but John insists that the reality they all encountered was the same, the truth:

---

[32] Maximos, *qu. dub.* 191 (Declerck, 133): Peter symbolizing faith, James hope, and John love.

He was transfigured then, not, assuming what he was not, nor changing into something that he was not, but what he was was revealed to his own disciples, opening their eyes and changing their blindness into sight. This, therefore, is what is meant by 'he was transfigured before them': remaining the same in himself, he now manifested himself to his disciples in another aspect than that in which he had manifested himself before. (*Transfig.* 12. 17–22)

John now comes to the transfigured Christ himself (*Transfig.* 13). Jesus' face 'shone like the sun'. John's interpretation is very like that of Maximos, though he presents it differently. The radiance of the face is the radiance of the divine Person he is: 'For he is the true light begotten eternally from the true and immaterial light, the Father's Word existing personally, the effulgence of his glory, the natural stamp of the person of God the Father. His is the face that shone like the sun' (*Transfig.* 13. 3–7). (In Greek, the echo of the Nicene Creed, 'true light from true light', is much clearer.) John then launches into an apostrophe of the evangelist. He follows this with a corollary important for his understanding of the icon, which, in fact, anticipates the objections of the iconoclasts of the Synod of Hiereia:[33]

The holy body is therefore circumscribed—for, standing on Tabor, it did not stretch outside the mountain—the Godhead being uncontained by anything and beyond everything. And the body shines like the sun; for the radiance of light comes from the body. For all the properties of the one incarnate Word of God have become common, those of the flesh and those of the uncircumscribable Godhead. (*Transfig.* 13. 23–8)

Moses and Elias are introduced (*Transfig.* 14), demonstrating the unity of the Old Testament with the New. Moses further symbolizes the unity of God (John refers to the *Shema* (Deut. 6: 4)), and Elias (to whom God appeared as a 'gentle breeze': 3 Kgd. 19: 12) his hiddenness (*Transfig.* 15). Peter's words—'it is good for us to be here'—are treated as an understandable response to the wonder of the Transfiguration, but out of place: 'if Adam had not sought deification before the time, he would have achieved his desire. Do not seek good things before the time, O Peter' (*Transfig.* 16. 29–30).

The cloud descends—not a dark cloud as on Sinai, but a cloud of light (*Transfig.* 17. 7–8). And a voice is heard from the cloud: 'The voice of the Father has come from the cloud of the Spirit, "This is my beloved Son": this man you see, who looks like a man, who yesterday became man, who humbly walked among you, whose face now shines. This is my beloved

[33] See the Definition of the 754 Synod: Hennephof 1969, 222, 223, 225.

son, the one before the ages, the only-begotten, who alone came forth from the alone timelessly and eternally, from me, his progenitor, who is eternally from me and in me and with me, no later in his existence' (*Transfig.* 18. 2–9). The voice further proclaims his good pleasure in his Son:

For by the Father's good pleasure, his only-begotten Son and Word was incarnate; by the Father's good pleasure, in his only-begotten Son the salvation of the whole cosmos was wrought; by the Father's good pleasure, in the only-begotten Son the harmony of all was welded together. For if human kind is a little cosmos, naturally bearing in itself the bond of all being, visible and invisible, being both one and the other, the master and creator and ruler of all was truly well-pleased in his only-begotten and consubstantial Son of divinity and humanity, and through this to bring about the harmony of the whole creation, 'that God might be all in all' (1 Cor. 15. 28). (*Transfig.* 18. 13–23)

The cloud lifts: Moses and Elias have gone; only Jesus is seen by the disciples. As they descend, he commands them not to reveal what they have seen, for not all the disciples have yet attained perfection. John then draws his homily to a close by meditating on the rest of the words from the cloud: 'Hear him'. Hear him who said: 'You shall love the Lord your God with all your heart'; 'Be reconciled with your brother beforehand, and then go and offer your gift'; 'Love your enemies'; 'Judge not, and you will not be judged'. If we follow these commands, we shall ourselves be brought to taste the divine glory here on earth, and behold its fulfilment in heaven.

It is a lengthy homily, though I do not think it would take more than an hour to deliver (which 'all ages have thought a competency', as George Herbert remarked[34]). But it is a slow-moving, meditative sermon, full of repetition, which enables complex theological considerations to be developed. It moves back and forth from image to idea, building up before the minds of his congregation the implications of what is involved in the whole tableau of the Transfiguration. It is, in fact, a kind of audible icon, in which biblical imagery and the technical terminology of Chalcedonian theology are used to draw out the significance of the subject of our contemplation: the transfigured Christ. Here, in the contemplation of Christ, as Keetje Rozemond rightly remarks, we are at the heart of John's Christology.

It is very much a part of the tradition of Byzantine interpretation of the Transfiguration. Two ideas, however, he brings out more clearly than his

[34] George Herbert, *A Priest to the Temple*, ch. 7, in *The Works of George Herbert*, ed. F. E. Hutchinson (Oxford: Clarendon Press, 1941), 235.

forebears: first, the Trinitarian aspect of the Transfiguration (on the analogy, as his parallel of Hermon and Tabor suggests, of the long-standing Trinitarian interpretation of the baptism of Christ); secondly, that the radiance of Christ comes from within—which was to be of importance when the interpretation of the Transfiguration became a matter for dispute in the hesychast controversy of the fourteenth century. We also note the contrast, to which he returns again and again, between the Old Testament and the New, Sinai and Tabor, darkness and light.

(c) The Homilies on the Dormition of the Mother of God

As already noted, the three homilies on the Dormition (or Koimesis, or Falling Asleep) of the Mother of God were delivered as a trio, as part of an all-night vigil, and the three homilies themselves give evidence of the exigences of such a strenuous occasion.[35] They are among the most carefully crafted of his homilies, with much use of rhetorical devices to (it seems to me) considerable effect, both dramatically and also theologically: the rhetoric reflects the theological reality it is expounding. The structure of the homilies taken as a trio is clearly significant: homily 1 is mainly concerned with the Incarnation, including the events of Mary's life that led up to the Nativity of the Lord (especially her Presentation in the Temple and the Annunciation), as well as the prophetic foreshadowing of the Incarnation; homily 2 moves to the event of the Dormition and Assumption itself, and founds this theologically on the fact of Mary's perpetual virginity, an entailment of the Incarnation already drawn out in homily 1; homily 3 is a celebration of the Assumption, worked out through elaborate imagery, the guiding thread of which is the metaphor of Mary as the ark that bore God. Throughout, the burden of the theological exposition is borne by imagery almost entirely inspired by the Old Testament (and already current in Byzantine poetry, not least in the Akathist Hymn and the canon that accompanies it liturgically). Another striking feature of these homilies is the use John makes of the Song of Songs in relation to Mary (such use is often alleged to be less common in the Byzantine East than in the Latin West: and it is certainly

---

[35] For John's Mariology in general, see Chevalier 1936; for the homilies on the Dormition, in particular, see ibid. 83–93, 198–206 (Chevalier's book suffers, as do many Roman Catholic works on Mariology published between the proclamation of the two Marian dogmas in 1854 and 1950, from a tendency to read back later developments; but he draws widely on the works of the Damascene, and gathers together a great deal of material).

true that the veritable explosion of commentaries on the Song in the twelfth century in the West has no parallel in the East[36]).

Although the tradition into which John enters in his homilies on the Dormition does not stretch back so far historically as meditation on the Transfiguration—the earliest homily on the Dormition is no earlier than the late sixth century, around the time when the emperor Maurice decreed that 15 August was to be observed as the feast of the Dormition—it is scarcely less developed, for the themes of the feast are clearly stated in the earliest of the surviving homilies; development was a matter of greater density of imagery, rather than new ideas.[37] A more significant tradition is that of devotion to the Mother of God, for though that can be traced back much earlier (the earliest prayer to the Mother of God being preserved on Papyrus John Rylands no. 470, which is dated no later than the early fourth century[38]), from the fifth century onwards, and especially after the Synod of Ephesus gave oecumenical authority to her title of *Theotokos*, devotion to the Mother of God had found wider and wider expression, both in icons and in celebrations of her in hymns and other forms of liturgical poetry (for instance, the kontakion, not least those of the greatest poet of the kontakion, Romanos the Melodist).

The first homily begins with three biblical quotations, one each from Proverbs and Psalms which bear directly on the death of the saints (Prov. 10: 7 and Ps. 115: 6), and another rather different one from the Psalms—'Glorious things are spoken of you, city of God' (Ps. 86: 3). The city of God, the dwelling-place of God, is the Mother of God herself, who 'alone truly contained, uncircumscribably and in a way transcending nature and being, the Word of God who is beyond being' (*Dorm.* 1. 1). John then turns to his customary use of the literary figure of adynaton at the beginning of a passage of theological exposition, in which he includes an exemplum of a peasant who, while ploughing, sees a king passing by, and having nothing else to offer, offers him water in his cupped hands, thus offering from his neediness nothing more than his courage in approaching him (*Dorm.* 1. 2). After a brief apostrophe to Mary herself, John embarks on a brief, dense exposition of the doctrine of the Incarnation, in an apostrophe addressed to Christ (*Dorm.* 1. 3). Turning to address his audience directly, in an anaphora based on 'behold' and 'blessed [are you]' (the combination itself recalls the sixth beatitude and other sayings of the

---

[36] See Matter 1990.

[37] See most recently Daley 1998, which contains fine translations of early homilies on the Dormition (up to Theodore of Stoudios) and an excellent introduction.

[38] See Mercenier 1939, Stegmüller 1952.

Lord about seeing and blessedness), he calls on his audience to behold the consequences of the birth of the Son of God to the Mother of God manifest in her Dormition and Assumption (*Dorm.* 1. 4). John then turns to the events that led up to the Nativity: he tells of Mary's parents, Joachim and Anna, of Mary's Presentation in the Temple and her life there as a young girl, and her betrothal to Joseph (*Dorm.* 1. 5). Though all this is based on apocryphal material, John's account is sober, and avoids the fabulous. He now reaches the Annunciation, reciting the biblical account and commenting on it, often using anaphora: on the angel's words 'You have found grace with God', John comments of Mary,

Truly she found grace, she who was worthy of grace. She found grace, she who had worked hard in the field of grace and brought forth a heavy ear of corn. She found grace, she who had given birth to the seeds of grace, and brought forth a fat corn of grace. She found the abyss of grace, she who preserved sound the vessel of double virginity, and kept the soul virgin, no less than the body, whence also the virginity of the body has been preserved. (*Dorm.* 1. 7. 10–14)

John moves on through the dialogue between Mary and the angel, and as she realizes from the angel's words that it is God who is calling her, John introduces her *fiat* thus: 'she, hearing the name that she had always longed for and feared with sacred reverence, undid the penalty of disobedience and said with words full of fear and joy, "Behold the slave-girl of the Lord. Be it to me according to your word"' (*Dorm.* 1. 7. 29–32). This releases the power of God, and he 'accomplishes in her that mystery newer than all new things' (*Dorm.* 1. 8. 7), a phrase echoing John's characterization of the Incarnation in his *On the Orthodox Faith* as 'the newest of all new things, the only new thing under the sun' (*Expos.* 45. 44–5).

There follows immediately an apostrophe to Mary using a series of titles: the royal throne, the spiritual (*noētē*) Eden, and then, more precisely as the one prefigured by the ark (of Noah), the Burning Bush, the tablets of stone written on by God, the ark of the Law, the golden urn, the candelabra, the table, and the rod of Aaron that blossomed. The one born of Mary is called the flame of divinity, the 'definition and Word of the Father' (an expression taken from one of Gregory Nazianzen's homilies[39]), the manna, the unknown name 'that is above every name' (Phil. 2: 9), the eternal and unapproachable light, the heavenly bread of heaven, the uncultivated fruit. John then says that Mary was prefigured by the fire of the furnace, a fire at once dewy and burning (*pyr drosizon hama kai phlogizon*)—the furnace of the three holy children (Dan. 3: 49–50)—

---

[39] Gregory Nazianzen, *or.* 38. 13. 18–19 (Moreschini).

and also by the tabernacle in which Abraham had Sarah prepare a loaf baked in the ashes (according to the LXX: *enkryphios*) for the Lord, manifest as three angels at the oak of Mamre. Out of these John develops what one can only call a 'conceit' (as in the Metaphysical poets):

> human nature offered to God the Word who tabernacled in your womb, the first-fruits of your pure blood, the loaf baked in the ashes, baked as it were and made bread by the divine fire, which thus found its subsistence in the divine Person, and came truly to exist as a body animated by a rational and intellectual soul. (*Dorm.* 1. 8. 35–40)

Like the conceits of John Donne, this conceit of the Damascene gives a precise statement of (in this case) Christological doctrine through imagery closely perceived. John then introduces the image of Jacob's ladder—as if he had nearly forgotten it!—and passes on to consider other imagery provided by the oracles of the prophets. There is the fleece on which the Son of God descended like rain (cf. Ps. 71: 6), the virgin, whose conception Isaiah foretold (Isa. 7: 14), the mountain, 'out of which the corner-stone, Christ, is cut without human hands'[40]—'Is not this the virgin who conceived without seed and remained a virgin?' (*Dorm.* 1. 9). Then there is Ezekiel's closed door, through which the Saviour passed without opening it (Ezek. 44: 2). There are two things striking about all this imagery. First, it is all drawn from the Old Testament; the Virgin Mary is seen as the fulfilment of all Israel's hopes and longings; the Old Testament is ransacked for Marian imagery; we are a long way from the kind of anti-Jewish rejection of the Old Testament to which John is sometimes inclined. And secondly, how familiar all these images are! Most of them appear in the Akathist Hymn, already at least two centuries old by the time John preached this homily; even more are to be found (and this may be significant, for the canon is later than the hymn) in the canon that accompanies the liturgical singing of the Akathist.[41]

John brings this section to a conclusion with an apostrophe to the Mother of God in the form of an anaphora: 'It was you whom the prophets preached, you whom the angels serve, you to whom the Apostles minister, the virgin theologian serving the ever-virgin Theotokos' (*Dorm.* 1. 9. 16–18)—which brings John to the gathering

[40] Cf. Dan. 2: 34, 44; cf. also Isa. 28: 16, Ps. 117: 22, Luke 20: 17, and Eph. 2: 20.

[41] The Akathist Hymn speaks of Mary as ladder, bridge, (tilled) ground, table, tabernacle, ark, treasury, and bridal chamber; in addition, the canon that accompanies the hymn (somewhat later than it, perhaps more nearly contemporary with John) uses imagery of the queen, fiery throne of the Almighty, source of living water, rose, apple, lily, city, fleece (in this case Gideon's), Eden, dove, dwelling-place of light.

together of the Apostles to attend Mary in her last earthly moments. There may be a veiled reference to Dionysios's account of the Assumption in John's use of the Dionysian term *zôarchikos* to describe the body that she bore: whether or not that is so, this word is the key term in the transition to what follows.

For if the body that Mary bore is *zôarchikos*—flowing as a source of life—what must be the case with Mary's body that bore that body? This points to an infinite difference between Mary and the other servants of God.

What then should we call this mystery that concerns her? Death? But if your all-sacred and blessed soul is naturally separated from your all-blessed and immaculate body, and the body placed in the customary tomb, it will not then remain in death, nor will it be dissolved by corruption. For if the virginity of the one who gave birth remained intact, then the body of this one, when she passes away, will be guarded undissolved, and transferred to a better and more divine tabernacle, not broken off by death, but continuing forever to ages of ages without end. (*Dorm.* 1. 10. 17–24)

It is as he celebrates the assumption of Mary's body that John turns to the Song of Songs: 'you have flourished "like an apple in the trees of a thicket" [Cant. 8: 5], and your fruit is sweet in the throat of the faithful' (*Dorm.* 1. 10. 36–8). Therefore, instead of 'death' we should speak rather of sleep, passage, or entry (*koimêsis, ekdêmia, endêmia*: *Dorm.* 1. 10. 39). As he contemplates the reception of Mary's soul (so he specifies: *Dorm.* 1. 11. 3) into heaven, he hears the angelic beings greeting Mary in the words of the Song:

'Who is this who ascends shining white?' 'Looking forth like the dawn, fair as the moon, bright as the sun?' How beautiful you have become, how gentle! You are 'a flower of the meadow', 'like a lily among thorns', 'therefore the maidens love you'. 'Let us run after the fragrance of your ointments. The king has brought you into his secret chamber': and authorities bear you within, principalities bless you, thrones hymn you, the rejoicing cherubim are astonished, and the seraphim glorify the one who has been revealed in the economy as the true and natural mother of our own Lord. (*Dorm.* 1. 11. 5–13)[42]

Death has now taken on a new meaning: no longer an occasion for grief and sorrow, but a cause of joy and celebration. As well as her soul, Mary's body—the true ark, prefigured by the ark of the covenant—is not abandoned on earth, but assumed into heaven (*Dorm.* 1. 12). The tomb itself has become glorious (*Dorm.* 1. 13). The homily ends with a prayer consecrating John and his hearers to the Mother of God.

---

[42] Quoting Cant. 8: 5; 6: 10; 2: 1, 2; 1: 3, 4.

The second and third homilies build on this basis. The second homily focuses on the account of the Assumption itself, based on traditions that have been handed down 'from father to child' (*Dorm.* II. 4. 4),[43] presumably in Jerusalem, where John may well have been preaching. This is introduced by an elaborate reprise, in an anaphora of the word 'today', of the biblical imagery of the Virgin Mother of God: ark, dove, Eden of the new Adam, the truly ensouled heaven, the treasury of life, the abyss of grace, and finally, the living city of God, the heavenly Jerusalem (*Dorm.* II. 2–3). In his account of the Assumption, John imagines the dialogue between Mary and her Son, as she lies on her deathbed: here, too, John draws heavily on the Song of Songs to represent their encounter. Then John moves on to consider its significance. A long anaphora draws out the necessity of the Assumption, entailed by Mary's perpetual virginity and divine motherhood: *edei . . ., edei . . ., edei.* One of these acclamations includes the idea that the pains that Mary was spared in her virginal birth-giving she experienced at the foot of the Cross: 'It was necessary that the one who beheld her own Son on the cross, and received in her heart the sword of the pain that she had been spared when she gave birth, should contemplate him seated beside his Father' (*Dorm.* II. 14. 27–9). John dwells on the reality of the Incarnation and the divine motherhood, to which there corresponds the reality of the Assumption, and leads into a prosopopeia of the tomb which has become a source of grace: as in Christ's case, so in that of his mother (*Dorm.* II. 17). In between the tomb's words and the response of John and his audience, there has been incorporated in all manuscripts (and explicitly) a long extract from the *Euthymiac History* which itself is bound up with the legend of the discovery of the robe of the Virgin. But it is so evidently an interpolation that we can omit any consideration of it here. The response of John and his audience to the tomb brings the homily to a close.

The final homily is very brief, and expressed almost entirely in terms of encomiastic imagery. He begins by saying that it is not difficult to give a third homily in one night on the Dormition of the Mother of God, for lovers always have the name of their beloved on their lips, and picture her in their mind's eye day and night. It is a celebratory recall of the earlier homilies: the imagery is the same, there are the same anaphorae, including another based on *edei.* He introduces one section with a striking antimetabole: 'Today she receives the beginning of her second existence from him who gave her her first existence, she who gave him the beginning of his second, I mean his bodily existence' (*Dorm.* III. 4. 1–3).

[43] Cf. *Imag.* I. 23. 35–7/II. 16. 35–7, which also relates to Jerusalem traditions.

This final homily ends with an elaborate encomium of the Mother of God.

From this account it will be evident that John expresses his theology in these homilies in a way that, far from aspiring to the condition of a florilegium, aspires rather to that of poetry, but poetry that expresses quite as precisely as any prose a carefully formulated doctrine of the Incarnation.

Interlude: Steps to the Altar:
John the Monk at prayer

In the homilies of John Damascene, or at least some of them, we seem to be able to peer beyond the teacher and the controversialist, and glimpse something of what moved his heart, his inner devotion. We shall discern more of this in the final chapter when we look at how his mind and heart found expression in song. But before we do that, let us look briefly at his prayer. This we have already encountered, for there are several occasions in his more formally didactic works when John seems to pause and give us a glimpse of what moved him. We noticed this in the first chapter of the fuller version of the *Dialectica*, where he seems to invite his reader to embark on an ascetic and mystical search for the truth, a demanding way of prayer. We encountered this again in his exposition of Christology, when he paused to consider the prayer of the Lord (*Expos.* 68), and again when he dwelt on the meaning of our encounter with Scripture (*Expos.* 90). We also discovered this side of John in the course of his account of the divine mysteries, the holy Eucharist (*Expos.* 86). This last is significant, for the three prayers ascribed to John Damascene, printed in the *Patrologia Graeca*, are all prayers of preparation for receiving Holy Communion.[1]

The first two are familiar to all Orthodox Christians, as they are included in the Office of Preparation for Holy Communion.[2] They are short, simple prayers, in the first of which the communicant prays for absolution from his sins, so as to be counted worthy to receive the sacred mysteries without condemnation. In the second, a prayer to be said when already in church, the communicant confesses that, even standing before the holy doors, his mind is still distracted by evil thoughts, and appeals to Christ our God, 'who justified the publican, had mercy on the woman of Canaan, and opened the gates of Paradise to the Thief', to 'open for me the compassion of your love for human kind, and receive me as I draw near and touch you, like the Harlot and the woman with an issue of blood.

---

[1] PG 96. 816–17. Geerard lists them under *dubia* (*CPG* 8081), following Hoeck (1957, 29 n. 5). The fact that the prayers also exist in Arabic and (thence, presumably) in Georgian, as Hoeck mentions, seems to me to make their authenticity more, rather than less, plausible.

[2] See, e.g., Lash 1999, 49, 55–6.

For the one touched your hem and readily received healing, while the other clasped your most pure feet and obtained remission of her sins.' The communicant continues, 'But may I, poor wretch, who dare to receive your whole Body, not be burned up; but receive me like them, enlighten the senses of my soul, and burn up the indictment of my sin, at the intercessions of her who gave birth to you without seed, and of the heavenly Powers, for you are blessed to the ages of ages.'[3]

The third prayer is not included in the current Office of Preparation for Holy Communion, but is a prayer to be said immediately before receiving Communion. As it is less well known, it is given in full:

I am wounded in my heart. Your fervour made me melt, your love changed me, O Master; I am a prisoner of your love. Let me be filled with your flesh; let me be satiated with your life-giving and deifying blood; let me have enjoyment of your good things; let me be filled with the delights of your Godhead! Make me worthy to meet you, when you come in glory, caught up in the air in the clouds with all your chosen ones, as I hymn and worship and glorify you with thankgiving and confession, together with your Father without beginning and your all-holy and good and life-giving Spirit, now, and for ever, and to the ages of ages. Amen.

These prayers give us a glimpse of John's devotion to the Eucharistic mystery, in which his love for the Lord was deepened and purified, as he looked to the final meeting with the Lord 'coming in his kingdom', experienced in anticipation at the Eucharistic banquet.

[3] Trans. by Fr Ephrem Lash, ibid.

Γλυκορρήμων ('sweetly speaking'): John the Poet

What shall I call you, divine sweetly-speaking John: most radiant star, one whose sight is illuminated by the lightning flash of the Trinity? You entered into the dark cloud of the Spirit; you were initiated into the ineffable mysteries of the Divine; like Moses you made things clear in the beautiful language of the Muses. Intercede that our souls may be saved.[1]

So far we have looked at John Damascene's theological *œuvre* and his homilies. We have seen that John was famous as a preacher in his own lifetime, and that his fame as a theologian was felt throughout the Middle Ages and beyond, not least in the West, but also in most parts of the world where Christianity took root. But, so far as the Byzantine world is concerned, all this is peripheral. Certainly, John's fame as a theologian was felt in that world, too, but much greater fame attached to his liturgical poetry. A few learned scholars—perhaps even many learned scholars—knew about John's *On the Orthodox Faith*; only a few of the learned knew of his polemical works, his introduction to logic, his sermons. But everyone in the world touched by Byzantium knows John's great Easter canon, 'The Day of Resurrection' (*Anastaseôs hêmera*), sung at midnight as part of the Easter Vigil; and many know that it is John's. And any singer (or *psaltes*) knows many more pieces attributed to John, many of which are genuinely his. Such was his fame as a liturgical poet that within a few centuries of his death he was thought of as *the* liturgical poet, and credited with the whole of the *Paraklitiki*, the service-book which contains the texts for the basic eight-week cycle on which the Byzantine liturgical year is based. Perhaps three centuries after his death, another Damascene, Peter, in a large compilation of Byzantine ascetical and theological wisdom eventually included in the *Philokalia*, several times

---

1 Second sticheron at vespers on the feast of St John Damascene: *Menaion* (4 Dec.), 37.

quotes from John, and in virtually every case it is the *Paraklitiki* that he is quoting.[2]

Scholarly work on the riches of Byzantine liturgical poetry is in its infancy, and much uncertainty remains about the attributions found in the service-books, but there is little doubt about the important role that John played in building up this literary heritage. The Easter canon is certainly his, and so are many others.[3] It is with the canon that his fame is especially associated, so we shall begin this chapter by discussing the development of the canon and John's role in it.

(a) Palestinian Monasticism and the Development of the Canon

There is a tradition, the influence of which we have already met in the *Life of St John Damascene*, that monasticism was initially opposed to singing. It is now held that this idea of monastic opposition to singing is a later development, as there are no such stories from the early Desert Fathers.[4] Nevertheless, the first form of liturgical poetry to develop in the Byzantine world emerged, not in the monastic office, but in the services in the great city churches, in the so-called Cathedral Office.[5]

This was the kontakion, a kind of verse sermon, that formed part of the vigil service for Sundays and great feasts and during Lent.[6] Its origins appear to be Syrian,[7] and its first great exponent—indeed, the greatest composer of kontakia ever—was Romanos the Melodist, a native of Emesa (modern Ḥimṣ in Syria), who spent most of his adult life in Constantinople, his time there coinciding roughly with the reign of the Emperor Justinian. The name for this kind of liturgical verse, kontakion, is late, not found before the ninth century; those who composed these verses called them hymns or psalms, poems, songs, praises, or prayers. The form of the kontakion consists of an initial stanza, called in Greek the *koukoulion*, followed by a number of longer stanzas, all in identical metre, called *oikoi* ('houses', a term used in Syriac for stanzas of liturgical poetry; the modern transliteration of *oikos* is *ikos*, which is more commonly used). The stanza, after which the others are modelled, is called the *heirmos* (or

[2] For Peter of Damascus, see *Philokalia* 1979 ff., iii,74–281, with introductory note, 70–3.

[3] For a start in assessing John's contribution, see the remarkable series of articles by Eustratiades based on study of liturgical manuscripts: Eustratiades 1931–3.

[4] McKinnon 1994, 508.

[5] On which see Taft 1986, 31–56, 165–90.

[6] For the kontakion, see Wellesz 1961, 179–97, and also, with special reference to Romanos, Lash 1995, pp. xxiii–xxxii.

[7] See Brock 1989.

irmos), which may be specially composed for the kontakion (in which case it is the first *ikos*), or is a standard one (giving the metre, and probably the tune as well), referred to by its first line. The initial letters of the stanzas either form an acrostic (in Romanos's case, often, TOU TAPEINOU ROMANOU: 'of the humble Romanos') or are arranged in alphabetical order, or are a combination of both. The last line of the *koukoulion* provides the last line of each of the following stanzas, forming a kind of refrain. It is likely that, when originally performed, the chanter sang the stanzas, with the whole choir (or perhaps the whole congregation) picking up the refrain.

The kontakion formed part of the vigil service until the end of the twelfth century; in Constantinople itself it seems to have continued until 1204, when continuity was broken with the sacking of the city by the crusaders.[8] But by that time kontakia were no longer being composed, Joseph the hymnographer (812/18–*c*.886) being the last known composer of kontakia. For liturgical inspiration had migrated from the great city churches to the monasteries, where, from the time of John of Damascus, there developed another form of liturgical poetry, called the canon. This formed part of the monastic vigil service, which included the singing of the nine biblical odes, or canticles, which are normally included in psalters after the psalms, and therefore printed after the psalms in editions of the Septuagint. These nine odes are:

1. The Song of Moses: Exod. 15: 1–19
2. The Song of Moses: Deut. 32: 1–43
3. The Song of Anna (or Hannah): 1 Kgd. [1 Sam.] 2: 1–10
4. The Prayer of Avvakum (or Habakkuk): Hab. 3: 1–19
5. The Prayer of Isaias: Isa. 26: 9–20
6. The Prayer of Jonas: Jonas 2: 3–10
7. The Prayer of the Three Holy Children: Dan. 3: 26–56 (LXX)
8. The Song of the Three Holy Children (the 'Benedicite'): Dan. 3: 57–88 (LXX) + three further verses[9]
9. The Song of the Mother of God (the *Magnificat*): Luke 1: 46–55, and the Song of Zacharias (the *Benedictus*): Luke 1: 68–79

The canon consists of stanzas (called troparia) corresponding to each of these odes, which were sung between the last few verses of each ode

[8] Lingas 1995.

[9] The three further verses are: 'Bless the Lord, Apostles, Prophets and Martyrs of the Lord, praise him and exalt him to the ages. Let us bless the Lord, Father, Son and Holy Spirit; let us praise him and exalt him to the ages. Let us praise, bless and worship the Lord, praising him and exalting him to the ages.'

(all of which, save the eighth ode, end with the little doxology: Glory to the Father, and to the Son, and to the Holy Spirit; Both now and for ever and to the ages of ages. Amen). The second ode, probably because of its length and its minatory tone, soon dropped out, except during the penitential season of Lent, with the result that very few canons, except those for Lent, contain any stanzas for the second ode.[10] The troparia generally have some reference to the ode in which they are inserted, though it is sometimes very slight, particularly in the later canons.

Though the canon developed in a different liturgical context, it shows the influence of the kontakion. The initial letters of the troparia of the canon frequently form an acrostic, though it is rare for the canon to have a refrain (the endings of some of the troparia, however, often echo the ending of the irmos). But generally the canon is a different sort of liturgical verse from the kontakion. Whereas the kontakion is a chanted sermon, the canon is much more like a series of meditations, though this contrast is by no means absolute; later kontakia are generally much more meditative than Romanos's chanted sermons, but some of the earlier canons retain elements of the kontakion (for instance, the dramatic dialogue in Cosmas's canon for the Annunciation). The most far-reaching difference between the kontakion and the canon, however, as Wellesz points out, lies 'in the increased use, and the greater variety, of the music in the new poetical genre'.[11] Cathedral vigils were relatively infrequent: the tenth-century typikon of the Great Church prescribes kontakia for only twelve vigils,[12] and even if this represents a decline from earlier usage, it is a long way short of the frequency of the canon, which came to be used daily in monastic services. The variety of the music for the canon is inherent in it, in that whereas the kontakion was sung throughout to one tune, the troparia of the canon were sung to different tunes corresponding to each ode. More than this it is difficult to say, as manuscripts with musical notation do not date back as far as the origin of the canon.

Gradually monastic usage influenced the liturgical practice in non-monastic churches, though this process took place much more slowly than was once thought, and with the break in continuity of liturgical tradition at the Great Church of Hagia Sophia in 1204, monastic models became virtually universal throughout the Byzantine world (though the

[10] See Gahbauer 1995, 148, for some exceptions. For weekdays in Lent, the canon takes a different form, having stanzas for only three of the odes (the first varying according to the day of the week and the last two); the service-book for Lent is thus called the *Triodion*.

[11] Wellesz 1961, 202.

[12] See the table in Lingas 1995, 55.

Cathedral Office was still in use in Thessaloniki at the beginning of the fifteenth century). Of particular importance in this growing influence of monastic liturgy was the Stoudios monastery in Constantinople, after its renewal under Theodore of Stoudios at the beginning of the ninth century.

The beginnings of the distinctive monastic liturgical practice that was eventually to be determinative for the Byzantine world are to be found not in Byzantium itself, but in the monasteries of Jerusalem and the Judaean desert, not least the monastery of Mar Saba, where John may well have been a monk. It was Sabaïte practice that Theodore introduced to the Stoudios monastery, something very likely encouraged by the influence of the small group of monks led by Michael the Synkellos, who arrived in Constantinople from Palestine at the beginning of the second period of iconoclasm and, throwing in their lot with the iconophiles led by Theodore, made Constantinople their home.[13]

It was not just in refining and defining Orthodox theological doctrine that the monks of Palestine played such an important role in the first century under Arab rule, therefore, but also in the development of liturgical forms, especially the canon, that were to become characteristic of the Byzantine Christian tradition. And in both aspects of this development of what was to be characteristic of Byzantine Orthodoxy, John played a central part. There are three names associated with the creation of the canon: Andrew of Crete, Cosmas the Melodist, and John Damascene. They were contemporaries, and all had links with Jerusalem and its monasteries. Further, they may all have come from Damascus. Andrew was born there, like John, and according to legend, Cosmas was John's schoolmate in Damascus. Andrew was tonsured a monk at the monastery connected with the Church of the Anastasis in Jerusalem, with which, as we have seen, John as a preacher might have been associated, before administering an orphanage in Constantinople, and then, sometime between 692 and 713, becoming bishop of Gortyna and metropolitan of Crete. Cosmas is said to have been a monk in Palestine before becoming bishop of Maïuma, by tradition at the same monastery as John (according to the *Synaxarion of Constantinople*, John embraced the monastic life 'together with Cosmas'[14]), perhaps the monastery of Mar Saba.

---

[13] Michael's two most famous companions were the 'graptoi' (branded) brothers, Theophanes and Theodore, so-called from having had verses cut into their faces at the order of the Emperor Theophilos because of their staunch opposition to iconoclasm. See Cunningham 1991.

[14] *Synaxarion* 279, 1–2. As already noted (in Ch. 1), the *Synaxarion* does not mention the name of the monastery.

Andrew of Crete composed a number of canons, notably the 'Great Canon', an immensely long penitential canon, sung during the first week of Lent (divided over four days) and on the Thursday of the fifth week of Lent. For many of the greater feasts of the liturgical year, there are two canons: in the case of the feasts of Christmas and the Theophany, the Transfiguration and the Dormition, one is ascribed to Cosmas, and the other to John. According to Nikodimos, both Cosmas and John composed canons for Easter, too, but only John's has ever been used, since Cosmas felt that his canon did not bear comparison with John's.[15] Andrew has sometimes been claimed to be the inventor of the canon.[16] Eustratiades dismissed this claim, arguing that 'only the musical and poetic power of the Damascene John would have been adequate to introduce into the Church these new forms of song and effect the change without causing a scandal'.[17] Eustratiades, however, like most scholars until very recently, seems to have envisaged the canon immediately overthrowing the kontakion at the turn of the seventh century. As I have argued above, this notion rests upon a misunderstanding, for the canon emerged in a different liturgical context from the kontakion, and only very gradually supplanted it. Furthermore, even if John's poetic talent is in some respects greater than that of Andrew or Cosmas, we should perhaps look to the circle of the three for the emergence of the canon, rather than to the creative genius of any individual.

Our concern, however, is with John and his liturgical poetry. Eustratiades characterizes John's poetical gifts in these terms: 'he does not have the spontaneity nor the lyricism of Romanos or Cosmas, but there is sweetness in his rhythm and diction and simplicity in his description. His lyre is inspired by the life-giving tomb and floods the souls of Christians with joy and happiness. The resurrection of the Lord is the subject of his greatest song, and his grace-filled flute plays about it.'[18] This echoes what is said in the troparion quoted at the beginning of the chapter: the sweetness of his poetry, and the clarity of its description, in the latter case comparing John to Moses, seen less as lawgiver and prophet, or the one who recounted the creation of the world, as one who expressed himself in song, not least the songs that constitute the first two odes. We shall see something of this in the rest of this chapter, which will

[15] See Nikodimos 1987, ii. 289 n. Nikodimos asserts that Cosmas's canon survives (or survived in the eighteenth century) in a manuscript at the monastery of Vatopedi.

[16] Wellesz 1961, 204.

[17] Eustratiades 1931, 501.

[18] Ibid. 500.

be devoted to exploration of three of John's canons: first, his most famous canon, the 'Queen of Canons', the canon for Pascha; and then the canons devoted to those mysteries we have already explored in his homilies, the Transfiguration of the Lord and the Dormition of the Mother of God. In doing so, we shall look simply at the troparia of the canons, glancing back to the odes that they accompany. In fact, there is both more and less when they are performed liturgically: more, in that various other troparia are added, including the final remnant of the kontakion, the *koukoulion* (now called simply the kontakion) and the first *ikos* (called simply the *ikos*), as well as litanies, and the commemorations of the day from the *synaxarion*; and less, in that (save during Lent, and in some monasteries) the odes themselves are omitted, except for the Song of the Mother of God, the *Magnificat*, which is sung before the stanzas of the canon. In each case, I shall first give an English translation of the canon, and then a brief commentary, ode by ode.[19]

John did, in fact, compose liturgical verse in other forms than the canon; Eustratiades lists as authentic many *irmoi*, a great number of troparia for Easter and the week following ('Bright Week', or the 'Week of Renewal'), most of which have not found their way into the service books, 'dogmatic theokotia' (troparia to the Mother of God that praise her in elaborately theological reflections on the Incarnation), other troparia in honour of the Mother of God, and many of the so-called anatolika, troparia interspersed in the set psalms for vespers on Saturday and lauds on Sunday. But it is in the canons that his poetic imagination gives expression to his theological insight most strikingly.

(b) The Paschal Canon

Ode 1 (Song of Moses). *1st Tone. Irmos*

The day of resurrection, let us be radiant, O peoples, Pascha, the Lord's Pascha; for from death unto life, and from earth unto heaven, Christ our God has brought us over, as we sing the triumphant song.

Troparia

Let us purify our senses and then we shall see in the light unapproachable of the Resurrection Christ shining forth, and we shall clearly hear him say 'Rejoice!', as we sing the triumphant song.

[19] The commentary is mostly indebted to that of Nikodimos (1987), which frequently indicates the sources that John used. What little commentary there is on this verse generally seems ignorant of Nikodimos's immense learning: unaccountably, neither Wellesz nor Eustratiades nor Gahbauer seems aware of him.

1. The Anastasis, Theophanis the Cretan (1546),
Stavronikita

Let the heavens, as is fitting, rejoice, and let the earth be glad; now let the universe entire, both seen and unseen, celebrate the feast; for Christ has risen, Christ our eternal joy.[20]

Nikodimos points out how the *irmos* is constructed by John from two passages from Gregory Nazianzen's two homilies for Easter, his first homily (on Easter and his lateness) and the last.[21] From the first homily,

[20] Text in *Pentekostarion*, 17–24. 'Critical' text with German translation in Gahbauer 1995, 135–46. Text and English translation in Wellesz 1961, 207–14. French translation in Roze-mond 1959, 84–6. For the English translation, I have used that by Fr Ephrem in Lash 2000, 5–16 (with some slight modifications). Nikodimos's commentary: 1987, ii. 277–336.

[21] Nikodimos 1987, ii. 280.

John takes the opening words: 'The day of resurrection, . . . let us be radiant'.[22] From the last homily, John takes, 'Pascha, the Lord's Pascha'; in fact, as Nikodimos points out, in Gregory's original homily, his words are: 'The Lord's Pascha, Pascha, and again I say Pascha, in honour of the Trinity.'[23] John also takes from Gregory the explanation of the word *pascha*, derived not from the Greek word, *paschein*, to suffer, but from the Hebrew, *pesach*, 'passover', referring to the passing over from Egypt to Canaan, but spiritually 'to the passage from below to above, and the procession and ascent to the land of the promise'.[24] This makes the link with the first ode, Moses' song of deliverance after crossing the Red Sea. A few words and an idea from Gregory provide John with the materials for his first *irmos*, which sets the tone for the whole canon.

According to Nikodimos, the first of the troparia is based on the notion that human kind is a twofold being, with both bodily and spiritual senses: a theme close to John's heart, as we have seen.[25] More precisely, Nikodimos finds in Gregory's last homily the notion that the paschal sacrifice is offered 'for the purification of the senses'.[26] Only if purified can we see Christ 'the light unapproachable of the Resurrection'.

For the second troparion, Nikodimos again refers us to Gregory Nazianzen,[27] this time his homily on the Theophany, where he quotes Psalm 95: 11: 'let the heavens rejoice and let the earth be glad',[28] and to the last homily for the rejoicing of the whole cosmos, seen and unseen.[29] The whole universe, seen and unseen, refers either to the angels and human kind, or perhaps, Nikodimos suggests, even to the inanimate elements.[30] We have seen that John, in common with other Fathers such as Maximos, affirms the truly cosmic dimension of Christ's victorious resurrection.

The tone of triumph and rejoicing that runs through these troparia chimes in well with the theme of the biblical ode they accompany, the Song of Moses: 'I will sing to the Lord, for he has triumphed gloriously; the horse and the rider he has thrown into the sea. My strength and my song, he has become my salvation!' (Exod. 15: 1–2). These are themes

[22] Gregory Nazianzen, *or.* 1. 1. 1–2 (Bernardi, 72).
[23] Gregory Nazianzen, *or.* 45. 2 (PG 36. 624D).
[24] Ibid. 45. 10 (PG 36. 636CD).
[25] Nikodimos 1987, ii.283.
[26] Gregory Nazianzen, *or.* 45. 14 (PG 36. 641C).
[27] Nikodimos 1987, ii. 285–6.
[28] Gregory Nazianzen, *or.* 38. 1. 4 (Moreschini, 104).
[29] Gregory Nazianzen, *or.* 45 (PG 36. 626B).
[30] Nikodimos 1987, ii. 286.

that are fresh in the memories of those who hear and sing this canon, for the Song of Moses is part of the vesperal liturgy of Holy Saturday.

Ode 3 (Song of Anna). *Irmos*

Come, let us drink a new drink, not one wondrously brought forth from a barren rock, but incorruption's source, which pours out from the sepulchre of Christ, in whom we are established.

Troparia

Now all things have been filled with light, both heaven and earth and all things beneath the earth; let all creation sing to celebrate the rising of Christ, by which it is established.[31]

Buried yesterday with you, O Christ, and today, as you arise, I am raised with you. I was crucified with you; O Saviour, grant me glory with you in your kingdom.

The third ode is the Prayer of Anna. The reference to the 'new drink' is possibly meant to recall that when Eli, finding Anna in the Temple, accused her of being drunk, she replied, 'I have been pouring out my soul before the Lord' (1 Kgd. 1: 15). More immediately it relates to the water Moses struck from the rock during the desert wandering (Num. 20: 10–11), but this is 'incorruption's source', echoing (or more probably the origin of) the communion hymn during Easter: 'Receive the body of Christ, taste the immortal source, Alleluia'. 'In whom we are established' is a reference to the beginning of Anna's song: 'My heart is established in the Lord' (1 Kgd. 2: 1).

The first troparion returns to the cosmic theme, introduced in the first ode. With the Resurrection, light has come, not just to heaven and earth, but also to the region beneath the earth, Hades, which was redeemed by Christ's descent there on Holy Saturday. Here we have a first allusion to the theme of the icon of the Resurrection, in which Christ is seen, breaking the gates of Hades, and bringing out those imprisoned there, beginning with Adam and Eve.[32]

The second troparion, as Nikodimos points out,[33] is derived from a passage in Gregory's first homily: 'Yesterday I was crucified with Christ, today I am glorified with him; yesterday I died with him, today I am given life with him; yesterday I was buried with him, today I am raised with him.'[34] But John has altered the order, unhistorically placing burial before

[31] Nikodimos argues that this last clause should read 'in whom it is established': 1987, ii. 289.

[32] For the development of the icon of the Resurrection, or Anastasis, see Kartsonis 1986.

[33] Nikodimos 1987, ii. 290.

[34] Gregory Nazianzen, *or.* 1. 4. 1–3 (Bernardi, 76).

crucifixion. The reason, Nikodimos suggests, is that John is concerned with what happens to us, with whom resurrection precedes glorification. This sharing with Christ in burial and crucifixion has three references, Nikodimos suggests: first, to our ascetic burial with Christ through the Lenten Fast; secondly, to Christ's identification with us in the Incarnation; and thirdly, to those baptized during Easter night.[35]

Ode 4 (Prayer of Avvakum). *Irmos*

Now let the prophet Avvakum inspired by God keep godly watch as sentinel with us; let him point out an angel bearing blazing light, who with resounding voice declares, 'Today is salvation for the world; for Christ has risen, as Omnipotent'.

Troparia

As a firstborn son, Christ appeared as a 'male', opening the virgin womb; as our food he is called 'lamb'; as our Pascha free from stain unblemished he is named, and is designated, 'perfect', as he is true God.

As a yearling lamb, blessed for us, the good crown, of his own free will and for all Christ our God was sacrificed, the Passover which purifies; from the tomb once again the fair Sun of Justice has shone for us.

God's forebear David dancing leaped before the sacred Ark; shadow was the Ark, but now seeing the fulfilment of the types, and full of God, let us God's holy people rejoice; for Christ has risen as Omnipotent.

The fourth ode is the Prayer of Avvakum (or Habakkuk). But, as is often the case in the canons, the reference is more immediately to where Avvakum was standing when he made his prayer, which is found in Habakkuk 2: 1: 'I will stand on my watch, and get up on a rock' (LXX). But, as Nikodimos notes, John arrives at this reference by way of the opening of Gregory's last homily.[36] Gregory opens by quoting Avvakum's words about standing at his watch, and says what he sees today, that is the day of Pascha: a vision of a man raised on the clouds, looking like an angel, with his clothes shining like lightning, crying out in a loud voice, 'Today is salvation for the world. . . . Today, Christ is risen from the dead, let us be raised with him.'[37]

The first troparion dwells on Christ our Pascha, sacrificed for us (cf. 1 Cor. 5: 7). The paschal lamb was to be 'without blemish, male, a year old' (Exod. 12: 5); John glosses this with Exodus 34: 19, about the male that opens the womb belonging to God. He also recalls another passage from Gregory's Easter homily: 'for us the lamb is eaten'.[38] With these

---

[35] Nikodimos 1987, ii. 290–1.   [36] Ibid. 291–2.

[37] Gregory Nazianzen, *or.* 45. 1 (PG 36. 624A).   [38] Ibid. 45. 16 (PG 36. 644D).

references, John puts together his troparion, meditating on Christ's sacrifice.

The second troparion continues this theme, laying stress on the voluntary nature of Christ's sacrifice. Again, John draws on Gregory's Easter homily, where he says of Christ as the paschal sacrifice: 'a year old, like the sun of justice, setting out from there [heaven], circumscribed in his visible nature, and returning to himself, and the "blessed crown of goodness",[39] being on every side equal to himself and alike; and not only this, but also as giving life to the circle of the virtues, gently mingled and mixed with each other, by the law of love and order'.[40] Here are all John's themes for this troparion. There is also a play on words, as Nikodimos points out,[41] in that the word translated 'good' in the troparion, is pronounced exactly like the word Christ (*christos/chrêstos*).

The last troparion refers to David dancing before the ark (2 Kgd. 6: 16–19). David celebrated what was simply a shadow of what was to come; Christians celebrate the fulfilment. 'Full of God, let us rejoice': for this Nikodimos refers to a passage in Gregory's homily for the Theophany: 'Let us celebrate, not as for a pagan festival, but divinely, not in a worldly manner, but in a manner that transcends the world.'[42]

Ode 5 (Prayer of Isaias). *Irmos*

Come let us arise in the early dawn, and instead of myrrh, the hymn of praise we shall offer to the Master; Christ himself we then shall see, the risen Sun of Righteousness, who causes life to dawn for all.

Troparia

Seeing your measureless compassion, those who were straitly constrained by the bindings and cords of Hades, pressing forward to the light, O Christ, they move with joyful steps, loudly they greet an eternal Pasch.

Let us go out bearing torches, and meet Christ as he comes from the sepulchre like a Bridegroom; with the Angels' festive ranks, together let us celebrate, feasting with them the saving Passover of God.

The fifth ode, the Prayer of Isaias, begins, 'By night my spirit watches for you, O God' (Isa. 26: 9 (LXX)). John's mind naturally goes to the myrrh-bearing women, the first witnesses of the Resurrection. The watching by night of the vigil, in which this canon is sung, is related to women coming to the sepulchre 'in the early dawn' (Luke 24: 1).

[39] Cf. Ps. 64: 12.
[40] Gregory Nazianzen, *or.* 45. 13 (PG 36. 641AB).
[41] Nikodimos 1987, ii. 296.
[42] Ibid. 298, quoting Gregory Nazianzen, *or.* 38. 4. 13–14 (Moreschini, 110).

Isaias's prayer closes by celebrating the redemption of the dead: 'the dead shall be raised, those in the graves will come out, and those on earth shall rejoice' (Isa. 26: 19). This theme is picked up in the troparia, the first of which returns to the theme of the redemption of Hades; John sees those who were bound pressing forward to Christ, as they are depicted in the icon of the Anastasis. The theme of rejoicing is tied to that of a wedding banquet, a favourite symbol of the coming of the Kingdom in the Gospel parables. Christ's tomb becomes a bridal chamber, from which he emerges as in the verse of the psalm (Ps. 18: 6). The bride he has made his own is the Church.

Ode 6 (Prayer of Jonas). *Irmos*

You went down to the deepest parts of the earth, and the everlasting bars you shattered, which held imprisoned those fettered there; O Christ, on the third day, like Jonas from the whale, you arose from the sepulchre.

Troparia

Unbroken you preserved the seals, O Christ, in your rising from the tomb, nor injured the locks of the virgin womb in your birth, and have opened to us the portals of Paradise.

My Saviour, living victim, and as God unsacrificed, yet to the Father willingly offering yourself, you raised with yourself all Adam's race, in your rising from the sepulchre.

The sixth ode is the Prayer of Jonas from the belly of the whale. The Lord's reference to the 'sign of Jonas', the prefiguring of his death and resurrection after three days by Jonas's three days in the whale (Matt. 12: 29–30), provides the obvious link between the ode and the Resurrection, the subject of the the Easter canon. Jonas himself says, 'I went down into the earth, whose bars held me fast eternally' (Jonas 2: 7 (LXX)), thus comparing his fate with descent into Hades. It is this that John picks up here: for Christ went down into the 'deepest parts of the earth' and shattered the bars that held fast those in Hades. Again, in this *irmos*, it is the theme of the Resurrection icon to which John returns.

The first troparion draws a parallel between Christ's rising from the sepulchre without breaking the seals and his being born from the Virgin Mother of God without harming her virginity, her *virginitas in partu*, which the Fathers saw prefigured in the gate of the Temple in Ezekiel's vision, which 'shall remain shut, . . . for the Lord, the God of Israel, has entered by it' (Ezek. 44: 2), as Nikodimos points out.[43] By passing through what remains sealed, Christ has opened for us the gates of Paradise.

[43] Nikodimos 1987, ii. 308.

The second troparion again draws on Gregory's second Easter homily, this time a passage in which Gregory is comparing Christ's sacrifice with sacrifices of the Old Covenant. These latter were not useless, a mere shedding of blood, 'but the great and, if I may say so, in its first [i.e., divine] nature, unsacrificed sacred offering [*athyton hiereion*, exactly as in the troparion] was mingled with the sacrifices of the law, and was a purification not for a small part of the world, nor for a brief period of time, but for the whole cosmos and for ever'.[44] John picks up Gregory's reference to cosmic salvation with his reference to 'all Adam's race'.

Ode 7 (Prayer of the Three Holy Children). *Irmos*

He who of old freed the young men from the furnace, becoming human suffers as a mortal, and through suffering he clothes the mortal with the glory of incorruption, the only blessed and most glorious God of our fathers.

Troparia

With fragrant myrrh, godly minded women hastened after you; the One they sought with tears as mortal man they adored with joy as the Living God; good tidings they then proclaimed of the mystical Pasch to your disciples, O Christ.

Now as a corpse death lies before us and we feast, Hell's destruction, and the first-fruits of the new eternal life: as we leap for joy, we sing praises to the cause, the only blessed and most glorious God of our fathers.

How truly holy and all festive this night of salvation, night yet full of light, the herald of the day of light, night the messenger which proclaims the Resurrection, in which the timeless light from the sepulchre shone bodily for all.

The seventh ode is the Prayer of the Three Children (or young men) from the burning fiery furnace, where Nabuchodonosor (Nebuchadnezzar) had condemned them. The angel of the Lord appeared to them (whom Nabuchodonosor saw as a fourth man 'like a son of God'[45]), and made the centre of the furnace like a 'whistling wind of dew' (Dan. 3: 50 (LXX)). For the Fathers, the angel of the Lord was the Word of God, so John sees the saving of the three children as an earlier act of salvation by the Word, who later became incarnate, and through suffering gives human kind incorruption.

The first troparion returns to the myrrh-bearing women, only this time, as Nikodimos points out, they are understood in the light of the Song of Songs: 'your anointing oils[46] are fragrant, your name is oil poured

---

[44] Gregory Nazianzen, *or.* 45. 13 (PG 36. 640D).

[45] Dan: 3. 92 (LXX), in the form in which Nikodimos quotes it.

[46] The word translated 'myrrh' in the Easter canon and the word here for 'anointing oils' are the same in Greek.

out; therefore your maidens love you. Draw me after you, let me run after the fragrance of your oils' (Cant. 1: 3).[47] They are seeking with tears the one they love. Finding him risen as God, they take the good tidings to his disciples. The second troparion continues this meditation: the women were seeking a corpse, but discovered the death of death.

The final troparion returns to celebration of the night, the night of salvation, the night of the Resurrection. Nikodimos again refers to a passage from Gregory's second Easter homily in which Gregory contrasts yesterday, 'beautiful' with its celebrations with candles and fires, with today, 'even more beautiful', since we celebrate the Resurrection itself, 'no longer as something hoped for, but already happened and drawing the whole world to itself'.[48] Nikomidos comments on how the Church begins the day in the evening, so that the day moves from darkness to light.[49]

Ode 8 (Song of the Three Holy Children). *Irmos*

This is the chosen and holy day, the first of all Sabbaths, it is the Queen and Lady, the Feast of Feasts, and the Festival it is of Festivals, on which we bless Christ to all the ages.

Troparia

Come, let us share the new fruit of the vine, of gladness divine, on this resplendent and refulgent day of the rising of Christ, on this day of the Kingdom of Christ our Lord, while praises we sing to him as God to all the ages.

Lift your eyes around you, O Sion, and see, for behold they have come like beacons blazing forth with light divine from the West and from the North, from the East and from the Sea, your children come to you, blessing Christ in you to all the ages.

Father almighty, Word of God, and Spirit, nature united in trinity of persons, transcending being, and transcending Godhead, into you we have been baptized, and we bless you to all the ages.

The Song of the Three Children is a song in which all creation is called on to praise God. This gives John the cue for these verses, which develop this theme of praise. The *irmos* is drawn from Leviticus 24: 36, which speaks of the 'eighth day [as] a chosen and holy day for you'; Gregory's second Easter homily, which praises Easter as 'the feast of feasts and the festival of festivals';[50] and a passage from his homily on New Sunday

---

[47] Nikodimos 1987, ii. 311.

[48] Gregory Nazianzen, *or.* 45. 2 (PG 36. 624D–625A).

[49] Nikodimos 1987, ii. 318–19.

[50] Gregory Nazianzen, *or.* 45. 2 (PG 36. 624C).

where he says that 'the queen of hours pays homage to the queen of days and bestows on her all that is most beautiful and pleasant'.[51]

The first troparion starts with a reference to the 'fruit of the vine', of which Jesus said to his disciples at the Last Supper, 'I shall not drink again of the fruit of the vine, until that day when I drink it new with you in my Father's kingdom' (Matt. 26: 29). The Father's kingdom is the Resurrection, says Nikodimos, following the interpretation of John Chrysostom.[52] The second troparion picks up more directly the theme of the ode, seeing people coming from the four corners of the earth to praise Christ. The final troparion recalls the Lord's final command in Matthew's Gospel (28: 19) to make disciples of all nations, baptizing them in the name of the Trinity. It is worth noting that the *irmos* and all the troparia end by praising God or Christ 'to the ages', which underlines the eschatological nature of the Resurrection.

Ode 9 (Songs of the Mother of God and of Zacharias). *Irmos*

Enlightened, be enlightened, O New Jerusalem, for the glory of the Lord has risen upon you, dance now, O Sion, rejoice and be glad, you too rejoice, all pure Mother of God, as he arises, to whom you gave birth.

Troparia

O divine! O beloved! O your sweetest voice! True the promise you made to us, to be with us evermore, even, O Christ, until time finds its end; this we possess as an anchor of hope, and we, the faithful, rejoice therein.

O Pascha, great Pascha, great and most sacred Pascha, Christ! O Wisdom, O Word of God, and Power of God! Grant us, O Lord, to partake of you yet more clearly in the day which has no evening, of your Kingdom.

The final ode consists of the two New Testament odes, the Song of the Mother of God and the Song of Zacharias, the father of St John the Forerunner. The opening word—'Enlightened, be enlightened' (*Phôtizou, phôtizou*)—very likely contains a reference to baptism, the sacrament of *phôtismos*, or enlightenment (as it is frequently called in the Fathers: John himself mentions this aspect of baptism in *Expos.* 82. 57), which was anciently celebrated as part of the Easter Vigil.[53] The beginning of the *irmos* is from Isaiah 50: 1, interpreted as looking beyond the end of the exile (its historical reference) to the lasting redemption of the Resurrection. It is an occasion for dancing and rejoicing. The word for 'rejoice' is cognate with that used in the *Magnificat* ('my spirit has rejoiced

---

[51] Gregory Nazianzen, *or.* 44. 10 (PG 36. 617C).

[52] Nikodimos 1987, ii. 323 and 287.

[53] I owe this observation to Fr Ephrem Lash.

in God my saviour': Luke 1: 44), which leads John to call on the 'all-pure Mother of God' to rejoice in the Resurrection. The first troparion is an ecstatic recalling of the promise of Christ, recorded at the end of Matthew, already alluded to in the last troparion of the previous ode. The final troparion John draws from the conclusion of Gregory's second Easter homily: 'But, O Pascha, great and sacred and cleansing the whole cosmos—for I will speak to you as to a living person! O Word of God, and Light and Life and Wisdom and Power! I rejoice in all your names.'[54] And calling upon the Pascha, John prays to 'partake of you yet more clearly in the day which has no evening, of your Kingdom'. The canon begins acclaiming the 'day of resurrection', which foreshadows the 'day without evening' of the Kingdom.

(c) The Canon on the Transfiguration of the Lord

Nikodimos prefaces his commentary on this canon[55] by referring to the icon of the Transfiguration, with Christ transfigured standing on a peak of the mountain, and Moses and Elias standing on either side on similar peaks, with the Apostles lower down, Peter and James still partly upright, while John is completely overcome by the vision.[56] The Transfiguration was a popular subject for icons, there being two famous examples from the sixth century: the apsidal mosaic in the church of the monastery of St Catherine at the base of Mount Sinai (originally, in the sixth century, the monastery was dedicated to the Burning Bush[57]), and the apsidal mosaic in the church of Sant' Apollinare in Classe in Ravenna. The development of the icon is of considerable interest, Christ sometimes surrounded by light and sometimes irradiating light, and his aureole sometimes separating him from the prophets and sometimes embracing them. John's canon, together with his homily, is probably one of the factors affecting this development. Unlike in the Easter canon, John mostly used existing *irmoi* (save for the fourth ode) and composed troparia modelled on their metrical form; the initial letters of these troparia (including the *irmos* of the fourth ode) form an acrostic which reads: MOSES THEOU PROSOPON EN THABOR IDE ('Moses saw the Face of God on Tabor').

---

[54] Gregory Nazianzen, *or.* 45. 30 (PG 36. 664A).

[55] Text in *Menaion* (6 Aug.), 89–98. English translation in Mary and Ware 1969, 482–94. French translation in Rozemond 1959, 90–3. The English translation used is my own. Nikodimos's commentary: 1987, iii. 279–320.   [56] Nikodimos 1987, iii. 279.

[57] See the extended treatment of this in Elsner 1995, 97–124.

2. The Transfiguration, Theophanis the Cretan (1546),
Stavronikita

Ode 1 (Song of Moses). *Troparia*

Moses of old saw prophetically the glory of the Lord in the sea, in the cloud, and in
the pillar of fire, and he shouted out: let us sing to our God and Redeemer.

Protected by the deified body, as by a rock, and seeing Him who is invisible, Moses
shouted out: let us sing to our God and Redeemer.

You appeared to Moses on the Mountain of the Law and on Tabor, of old in a dark
cloud, and now in the unapproachable light of the Godhead.

These verses serve to introduce Moses. The refrain sums up the burden
of the first ode, the Song of Moses. The first troparion refers back to the

events celebrated by the first ode, but does it by way of the Apostle Paul's summary in 1 Corinthians 10: 1–4, with its identification of the rock with Christ. This provides the first image of the second troparion, the 'deified body' being Christ's, identified with the rock; not, however, the rock Paul referred to, but the rock, in the cleft of which Moses hid, to see God's behind as he passed by: the nearest Moses got to seeing God in his lifetime (Exod. 33: 17–23). The last troparion draws the contrast between God's revelation on the two mountains, Sinai and Tabor: on Sinai in darkness, on Tabor in light (cf. *Transfig.* 4).

Ode 3 (Song of Anna). *Troparia*

The glory that formerly overshadowed the tabernacle and spoke to Moses your servant has become a figure of your Transfiguration, O Lord, that shone forth ineffably, like lightning, on Tabor.

The leaders of the Apostles went up with you, Only-begotten Word most high, on to Mount Tabor, and Moses and Elias were both present, as servants of God, only Lover of human kind.

Being complete God, you have become a complete mortal, having mixed humanity with complete divinity in your Person, which Moses and Elias saw on Mount Tabor in two essences.

The link between these verses and their ode, the Prayer of Anna, is quite slender, nothing much more than the fact that Anna was praying in the Temple, where the glory of God rested, referred to in the first troparion. But the glory of God that overshadowed the tabernacle, so central to John's defence of icons, is seen as a figure of the Transfiguration, here of the radiance that shone from Christ, later of the cloud that descended (cf. *Transfig.* 17). The canon begins, therefore, in much the same way as the homily: 'Today, the abyss of unapproachable light! Today the boundless outpouring of divine radiance is clearly seen by the apostles on Mount Tabor!' (*Transfig.* 2. 1–2). The second troparion introduces the witnesses to the Transfiguration, and the final troparion reflects on the dogmatic truth of the Incarnation that is revealed in the Transfiguration.

Ode 4 (Prayer of Avvakum). *Irmos*

Lightning flashes of divinity proceeded from your flesh; those chosen from the Apostles and Prophets sing and shout out: Glory to your power, O Lord.

Troparia

You preserved the bush unharmed, though it was united with fire, O Master, and showed to Moses the flesh shining with divine radiance, as he sang: Glory to your power, O Lord.

The visible sun was eclipsed by the rays of divinity, when on Mount Tabor it saw you transfigured, my Jesus. Glory to your power, O Lord.

Seen as immaterial fire that did not burn the matter of the body, when you appeared to Moses and the Apostles and Elias, Master, as one, out of two, in two perfect natures.

The link with the ode, the Prayer of Avvakum, is to the verse that speaks of God's 'lightning flashes' that proceeded into light, to the astonishment of the sun and moon (Hab. 3: 11). This gives the words of the *irmos*, and also the incomparable contrast between the uncreated and the created that runs through the verses, and provokes the refrain: 'Glory to your power, O Lord'. But, though incomparable, the uncreated does not annihilate the created. The Burning Bush was unharmed (Exod. 3: 2); hence it is a prefiguration of the Incarnation, in which the divine presence did not harm the integrity of the human nature: a theme that runs through all the troparia. There is perhaps also a reference to the sun's being eclipsed by that other manifestation of the glory of the Son on the Cross (cf. Matt. 27: 45; John 12: 23–33).

Ode 5 (Prayer of Isaias). *Troparia*

Even an eloquent tongue cannot declare your mighty works; for, ruling life and mastering death, you were present on Mount Tabor to Moses and Elias, who bore witness to your divinity.

You made human kind in your image with your invisible hands, O Christ, and now manifest your original beauty in created humanity; not as in the image, but as you are yourself in essence, God who are also called human.

In a union without confusion, you showed us on Mount Tabor the coal of divinity, that consumes sins, but enlightens souls, and you caught up Moses and Elias and the chief of the disciples in ecstasy.

The link with the ode does not occur until the final troparion, and then it is a link to the prophet Isaias, rather than to his prayer. It refers to Isaias's vision of God, in which his lips are purified by a burning coal, brought by one of the seraphim. The first troparion reflects on the ineffability of God's mighty works, and draws attention to how what happened on Tabor transcended the frontier of death, as Moses and Elias appeared together with the Apostles. The second troparion sees in the Trans-figuration the revelation of the true, primordial beauty of humanity, made in the image of God. For that image, in accordance with which human kind is made, is Christ himself, not 'in the image' but the original itself. Nikodimos, commenting on this revelation of beauty, quotes

St Augustine's famous exclamation: 'Late have I loved you, beauty so ancient and so new, late have I loved you!'[58] (in a slightly elaborated form, found by Nikodimos in a volume bearing the title 'Lovers' prayers'[59]).

Ode 6 (Prayer of Jonas). *Troparia*

How great and fearful is the vision seen today! The visible sun shone from heaven, but on Mount Tabor there shone forth, beyond compare, the spiritual Sun of righteousness.

'The shadow of the Law has grown weak and passed away, while Christ the Truth has plainly come': shouted out Moses, when he beheld your divinity on Tabor.

As the pillar showed Moses Christ transfigured, so the cloud pointed most clearly to the grace of the Spirit, overshadowing Mount Tabor.

John continues in these verses the theme from the last ode, and makes no reference that I can detect to the Prayer of Jonas. That theme is the contrast between uncreated and created, here the visible sun and the spiritual Sun of righteousness (cf. Mal. 4: 2). This gives way to another contrast, already noted by John, between the shadows of the Old Testament and the reality of the New, a theme he also develops in his homily. In the last troparion there is a hint of the Trinitarian interpretation of the Transfiguration, drawn out of the fulfilment of the types of the pillar of fire and the pillar of cloud that led the people of Israel through the desert (Exod. 13: 21–2) in Christ and the Spirit.

Ode 7 (Prayer of the Three Holy Children). *Troparia*

Now the invisible has been seen by the Apostles, the Godhead shining forth in the flesh on Mount Tabor, and they shout: Blessed are you, Lord God, to the ages.

Trembling with fear, and amazed at the majesty of the divine Kingdom on Mount Tabor, the Apostles shouted: Blessed are you, Lord God, to the ages.

Now the unheard of has been heard. For the fatherless Son of the Virgin receives glorious witness from the paternal voice, that he is divine and human, the same to the ages.

Not made by adoption, but being by essence from before all existence, the beloved Son of the Most High, unchangeably you dwelt with us, who cry out: Blessed are you, O God, to the ages.

The link with the ode, the Prayer of the Three Children, is found in the refrain: 'Blessed are you, Lord God, to the ages'. The theme here, possibly with reference to the miraculous deliverance of the three young men from the burning fiery furnace, is the paradox of God's works,

---

[58] Augustine, *Conf.* x. 27. 38.   [59] Nikodimos 1987, iii. 300.

pre-eminently the Transfiguration: the invisible seen, the unheard-of heard. And the response to this paradox of fear and awe. The 'majesty of the divine Kingdom' recalls, appropriately for the Transfiguration, the first verse of Psalm 92: 'The Lord reigns, he is clothed in majesty'; his majesty (*euprepeia*) manifest in the clothing that became 'white as the light' (Matt. 17: 2). The last two troparia reflect on the paradox of the Incarnation: 'the fatherless Son of the Virgin' acclaimed by his divine Father, the essentially divine Son living among those whom he makes children of God by adoption.

Ode 8 (Song of the Three Holy Children). *Troparia*

Having heard, O Master, the witness of the Father, but unable to bear to see the lightning flash of your face, too strong for human sight, your Disciples fell to the ground, singing: Priests, bless, people, highly exalt Christ to the ages.

Most fair king of kings, Lord of all who everywhere exercise lordship, blessed sovereign, dwelling in light unapproachable, which struck with wonder the Disciples, who shouted: Children, bless, priests raise a hymn, people highly exalt Christ to the ages.

You hold mastery over heaven, exercise kingship over the earth, and hold lordship over things beneath the earth, O Christ, so there were present with you, from the earth the Apostles, from heaven Elias the Thesbite, and from the slain Moses, all singing in harmony: People, highly exalt Christ to the ages.

Idle cares were left behind them on the earth by the chosen band from the Apostles, O Lover of human kind, as they followed you to the divine way of life that is far above this earthly world. Thus, accounted worthy of your Theophany, they sing: People, highly exalt Christ to the ages.

The link with the eighth ode, the Song of the Three Children, is again provided by the concluding acclamation, which echoes the closing verses of the ode. The first troparion is based on a passage in Gregory Nazianzen's homily on baptism: 'The Godhead manifest as light to the apostles on the mountain, too strong for their little sight.'[60] Blinded by the light of the Godhead, they fall to the ground in awe (see above Nikodimos's comments on the icon of the Transfiguration). The second troparion reworks 1 Timothy 6: 15–16, adding to its description of Christ the epithet 'fair', taken, Nikodimos suggests, from Psalm 44: 3 ('fair with beauty beyond the sons of men') or Song of Songs 1: 16 ('Behold you are beautiful, my beloved, and fair').[61] The majesty of Christ, expressed in 1 Timothy 6: 15, is developed in the next troparion, spelling out his

---

[60] Gregory Nazianzen, *or.* 40. 6. 18–20 (Moreschini, 208).

[61] Nikodimos 1987, iii. 311.

sovereignty over heaven, earth, and Hades, manifest in the Transfiguration in the presence of the Apostles (from earth), Elias (from
heaven, whither he was assumed on a fiery chariot: 4 Kgd. 2: 11–12), and
Moses (from 'the slain': John, as is not uncommon, uses a rare literary
word). The final troparion sees the Apostles, laying aside idle cares (an
echo, perhaps, of the Cherubic hymn of the Byzantine Liturgy), and
following Christ up Mount Tabor, to a new, divine way of life: a theme
that recurs in his homily (e.g. *Transfig.* 5, 10).

Ode 9 (Songs of the Mother of God and of Zacharias). *Troparia*

That you might show plainly your unutterable Second Coming, how God Most
High will be seen, standing in the midst of gods, you shone forth ineffably to the
Apostles on Tabor, to Moses with Elias; therefore we all magnify you, O Christ.

Come and listen to me, people: ascending the holy and heavenly Mount, let us stand
immaterially in the city of the living God, and contemplate with our minds
the immaterial Godhead, of the Father and the Spirit, shining forth in the only-
begotten Son.

You have cast a spell of longing over me, O Christ, and changed me with your
divine yearning; but burn up my sins in immaterial fire, and make me worthy to be
filled with delight in you, that, dancing, I may magnify your two comings, O Good
One.

The troparia of the ninth ode dwell on the Second Coming in glory, of
which the Transfiguration is an anticipation. For this we need to prepare
by ascending the Mount of Virtues to behold the Trinity itself, manifest
in the Incarnate Son. The final troparion is a prayer to be purified by longing for Christ, so that we can celebrate with delight the two comings of
Christ, the first in humility, the second in glory.

(d) The Canon on the Dormition of the Mother of God

Like the Easter canon, and unlike the canon for the Transfiguration, this
canon has no acrostic.[62] As with the canon on the Transfiguration, John
uses already existing *irmoi*. Our commentary (following Nikodimos) is
restricted to his troparia.[63]

---

[62] Text in *Menaion* (15 Aug.), 197–206. English translation in Mary and Ware 1969, 515–25.
English metrical translation in Daley 1998, 241–6. I have used Fr Ephrem's English translation (unpublished). Nikodimos' commentary: 1987, iii. 375–406.

[63] As well as Nikodimos's commentaries, see Chevalier 1936 and Ledit 1979.

3. The Koimesis, Theophanis the Cretan (1546), Stavronikita

Ode 1 (Song of Moses). *Troparia*

Young maidens with Miriam the Prophetess, now raise the song of departure; for the Virgin and only Mother of God is being taken over to her appointed place in heaven.

The divine tabernacles of heaven fittingly received you as a living heaven, all-pure Virgin; and as a blameless bride you stand radiantly adorned before your King and God.

Moses' song of victory was, in the biblical account, picked up by his sister Miriam, who led a dance singing the refrain of the song (Exod. 15: 20–1); this provides the theme for the first troparion. In the last of his homilies,

John sees in Miriam and her companions a type of the Church, rejoicing at the passing over into life of the Mother of God (*Dorm.* III. 3. 3–8). The final troparion introduces the theme of the Mother of God as a 'living heaven', which we also find in John's second homily, where, after calling her a living heaven, he exclaims, 'For who could err in calling her heaven, unless one were to say, and say rightly, that she has been lifted even above heaven in her incomparable privileges?'[64]—a sentiment echoed in one of the most famous troparia about the Mother of God, ascribed to John's fellow-monk Cosmas: 'Greater in honour than the Cherubim and beyond compare more glorious than the Seraphim, without corruption you gave birth to God the Word. Truly the Mother of God, we magnify you!'

Ode 3 (Song of Anna). *Troparia*

Pure Virgin, sprung from mortal loins, your final departure was in conformity with nature; but, as you gave birth to the true life, you have passed over to the One who is the divine life in person.

A company of theologians from the ends of the earth and a multitude of Angels hastened to Sion at an all-powerful command, that they might fittingly minister at your burial, Sovereign Lady.

The link with the third ode is again very slender, but the Anna of the ode bore the same name as the Mother of the Virgin, and the theme of barrenness made miraculously fertile is common to both: hence the reference to the Virgin's birth 'from mortal loins'. The rest of the first troparion introduces the theme of the Virgin as the Mother of the One who was life in person (cf. John 14: 16), to whom she passed over in death. It is a central theme of both the apolytikion and the kontakion for the feast: 'you passed over into life, for you are the Mother of Life'; 'for as Mother of Life she has been taken over into life by him who dwelt in her ever-virgin womb'.[65] The second troparion refers to the account in Dionysios the Areopagite's *Divine Names* of the Dormition, where he tells of the gathering together of many of the early Christian leaders, including himself and his mentor, Hierotheos, as well as James and Peter and the other Apostles, to see the 'God-bearing body, the source of life' before her burial. Those thus gathered together Dionysios refers to as 'theologians'.[66] This passage, with its reference to the Virgin's body as the source of life, plays a pivotal role in the canon, as it did in the first of John's homilies on the Dormition.

[64] *Dorm.* II. 2. 34–6; trans. Daley 1998, 206.
[65] For the full text of these troparia, see Lash 1999, 92.
[66] Dionysios the Areopagite, *d.n.* 3. 2 (Suchla, i. 141. 4–14).

Ode 4 (Prayer of Avvakum). *Troparia*

Strange marvel it was to see the living heaven of the universal King going down below the hollows of the earth. How wonderful are your works! Glory to your power, O Lord!

At your translation, Mother of God, the hosts of Angels in fear and joy covered with hallowed wings your body that had been spacious enough to receive God.

If her fruit, who is beyond understanding, because of whom she was called Heaven, willingly underwent burial as a mortal, how will she refuse burial, who bore him without wedlock?

The fourth ode, Avvakum's prayer, is full of the wonder and mystery of God, and it is on this mystery manifest in the Dormition of the Mother of God that these troparia dwell. The 'living heaven' goes down into the 'hollows' of the earth. The word translated 'hollows' is a rare Greek word, *keneônes*. According to Nikodimos, this refers to the tomb in Gethsemane, where the Virgin was buried; but he contrasts this with what John's contemporary Andrew of Crete said in one of his homilies on the Dormition,[67] namely that, after her death, the Mother of God descended into Hades.[68] Although Andrew does not use the word *keneôn*, one might be tempted to read his interpretation of Mary's descent into this troparion; but such a temptation is probably to be resisted, as John specifically excludes the idea that the Virgin descended into Hades after her death in his second homily on the Dormition (*Dorm.* II. 3. 9–22). The next troparion turns to Mary's reception in heaven by the angels, the reception of one 'wider than the heavens', since she contained in her womb the uncontainable God. This had formed a point of meditation in John's first homily (*Dorm.* I. 13. 1–11). The image of the angels covering the Virgin's body with their wings recalls the icon of the Dormition in which Christ, standing above his Mother lying on her bier, is enclosed in an auriole that reaches down to the body of his Mother. This auriole is not simply one of light, but is filled with angelic forms: the glory that surrounds Christ and reaches down to his Mother is a glory consisting of the hosts of heaven. The last troparion brings out the parallel between the destiny of the Mother of God and that of her Son: as he underwent death

[67] The first one printed in Migne (PG 97. 1045–72), but numbered the second in Daley's translation (1998, 117–36).
[68] Nikodimos 1987, iii. 381–2, where he illustrates Andrew's teaching by quoting three passages from his second homily on the Dormition (PG 97. 1049D1–1052C1, 1052C3–6, 1053A15–B7).

and burial, so did his Mother (which confirms the interpretation of the first troparion given above). The reference to Christ as the Virgin's fruit recalls Elizabeth's acclamation to her cousin, 'Blessed are you among women, and blessed is the fruit of your womb' (Luke 1: 42). Nikodimos refers, as well, to passages in the prophets: 'The world is filled with his fruit' (Isa. 27: 6), 'the vine gives its fruit' (Zach. 8: 12), 'eat the fruit of life' (Hos. 10: 12 (LXX)).[69] But why a 'fruit who is beyond understanding'? For Nikodimos, this refers to the way in which, in the Incarnation, God reveals himself precisely as beyond understanding, an idea expressed by Dionysios the Areopagite in his third letter, which Nikodimos quotes, where Jesus is spoken of as 'also hidden after his manifestation, or, to speak more divinely, in his manifestation'.[70]

Ode 5 (Prayer of Isaias). *Troparia*

Let the trumpets of the theologians ring out today, and let the human tongue now sound praises with many voices. Let the air re-echo, shining with infinite light. Let Angels honour with hymns the Virgin's Falling Asleep.

The vessel of election, wholly beside himself, wholly transported, surpassed himself in hymns to you, O Virgin; wholly consecrated to God, he truly was and proved himself to all to be possessed by God, O all-praised Mother of God.

The link with the fifth ode, Isaias's Prayer, is imperceptible. The troparia join the celebration of the 'theologians' at the bier of the Mother of God, and the rejoicing of the angels who welcome her in heaven. This is the theme with which John ends his final homily on the Dormition (*Dorm.* III. 4–5). The last troparion echoes verbally Dionysios's account of Hierotheos's superlative praise of the Mother of God, in which he was 'wholly beside himself, wholly transported'.[71] The designation 'vessel of election' might seem to suggest the Apostle Paul (cf. Acts 9: 15), who is mentioned in the account in the *Synaxarion* as being present at the death of the Virgin.[72] However, John also described Hierotheos as a 'vessel of election' (after his master Paul, so Nikodimos suggests[73]), so it is likely that he is referring to Dionysios's account of Hierotheos here.[74]

---

[69] Nikodimos 1987, iii. 384.

[70] Ibid. iii. 384–5, quoting Dionysios the Areopagite, *ep.* 3 (Ritter, ii. 159. 6–7).

[71] Dionysios the Areopagite, *d.n.* 3. 2 (Suchla, i. 141, 11–12).

[72] *Synaxarion* 893, 33.

[73] Nikodimos 1987, iii. 390.

[74] See *Dorm.* III. 4. 16–18.

Ode 6 (Prayer of Jonas). *Troparia*

Life dawned from you without loosing the keys of your virginity. How then has your spotless tabernacle, source of life, become a partaker in the experience of death?

Once the sacred enclosure of life, you have found eternal life; for through death you, who gave birth to life in person, have passed over to life.

The reference to the sixth ode is again imperceptible. The first troparion, like the homilies, relates the passage of the Mother of God through and beyond death to her perpetual virginity: as her virginity was unharmed by giving birth to Life, so she retains her bodily integrity in death. The reference to the 'keys of virginity' recalls the passage in Ezekiel's vision about the 'locked door' (Ezek. 44: 2, quoted above), which we have already noted as a figure of Mary's perpetual virginity. This troparion also applied to Mary's body the adjective *zōarchikos* ('source of life'), borrowed from Dionysios's account of the Dormition. Nikodimos points out that, according to Dionysios, this adjective properly applies to God alone, being denied even to the angels.[75] Its significance, applied to the body of the Virgin Mother, is thus further enhanced. As in the first homily, where this adjective has pivotal significance, this recognition of the significance of the life-giving quality of her body transforms for her the meaning of death. As John says in his homily, 'O how may the fount of life be transferred to life by means of death?' (*Dorm.* 1. 10, 1–2, and see the whole paragraph).

Ode 7 (Prayer of the Three Holy Children). *Troparia*

Young men and maidens, old men and rulers, kings with judges, as you honour the memory of the Virgin and Mother of God, sing out, Lord and God of our fathers, blessed are you!

Let the mountains of heaven resound with the trumpet of the Spirit; let hills now rejoice, and let the godlike Apostles leap for joy, the Queen is being translated to her Son, with whom she rules for ever.

The most sacred translation of your godlike and undefiled Mother has gathered the celestial ranks of the Powers on high to rejoice together with those on earth who sing to you, O God, blessed are you!

John follows up the prayer of praise of the Three Holy Children, which constitutes the seventh ode, by drawing on one of the psalms (Ps. 148:

11–12) for his first troparion, a verse he has also used in his final homily on the Dormition (*Dorm.* III. 3. 9–12). In the next troparion, John refers, hyperbolically, to the 'mountains of heaven', before calling on the 'hills', mentioned in the same psalm (Ps. 148: 9). The 'mountains of heaven' refer allegorically to the highest of the angelic orders, authority for which Nikodimos finds in Gregory Nazianzen's homily on baptism.[76] All the ranks of the angels gather together for the translation of the Mother of God into heaven.

Ode 8 (Song of the Three Holy Children). *Troparia*

Immaculate Virgin, Rulers and Dominions with Powers, Angels, Archangels, Thrones, Principalities, the Cherubim and the dread Seraphim glorify your memory; while we, the human race, praise and highly exalt you to all the ages.

He, who when taking flesh made his dwelling strangely in your immaculate womb, himself received your all-holy spirit and, as a dutiful Son, gave it rest with himself. And so we praise you, O Virgin, and exalt you above all to all the ages.

O the wonders beyond understanding of God's Ever-Virgin Mother! For, dwelling in the tomb, she showed it to be Paradise. Standing beside this tomb today, we sing with joy: Praise the Lord, his works, and highly exalt him to all the ages.

Again, the eighth ode, the Song of the Three Holy Children from the burning, fiery furnace, recalls the presence among them of the Word of God, who was to be the offspring of the Virgin Mother of God. That event of redemption prefigured what now takes place in reality for the whole world, which rejoices in the words of their song, that provides the refrain for these troparia. The first troparion lists the angelic ranks, reproducing Dionysios the Areopagite's list,[77] though not in his order of three ranks of three, the reason being most likely metrical. The last troparion refers to Christ's receiving the Virgin's soul or spirit in heaven at her death. This is the moment depicted in the icon of the Dormition, and is clearly distinguished, both in John's canon and his homilies,[78] from the assumption of her body. It is the assumption of the body that is celebrated in the final troparion: her tomb is shown to be Paradise. In his second homily, John addresses the tomb, as if it were alive, and imagines the tomb replying: 'Now angels take care of me; now divine grace dwells in me. I have been revealed as a source of healing, a remedy for pain. I am a constant source of health; I put demons to flight.'[79]

[76] Nikodimos 1987, iii. 395, referring to Gregory Nazianzen, *or.* 40. 36. 7–9 (Moreschini, 280).

[77] Dionysios the Areopagite, *c.h.* 6. 2 (Heil, ii. 26. 11–27. 3).

[78] The reception of Mary's soul: *Dorm.* I. 11. 3; of her body: I. 13.

[79] *Dorm.* II. 17. 15–18; trans. Daley 1998, 221.

Ode 9 (Songs of the Mother of God and of Zacharias). *Troparia*

Come now, on Sion, the divine and fertile mountain of the living God, let us be glad as we gaze on the Mother of God. For as his Mother Christ translates her to a better and more divine tabernacle, the Holy of Holies.

Come, you faithful, let us approach the tomb of God's Mother, and let us embrace it, touching it sincerely with the lips, eyes and brows of the heart; and let us draw abundant gifts of healings, which flow from an ever-flowing fount.

Receive from us this burial hymn, O Mother of the living God; and overshadow us with your light-bearing and divine grace. Grant victories to our Sovereign, peace to the people that loves Christ, and to us who sing, forgiveness and salvation of our souls.

The celebration of the Assumption of the Mother of God continues in the troparia for the final ode, the Song of the Mother of God (the Song of Zacharias being, as usual, more or less ignored). The first two troparia draw on the imagery already used by John in his celebration of the Assumption of the Virgin's body in his first homily on the Dormition. The Assumption, for John, is the fulfilment of the moving of the ark of the covenant into the Temple of Solomon (3 Kgd. 8: 1–7).[80] The ark, Mount Sion, the tabernacle, the Temple: all these prefigure the body of the Mother of God that bore the divine presence. Psalm 67, the psalm that was at first probably sung as the ark of the covenant was borne into battle, speaks at one point of 'the mountain of God, the fertile mountain, the mountain of cheese, the fertile mountain, . . . the mountain, that it pleased God to dwell in her' (Ps. 67: 16–17 (LXX); quoted by John at *Dorm.* II. 12. 25–6, this verse provides a rich source of imagery for the Mother of God, some of it at first sight somewhat puzzling[81]). This is the verse that forms the first part of the first troparion, the second part seeing the Assumption of the Mother of God as her translation into the 'better and more divine tabernacle' (cf. Heb. 9: 11), the 'Holy of Holies', no longer a shadow, but reality. The next troparion draws on John's first homily directly, where he says of the tomb: 'O sacred, wonderful, august and adorable monument! Angels come to venerate it, standing by in much reverence and holy fear; the demons tremble; human beings come forward in faith, showing it honour and worship, venerating it with eyes and lips and yearning of soul, and drinking deep of its inexhaustible store

---

[80] Cf. Nikodimos's general preface to the canons on the Dormition, which dwells on this event and its fulfilment: 1987, iii. 321–3.

[81] See Lash 1990, 70–2. The whole article is very illuminating about the way in which imagery from the Old Testament is applied to the Mother of God, especially in liturgical texts.

of blessings.'[82] This apostrophe to Mary's tomb, and the directness with which the second troparion of the ninth ode exhorts the faithful to venerate it, would suggest that John's words were composed specifically for the pilgrimage shrine of the tomb of the Virgin Mother of God in Gethsemane, outside the city of Jerusalem.[83]

The final troparion asks the Mother of God to receive this funeral hymn—no lament, but a song of rejoicing. As the poet thinks of the over-shadowing protection of the Mother of God, he turns to the traditional themes of that protection: protection for the Emperor, the *Basileus*, for the 'Christ-loving people', and for 'us who sing'. One is left with a picture of our priest-poet, singing for the protection of his Emperor, under whose rule he had never lived, and with whom his only encounter, and that but a literary one, was in terms of unqualified rebuke.

From these comments (drawn largely from the erudition of St Nikodimos of the Holy Mountain), it becomes evident how, by drawing on Scripture and the Fathers, especially St Gregory the Theologian, John has turned doctrine into images and images into poetry, teaching into doxology, and confession into praise.

[82] *Dorm.* I. 13. 7–11; trans. Daley 1998, 198.

[83] On the early Palestinian cult of the Mother of God, first at the shrine of the Kathisma, between Jerusalem and Bethlehem, marking the place where the pregnant Mother of God rested on her way to Bethlehem, and then also at the tomb in Gethsemane, see most recently Shoemaker 2001.

Epilogue

In 735 the Venerable Bede died in Jarrow in the north-east of England, almost as close as one could be to the Roman wall built at the Emperor Hadrian's command to mark the northernmost frontier of his Empire. Bede the Northumbrian and John the Damascene were therefore contemporaries; they may, indeed, have been coevals, though we are more sure of the date of Bede's birth, 673, than we are of John's. In Western scholarship they are both conventionally regarded as marking the end of the patristic period: Bede for the Latin world and John for the Greek.[1] Neither was aware of the other, though both thought of themselves as belonging to the same *oikoumene*, constituted by the Roman (or Byzantine) Empire. John was just about aware of the region that Bede inhabited: he speaks of an 'Iberian Sea' beyond the Pillars of Hercules, names the two British provinces of the Roman Empire, and knows of the Celts, who live in the remote north-north-west corner of the Empire (though all these references occur in appendices to chapters in *On the Orthodox Faith*, that may have been added by a later hand[2]). Bede, on the other hand, was well aware of the region in which John lived his monastic life, and indeed wrote a short treatise on the Holy Places, which not only discusses the Holy Places of Jerusalem, but also briefly mentions John's birthplace, Damascus, as well as having a chapter on Constantinople, principally because it was in the Great Church of Hagia Sophia that there was preserved, in Bede's day, the relic of the True Cross. Nevertheless, in relation to the great Christian Empire to which they felt themselves to belong, more in imagination than in political reality, they both lived on the periphery, though that empire was by then fragmented and already undergoing a process of transmogrification, which would result in the Roman Empire of their individual imaginations soon becoming quite

---

[1] This is neatly evidenced by the concluding volumes of Quasten's *Patrology*, just brought to completion by scholars under the direction of Angelo di Berardino of the Institutum Patristicum Augustinianum in Rome: vol. IV (1996) ends with Bede, vol. V (2000, though published too late for me to use for this book) ends with John Damascene.

[2] *Expos.* 23b. 4; 24b. 2–3, 34–5.

separate political realities (already foreshadowed in the fact that 'Roman', for Bede, evokes the pope, whereas 'Roman', for the Damascene, means the Emperor in Constantinople).

In his history of the church of Durham, the monk Symeon says of Bede: 'Now Bede lived hidden away in an extreme corner of the world, but after his death he lived on in his books and became known to everyone all over the world.'[3] As we have seen, much the same could be said of John of Damascus—but with this difference, that whereas Bede would have recognized himself in Symeon's words, John would have been surprised that Jerusalem and the Holy Places could ever appear to be an 'extreme corner' of the world. However, as we have seen, knowledge of John, other than awareness of the fact of his protest against iconoclasm, seems to have taken generations to make any impact at the centre of the Byzantine world; the events of the seventh century had rendered the religious centre of the Christian world (both for John and for Bede) peripheral to political reality of what survived of the Roman (or Byzantine) Empire.

There are, then, more points of similarity between these two contemporary monk-theologians than might appear at first sight. Living at two extreme corners of the original Christian world, that had been conterminous with the Roman Empire, but which was now disintegrating, John and Bede were grappling with problems that were similar in general terms, though in many ways different in detail. As a conclusion to this book on the Damascene who became a monk of the Judaean desert, a brief comparison of the two may perhaps be illuminating.

They were both monks, and both teachers, though there seem to have been significant differences in their lives as monks and teachers. Bede had known no other life; as a child, he had become an oblate of the twin monastery of Jarrow–Monkwearmouth, and he remained there all his life.[4] John, by contrast, had a secular education and pursued a secular career in the service of the Caliph in Damascus, before renouncing it for the monastic life. Both were teachers; but Bede seems isolated in his teaching office, and there is a sense in his writings that he was rebuilding in England the foundations of Christian Latin education for those who would come after, whereas John clearly belonged to an established and developing tradition, being educated in Damascus in the traditional Hellenic way (though perhaps one of the last to benefit from this then still unbroken tradition), and, as a theologian, forming part of a tradition of

---

[3] Symeon of Durham, *lib. Dun. Eccl.* 1. 14 (Rollason, 64).

[4] Ward 1990, 4–5.

defence and exposition of Chalcedonian Orthodoxy that the monks of
Palestine (and also of Sinai) had established in the centuries since
Chalcedon, and in particular in the decades since the Arab conquest.

This contrast takes on a sharper profile if we look at the writings of
Bede and John. Bede gives a list of his works (not all of which have
survived) at the end of his *Ecclesiastical History of the English People*.[5] It
begins with an impressive list of works of biblical exegesis, mainly on
particular biblical books, though including two works, on the tabernacle
and on the Temple, determined by the arrangements for worship detailed
in the Pentateuch. In placing this long list first, Bede makes clear that he
regards these as his most important writings. The biblical works are
followed by various letters on particular issues, both exegetical and
calendrical. He then lists his works of hagiography, especially the two
lives, one in verse and one in prose, of St Cuthbert, the famous monk
and bishop of Lindisfarne. Then follow two works of history: a history
of the abbots of his monastery, and then, certainly his most famous
work, his *Ecclesiastical History of the English People*. Bede then mentions a
martyrology, a book of hymns, and another of epigrams, two short books
on cosmology and on chronology, and a larger work on chronology. The
list closes with some introductory works on grammar and rhetoric. For
John there is no such list: we are limited to what has survived. But there
are striking parallels between the works of the two men: both compiled
textbooks (John on logic, Bede on grammar and rhetoric), both are
interested in cosmology and chronology (John in his *On the Orthodox
Faith*, Bede in various works), both composed lives of saints (in both
cases there is an interest in local saints: Artemios and John Chrysostom
associated with Antioch, most of Bede's saints belonging to the north-
east of England), both were historians (though Bede incomparably
greater than John; John's *Passion of St Artemios*, however, contains a great
deal of well-digested historical narrative, drawn from valuable sources),
and both were poets (though here John's fame far exceeds that of Bede).

The most striking contrast lies in the area of biblical exegesis: it is
central to Bede, whereas its place in John's *œuvre* is more difficult to
determine. Save for the exegesis contained in his homilies, the only
works of exegesis of John's that survive are the *Hiera* (or *Sacra Parallela*)
and a commentary on the Pauline Epistles, the latter probably not
authentic, the former surviving only in imperfect forms.[6] The *Hiera*
is clearly an important part of the Damascene's *œuvre*, however difficult

[5] Bede, *Hist.* 5. 24 (Colgrave and Mynors, 566–70).
[6] See above, Ch. 2.

it is for us now to make much of John's method and intentions in compiling it.

Even on this slender basis, however, it is possible to draw some contrasts between Bede's approach to the Scriptures and that of the Damascene. Bede's exegetical works seem to be guided by two principles: first, making accessible to his contemporaries the learning of the earlier patristic period (Ambrose, Jerome, Augustine, Gregory the Great), which was expressed in a style probably more elaborate than they could easily cope with (this is especially true of his commentary on Genesis, which had already been much commented on by earlier Fathers); and secondly, filling in the gaps in the tradition of Latin biblical commentaries (e.g., his commentaries on Kings, Esdras, Nehemias, and Acts—though with these we may also discern the interests of Bede the historian— Proverbs, Mark, and the Apocalypse[7]). John Damascene's motives seem to have been quite different (though he perhaps adopts something of the former principle in the commentary on the Pauline Epistles, if authentic, where, however, it is brevity he is seeking rather than simplicity of style). In the *Hiera*, John takes for granted the early tradition, and its sufficiency, and draws on its riches to deal with a series of doctrinal and ascetical issues; this is essentially the same as his method in *On the Orthodox Faith* (though there are puzzling differences between the patristic resources he uses in these two works). In contrast, what Bede achieves in his exegetical works is essentially what his predecessors in the Latin Patristic tradition of biblical exegesis achieved, albeit tempered to his expectations of those he seeks to instruct; this identity of purpose is especially apparent in his attempt to complete the exegetical resources available in Latin. One is tempted to characterize the difference between Bede and John by appealing to threadbare caricatures of East and West: whereas John is conscious of inheriting a highly sophisticated tradition of reflection on the Christian faith, which is entirely adequate, Bede seems conscious of a new beginning, for which he is concerned to provide an adequate foundation. This contrast is confirmed by the fact that, while both Bede and John were standing at a watershed between a classically formed culture, expressed in Greek or Latin, and a new culture, expressed in the vernacular of everyday life, whether Arabic or English, and while both of them were fluent in both the old and the new languages, it is only Bede, so far as we know, who is at all interested in making the transition from the old to the new. It was John's successors, for instance, Theodore Abū Qurrah—who sought to make Christianity accessible in Arabic; whereas Bede himself

---

[7] See Ward 1990, 41–87.

made a start by providing Anglo-Saxon translations of the Lord's Prayer, the Creed, and—his last work—a translation of one of the Gospels.

In another way, Bede and John may be seen as standing on the borders: Bede between the worlds of Roman and Irish Christianity, John between the realms of Greek and Syriac Christianity. Bede's attachment to Christianity in its Roman form, of which the controversy over the date of Easter was a symptom, is evident, both from his *Ecclesiastical History* as well as from his painstaking attempts to explain the calendrical issues involved in the calculation of the date of Easter.[8] But his attachment to the ascetical traditions of Northumbrian monasticism is equally evident in the *Ecclesiastical History*, as well as in his two lives of Cuthbert of Lindisfarne. John was similarly placed between two traditions: the traditions of Greek and Syriac Christianity. His attachment to the Byzantine tradition is manifest, but, however Hellenized, his family was doubtless of Syrian stock, and it is not unlikely that he knew Syriac. But it is in his great poetical work that his openness to the Syriac tradition is most evident. We have already seen that the early Byzantine poetical tradition of the kontakion had Syriac roots, and though these roots are less easily detected in the case of the canon, it can hardly be without significance that not only John, but the other two early composers of canons, Cosmas and Andrew of Crete, were of Syrian origin.

But neither Bede nor John can be confined to the particular historical situation in which each found himself. Each lived on in his books and became known to everyone all over the world. One notable way in which this became true of Bede is through his influence on the *Glossa Ordinaria*, the 'ordinary gloss', or commentary, on the Scriptures, that provided the basis for medieval understanding of the Bible.[9] Similarly, John's influence, as we have seen, was destined to be widespread, both in the Byzantine world and beyond. If Bede's influence on Western medieval theology was spread through the *Glossa Ordinaria*, John's was no less profound through the translation of *On the Orthodox Faith*. John's influence can perhaps be characterized in two ways. First, and most obviously, his influence is manifest in the way in which, especially through *On the Orthodox Faith*, he harvested the wisdom of the formative centuries of doctrinal clarification in the Greek Christian world; this harvest of patristic theology shaped much later Christian theology, both in the Middle Ages and beyond, and has a value that modern theology—both Orthodox and Western, whether Catholic or Protestant—has yet fully to recover. But secondly, and more profoundly, John's influence is felt

[8] See, most recently, Wallis 1999.   [9] Ward 1990, 144.

through his liturgical poetry, in which this harvest of patristic theology is turned into song and celebration. This is not a matter of mere poetical embellishment; rather, in this disciplined praise and confession, theology finds its most fundamental role, in interpreting, as it were,[10] the return of the whole human being, both soul and body, to God, the beginning and end, the alpha and omega.

[10] Cf. Thomas Aquinas, *Summa Theologiae*, IIa IIae. 83. 1 *ad primum*, where Aquinas suggests that prayer be understood as *quodammodo . . . desiderii interpres* ('in a way, an interpreter of desire').

BIBLIOGRAPHY

Editions of texts used

ALEXANDER OF ALEXANDRIA, Letter to Alexander of Constantinople, in H.-G. Opitz, *Athanasius Werke*, iii/1, Urkunde zur Geschichte des Arianischen Streites, Berlin and Leipzig: Walter de Gruyter, 1934, 19–29.

AMBROSE, *Expositio Evangelii secundum Lucam*, ed. C. Schenkl (completed by H. Schenkl), CSEL 32, pt. 4, 1902.

ANASTASIOS OF SINAI, *Viae Dux (Hodegos)*, ed. Karl-Heinz Uthemann, CCSG 8, 1981.

ARISTOTLE, *Physica*, ed. W. D. Ross, OCT, 1950.

——*Aristotle's Metaphysics*, a revised text with introduction and commentary, W. D. Ross, 2 vols., Oxford: Clarendon Press, 1924.

(PSEUDO-)ARISTOTLE, *On the Cosmos*, ed. D. J. Furley, LCL 400, 1955, 331–409.

ATHANASIOS OF ALEXANDRIA, *Contra Arianos*, ed. William Bright, 2nd edn., Oxford: Clarendon Press, 1884.

——*Contra Gentes* and *De Incarnatione*, ed. and trans. R. W. Thomson, Oxford: Clarendon Press, 1971.

——*De Decretis Nicaenae Synodis*, in H.-G. Opitz, *Athanasius Werke*, ii/1, Berlin: Walter de Gruyter, 1935–41, 1–45.

AUGUSTINE, *Confessiones*, ed. M. Skutella, rev. edn., Stuttgart: Teubner, 1969.

——*De utilitate credendi*, in BA 8, ed. J. Pegon, SJ, 1951, 195–301.

BASIL, *Contre Eunome*, ed. Bernard Sesboüé, SJ, Georges-Matthieu de Durand, OP, and Louis Doutreleau, SJ, SC 299, 305, 1982–3.

——*Homélies sur l'Hexaéméron*, ed. Stanislas Giet, SC 26*bis*, 1968.

——*The Letters*, ed. and trans. Roy J. Deferrari, 4 vols., LCL 190, 215, 243, 270, 1926–34.

——*Sur le Saint-Esprit*, ed. Benoît Pruche, OP, SC 17*bis*, 1968.

——*Sur l'origine de l'homme*, ed. A. Smets-Michel Van Esbroek, SC 160, 1970.

BEDE, *Bede's Ecclesiastical History of the English People*, ed. Bertram Colgrave and R. A. B. Mynors, Oxford: Clarendon Press, 1969.

BOETHIUS, *The Theological Tractates, The Consolation of Philosophy*, ed. and trans. E. K. Rand, H. F. Stewart, and S. J. Tester, LCL 74, 2nd edn. 1973 [cited as Rand *et al.*].

Chronicon Paschale, ed. L. Dindorf, 2 vols., Bonn, 1832. Eng. trans.: M. and M. Whitby, *Chronicon Paschale 284–628 AD*, Translated Texts for Historians, 7, Liverpool: Liverpool University Press, 1989.

CLEMENT OF ROME, in *Die Apostolischen Väter*, pt. 1, ed. F. X. Funk, Karl Bihlmeyer, and Wilhelm Schneemelcher, 3rd edn., Tübingen: J. C. B. Mohr, 1970.

Codex Iustinianus, in *Corpus Iuris Civilis (Digest, Codex, Novellae)*, ed. T. Mommsen, P. Krueger, *et al.*, 3 vols., 2nd edn., Berlin, 1928–9.

CYRIL OF ALEXANDRIA, S. Cyrillus, *Opera*, ed. P. E. Pusey, vols. i–vii, pt. 1, Oxford: Clarendon Press, 1868–77.

——*Select Letters*, ed. and trans. Lionel R. Wickham, Oxford: Clarendon Press, 1983.

CYRIL OF JERUSALEM, *St Cyril of Jerusalem's Lectures on the Christian Sacraments*, ed. Frank Leslie Cross, London: SPCK, 1961 [contains *Procatechesis, Catecheses* 19–23].

CYRIL OF SCYTHOPOLIS, *Life of St Sabas*, in E Schwartz, *Kyrillos von Skythopolis*, TU 49/2, Leipzig: Walter de Gruyter, 1939.

DIADOCHOS OF PHOTIKI, *Oeuvres Spirituelles*, ed. Édouard des Places, SJ, SC 5*bis*, 1966.

DIONYSIOS THE AREOPAGITE, *Corpus Dionysiacum*, ed. Beata Suchla, G. Heil, and A. M. Ritter, 2 vols., PTS, 33, 36, Berlin and New York: Walter de Gruyter, 1990–1.

Doctrina Patrum de Incarnatione Verbi: Ein griechisches Florilegium aus der Wende des 7. und 8. Jahrhunderts, ed. Franz Diekamp, 2nd edn., Basileios Phanourgakis-Evangelos Christos, Münster: Aschendorff, 1981; first published 1907.

EPIPHANIOS, *Panarion*, ed. Karl Holl, 3 vols., GCS 25, 31, 37, 1915–33 (vols. ii and iii rev. J. Dummer, 1980–5).

EUSEBIOS, *Eusebius Werke*, vol. 2, pts.1–3, ed. Eduard Schwartz, GCS 9, pts. 1–3, 1903–9.

EUTYCHIOS, *Annals: Das Annalenwerk des Eutychios von Alexandrien*, ed. and trans. Michael Breydy, CCSO 471–2, Scriptores Arabici, 44–5, Louvain: E. Peeters, 1985.

EVAGRIOS, *De oratione*, in *Philokalia* (1782), 155–65; (1979), i. 55–71.

——*Traité pratique ou le Moine*, ed. A. and C. Guillaumont, 2 vols., SC 170–1, 1971 (with continuous pagination).

EVERGETINOS, Εὐεργετινός ἤτοι Συναγωγή . . ., 4 vols., 6th edn., Athens: Mattaios Langi, 1993 (first published in Venice, 1783).

GIBBON, *The History of the Decline and Fall of the Roman Empire*, ed. with an intro-duction and appendices by David Womersley, 3 vols., London: Allen Lane, The Penguin Press, 1994 (with continuous pagination).

GREGORY NAZIANZEN, *Discours 1–3*, ed. Jean Bernardi, SC 247, 1978.

——*Discours* 27–31, ed. Paul Gallay, SC 250, 1978. English trans. of Theological Orations (*Or.* 27–31) in Frederick W. Norris, *Faith Gives Fullness to Reasoning: The Five Theological Orations of Gregory Nazianzen*, with trans. by Lionel Wickham and Frederick Williams, Supplements to *Vigiliae Christianae*, 13, Leiden, New York, Copenhagen and Cologne: E. J. Brill, 1991.

——*Discours* 38–41, ed. Claudio Moreschini, SC 358, 1990.

——*Lettres Théologiques*, ed. P. Gallay, SC 208, 1974 [includes *epp.* 101, 102, 202].

GREGORY OF NYSSA, *Opera (Dogmatica Minora)*, iii/1, ed. Fridericus Mueller, Leiden: Brill, 1958.

—— *Oratio Catechetica, Opera (Dogmatica Minora)*, iii/4, ed. Ekkehardus Mühlenberg, Leiden: Brill, 1996.

—— *In Canticum Canticorum, Opera*, vi, ed. Hermannus Langerbeck, Leiden: Brill, 1960.

GREGORY PALAMAS, *The One Hundred and Fifty Chapters*, ed. Robert E. Sinkewicz, Studies and Texts, 83, Toronto: Pontifical Institute of Medieval Studies, 1988.

HEGEMONIOS, *Acta Archelai*, ed. Charles Henry Beeson, GCS 16, 1906.

IRENAEUS, *Adversus Haereses*, ed. W. W. Harvey, 2 vols., Cambridge: Typis Academicis, 1857.

JEROME, *Commentarii in Matheum*, CCSL 77, pt. 1/7, ed. D. Hurst and M. Adriaen, 1969.

——*Lettres*, ed. Jérôme Labourt, 8 vols., Paris: Société d'Édition 'Les Belles Lettres', 1949–63.

JOHN CHRYSOSTOM, *Sur l'Incompréhensibilité de Dieu*, i (Homélies 1–5), ed. Anne-Marie Malingrey, trans. Robert Flacelière, SC 28*bis*, 1970.

JUSTIN MARTYR, *The Apologies of Justin Martyr*, ed. A. W. F. Blunt, Cambridge: Cambridge University Press, 1911.

MAKARIOS, *Die 50 geistliche Homilien des Makarios*, ed. H. Dörries, E. Klostermann, and M. Kroeger, PTS, 4, Berlin: Walter de Gruyter, 1964.

MAXIMOS THE CONFESSOR, *Capitoli sulla carità*, ed. Aldo Ceresa-Gastaldo, Verba Seniorum, NS 3, Rome: Editrice Studium, 1963.

—— *Quæstiones ad Thalassium*, ed. Carl Laga-Carlos Steel, CCSG 7, 22, 1980–90.

—— *Quæstiones et dubia*, ed. J. H. Declerck, CCSG 10, 1982.

Menaion, Μηναία (12 vols., one for each month of the year), Ἀθηναί Ἔκδοσις τῆς Ἀποστολικῆς Διαχονίας τῆς Ἐκκλησίας τῆς Ἑλλάδος (1993 edition).

NEMESIOS, *De natura hominis*, ed. Moreno Morani, Leipzig: Teubner, 1987.

NESTORIOS, *Le Livre d'Héraclide de Damas*, trans. F. Nau, Paris: Letouzey et Ané, 1910.

ORIGEN, *Origenes Matthäuserklärung*, ed. E. Klostermann with E. Benz, GCS 40, 1935.

Paraklitiki, Παρακλητικὴ ἤτοι Ὀχτώηχος ἡ Μεγάλη, Ἀθηναί: Ἔκδοσις τῆς Ἀποστολικῆς Διακονίας τῆς Ἐκκλησίας τῆς Ἑλλάδος (1994 edn.).

PASCAL, *Pensées*, ed. Philip Sellier, Paris: Mercure de France, 1976.

Pentekostarion, Πεντηκοστάριον χαρμόσυνον, Ἀθηναί: Ἔκδοσις τῆς Ἀποστολικῆς Διακονίας τῆς Ἐκκλησίας τῆς Ἑλλάδος(1994 edn.).

PHILO THE JEW, *On the Giants*, in *Philo*, ed. F. H. Colson and G. H. Whitaker, vol. ii, LCL, 1929, 446–479 [= *gig.*].

Philokalia (1782), *Φιλοκαλία τῶν Ἱερῶν Νηπτικῶν*, Venice: Antonio Bortoa.

Philokalia (1979 ff.), *The Philokalia: The Complete Text Compiled by St Nikodimos of the Holy Mountain and St Makarios of Corinth*, 4 vols. so far (out of 5), trans. and ed. G. E. H. Palmer, Philip Sherrard, and Kallistos Ware, London: Faber and Faber.

PLATO, *Opera*, ed. J. Burnet, 5 vols., OCT, 1905.

PROKLOS DIADOCHOS, Proclus, *Elements of Theology*, see Dodds 1963.

Qur'ān, *The Koran*, trans. with notes by N. J. Dawood, Penguin Classics, Harmondsworth, 1990.

Socrates, *Historia Ecclesiastica*, ed. G. C. Hansen and M. Sirinjan, GCS NF 1, 1995.

Symeon the New Theologian, *Traités Théologiques et Éthiques*, ed. and trans. Jean Darrouzès, 2 vols., SC 122, 129, 1966–7.

Symeon of Durham, *Libellus de Exordio atque Procursu istius hoc est Dunhelmensis Ecclesie*, ed. and trans. David Rollason, Oxford Medieval Texts, Oxford: Clarendon Press, 2000.

Synaxarion, Synaxarium Ecclesiae Constantinopolitanae, Propylaeum ad Acta Sanctorum Novembris, ed. H. Delehaye, Brussels: Société des Bollandistes, 1902.

Tertullian, *Tertullian's Treatise against Praxeas*, ed. Ernest Evans, London: SPCK, 1948.

Theodore Abū Qurrah, *A Treatise on the Veneration of the Holy Icons*, see Griffith 1997.

Theodore of Raïthu, *Proparaskeué*, in Diekamp 1938, 173–222.

Theodore of Stoudios, *Epistulæ*, ed. Georgios Fatouros, 2 vols. (with continuous pagination), Corpus Fontium Historiæ Byzantinæ 31/1, 2, Berlin and New York: Walter de Gruyter, 1992.

Theodoret, *Historia Ecclesiastica*, ed. L. Parmentier, GCS 19, 1911.

Theophanes, *Chronographia*, ed. C. de Boor, 2 vols., Leipzig, 1883–5, repr. Hildesheim, 1963. English trans.: *The Chronicle of Theophanes Confessor: Byzantine and Near Eastern History AD 284–813*, trans. with introduction and commentary by C. Mango and R. Scott, with the assistance of G. Greatrex, Oxford: Clarendon Press, 1997.

Thomas Aquinas, *Summa Theologiae*, Leonine edn., 6 vols., Rome: Typographia Forzani et Sodalis, 1894.

Triodion, Τριώδιον Κατανυκτικόν, Ἀθηναί: Ἔκδοσις τῆς Ἀποστολικῆς Διακονίας τῆς Ἐκκλησίας τῆς Ἑλλάδος (1994 edn.).

Secondary Literature

Alexakis, Alexander (1996), *Codex Parisinus Graecus 1115 and its Archetype*, Dumbarton Oaks Studies, 35, Washington: Dumbarton Oaks Research Library and Collection.

Alexander, Paul J. (1958), *The Patriarch Nicephorus of Constantinople: Ecclesiastical Policy and Image Worship in the Byzantine Empire*, Oxford: Clarendon Press.

——— (1985), *The Byzantine Apocalyptic Tradition*, Berkeley, Los Angeles, and London: University of California Press.

Allatus, Leo (1860), *De Sancto Joanne Damasceno Prolegomena et Dissertationes*, PG 94. 117–43.

Allies, Mary H. (1898) (trans.), *St John Damascene on Holy Images, followed by Three Sermons on the Assumption*, London: Thomas Baker.

ALTANER BERTHOLD, and STUIBER, ALFRED (1978), *Patrologie: Leben, Schriften und Lehre der Kirchenväter*, 8th rev. and expanded edn., Freiburg, Basle, and Vienna: Herder.

ANASTOS, MILTON (1968), 'Leo III's Edict against the Images of the Year 726–7 and Italo-Byzantine Relations between 726 and 730', *Byzantinische Forschungen*, 3, 5–41.

ANDERSON, DAVID (1980) (trans.), St John of Damascus, *On the Divine Images*, Crestwood, NY: St Vladimir's Seminary Press.

ATIYA, AZIZ S. (1968), *A History of Eastern Christianity*, London: Methuen.

AUZÉPY, MARIE-FRANCE (1990), 'La Destruction de l'icône du Christ de la Chalcé par Léon III: propagande ou réalité?', *Byzantion*, 60, 445–92.

——(1994), 'De la Palestine à Constantinople (VIIIᵉ–IXᵉ siècles): Étienne le Sabaïte et Jean Damascène', *Travaux et Mémoires*, 12, 183–218.

BALTHASAR, HANS URS VON (1961), *Kosmische Liturgie: Das Weltbild Maximus' des Bekenners*, 2nd completely rev. edn., Einsiedeln: Johannes-Verlag.

BARKER, ERNEST (1957), *Social and Political Thought in Byzantium from Justinian I to the last Palaeologus: Passages from Byzantine Writers and Documents*, Oxford: Clarendon Press.

BARNES, MICHEL RENÉ (1995), 'De Régnon Reconsidered', *Augustinian Studies*, 26/2, 51–79.

BARNES, TIMOTHY D. (1993), *Athanasius and Constantius: Theology and Politics in the Constantinian Empire*, Cambridge, Mass., and London: Harvard University Press.

BARTHES, ROLAND (1977), *Image–Text–Music*, selected and trans. by Stephen Heath, London: Fontana Press.

BECK, HANS-GEORG (1959), *Kirche und Theologische Literatur im Byzantinischen Reich*, Munich: C. H. Beck'sche Verlagsbuchhandlung.

BILZ, JAKOB (1909), *Die Trinitätslehre des hl. Johannes von Damaskos*, Forschungen zur Christlichen Literatur- und Dogmengeschichte, 9, Paderborn: Ferdinand Schöningh.

BOWMAN, ALAN, and WOOLF, GREG (1994) (eds.), *Literacy and Power in the Ancient World*, Cambridge: Cambridge University Press.

BRATKE, P. (1899) (ed.), *Das sogenannte Religionsgespräch am Hofe des Sasaniden*, TU 19/3; NF 4/3.

BROCK, SEBASTIAN (1980), 'The Orthodox–Oriental Orthodox Conversations of 532', *Apostolos Varnavas*, 41, 219–27; repr. in Brock 1984, item XI.

——(1984), *Syriac Perspectives on Late Antiquity*, London: Variorum.

——(1989), 'From Ephrem to Romanos', SP 20, 139–51.

BUCKTON, DAVID (1994) (ed.), *Byzantium, Treasures of Byzantine Art and Culture from British Collections*, London: British Museum Press.

BURKITT, F. C. (1925), *The Religion of the Manichees*, Cambridge: Cambridge University Press.

CAMERON, AVERIL (1979), 'Images of Authority: Elites and Icons in Late Sixth-Century Byzantium', *Past and Present*, 84, 3–35; repr. in Cameron 1981, item XVIII.

CAMERON, AVERIL (1981), *Continuity and Change in Sixth Century Byzantium*, London: Variorum.

—— (1993), *The Mediterranean World in Late Antiquity AD 395–600*, London and New York: Routledge.

—— (1994), 'Texts as Weapons: Polemic in the Byzantine Dark Ages', in Bowman and Woolf 1994, 198–215.

—— (1996), 'Byzantines and Jews: Some Recent Work on Early Byzantium', *Byzantine and Modern Greek Studies*, 20, 249–74.

—— and CONRAD, LAWRENCE I. (1992) (eds.), *The Byzantine and Early Islamic Near East, 1: Problems in the Literary Source Material*, Studies in Late Antiquity and Early Islam, 1, Princeton: The Darwin Press Inc.

CHADWICK, H. (1969), 'Florilegium', in *Reallexikon für Antike und Christentum*, ed. T. Klauser *et al.*, vol. vii, Stuttgart: Anton Hiersemann, 1131–60.

—— (1981), *Boethius: The Consolations of Logic, Music, Theology, and Philosophy*, Oxford: Clarendon Press.

—— (1987), 'Philoponus the Christian Theologian', in Richard Sorabji (ed.), *Philoponus and the Rejection of Aristotelian Science*, London: Duckworth, 41–56.

CHASE, FREDERIC H. (1958) (trans.), Saint John of Damascus, *Writings*, with introduction, Fathers of the Church, 37, New York: Fathers of the Church, Inc.

CHEVALIER, C., SJ (1936), *La Mariologie de saint Jean Damascène*, Orientalia Christiana Analecta, 109, Rome: Pontificale Institutum Orientalium Studiorum.

COLEMAN-NORTON, P. R. (1966), *Roman State and Christian Church*, 3 vols., London: SPCK (cited by document number).

CORBIN, HENRY (1993), *History of Islamic Philosophy*, trans. Liadain Sherrard (French original, 1964), London and New York: Kegan Paul International, in association with Islamic Publications of the Institute for Ismaili Studies.

CORMACK, ROBIN (1985), *Writing in Gold: Byzantine Society and its Icons*, London: George Philip.

CONTICELLO, VASSA L. (1995), 'Pseudo-Cyril's "De SS. Trinitate": A Compilation of Joseph the Philosopher', *Orientalia Christiana Periodica*, 61, 117–29.

CORRIGAN, KATHLEEN (1992), *Visual Polemics in the Ninth-Century Byzantine Psalters*, Cambridge: Cambridge University Press.

COUNE, MICHEL, OSB (1985) (ed.), *Joie de la Transfiguration*, Spiritualité Orientale, 39, 2nd edn., Bégrolles-en-Mauges: Abbaye de Bellefontaine.

CRONE, PATRICIA (1980), *Slaves on Horses: The Evolution of the Islamic Polity*, Cambridge: Cambridge University Press.

—— (1987), *Meccan Trade and the Rise of Islam*, Oxford: Basil Blackwell.

—— and COOK, MICHAEL (1977), *Hagarism: The Making of the Islamic World*, Cambridge: Cambridge University Press.

CUNNINGHAM, MARY B. (1991) (trans. and ed.), *The Life of Michael the Synkellos*, Belfast Byzantine Texts and Translations, 1, Belfast: Belfast Byzantine Enterprises.

DAGRON, GILBERT (1996), *Empereur et prêtre: Étude sur le 'césaropapisme' byzantin*, Paris: Gallimard.

———Riché, Pierre, and Vauchet, André (1993), *Histoire du christianisme des origines à nos jours*, iv: *Évêques, moines et empereurs (610–1054)*, Paris: Desclée.

Daley, Brian E., SJ (1998), *On the Dormition of Mary: Early Patristic Homilies*, Crestwood, NY: St Vladimir's Seminary Press.

Daniélou, Jean, SJ (1952), *Les Anges et leur mission d'après les Pères de l'Église*, Gembloux: Éditions de Chevetogne.

Dawes, Elizabeth, and Baynes, Norman H. (1948) (trans.), *Three Byzantine Saints*, London and Oxford: Mowbrays.

de la Taille, Maurice, SJ (1934), *The Mystery of Faith and Human Opinion Contrasted and Defined*, London: Sheed and Ward (first published 1930).

Diekamp, Franz (1938), *Analecta Patristica: Texte und Abhandlungen zur griechischen Patristik*, Orientalia Christiana Analecta, 117, Rome: Pontificale Institutum Orientalium Studiorum.

Dodds, E. R. (1963) (ed.), Proclus, *The Elements of Theology*, ed. with trans., introduction and commentary, 2nd edn., Oxford: Clarendon Press.

Dölger, F. (1953), *Der griechische Barlaam-Roman ein Werk H. Johannes von Damaskos*, Studia Patristica et Byzantina, 1, Ettal: Buch-Kunstverlag.

Dörries, Hermann (1941), *Symeon von Mesopotamien: Die Überlieferung der messalianischen 'Makarios'-Schriften*, TU 55/1.

Douglas, Mary (1970), *Purity and Danger*, Harmondsworth: Pelican Books (first published 1966).

Ebied, R. Y., and Wickham, L. R. (1985), 'Timothy Aelurus: Against the Definition of the Council of Chalcedon', in Laga *et al.* 1985, 115–66.

———Van Roey, A., and Wickham, L.R. (1981), *Peter of Callinicum, Anti-Tritheist Dossier*, Orientalia Lovaniensia Analecta, 10, Leuven: Departement Oriëntalistiek.

Elsner, Jás (1995), *Art and the Roman Viewer: The Transformation of art from the Pagan World to Christianity*, Cambridge: Cambridge University Press.

Englezakis, Benedict (1995), 'An Unpublished Commentary by St Neophytos the Recluse on the Apocalypse', in *idem, Studies on the History of the Church of Cyprus, 4th–20th Centuries*, trans. Norman Russell, Aldershot: Variorum, 105–45.

[Eustratiades], Sophronios (1931, 1932, 1933), 'Ὁ Ἅγιος Ἰωάννης ὁ Δαμασκήνος καὶ τὰ ποιητικὰ αὐτοῦ ἔργα', *Νέα Σίων* 26, 385–401, 497–512, 530–8, 610–17, 666–81, 721–36; 27, 28–44, 111–23, 165–77, 216–24, 329–53, 415–22, 450–72, 514–34, 570–85, 644–64, 698–719; 28, 11–25.

Festugière, André-Jean, OP (1970), *Vie de Théodore de Sykéôn*, 2 vols., Subsidia Hagiographica, 48, Brussels: Société des Bollandistes.

Finney, Paul Corby (1994), *The Invisible God: The Earliest Christians on Art*, New York and Oxford: Oxford University Press.

Fitschen, Klaus (1998), *Messalianismus und Antimessalianismus: Ein Beispiel ostkirchlicher Ketzergeschichte*, Forschungen zur Kirchen- und Dogmengeschichte, 71, Göttingen: Vandenhoeck und Ruprecht.

Fletcher-Louis, Crispin H. T. (2001), 'The Revelation of the Sacral Son of Man:

The Genre, History of Religions Context and the Meaning of the Transfiguration', in F. Avemarie and H. Lichtenberger (eds.), *Auferstehung-Resurrection: The Fourth Durham–Tübingen Symposium: Resurrection, Exaltation, and Transformation in Old Testament, Ancient Judaism, and Early Christianity*, Wissenschaftliche Untersuchungen zum Neuen Testament, 135, Tübingen: Mohr–Siebeck.

FLOROVSKY, GEORGES (1972), *Bible, Church, Tradition: An Eastern Orthodox View*, in *Collected Works*, i, Belmont, Mass.: Nordland Publishing Company.

—— (1987), *The Byzantine Fathers of the Fifth Century*, in *Collected Works*, viii, Vaduz: Büchervertriebsanstalt.

FLUSIN, BERNARD (1992), *Saint Anastase le Perse et l'histoire de la Palestine au début du VIIe siècle*, 2 vols., Paris: Éditions du Centre National de la Recherche Scientifique.

FOWDEN, GARTH (1993), *Empire to Commonwealth: Consequences of monotheism in late antiquity*, Princeton: Princeton University Press.

FRAIGNEAU-JULIEN, B. (1961), 'Un Traité anonyme de la sainte Trinité attribué à saint Cyrille d'Alexandrie', *Recherches de science religieuse*, 49, 188–211, 386–405.

GAHBAUER, FERDINAND, OSB (1995), 'Der Osterkanon des Johannes von Damaskos: Text, Übersetzung und Kommentar', *Studien und Mitteilungen zur Geschichte des Benediktinerordens*, 106, 133–74.

GAUTHIER, R. A. (1954), 'Saint Maxime le Confesseur et la psychologie de l'acte humain', *Recherches de théologie ancienne et médiévale*, 21, 51–100.

GOUILLARD, J. (1968), 'Aux origines de l'iconoclasme: le témoignage de Grégoire II?', *Travaux et Mémoires*, 3, 243–307.

GRÉGOIRE, JOSÉ (1969), 'Le Relation éternelle de l'Esprit au Fils d'après les écrits de Jean de Damas', *Revue d'histoire ecclésiastique*, 64, 713–55.

GREGORIOS, PAULOS, LAZARETH, WILLIAM H., and NISSIOTIS, NIKOS A. (1981), *Does Chalcedon Divide or Unite? Towards Convergence in Orthodox Christology*, Geneva: World Council of Churches.

GRIFFITH, SIDNEY H. (1986), 'Greek into Arabic: Life and Letters in the Monasteries of Palestine in the Ninth Century: The Example of the *Summa Theologiae Arabica*', *Byzantion*, 56, 117–138; repr. in Griffith 1992, item VIII.

—— (1987), 'Anastasius of Sinai, the *Hodegos* and the Muslims', *Greek Orthodox Theological Review*, 32, 341–58.

—— (1992), *Arabic Christianity in the Monasteries of Ninth-Century Palestine*, Aldershot: Variorum.

—— (1997) (ed. and trans.), Theodore Abū Qurrah, *A Treatise on the Veneration of the Holy Icons*, Eastern Christian Texts in Translation, 1, Louvain: Peeters.

GRILLMEIER, ALOYS, SJ (1975, 1987, 1995), *Christ in Christian Tradition*, vol. i, vol. ii, pts. 1 and 2, London and Oxford: Mowbray.

—— and BACHT, HEINRICH, SJ (1951), *Das Konzil von Chalkedon: Geschichte und Gegenwart*, 3 vols., Würzburg: Echter-Verlag.

HAHN, AUGUST (1897), *Bibliothek der Symbole und Glaubensregeln der alten Kirche*, 3rd edn., by G. L. Hahn, Breslau: Verlag von E. Morgenstern (cited by item number).

HALDON, JOHN (1992), 'The Works of Anastasius of Sinai: A Key Source for the History of Seventh-Century East Mediterranean Society and Belief', in Cameron and Conrad 1992, 107–47.

HALEEM, M. ABDEL (1996), 'Early *kalām*', in Nasr and Leaman 1996, 71–88.

HALKIN, F. (1953), review of Dölger 1953, *Analecta Bollandiana*, 71, 475–80.

HALLEUX, ANDRÉ DE (1984), '"Hypostase" et "personne" dans la formation du dogme trinitaire', *Revue d'histoire ecclésiastique*, 79, 311–69, 623–70; repr. in Halleux 1990, 113–214.

—— (1986), 'Personnalisme ou Essentialisme trinitaire chez les Pères Cappadociens', *Revue théologique de Louvain*, 17, 129–55, 265–292; repr. in Halleux 1990, 215–68.

—— (1990), *Patrologie et Oecuménisme: Recueil d'Études*, Bibliotheca Ephemeridum Theologicarum Lovaniensium, 93, Leuven: Uitgeverij Peeters/Leuven University Press.

HAMILTON, JANET, and HAMILTON, BERNARD (1998), *Christian Dualist Heresies in the Byzantine World c.650–c.1405*, Manchester and New York: Manchester University Press.

HARNACK, ADOLPH (1884–9), *History of Dogma*, English trans., 7 vols., London: Williams and Norgate.

HENNEPHOF, HERMAN (1969), *Textus Byzantini ad iconomachiam pertinentes*, Leiden: E. J. Brill (cited by item number).

HENRY, PATRICK (1976), 'What was the Iconoclast Controversy about?', *Church History*, 45, 16–31.

HIRSCHFELD, YIZHAR (1992), *The Judean Desert Monasteries in the Byzantine Period*, New Haven and London: Yale University Press.

HOECK, JOHANNES M. (1951), 'Stand und Aufgaben der Damaskenos-Forschung', *Orientalia Christiana Periodica*, 17, 5–60.

HOLL, KARL (1897), *Die Sacra Parallela des Johannes Damascenus*, TU 16.

—— (1898), *Enthusiasmus und Bussgewalt beim griechischen Mönchtum: Eine Studie zu Symeon dem Neuen Theologen*, Leipzig: J. C. Heinrich'sche Buchhandlung.

HOYLAND, ROBERT G. (1997), *Seeing Islam As Others Saw It: A Survey and Evaluation of Christian, Jewish and Zoroastrian Writings on Early Islam*, Studies in Late Antiquity and Early Islam, 13, Princeton: Darwin Press Inc.

HUMPHREYS, R. STEPHEN (1991), *Islamic History: A Framework for Inquiry*, rev. edn., London and New York: I. B. Tauris.

HUSSEY, J. M. (1986), *The Orthodox Church in the Byzantine Empire*, Oxford: Clarendon Press.

ICĂ, IOAN I., JUN. (1995), '"Dialectica" Sf. Ioan Damaschinul—prolegomenā logico-filosoficā a "Dogmaticii"', *Studia Universitatis Babeş-Bolyai, Theologia Orthodoxā*, 40/1–2, 85–140.

IVÁNKA, ENDRE VON (1954), '*ΚΕΦΑΛΑΙΑ*: Eine byzantinische Literaturform und ihre antiken Wurzeln', *Byzantinische Zeitschrift*, 47, 285–91.

JOANNOU, PÉRICLÈS-PIERRE (1962), *Discipline Générale Antique (IIᵉ–IXᵉ siècles)*, i/1:

Les Canons des conciles œcuméniques, Fonti, fasc. IX, Grottaferrata: Tipografia Italo-Orientale 'S. Nilo'.

JONES, DAVID (1959), 'Art and Sacrament', in *idem, Epoch and Artist*, New York: Chilmark Press, London: Faber and Faber, 143–79.

JUGIE, M. (1924), 'La Vie de saint Jean Damascène', *Echos d'Orient*, 23, 137–61.

—— (1926–35), *Theologia Dogmatica Christianorum Orientalium ab Ecclesia Catholica Dissidentium* [sic], 5 vols., Paris: Letouzey et Ané.

KARTSONIS, ANNA D. (1986), *Anastasis: The Making of an Image*, Princeton: Princeton University Press.

KAZHDAN, A. (1988), 'Where, When and by Whom was the Greek Barlaam not written?', in W. Wolfgang and W. Gerhard (eds.), *Zu Alexander dem Grossen Festschrift G. Wirth*, Amsterdam: Verlag Adolf M. Hakkert, ii. 1187–1207.

KAZHDAN, ALEXANDER P. (1991) (ed.), *Oxford Dictionary of Byzantium*, 3 vols., New York and Oxford: Oxford University Press.

—— and GERO, S. (1989), 'Kosmas of Jerusalem: A More Critical Approach to his Biography', *Byzantinische Zeitschrift*, 82, 122–32.

KELLY, J. N. D. (1964), *The Athanasian Creed*, London: Adam and Charles Black.

—— (1972), *Early Christian Creeds*, 3rd edn., London: Adam and Charles Black.

KHOURY, ADEL-THÉODORE (1969), *Les Théologiens byzantins et l'Islam: Textes et auteurs (VIIIᵉ–XIIIᵉ S.)*, 2nd edn., Louvain: Éditions Nauwelaerts/Paris: Béatrice-Nauwelaerts.

KHOURY, PAUL (1957–8), 'Jean Damascène et l'Islam', *Proche-Orient Chrétien*, 7, 44–63; 8, 313–39.

KITZINGER, ERNST (1954), 'The Cult of Images in the Age before Iconoclasm', *Dumbarton Oaks Papers*, 8, 83–150.

KNORR, ORTWIN (1998), 'Zur Überlieferungsgeschichte des "Liber de Haeresibus" des Johannes von Damaskus (um 650–vor 754): Anmerkungen zur Edition B. Kotters', *Byzantinische Zeitschrift*, 91, 59–69.

KOLBABA, TIA M. (2000), *Byzantine Lists: Errors of the Latins*, Urbana, Ill., and Chicago: University of Illinois Press.

KOTTER, BONIFAZ (1959) *Die Überlieferung der Pege Gnoseos des hl. Johannes von Damaskos*, Studia Patristica et Byzantina, 5, Ettal: Buch-Kunstverlag.

KOTTER, BONIFATIUS (1988), 'Johannes von Damaskos', in Gerhard Müller (ed.), *Theologische Realenzyklopädie*, xvii, Berlin and New York: Walter de Gruyter, 127–32.

KRIVOCHÉINE, BASILE (1980), *Dans la lumière du Christ: S. Syméon le nouveau théologien*, Chevetogne: Éditions de Chevetogne.

LAGA, C., MUNITIZ, J. A., and VAN ROMPAY, L. (1985) (eds.), *After Chalcedon: Studies in Theology and Church History Offered to Professor Albert Van Roey for his Seventieth Birthday*, Orientalia Lovanensia Analecta, 18, Leuven: Uitgeverij Peeters.

LAMPE, G. W. H. (1961) (ed.), *A Patristic Greek Lexicon*, Oxford: Clarendon Press.

LANG, DAVID M. (1955), 'St Euthymius the Georgian and the Barlaam and Ioasaph Romance', *Bulletin of the School of Oriental and African Studies*, 17, 306–25.

LANG, U. M. (1998), 'Anhypostatos-Enhypostatos: Church Fathers, Protestant Orthodoxy and Karl Barth', *Journal of Theological Studies*, NS 49, 630–57.

LANGE, GÜNTHER (1969), *Bild und Wort: Die katechetischen Funktionen des Bildes in der griechischen Theologie des sechsten bis neunten Jahrhunderts*, Würzburg: Echter Verlag.

LANGEN, J. (1879), *Johannes von Damaskus*, Gotha: Friedrich Andreas Perthes.

LARCHET, JEAN-CLAUDE (1998), *Maxime le Confesseur, médiateur entre l'Orient et l'Occident*, Cogitatio Fidei, 208, Paris: Cerf.

——(2000), 'La Question christologique: À propos du projet d'union de l'Église orthodoxe et des Églises non chalcédoniennes: problèmes théologiques et ecclésiologiques en suspens', *Le Messager Orthodoxe*, 134, 3–103.

LASH, FR. EPHREM (1990), 'Mary in Eastern Church Literature', in Alberic Stacpoole, OSB, *et al.*, (eds.), *Mary in Doctrine and Devotion*, Blackrock, Co. Dublin: Columba Press, 58–80.

——(1995), St Romanos, *On the Life of Christ: Kontakia*, Sacred Literature Series, San Francisco, London, and Pymble, NSW: HarperCollins.

——(1999), *An Orthodox Prayer Book*, Oxford: Oxford University Press.

——(2000), *The Services for the Holy and Great Sunday of Pascha*, Manchester: Saint Andrew's Monastery.

LE COZ, RAYMOND (1992), Jean Damascène, *Écrits sur Islam,* présentation, with introduction, translation, and commentaries, SC 383.

LEDIT, JOSEPH (1979), *Marie dans la liturgie de Byzance*, Théologie Historique, 39, rev. edn., Paris: Beauchesne.

LEMERLE, P. (1979, 1981), *Les Plus Anciens Recueils des miracles de saint Démétrius*, 2 vols., Paris: Éditions de la Centre Nationale de la Recherche Scientifique.

LÉTHEL, FRANÇOIS-MARIE (1979), *Théologie de l'Agonie du Christ*, Théologie Historique, 52, Paris: Beauchesne.

LEVINE, LEE I. (1999), *The Ancient Synagogue: The First Thousand Years*, New Haven and London: Yale University Press.

LIDDELL, HENRY GEORGE, and SCOTT, ROBERT (1996) (eds.), rev. Sir Henry Stuart Jones and Roderick McKenzie, *A Greek–English Lexicon*, with a revised supplement, ed. P. G. W. Glare and A. A. Thompson, Oxford: Clarendon Press.

LIEU, SAMUEL N. C. (1988), *Manichaeism in the Later Roman Empire and Medieval China: A Historical Survey*, repr. with corrections (first published 1985), Manchester: Manchester University Press.

LINGAS, ALEXANDER (1995), 'The Liturgical Place of the Kontakion in Constantinople', in Constantin C. Akentiev (ed.), *Liturgy, Architecture, and Art in the Byzantine World*, Papers of the XVIII International Byzantine Congress (Moscow, 8–15 August 1991) and Other Essays Dedicated to the Memory of Fr John Meyendorff, St Petersburg: Byzantinorossica, 50–7.

LITTLEWOOD, A. R. (1995) (ed.), *Originality in Byzantine Literature, Art and Music*, Oxbow Monograph, 50, Oxford: Oxbow Books.

LOOFS, F. (1887), *Leontius von Byzanz und die gleichnamigen Schriftsteller der griechischen Kirche*, TU 3/1–2.

LORENZATOS, ZISSIMOS (2000), *The Drama of Quality*, Romiosyni Series, 16, Evia, Greece: Denise Harvey.

LOUTH, ANDREW (1981), *The Origins of the Christian Mystical Tradition: From Plato to Denys*, Oxford: Clarendon Press.

——(1989*a*), *Denys the Areopagite*, London: Geoffrey Chapman/Wilton, Conn.: Morehouse-Barlow.

——(1989*b*), 'The Use of the Term ἴδιος in Alexandrian Theology from Alexander to Cyril', *Studia Patristica*, 19, 198–202.

——(1995), 'Paradies: IV Theologiegeschichtlich' in Gerhard Müller (ed.), *Theologische Realenzyklopädie*, xxv, Berlin and New York: Walter de Gruyter, 714–19.

——(1996), *Maximus the Confessor*, London: Routledge.

——(1997), 'St Denys the Areopagite and the Iconoclast Controversy', in Ysabel de Andia (ed.), *Denys l'Aréopagite et sa postérité en orient et en occident*, Actes du Colloque International, Paris, 21–24 septembre 1994, Collection des Études Augustiniennes, Série Antiquité, 151, Paris: Institut d'Études Augustiniennes, 329–39.

——(with Dr C. T. R. Hayward) (1998), 'Sanctus', in Gerhard Müller (ed.), *Theologische Realenzyklopädie*, xxx, Berlin and New York: Walter de Gruyter, 20–9.

——(2002), 'Trishagion', in Gerhard Müller (ed.), *Theologische Realenzyklopädie*, xxxiv, Berlin and New York: Walter de Gruyter, 121–4.

——(2003*a*), 'The Πηγὴ Γνώσεως of St John Damascene: Its Date and Development', in Jonathan Harris *et al.* (eds.), *Porphyrogenita: Essays on the History of Literature of Byzantium and the Latin East in Honour of Julian Chrysostomides*, Aldershot: Ashgate, 335–40.

——(2003*b*), St John of Damascus, *Three Treatises on the Divine Images*, translation with introduction and notes, Crestwood, NY: St Vladimir's Seminary Press.

MADDEN, J. D. (1982), 'The Authenticity of Early Definitions of Will (Thelesis)', in F. Heinzer-C. Schönborn (ed.), *Maximus Confessor: Actes de Symposium sur Maxime le Confesseur, Fribourg, 2–5 septembre 1980*, Paradosis, 27, Fribourg-en-Suisse: Éditions Universitaires, 61–79.

MANGO, CYRIL (n.d.), 'Greek Culture in Palestine after the Arab Conquest', in G. Cavallo, G. de Gregorio, and M. Maniaci (eds.), *Scritture, Libri e Testi nelle Aree Provinciali di Bisanzio Atti del seminario di Erice, 18–25 settembre 1988*, Spoleto: Centro Italiano di Studi sull'Alto Medioevo, 149–60.

MARY, MOTHER, and WARE, ARCHIMAUDRITE KALLISTOS (1969), The Festal Menaion, London: Faber and Faber.

MATEOS, JUAN, SJ (1962), *La Typikon de la Grande Église, Ms Sainte-Croix n° 40, X° siècle*, 2 vols., Orientalia Christiana Analecta, 165–6, Rome: Pontificale Institutum Orientalium Studiorum.

MATHEW, GERVASE (1963), *Byzantine Aesthetics*, London: John Murray.

MATSOUKAS, NIKOS (1988) (ed.), *Ἰοάννου Δαμασκηνοῦ, Κατὰ Μανιχαίων Λόγος, Πρὸς τοὺς διαβάλλοντας τὰς ἀγίας εἰκόνας Λόγοι τρεῖς*, Thessaloniki: Ekdoseis P. Pournara.

MATTER, E. ANN (1990), *The Voice of My Beloved: The Song of Songs in Western Medieval Christianity*, Philadelphia: University of Pennsylvania Press.

MAY, GERHARD (1994), *Creatio ex nihilo: The Doctrine of 'Creation out of Nothing' in Early Christian Thought*, Edinburgh: T. & T. Clark.

McGUCKIN, JOHN A. (1986), *The Transfiguration of Christ in Scripture and Tradition* Studies in the Bible and Early Christianity, 9, Lewiston, Me., and Queenston: Edwin Mellen Press.

——(1993), 'The Theology of Images and the Legitimation of Power in Eighth-Century Byzantium', *St Vladimir's Theological Quarterly*, 37, 39–58.

McKINNON, JAMES (1994), 'Desert Monasticism and the Later Fourth-Century Psalmodic Movement', *Music and Letters*, 75, 505–21.

MENGES, H. (1938), *Die Bilderlehre des hl. Johannes von Damaskus*, Münster: Aschendorffische Verlagsbuchhandlung.

MERCENIER, F. (1939), 'L'Antienne Mariale grecque la plus ancienne', *Le Muséon*, 52, 229–33.

MULLETT, MARGARET, and KIRBY, ANTHONY (1994) (eds.), *The Theotokos Evergetis and Eleventh-Century Monasticism*, Belfast Byzantine Texts and Translations, 6/1, Belfast: Belfast Byzantine Enterprises.

——(1997) (eds.), *Work and Worship at the Theotokos Evergetis*, Belfast Texts and Translations, 6/2, Belfast: Belfast Byzantine Enterprises.

MUNITIZ, J. A., (1997), with Chrysostomides, J., Harvalia-Crook, E., Dendrinos, Ch. *The Letter of the Three Patriarchs to Emperor Theophilos and Related Texts*, Camberley: Porphyrogenitus.

MURDOCH, IRIS (1970), *The Sovereignty of Good*, London: Routledge and Kegan Paul.

MURRAY, MARY CHARLES (1977), 'Art and the Early Church', *Journal of Theological Studies*, NS 28, 304–45.

NASR, SEYYED HOSSEIN, and LEAMAN, OLIVER (1996) (eds.), *History of Islamic Philosophy*, 2 vols., London: Routledge.

NASRALLAH, JOSEPH (1950), *Saint Jean de Damas: Son Époque—Sa Vie—Son Oeuvre*, Les Souvenirs Chrétiens de Damas, 2, Harissa: Imprimerie Saint Paul.

—— and HADDAD, RACHID (1996), *Histoire du mouvement littéraire dans l'Église Melchite du Vᵉ au XXᵉ siècle*, . ii, pt. 1, Damascus: Fondation Joseph Nasrallah.

NELLAS, PANAGIOTIS (1995), Ἁγίου Ἰωάννου Δαμασκηνοῦ Ἡ Θεοτόκος. Τέσσερις Θεομητορικὲς Ὁμολιές, Ἐπὶ τὰς Πηγάς 3, Ἀθήναι: Ἔκδοσις Ἀποστολικῆς Διακονίας, 3rd edn. (1st edn. 1970).

NIKODIMOS THE AGIORITE (1987), Ἑορτοδρόμιον, 3 vols., Θεσσαλονίκη: Ἔκδοσις Ὀρθόδοξος Κυψέλη (originally published in 1836). There is an abridged translation by Elizabeth Theokritoff of ii. 279–91 (the first two odes of the Easter Canon) in *Sourozh*, 71 (Feb. 1998), 40–9.

NOBLE, THOMAS F. X. (1987), 'John Damascene and the History of the Iconoclast Controversy', in T. Noble and Contreni (eds.), *Religion, Culture and Society in the Early Middle Ages: Studies in honor of Richard E. Sullivan*, Kalamazoo, Mich.: Western Michigan University Press, 95–116.

Nock, A. D. (1972), *Essays on Religion and the Ancient World*, ed. Zeph Stewart, 2 vols. (with continuous pagination), Oxford: Clarendon Press.

Odorico. P. (1990), 'La cultura della Συλλογή: 1. Il cosiddetto enciclopedismo bizantino, 2. Le tavole del sapere di Giovanni Damasceno', *Byzantinische Zeitschrift*, 83, 1–21.

Palmer, Andrew (1993), *The Seventh Century in the West-Syrian Chronicles*, Translated Texts for Historians, 15, Liverpool: Liverpool University Press.

Patrich, Joseph (1994), *Sabas, Leader of Palestinian Monasticism: A Comparative Study in Eastern Monasticism, Fourth to Seventh Centuries*, Dumbarton Oaks Studies, 32, Washington: Dumbarton Oaks Research Library and Collection.

Pavlin, James (1996), 'Sunni *kalām* and Theological Controversies', in Nasr and Leaman 1996, 105–18.

Payton, James R., jun. (1996), 'John of Damascus on Human Cognition: An Element in his Apologetic for Icons', *Church History*, 65, 173–83.

Pourkier, Aline (1992), *L'Hérésiologie chez Épiphane de Salamine*, Christianisme antique, 4, Paris, Beauchesne.

Prestige, G. L. (1952), *God in Patristic Thought*, 2nd edn. (first published 1936), London: SPCK.

Régnon, Th. de (1892–8), *Études de théologie positive sur la Saint Trinité*, 3 vols. in 4, Paris: Victor Retaux et fils.

Reinink, G. J. (1992), 'Ps.-Methodius: A Concept of History in Response to the Rise of Islam', in Cameron and Conrad 1992, 149–87.

Relton, H. Maurice (1934), *A Study in Christology*, London: SPCK.

Rich, John (1992) (ed.), *The City in Late Antiquity*, London and New York: Routledge.

Richard, Marcel (1950), 'Ἀπὸ φωνῆς', *Byzantion*, 20, 191–222; repr. in Richard 1976–7, iii. item 60.

—— (1951), 'Les Florilèges diphysites du Vᵉ et du VIᵉ siècle', in Grillmeier and Bacht 1951, i. 721–48; repr. in Richard 1976–7, i. item 3.

—— (1964), 'Florilèges grecs', in *Dictionnaire de Spiritualité*, v, Paris: Le Cerf, 475–512; repr. in Richard 1976–7, i. item 1.

—— (1976–7), *Opera Minora*, 3 vols., Turnhout: Leuven University Press.

Richter, Gerhard (1964), *Die Dialektik des Johannes von Damaskos: Eine Untersuchung des Textes nach seinen Quellen und seiner Bedeutung*, Studia Patristica et Byzantina, 10, Ettal: Buch-Kunstverlag.

—— (1982), Johannes von Damaskos, *Philosophische Kapitel*, Bibliothek der Griechischen Literatur, 15, Stuttgart: Anton Hiersemann.

Robertson, Archibald (1892) (ed. and trans.), *St Athanasius: Select Works and Letters*, Nicene and Post-Nicene Fathers, ser. 2, vol. iv, Oxford: Parker and Co./New York: Christian Literature Co.

Roey, A. Van (1944), 'La lettre apologétique d'Élie à Léon, syncelle de l'évêque chalcédonien de Harran. Une apologie monophysite du VIII–IXᵉ siècle', *Muséon*, 57, 1–52.

ROREM, PAUL, and LAMOREAUX, JOHN C. (1998), *John of Scythopolis and the Dionysian Corpus*, Oxford: Clarendon Press.

ROUECHÉ, MOSSMAN (1974), 'Byzantine Philosophical Texts of the Seventh Century', *Jahrbuch der Österreichischen Byzantinistik*, 23, 61–76.

——(1980), 'A Middle Byzantine Handbook of Logic Terminology', *Jahrbuch der Österreichischen Byzantinistik*, 29, 71–98.

——(1990), 'The Definitions of Philosophy and a New Fragment of Stephanus the Philosopher', *Jahrbuch der Österreichischen Byzantinistik*, 40, 107–28.

——(2002), 'Why the Monad is Not a Number: John Philoponus and *In De Anima* 3', *Jahrbuch der Österreichischen Byzantinistik*, 52, 95–123.

ROZEMOND, KEETJE (1959), *La Christologie de saint Jean Damascène*, Studia Patristica et Byzantina, 8, Ettal: Buch-Kunstverlag.

——(1984), 'La Lettre "De hymno trisagio" de Jean Damascène, ou Jean Mosche, patriarche de Jérusalem', SP 15 (= TU 108), 108–11.

RUNCIMAN, STEVEN (1947), *The Medieval Manichee: A Study of Christian Dualist Heresy*, Cambridge: Cambridge University Press.

RUNIA, DAVID T. (1989), 'Festugière Revisited: Aristotle in the Greek Patres', *Vigiliae Christianae*, 43, 1–34.

RUSSELL, NORMAN (2000), *Cyril of Alexandria*, London: Routledge.

SAHAS, DANIEL J. (1972), *John of Damascus on Islam: The 'Heresy of the Ishmaelites'*, Leiden: E. J. Brill.

——(1986), *Icon and Logos: Sources in Eighth-Century Iconoclasm*, Toronto Medieval Texts and Translations, 4, Toronto, Buffalo, and London: University of Toronto Press.

——(1992), 'The Arab Character of the Christian Disputation with Islam: The Case of John of Damascus (ca. 655–ca. 749)', in Bernard Lewis and Friedrich Niewöhner (eds.), *Religionsgespräche im Mittelalter*, Wolfenbütteler Mittelalter-Studien, 4, Wiesbaden: Otto Harrasowitz, 185–205.

SAVVIDIS, KYRIAKOS (1997), *Die Lehre von der Vergöttlichung des Menschen bei Maximos dem Bekenner und ihre rezeption durch Gregor Palamas*, Veröffentlichungen des Instituts für Orthodoxe Theologie, 5, St Ottilien: Erzabtei St Ottilien Verlag.

SCHICK, ROBERT (1995), *The Christian Communities of Palestine from Byzantine to Islamic Rule: A Historical and Archaeological Study*, Studies in Late Antiquity and Early Islam, 2, Princeton: Darwin Press Inc.

SCHÖNBORN, CHRISTOPH VON, OP (1976), *L'Icône du Christ: Fondements théologiques élaborés entre le Iᵉʳ et le IIᵉ Concile de Nicée (325–787)*, Paradosis, 24, Fribourg en Suisse: Édition Universitaires.

——(1982), 'Le Sainteté de l'icône selon S. Jean Damascène', *Studia Patristica*, 17/1, 188–93.

SCOTT, ALAN (1991), *Origen and the Life of the Stars: A History of an Idea*, Oxford: Clarendon Press.

SHARPLES, R. W. (1983), 'Nemesius of Emesa and Some Theories of Divine Providence', *Vigiliae Christianae*, 37, 141–56.

SHERWOOD, POLYCARP (1955), *The Earlier Ambigua of St. Maximus the Confessor*, Studia Anselmiana, 36, Rome: Herder.

SHOEMAKER, STEPHEN J. (2001), 'The (Re?)Discovery of the Kathisma Church and the Cult of the Virgin in Late Antique Palestine', *Maria*, 2 (Feb.), 21–72.

SPECK, PAUL (1981), *Artabasdos, der rechtgläubige Vorkämpfer der göttlichen Lehre, Ποίκιλα Βυζαντίνα* 2, Bonn: Dr Rudolf Habelt GmBH.

—— (1989), 'Eine Interpolation in den Bilderreden des Johannes von Damaskos', *Byzantinische Zeitschrift*, 82, 114–15.

ŠPIDLÍK, TOMÁŠ, SJ (1989), 'Le Concept de l'image chez les Pères jusqu'au Concile Nicée II', SP 23, 74–86.

STĂNILOAE, DUMITRU (1981), 'The Procession of the Holy Spirit from the Father and his Relation to the Son, as the Basis of our Deification and Adoption', in Vischer 1981, 174–86.

STEAD, G. CHRISTOPHER (1974), '"Homoousios" dans la pensée de Saint Athanase', in Charles Kannengiesser (ed.), *Politique et Théologie chez Athanase d'Alexandrie*, Théologie Politique, 27, Paris: Beauchesne.

STEGMÜLLER, O. (1952), 'Sub tuum praesidium: Bemerkungen zur ältesten Überlieferung', *Zeitschrift für katholischen Theologie*, 74, 76–82.

STEWART, COLUMBA (1991), *'Working the Earth of the Heart': The Messalian Controversy in History, Texts, and Language to* AD 431, Oxford: Clarendon Press.

STUDER, BASILIUS (1956), *Die theologische Arbeitsweise des Johannes von Damaskos*, Studia Patristica et Byzantina, 2, Ettal: Buch-Kunstverlag.

SUERMANN, HARALD (1998), *Die Gründungsgeschichte der Maronitischen Kirche*, Orientalia Biblica et Christiana, 10, Wiesbaden: Harrassowitz Verlag.

SWETE, H. B. (1876), *On the History of the Doctrine of the Procession of the Holy Spirit*, Cambridge: Deighton, Bell and Co./London: George Bell and Sons.

SWINBURNE, RICHARD (1994), *The Christian God*, Oxford: Clarendon Press.

TAFT, ROBERT, SJ (1986), *The Liturgy of the Hours in East and West*, Collegeville, Minn.: Liturgical Press.

TANNER, NORMAN P., SJ (1990), *Decrees of the Ecumenical Councils*, 2 vols. (with continuous pagination), London: Sheed and Ward/Washington: Georgetown University Press.

TELFER, WILLIAM (1955) (ed. and trans.), *Cyril of Jerusalem and Nemesius of Emesa*, Library of Christian Classics, . 4, London: SCM Press.

THOMAS, DAVID (1992), *Anti-Christian Polemic in Early Islam*, University of Cambridge Oriental Publications, 45, Cambridge: Cambridge University Press.

THÜMMEL, H. G. (1981), 'Zur Entstehungsgeschichte der sogenannten Pege gnoseos des Ioannes von Damaskos', *Byzantinoslavica*, 42, 20–30.

—— (1992), *Die Frühgeschichte der ostkirchlichen Bilderlehre: Texte und Untersuchungen zur Zeit vor dem Bilderstreit*, TU 139.

THUNBERG, LARS (1995), *Microcosm and Mediator: The Theological Anthropology of Maximus the Confessor*, 2nd rev. edn., Chicago and La Salle, Ill.: Open Court.

TORRANCE, IAIN (1988), *Christology after Chalcedon: Severus of Antioch and Sergius the Monophysite*, Norwich: Canterbury Press.

TWOMBLY, CHARLES C. (1992), *Perichoresis and Personhood in the Thought of John of Damascus*, Ph.D. diss. Emory University.

VAN DEN VEN, P. (1955–7), 'La Patristique et l'hagiographie au concile de Nicée de 787', *Byzantion*, 25–7, 325–62.

VISCHER, LUKAS (1981) (ed.), *Spirit of God, Spirit of Christ: Ecumenical Reflections on the Filioque Controversy*, Faith and Order Paper, 103, London: SPCK/Geneva: World Council of Churches.

VOULET, PIERRE, SJ, (1961) (ed.), S. Jean Damascène, *Homélies dur la Nativité et la Dormition*, SC 80.

WALLACE-HADRILL, D. S. (1968), *The Greek Patristic View of Nature*, Manchester: Manchester University Press.

WALLIS, FAITH (1999), *Bede: The Reckoning of Time*, trans. with introduction, notes, and commentary, Translated Texts for Historians, 29, Liverpool: Liverpool University Press.

WARD, BENEDICTA, SLG (1990): *The Venerable Bede*, London: Geoffrey Chapman.

WELLESZ, EGON (1961), *A History of Byzantine Music and Hymnography*, 2nd rev. edn., Oxford: Clarendon Press.

WIDENGREN, GEO (1961), *Mani and Manichaeism*, London: Weidenfeld and Nicolson.

WILKINSON, JOHN (1981), *Egeria's Travels to the Holy Land*, rev. edn., Warminster: Aris & Phillips.

——, with Joyce Hill and W. F. Ryan (1988), *Jerusalem Pilgrimage 1099–1185*, London: Hakluyt Society.

WOLFSON, HARRY AUSTRYN (1970), *The Philosophy of the Church Fathers*, 3rd rev. edn., Cambridge, Mass.: Harvard University Press.

WOLSKA, W. (1962), *La 'Topologie Chrétienne' de Cosmas Indicopeustès: Théologie et science au V* siècle*, Études, 3, Paris: Bibliothèque byzantine.

YANNARAS, CHRISTOS (1991), *Elements of Faith: An Introduction to Orthodox Theology*, Edinburgh: T. & T. Clark.

ZIZIOULAS, JOHN (1985), *Being as Communion: Studies in Personhood and the Church*, London: Darton, Longman and Todd.

INDEX OF CITATIONS

GENERAL INDEX

Theodore of Stoudios 14, 198, 204, 218, 227
Theodoret of Kyrrhos 72–5, 88–9, 227
Theodosians (Egyptian Monophysites) 10
Theodosius I, emperor 58, 96
Theodosius II, emperor 149
Theokatagnostai 60
theologia 113, 115
  distinguished from *oikonomia* (*q.v.*) 91, 92, 108, 114, 151, 153, 158, 159, 174
theology, *apophatic* and *kataphatic* 92, 94, 235–6
theopaschite formula 152, 153
Theophanes the Confessor 5, 6, 10, 33, 193, 197, 208, 224
Theophilos, emperor 193
Theophylact Simocatta 141
Theotokos, Mother of God 149, 173
  see also Mary, Mother of God
Thessaloniki 196, 256
Thnêtopsychitai 60
Thomas Aquinas 288
Thümmel, H. G. 195
time 119
  liturgical 231–2
Timothy of Constantinople 73–4
Tolstoy, Alexei 18 n.
tomb of Christ as bridal chamber 264
tomb of BVM 281–2
tradition 12–13, 15, 26, 35–7, 54–7, 87, 195–6
  unwritten traditions 183, 186, 202, 203, 205
Transfiguration of the Lord 234–43, 244, 257, 258, 268–74
tropos tês hyparxeôs 48, 95, 96, 97, 106, 113, 114, 162
Trinity, doctrine of 32, 39, 47–8, 51, 58, 66–7, 70–1, 89–118, 147, 158,

162, 166, 174, 179, 180, 236, 239, 243, 272
Trisagion 163–4
tritheists 99–100, 115
Trullan Synod (691–2) 60, 185, 196, 203, 212

Umar, Caliph 11
Umayyads 4, 70, 78, 82, 85, 155

Vahram I 62
Valens, emperor 204
Valentinus, Valentinianism 61, 64
Van den Ven, P. 213
Van Roey, A. 165–6
veneration (*proskynesis*) 201, 203, 206, 207–8, 210, 214, 215, 221
  expressing honour (*timê*) 201, 210
  expressing worship (*latreia*) 201, 210
Victoria and Albert Museum 195
vigil service 254–6
virginal conception of Christ 188
virginity 144, 188
Voulet, P. 226

water 129–30
Wellesz, E. 255
Wickham, Lionel 228
will, see *thelema*
woman 143
worship (*latreia*), *see* veneration

Yannaras, Christos 223
Yazīd II, caliph 197

Zeno, emperor 131, 206
Zizioulas, J. 51
zôarchikos 247, 279
zodiac 128
Zoroastrianism 62